There is no Supreme Constitution - A Critique of Statist-individualist Constitutionalism

Published by AFRICAN SUN MeDIA under the SUN PReSS imprint

This publication was subjected to an independent double-blind peer evaluation by the publisher.

First edition 2019

ISBN 978-1-928480-26-6
ISBN 978-1-928480-27-3 (e-book)
https://doi.org/10.18820/9781928480273

Set in Gentium Basic 9.5/13

Cover design, typesetting and production by AFRICAN SUN MeDIA
Cover image: © Juan Antonio Ribera's c.1806 Cincinnatus Leaves the Plough to Dictate Laws to Rome

SUN PReSS is a licensed imprint of AFRICAN SUN MeDIA. Scholarly, professional and reference works are published under this imprint in print and electronic formats.

This publication can be ordered from:
orders@africansunmedia.co.za
Takealot: bit.ly/2monsfl
Google Books: bit.ly/2k1Uilm
africansunmedia.store.it.si *(e-books)*
Amazon Kindle: amzn.to/2ktL.pkL

Visit africansunmedia.co.za for more information.

There is no *Supreme* Constitution

A Critique of Statist-individualist Constitutionalism

KOOS MALAN

SUN PRESS

CONTENTS

5   THE CONSTITUTION OF THE REPUBLIC OF SOUTH AFRICA IS NOT SUPREME AND ITS RIGHTS NOT ENTRENCHED - THE CHANGING SOUTH AFRICAN CONSTITUTION

In memory of
Oswald Davies and Lawrence Schlemmer

ACKNOWLEDGEMENTS

A book of this kind is the product of a considerable research effort. However, as important as the personal research and writing endeavour, the indispensable contribution of colleagues, friends, students and other acquaintances through the exchange of ideas and advice during numerous formal and informal conversations can never be underestimated.

The consistent advice and numerous exchanges with my friend of several decades, illustrious philosopher, Danie Goosen is hardly replaceable. Of great value too were exchanges with Hennie Strydom, Frank Judo, Stefan Hobe, Werner Human, Tiaan van Dyk, Johann Rossouw, Pieter Duvenage, Marinus Schoeman, Cerneels Lourens, Piet le Roux, Heinrich Matthee, Danie Malan, Ilze Grobbelaar-du Plessis, Charles Fombad, Johan Scott, Tsholofeko Chiloane, Steve Cornelius, Christo Botha, Bernard Bekink and Pieter Alberts to mention but a few important names. Particularly noteworthy is Johan Kok. His editing was that of the true diligens pater familias and the many instances of advice were priceless. Also a word of thanks to Chrisna Nel who conducted careful proof reading.

Many perspectives discussed in this book were honed in exchanges with post graduate students in class discussions of the master's course in constitutional law at the University of Pretoria that I have been offering for more than a decade now, and with several post graduate research students.

I am happy also to highlight the name of my father, Manie Malan. His splendid example unwittingly showed me already at a very early age the way towards responsible and valiant independent thinking. Even though he passed away more than a decade ago the sharp-wittedness of my late friend, Z.B. du Toit, remains an important influence to this day. This book is in memory of Oswald Davies and Lawrence Schlemmer. Oswald was a close friend whose intellectual company and encyclopaedic knowledge of several languages I tremendously gained from. Lawrence was an extremely knowledgeable and sharp-minded social scientist. He walked tall. I am grateful for the benefit to have learned from him. I am indebted to Marno Swart and Chrislie Thomas for their fine-tuning the footnotes and to Juanita Larkin, our departmental secretary whose reliable technical assistance I could always count on.

The working atmosphere at the department of public law where I spend most of my days is sound and pleasant. I am thankful to all my colleagues for that. The buoyant presence of my partner, Esley-Jane has been a constant inspiration. The cooperation with Emily Vosloo, Wikus van Zyl and Anina Joubert from AFRICAN SUN MeDIA towards the eventual finalisation of the book was constructive, friendly and effective.

Koos Malan
15 July 2019

About the Author

Koos Malan is professor of Public Law at the University of Pretoria, South Africa. He is the author of *Politocracy – An assessment of the coercive logic of the territorial state and ideas around a response to it.*

INTRODUCTION

This book is a critique of what is described as the doctrine of statist-individualist constitutionalism. Statist-individualist constitutionalism is the dominant current species of constitutionalism. It has so much traction that some might confuse it with the notion of constitutionalism as such. To do that, would be wrong, however. There is much more to constitutionalism than the statist-individualist doctrine. Statist-individualist constitutionalism is but one of various notions of constitutionalism. Moreover, as will be shown in the discussions in this book, there are some aspects of the statist-individualist constitutionalism that are in fact not as constitutional as one might tend to think and they might in fact fall short of what a more authentic view of constitutionalism requires.

In part this book builds on *Politocracy: An assessment of the coercive logic of the territorial state and ideas around a response to it.* The primary focus of *Politocracy* was the emergence of the territorial state followed by the coercive logic of statism. The logic of statism is divided into two aspects: first, how the territorial state set the framework for a scholarly paradigm in constitutional law and political science, political philosophy, other social sciences, as well as in general public discourse; and secondly how the territorial state has laid down the coercive parameters for enforcing particular statist identities on people.

Statist-individualist constitutionalism revolves around two entities: the state (the sovereign territorial state as described in *Politocracy*) and the individual (the abstract individual with universal human rights). Statist-individualist constitutionalism is premised on the exclusive twosome consortium of the sovereign territorial state described in *Politocracy* and the abstract individual with universal human rights.

Accordingly, statist-individualist constitutionalism dismisses anything but the territorial state and the individual as entities that qualify for a place in theorising on constitutionalism. More specifically, it refuses to account for communities on two fronts, namely that of power and that of rights. Communities cannot have governmental power, and they also cannot be vested with rights.

Statist-individualist constitutionalism is particularly pertinent in South Africa since 1994 – the year in which South Africa made its first great step in its internationally celebrated constitutional transition. The South African Constitution emphatically embodies all the ingredients of statist-individualist constitutionalism. That was the reason why it has been hailed as one of the best Constitutions in the world. Constitutional jurists in and outside South Africa, who embraced the doctrine of statist-individualist constitutionalism, have poured acclaim on the South African Constitution. Scores of politicians, followed by large coteries of journalists – locally and abroad – joined in the praises. So prodigious were the accolades bestowed on the South African Constitution – and implicitly on statist-individualist constitutionalism – that doubts could only be ventilated at the risk of pillory for insolent constitutional apostasy, both in academia and in the general public discourse.

However, these praises were often groundless, precisely because of their statist-individualist foundations being reproachable. The foundations of statist-individualist constitutionalism do not really provide the solid and comprehensive basis for sound constitutionalism.

The erstwhile exuberant praises for the South African Constitution have largely faded. This, however, is not in the first place due to lucid new insights gained on the true quality of South Africa's Constitution. It is largely because of the mediocre (if not out outright dismal) performance of the South Africa's government under the dominant African National Congress (ANC) that has been in government since the dawn of the constitutional transition. These failures include unabated large scale corruption, the deterioration of the public sector, poor public services, large scale wasting of public funds, a sustained high rate of violent crime and the attending inability of the relevant state agencies to deal with that issue, erratic economic policies that are destroying trust in the economic stability of the country, lack of economic growth, an upsetting high rate of unemployment and a decreasing level of trust in the country's judicial system. Hardly ever, however, does the focus shift to the more fundamental level, namely that of the foundations of the Constitution as such, and on that score, to the foundations of statist-individualist constitutionalism. The assumption, though not as expressly and gleefully proclaimed as before, is still that the Constitution is superb. It is only tragically let down by a mal-performing government. In the result, critical reflection on the proclaimed august virtue of the Constitution is dodged. By the same token, any critical consideration about the statist-individualist doctrinal foundations on which it is premised is also evaded. In fact, there seems to be an odd oblivion of the existence of this doctrinal basis, thus rendering critical reflection impossible.

The discussion in this book brings the doctrinal assumptions of statist-individualist constitutionalism in focus. Statist-individualist has significant merits. Many aspects are so important that they cannot be dispensed with without jeopardising the essentials of constitutionalism as such. Yet, it remains but one of a variety of trends in the broader tradition of constitutionalism. Moreover, statist-individualist constitutionalism has serious inadequacies and many of its claims and important attributes of its belief system are not plausible at all. It is also a limited form of constitutionalism in that it dispenses with important aspects from its belief system and in that way harms the very notion of constitutionalism.

In this book, statist-individualist constitutionalism will be critiqued. The validity of its core claims and beliefs will be demystified and debunked and its narrowness and shortcomings will be exposed. The discussion will mainly be conducted against the backdrop of the South African constitutional experience since the beginning of the country's constitutional transition in the middle of the 1990's. Many of the references in this book will therefore be to the South African Constitution and the discourse surrounding it.

The concern of this book, however, is not in the first place the minute detail of the South African Constitution but the belief system of statist-individualist constitutionalism that underpins the Constitution (and many other statist-individualist Constitutions). It is precisely because the South African Constitution so unequivocally subscribes to the doctrine of statist-individualist constitutionalism that it provides such an apt case study for critiquing statist-individualist constitutionalism. The (working of the) South African Constitution has revealed that statist-individualist constitutionalism is an implausible belief system which is not capable of securing the solid constitutionalism that statist-individualist constitutionalism claims to guarantee.

In rebutting the claims of statist-individualist constitutionalism it will be shown that:

σ   The so-called supremacy of the Constitution is in fact very tenuous, if not entirely groundless: the so-called supreme Constitution is subject to forces that often by far exceed the assumed potency of the supreme Constitution;

σ   The strategies that seek to guarantee the Constitution's supremacy, though possibly inculcating faith in the Constitution's supremacy claim, are feeble and ineffectual; the Constitution, regardless of its ostensible supremacy and attending stability, is changing continually, even though the text remains unchanged;

σ   The judiciary is far less independent and impartial than what statist-individualist constitutionalism sermonises. Ordinarily the judiciary, together with the executive and the dominant party in the legislature, is an essential part of the dominant political elite, and not an effective apparatus for the splendid checks and balances that statist-individualist constitutionalism claims it to be;

σ A bill of individual (human) rights (interpreted by the courts), fall way short of securing justice as claimed in terms of statist-individualist constitutionalism.

As the discussion will show, all the above holds true for statist-individualist constitutionalism in general and for South Africa's *supreme* Constitution.

Chapter 1 begins with an exposition of the essential core of the notion of constitutionalism. In Chapter 2 the belief system of statist-individualist constitutionalism and its accompanying structural strategies and mechanisms are expounded.

Chapter 3 shows that the present South African Constitution is a prime example of statist-individualist constitutionalism. Then follows five Chapters – 4-8 – in which the belief system of statist-individualist constitutionalism is rebutted and its mechanisms shown to be ineffectual to secure a plausible system of constitutionalism.

Chapter 4 shows that the claim of supremacy of the written Constitution is ill-founded and that strict amendment procedures that claim to guarantee the integrity, stability and permanency of the Constitution are ineffectual. Supremacy provisions and strict amendment procedures are no match for potent socio-political forces that create, recreate and change the (actual) constitution, which is a function of the changing balance of socio-political forces in the state concerned.

Chapter 5 applies the insights of Chapter 4 to the South African experience since 1994, more specifically since the *final* Constitution which took effect in 1997, showing that the Constitution is in fact not supreme and that it has undergone profound changes as a result of potent socio-political forces that have been operative in South Africa over recent decades.

Chapter 6 shows that separation of powers and the concomitant doctrines of judicial independence and impartiality are largely metaphorical and fall way short of establishing and securing a truly balanced constitution.

Chapter 7 deals with the judiciary from the vantage point of judicial interpretation and its effect on the claim that individual rights secure a system of justice. The highest courts – also those in South Africa – subscribe to the ideological convictions of the dominant political elite of which they are an integral element, and they interpret rights in accordance with the ideological commitments of the dominant elite, which at the same time violate the interests of sectors in society that are in disagreement with these commitments.

Chapter 8 debunks the statist-individualist belief that individual rights provide a fool-proof system of justice. Justice can often not be sustained without the protection of communities which serve as the prerequisite for the safeguarding of individual interests.

Chapter 9 goes back to the basic tenets of constitutionalism set out in Chapter 1 and makes observations on an improved constitutionalism beyond the confines of the doctrine of statist-individualist constitutionalism.

The largest part of this book is new. Most of the themes covered here have not, or only in part, been dealt with in previous publications. However, a selection of my previous writings form the basis of some of the topics now addressed more comprehensively in the book. The article entitled "Deliberating the rule of law and constitutional supremacy from the perspective of the factual perspective of law" *PER/PELJ*, 2015/4, Vol 18:1205-1250 has informed part of Chapter 4; "*Die versweë verandering van die Suid-Afrikaanse konstitusie* (The silent change of the South African constitution)" *TGW*, 2018 (Vol 58/2):387-410 is the original basis of the first part of Chapter 5; "Reassessing judicial independence and impartiality against the backdrop of judicial appointments in South Africa" *PER/PELJ*, 2014(17):1965-2040 is the original basis of some passages of Chapter 6; and "The deficiency of individual rights and the need for community protection" *THRHR*, 2008(3):415-437 forms the basis of the last quarter of Chapter 8.

Constitution and constitution

In this book, the term constitution is in some places spelt with a capital letter and in others not. The choice is deliberate because Constitution with a capital "C" means something different from the constitution with a small "c". Constitution with the capital refers to the Constitution as perceived in terms of the doctrine of statist-individualist constitutionalism. This is the Constitution that is believed to be supreme. It is the formal Constitution, namely the one captured in the written instrument of the Constitution Act/*Der Grundgesetz*/die Grondwet – the text. In contrast to this we have just the constitution – the small letter constitution – the constitution without the pretence of supremacy and the constitution that might in fact not be written, at least not in full. The salient feature of this constitution is that it is the actual constitution, that is, the constitution of the actual norms that govern a society. A constitution might be the same as or similar to the Constitution, but depending on the circumstances, it may have a vastly different content than the Constitution – the one with the capital letter. This small letter constitution does not have the pretence of supremacy but it encapsulates the actual constitution in a society. The differences between the constitution and the Constitution are fully discussed in Chapter 4, but the distinction between the two as reflected in the distinction between the Constitution with the capital, and the constitution without it, is important for the entire book. Hence, this clarification at the outset.

CONSTITUTIONALISM

1.1

Introduction

This chapter discusses the gist of constitutionalism. It does so by highlighting what I regard to be the four essential characteristics of the idea of constitutionalism. In our day constitutionalism, as will be shown in the next chapter, is statist-individualist constitutionalism, that is, constitutionalism as conceived and practiced within the framework of the contemporary territorial state and within the bounds set by the statist-individualist paradigm of political and legal, more specifically constitutional thinking. Statist-individualist constitutionalism represents only one version of constitutionalism even though the mal-conception might be harboured that it embodies the very idea of constitutionalism as such.

1.2

The core characteristics of constitutionalism

A good constitution – *politeia* – according to Aristotle, is a constitution that secures the happiness of the polis[1] and this happiness, Aristotle states, finds expression in an "activity and the complete utilization of all our powers, our goodness, not conditionally but absolutely."[2] On close analysis, constitutionalism is essentially

---

1   Aristotle, 1962:273.

2   Ibid, p.83.

concerned with two interrelated questions – one normative and the other structural. The second flows from the first. The normative question revolves around justice, more specifically justice on a comprehensive scale, that is, the quest for the just society or the just polity.[3] Justice in this sense is ethically inspired, not merely justice in the legal-technical sense.[4] The second – and structural – question revolves around governmental power and generally around public power: how should such power be allocated, exercised and controlled in order to best serve the achievement of justice, thus to achieve happiness? These are old questions which most probably arose with the emergence of the first human communities. Conscious reflection on politics which goes back to Classicism is inherently constitutional in nature, precisely because it grappled with questions regarding justice on the one hand and the allocation, exercise and control of public power on the other.[5] It is for this very reason that Harold Berman could state aptly that the notion of constitutionalism is much older than the term. The notion of constitutionalism in fact predated the currently dominant territorial state and the concomitant present statist-individualist doctrine of constitutionalism by millennia.[6]

History witnessed different and changing views on constitutionalism, that is, on what a just polity entails and how governmental power should be allocated and checked in order to achieve such polity. Possibly the biggest difference is the one between the premodern and the contemporary dominant statist-individualist doctrine of constitutionalism.[7] Notwithstanding the divergent concepts of constitutionalism, it is possible to distil constitutionalism's core or essential content. That is what I would regard as the fourfold essence of constitutionalism – all four flowing from the normative (justice) and the structural (public power) elements mentioned above. The first two of the four related elements are normative in nature and the second two are more structural. These essential elements are:

σ   justice (the identification of the constitutional idea with the quest for a just polity);

σ   fundamentality;

σ   the consensual basis of the rule of law;

---

3   Hence Aristotle 1962:29 asserts that justice is essential to the state – the polis.

4   It is justice as conceived in the German *Gerechtigkeit* and the Afrikaans *geregtigheid*, rather than in the (arguably) potentially restricted English *justice*. Compare the observation by P.S. Dreyer, 427-347:45-46.

5   The quest for justice goes back to the earliest roots of political thought. Thus Oakeshott, 2006:141 for example states: "Polis life is the pursuit of human excellence in 'justice'." Oakeshott, 2006:149 continues: "Justice according to the legend of Greek politics was the midwife of the polis ..." The polis was regarded as the only situation in which justice could be achieved. On the importance of justice at the root of legal and political thought, see for example Lane, 2014:18. The constitution (or the *politeia* which is the closest Greek equivalent of the constitution) was identified with justice. Therefore, Oakeshott, 2006:85 quite aptly stated that it cannot surprise us that the first classical work on politics, which is Plato's *Republic* was called *Concerning Justice* which is the proper title of his *political magnum opus*.

6   Compare the discussion of Medieval constitutionalism Malan, 2012a:21-32. See also Vincent, 1987:82-92 on the origins of the constitutional theory, 82-103 of the state in Greco-Roman, medieval and early modern thought and practice.

7   See McIlwain, 2007:1-2. See in this regard Paine, 1996:2-13.

σ   and limited government, to which is related division – diffusion – and balance of power, the notion of the mixed constitution and the notion of public office.

These four essentialia are mutually implied and reinforcing. Normativity and fundamentality together constitute the ideal element of constitutionalism. The rule of law, together with the diffusion and balance of power are both premised on the importance of (consensual) communities for sustaining constitutionalism. Power balance and limitation relate to the real or structural element of constitutionalism.

These four essential *elements* of constitutionalism will now be discussed.

1.2.1   Normativity – the commitment to justice

Pursuit of justice is the quintessence of constitutionalism. That is why *ius* and *iustitia* – law and justice – are indivisible, and why the essential connection between law and justice is proclaimed right at beginning of arguably the most famous legal documents of all times, the Digest (of Justinian's *Corpus Iuris Civilis*). Law is the art of goodness and fairness.[8] Hence, the prime responsibility of jurists, according to the classical Roman jurist, Celsus, is to:

> (c)ultivate the art of justice and claim awareness of what is good and fair, discriminating between fair and unfair, distinguishing lawful from unlawful, aiming to make men good not only through fear but also under allurement of rewards, and affecting a philosophy which, if I am not deceived, is genuine, and not a sham.[9]

This idea that the pursuit of justice is an essential element of law has been a significant driving force behind natural law thinking for ages. Hence, ideas on justice (and morality) have either been posited as normative standards to qualify as (positive) law or as a moral yardstick to evaluate the quality of positive law. The main tenet of natural law, according to Edgar Bodenheimer is that arbitrary will is not legally final.[10] Bodenheimer further states that "(t)here would, indeed, appear to exist some minimum postulates of justice which, independently of the will of the lawgiver, need to be recognised in any viable order of society."[11] Thus St Augustine proclaims as follows: "Justice being taken away then, what are Kingdoms but great robberies?"[12] This means that unjust law is no law at all.[13] St Thomas of Aquinas declares that a "human law ... in so far as it deviates from reason, is called an unjust law, and has the nature, not of law but of violence."[14] In tune with this, church authorities during the Middle Ages, often supported by civilian authorities, rejected the validity of those laws made by political authorities because they were

---

8   Mommsen & Krueger, 1985:1.

9   Ibid.

10   Bodenheimer, 1962:216.

11   Ibid.

12   Ibid, p.22-23.

13   Ibid, p.265.

14   Ibid.

considered to be incompatible with the divine or natural law.[15] The justice threshold might not, and in fact should not be particularly high in order to safeguard the stability of legal systems against trivial claims based on allegations that the law of such systems are unjust and for that reason are not constituting positive law at all. Too high a threshold could give licence to lawlessness and chaos. Still, there should at least be some threshold because tyrannical decrees permitting unbridled assault on life, body or property should not be allowed to pass as law. Such minimum justice threshold is necessary to ensure that not every expression of the will of a sovereign would qualify as law.[16]

This minimum justice requirement for law also resonates in modern legal theory, for example in the works of Gustav Radbruch and Robert Alexy, who are of the view that not all legislative enactments would qualify as law. They are of the view that state-made law based on due enactment providing for the enforcement of state power does constitute law even if it is unjust and contrary to the general welfare. However, according to them, an enactment may constitute such an egregious violation of justice that it is rendered lawless' for its failure to meet the minimum standard of justice.[17]

Justice and constitutionalism are as inseparable as law and justice.[18] Constitutionalism encapsulates the notion of justice on a grand – systemic – scale, that is, for the whole of the polity. Hence, the closer a constitution reaches the achievement of justice,

---

15 Ibid, p.264-265.

16 Law's commitment to justice also finds expression in the views developed in the thinking of Lon Fuller namely that the so-called internal morality is an indispensable ingredient of justice.

17 Alexy, 2008:290 refers here to Radbruch, 2006:7. This thesis is sometimes referred to as the extreme injustice hypothesis. See for example Aarnio, 2011:55. This view somehow also resonates the view of Ronald Dworkin, positing that in addition to rules there are also deep-seated principles that encapsulate the broad political philosophy of the institutional history of the legal order that serves as a comprehensive and coherent (contradiction-free), single collective moral agent and as such the most important source of law that enables principle-based decisions that give effect to the rights of legal subjects (involved in disputes) and that renders the exercise of discretion completely redundant. Dworkin, 1977:81-130; Dworkin, 1986:188. For Dworkin's distinction between principles (aimed at effectuating rights in contrast to policies which are *statistically defined* and directed toward the achievement of broad public goals), see Dworkin, 1986:223; 243.

18 Thus, classical politics was aimed in the first place at securing justice. Michael Oakeshott observes that justice was the "midwife of the polis". He further states that "(t)he polis was constituted in a judicial activity of dealing out of 'justice' to the various tribes and families that came together to compose it." So crucial was the question of justice in Greek politics that it induced Oakeshott to state: "No Greek, then, could fail to think first that the 'image' of 'justice' and 'injustice' was most profitably to be looked for in the structure of the polis." (Oakeshott, 2006:149). Large tracts of Plato's *Republic* concern the question of the polis as the way of answering the question of "What is justice?" (Oakeshott, 2006:149-150. See further 150-158.) Political office and the exercise of political authority has for long been identified not with law making and execution but with adjudication. Aside from protecting his community, the main responsibility of the medieval king was adjudicatory in nature. He had to deal out justice (*ius dicere*) on the basis of the existing (customary) law of his community and not make new law (*ius facere or ius dare*) or execute such law. Friedrich, 1974:122 explained that judicial power had been the core of royal government in the earlier Middle Ages. The king was above all the source of judgments by which right was announced. "The settling of disputes is the primordial function of a political order." Such judging was meant to establish justice. Medieval and early modern assemblies (such as parliaments and cortes) were adjudicators rather than lawmakers. Parliament (in this context the English parliament), which is nowadays fully identified with the legislature, was a judicial rather than a legislative body, which applied the existing common law to specific cases. Thence, parliament's capacity as a high court, (See McIlwain, 1910:51, 70, 86, 94 as well as the detailed discussion at 109-256. For Edward Coke, McIlwain, 1910:94 explained, the main responsibility of the parliament and the king (the king in parliament) was judicial – *ius dicere* and *not ius dare*.

the closer it approximates (the achievement of the ideal of) constitutionalism. Constitutionalism presupposes the pursuit of justice on a grand scale, that is, for the whole of the polity, and more specifically for all individuals and communities[19] within the polity. That is why the political community should not be viewed simply as an aggregate of any number of persons, but as a community bound together in its pursuit of justice and happiness.[20] What justice should entail, is always debatable and controversial. Moreover, it is not within the reach of inherently fallible humans to attain full-scale, complete and perpetual justice. Precisely for that reason the pursuit of justice remains the perpetual telos of law and constitutionalism. Once the pursuit of justice, which is the very purpose of constitutionalism, is lost, the idea of constitutionalism is also lost.

The commitment of constitutional law to the achievement of justice was well-known already in pre- and early modern constitutional (and political) thinking. Parliamentary action (of the English parliament) for example was not regarded as an expression of the sovereign will of a legislative body. On the contrary, parliament, which is today associated with the legislative function, that is, with the law-*making*, used to be a judicial body responsible for adjudication in terms of the precepts of the common law, rather than a body that made law through legislation.[21] Hence, Charles McIlwain declared that for Edward Coke (1552-1634) the duty of the English parliament (and of the king) was that of *ius dicere* and not *ius dare*,[22] that is, that it was a matter of adjudication directed towards the achievement of justice and not merely a matter of (arbitrary) law-making.

Being a judicial body, parliament was therefore associated with the pursuit of justice. Parliament also guarded over the integrity of the (fundamental) common law and claimed the authority to declare legislative acts (which were associated with acts of the prince) void for incompatibility with the common law.[23] The views of Edward Coke expressed during the famous constitutional struggle with King James I of England at the beginning of the seventeenth century, resonates this view of the adjudicative duties of parliament.[24]

---

19 In Chapter 8, I shall deal with the reason why justice to communities in addition to individuals is crucial.

20 In subscribing to this view, I agree with Aristotle, 1962:118-121, rather than Thomas Hobbes and John Locke, and echoed in modern definitions of the state, in terms of which the political community (currently the state) is simply any aggregate of persons, as long as it is a permanent population within fixed boundaries.

21 McIlwain, 1910:51, 70, 86, 94 and for a further detailed discussion 109-256.

22 Ibid, p.94.

23 Plucknett, 1927:50.

24 Coke's view that royal acts were subject to judicial review was based on the conviction that English common law was supreme. He articulated this as follows in 1613 in *Bonham's case*: "It appears in our books, that in many cases the common law will control acts of Parliament, and sometimes will adjudge them as utterly void: for when an act of Parliament was against common right and reason, or repugnant, or impossible to be performed, the common law will control it, and adjudge such acts to be void." Quoted by Sabine, 1971:452 from the Coke Reports Pt VIII, 118a.

1.2.2 Fundamental (higher) law

Constitutionalism presupposes a distinction between fundamental law or higher law in contrast to ordinary law. The constitution is embodied in the fundamental law. The constitution can assume a variety of forms. As will be shown in the next chapter, modern constitutions, in keeping with the doctrine of statist-individualist constitutionalism are by definition written instruments – more specifically a single document. A constitution, however, need not be fully written. It need not be contained in a document that bears the designation constitution. A set of unwritten binding precepts, practices, usages, conventions, etc. that are customarily adhered to and that deals with matters that are typically constitutional subject matter is as much a constitution as the single written constitution. Typical constitutional matters deal with the allocation, exercise and balance of public power and the relationship between government and the citizenry, all serving the common objective of promoting a just polity.[25]

Regardless of the form of the constitution – a single written instrument or otherwise – the notion of constitutionalism requires that such constitution be invested with higher status than ordinary law which means that it serves as a binding measure for ordinary law and for conduct of political office bearers.[26] Law or conduct failing to meet the precepts of the constitution is void and of no legal consequence. Precisely for that reason the constitution in order to serve as a durable standard of validity, need to be more permanent and stable than ordinary law.

The notion of higher law is of ancient origin. At present the idea of higher law is identified with the written supreme Constitution. However, a written instrument is not a prerequisite for fundamentality.

1.2.3 The consensual basis of the rule of law – customary law-abiding conduct

The rule of law is an essential element of constitutionalism. Hence public governance must be conducted on a consistent basis in terms of predetermined, properly promulgated general legal rules (and principles) thus ensuring for the citizenry guaranteed legal protection without the fear of unpredictable, arbitrary decision-making beyond the bounds of predetermined law.[27] Such law must be obeyed by the citizenry and all public office-bearers (government in the broadest sense of the word). Law and the constitution are bolstered by legitimate force so that instances of legal defiance can be remedied and the law be restored and enforced

---

25   See Malan, 2015b:254-258; Also see Malan, 2012a:22-32.

26   In modern written constitutions this certainly holds true for rigid constitutions that are not as easily amendable as flexible ones that can ordinarily be amended with a simple majority in the legislature.

27   See the illuminating discussion by Lon Fuller, summed up by Van Blerk, 1998:111, as well as the illuminating discussion by De Montesquieu:2002:165-169.

in instances of breach.[28] Law and the constitution are not conceivable without an effective power apparatus capable of remedying instances of legal disobedience. However, law and the constitution are not premised and defined on the basis and in terms of the rarity of (abnormal) unlawful behaviour, that is, on the transgressions of the norms of law. Therefore, force is law's and the constitution's last resort, reserved for the exceptional instances of disobedient behaviour, contrary to the norms of law that calls for coercive remedial action. Law and the constitution are premised on the legal *normality*, that is, of people and government acting in conformity with the law.[29] People do act in accordance with the law particularly when they are in agreement with the law. This is where the consensual basis of the rule of law comes into the picture. Broad consensus on the content of the law and the constitution prevails when there is a community of people bound together by their commitment to the law and the constitution. On that consensual basis the community voluntarily and habitually act in conformity with the law.[30] This has the effect that law assumes a customary character, even though it might be captured in written instruments such as legislation or a written constitution. Such community is not created artificially by way of individuals contracting to the law under which they will be living. On the contrary, it owes its existence to an already existing culture rooted in a common ethos of which the law is an element. Hence, the rule of law is not based in the first place on the law and the constitution which is an active and premeditated creation. The opposite is true. That is that the law and the constitution are aspects of the character of the community.[31] Constitutionalism is therefore primarily embodied in the general customary, consensual conduct in compliance with the law; in people of the same community (unwittingly) experiencing and living the law as an integral part of the identity of such community, instead of being imposed from outside or established for the first time by individuals who enter into a law-creating and constitution-creating contract.[32]

1.2.4 Limited government; diffusion and balance of power; the idea of the mixed constitution; public office

It is the responsibility of the government, consisting of the apparatus of public office-bearers of the polity, to safeguard justice through governing in the interest of the whole of the polity (the public good); to exert legitimate force as prescribed

---

28 One may argue that the law and the constitution are based by a perfect *imbalance* between the forces that sustain the law and the constitution in contrast to the deviating and challenging forces. See Malan, 2004:474-479.

29 See the illuminating observations by Bodenheimer, 1962:273-274. See also Malan, 2004:474-479.

30 The consensual basis of the law that will be featuring repeatedly in this book was clearly understood already by Aristotle, 1962:83 who stated that custom is the basis for the obedience of law.

31 As Pitkin, 1987:167 stated: "The constitution is less something that we have but rather something we are."

32 It is precisely because of this customary basis of the rule of law that pre-modern notions of the rule of law could combine the idea of the supremacy of the law and popular sovereignty into a single contradiction-free system. See on this regard Malan, 2015b:254-267.

by the applicable law when necessary in the event of unlawful conduct and to fend off external threats. However, governmental power may go astray. Power might be abused to the detriment of smaller or larger parts of the citizenry instead of serving the whole of the body politic, thus defeating the very purpose of constitutionalism, which is to uphold justice for all. It might be exercised for the benefit of only a particular person or group of persons within government: a single person (and his or her patronage) in the case of autocratic rule; a racial, religious, ethnic, economic or any other minority that forms an oligarchy, or any racial, class or ethnic group that constitutes the majority, or scenarios where democracy descends into majority domination.[33] All these cases defeat the idea of constitutionalism since government is benefitting only a part instead the whole of the polity. In such cases government which the notion of constitutionalism requires to be to the public good is corrupted and degenerates into a private concern for the benefit of only a part instead of the whole of the polity. This risk is present irrespective of the form of government (autocratic, aristocratic or democratic), that is, regardless of whether governmental power vests in a single person, a few persons or the majority of the populace. In fact the most tenacious challenge of democratic theory revolves around the question of how democracy is to be prevented from degenerating into majority domination, that is, how majority rule is to be prevented from descending into government for the exclusive benefit of the majority and the corresponding detriment of the minority.[34] Governmental power lapses into privateering, which in the final analysis defeats justice. James Madison's discussion in the tenth Federalist Paper[35] is particularly insightful in this context. To Madison, what he calls factious rule by a majority faction was one of the gravest vices that could occur in public life. Factious rule implies that government is conducted, not for the public good, but in the interest of a dominant faction and unjustly to the detriment of a powerless minority and/or in violation of the interests of individuals. A government formed by a politically organised ethnic, racial, religious, cultural or language group pursuing their own interests in a heterogeneous society would fall squarely within Madison's definition of a faction. He meant by a faction:

> ... a number of citizens, whether amounting to a majority or a minority of the whole, who are united and actuated by some common impulse or passion, or of interest, adverse

---

33 The distinction between authentic public office for the benefit of the whole, in contrast to perversions of public office for only a part, invokes the classical distinction the various forms of government made for example by Aristotle, 1962:116: One-man rule for the common good is kingship; rule by a few people for the common good is aristocracy; rule exercised by the bulk of the citizens for the good of the whole of the community is a polity. The corresponding deviation are tyranny (for the benefit of the ruler), oligarchy (for the benefit of the few) – those that have means; and democracy for the benefit of the many – those without means.

34 Sartori, 1962:99-100. Mill, 1962:256-257. Mill's distinction between two forms of democracy is also pertinent in this context. First there is genuine democracy, which entails government of all the people by all the people. The second and pernicious form is government by the majority, solely in the interest of the majority. For all practical purposes, only the majority in such dispensation has a say in the affairs of the state. At the same time, the effect of such majority government is tantamount to disenfranchising the minority, causing the majority to effectively rule over the minority and usually dominating them.

35 Madison, 1937:55-62.

to the rights of the other citizens, or to the permanent and aggregate interests of the community.[36]

The two normative (or ideal) elements of constitutionalism, namely the commitment to justice and the enhanced status of fundamental law are not sufficient for safeguarding constitutionalism. The normative element has to be complemented and shorn up by suitable structures of public power in general and governmental power in particular: structural arrangements for the suitable allocation of governmental power and checks on power in order to ensure that power be exercised for the benefit of the whole of the polity, instead of degenerating into privateering for the sake of but a segment – a minority or the majority. This structural element is essential to constitutionalism. For that reason questions around governmental power – its allocation, exercise, limitation and control – are and have always been essential for constitutionalism. In essence the answer to these questions is that there must never be a single centre of governmental power. There must be a distribution – a diffusion – of governmental power and generally of public power. Moreover, the various centres of power must be checked, controlled, balanced and limited by counter-power – counter governmental power and other sources of public power. No single centre of power must be absolved – released – from the checks of counter-power. When so absolved, absolutism (and arbitrary governmental decision-making), which is the arch antagonist of constitutionalism[37] sets in. The essence of the classical idea of the mixed (and balanced) constitution, which goes back to the very beginning of political theorising in for example the work of Plato (and thereafter in other sectors of classical, medieval and pre-modern thinking)[38] and actual practice provided for a multitude of centres of power as well as for suitable checks on power. George Sabine[39] explains, with reference to the mixed constitution, that "(t)his was the principle of the 'mixed' state which is designed to achieve harmony by a balance of forces, or by a combination of diverse principles of different tendency in such a way that the various tendencies shall offset each other."[40] The Roman Republic during some of its phases gave expression to the idea of the mixed constitution. Brian Tierney paid much attention to the political and constitutional thinking of the late High Middle Ages in both the church and the worldly sphere. He explains how the idea of the mixed and balanced constitution played an important part in both spheres. Even though forms of papal monarchism have been dominant at times, it was consistently controverted by thinking premised on the notion of the mixed

---

36 Madison, 1937:54. See in this regard further Malan, 2006:142-160.

37 Precisely for that reason Vincent, 1987:4, 5 and 79 observes that the constitutional theory of government has been developed against the backdrop and with a view to combat absolutism.

38 Sabine, 1971:112-115 in Aristotle; 154 in Polybius; 155 and 163 in Cicero; 323 in the Conciliar movement; 521 in Halifax; 535 in Locke and various others.

39 Sabine, 1971:77.

40 Compare further with reference to the notion of the mixed constitution in Plato (Sabine, 1971:77-80); in Aristotle (Sabine:112-115); in Polybius (Sabine, 1971:155); in Cicero (Sabine:155, 163); in Locke (Sabine, 1971:535); and in De Montesquieu (Sabine:558-560).

constitution. In the worldly sphere the idea of the mixed constitution has always been dominant during this period.[41] The work of Johannes Althusius at the beginning of the seventeenth century can be regarded as a plea for the adjusted continuation of the balanced constitution of the previous centuries in Western Europe.[42] The British constitutional dispensation of the eighteenth century has also been viewed as a leading example of a mixed constitution in which there was a sound balance of power.[43] The British (largely unwritten) constitution of the eighteenth constitution, American historian, Gordon Wood says, was the best embodiment of the mixed constitution since classical times. Wood states:

> The division of British society into the three estates of king, nobles and people and their constitutional embodiment in Crown, House of Lords, and House of Commons seemed almost miraculously to fulfil the ancient dream of balancing the simple forms of monarchy, aristocracy and democracy within a single constitution. No wonder theorists everywhere, including De Montesquieu, viewed the eighteenth British constitution with admiration and awe.[44]

Wood also explains that the theory of the mixed and balanced constitution dates back to classical Greece and has in fact been prevalent in Western political thinking for centuries. Monarchy, aristocracy and democracy all have their virtuous elements but if any of the three is left on its own, it descends either into faction rule or chaos.[45] Wood states:

> The mixed or balanced polity was designed to prevent these perversions by including each of these classic simple forms of government in the same constitution, the force pulling in one direction would be counterbalanced by other force and stability would result. Only through this reciprocal sharing of political power by the one, the few and the many would the desirable qualities of each be preserved.[46]

Even though the various constitutions in revolutionary America were republican and not monarchic, they gave expression to the same principle as embodied in the office of the governor, senate and houses of representatives.

When modern statist-individualist constitutionalism emerged towards the last part of the eighteenth century, John Adams tersely summarised the idea of constitutionalism's association with power diffusion and balance when he stated: "Power must be opposed to power, force to force, strength to strength, interest to interest, as well as reason to reason."[47] Constitutionalism therefore denotes a multitude of centres of power within the polity. Their responsibility is to exercise

---

41 Tierney, 1982.

42 Althusius, 1994. See further the discussions of Althusius' work in Malan, 2017b and Malan, 2017a.

43 See in this regard Burke, 2013:148; 189-199.

44 Wood, 1993:94.

45 Ibid, p.93-94.

46 Ibid.

47 Quoted by Loughlin, 2007:57.

the power vested in them, which includes that they have to weigh in against each other, thus mutually limiting each other and keeping each other in check. Hence, in order to safeguard the commitment to justice (and consequently to uphold constitutionalism) the constitution must necessarily be mixed and balanced.

This concludes the discussion on the essential elements of the notion of constitutionalism. In the next chapter the leading contemporary version of constitutionalism, which is statist-individualist in nature, is discussed. The discussion will distil the core elements of statist-individualist constitutionalism. The largest part of the book is then dedicated to a critique of statist-individualist constitutionalism.

STATIST-INDIVIDUALIST CONSTITUTIONALISM

2.1

Introduction

The designation statist-individualist constitutionalism encapsulates the distinctive gist of this species of constitutionalism. This is constitutionalism marked by an exclusive twosome consortium of the state and the individual, accompanied by a rejection of any other entity, more specifically the rejection of communities. Statist-individualist constitutionalism is the doctrine of constitutionalism conceived within the framework of the contemporary territorial state and within the bounds set by the statist paradigm of political and legal, more specifically constitutional, thinking. Statist-individualist constitutionalism is at present the object of the dominant discourse of constitutionalism. It nevertheless remains only one trend within the broader discourse of constitutionalism. Statist-individualist constitutionalism could, however, never establish a full scale monopoly of the constitutional discourse and practice. It has been challenged ever since its first appearance as the dominant trend of constitutionalism towards the last quarter of the seventeenth century. Moreover, it was internally challenged by elements of statist-individualist constitutions that were not completely statist-individualist, such as that of the United States of America (USA). In political theory, there has also always been a wide range of pluralist political thinking that emphasised the importance of a multitude of communities as a crucial prerequisite for constitutional government and for individual rights.[1] The federalism of the United States of America constitution is to an extent a distinctive

---

[1]   See for example the informative discussion by Vincent, 1987:180-217.

non-statist anomaly since it recognises political authorities alongside the national government, thus weakening the typical statist commitment to undivided state sovereignty. The same holds true for the federal elements in a handful of other constitutional dispensations.[2] Other forms of political pluralism pose a similar challenge to the dominance of statist-individualist constitutionalism, but they have never been strong enough to make notable inroads into the dominance of statist-individualist constitutionalism. The rise of the notion of the multi-communal state, together with the increased recognition of the rights of minorities as communities (and not merely the rights of individual members of communities), the devise of mechanisms for the internal self-determination of communities (on a corporate or geographic basis), the rise of so-called free cities and the general urge and increased ability of communities to rule themselves independently of state governments are now posing the strongest challenge that statist-individualist constitutionalism has ever faced. The present discussion recognises these anomalies in, and challenges to the doctrine of statist-individualist constitutionalism, but the focus is now on the core elements of statist-individualist constitutionalism.

The discussion of statist-individualist constitutionalism in this chapter proceeds as follows. It begins in the second part of this chapter under the heading *Statism - paving the way to statist constitutionalism* with a brief exposé of the backdrop of the emergence of statist-individualist constitutionalism, followed in the third part with an enunciation of constitutionalism's virtual monopolisation by the statist-individualist concept of constitutionalism. This is under the heading *The establishment of statist-individualist constitutionalism*, followed in the fourth part with a discussion of core elements of statist-individualist constitutionalism under the heading *The nine essential beliefs of statist-individualist constitutionalism*. This represents the basic belief system of statist-individualist constitutionalism. These beliefs are embodied in a set of three core mechanisms which are quintessential to constitutions that are conditioned by the doctrine of statist-individualist constitutionalism, which is the focus of the fifth and final part of the chapter under the heading *Statist constitutionalism's three key mechanisms*.

2.2

Statism – paving the way to statist constitutionalism

Statist-individualist constitutionalism represents a distinctive sector within the larger discourse of constitutionalism. It arose as part of *enlightenment rationalism*

---

2   It should also be noted that the territorial state and statist-individualist constitutions, even in Europe, arrived quite late on the historical scene. Arguably the best example is the empire of Austria-Hungary that was only dismantled at the end of World War I.

within the context of the territorial state (often incorrectly called the nation state)[3] that established itself in Western Europe – first in England and France – in the sixteenth and seventeenth centuries.[4] Within the framework of the territorial state, an intellectual endeavour, namely a specific modus of political and constitutional thinking was forged, which may be described as the paradigm of territorial statism or statism for short.[5] This endeavour, amongst other things, produced the distinctive conception of statist-individualist constitutionalism which is presently still dominant. Statist-individualist constitutionalism is interrelated with the modern concept of the territorial state[6] and intensely concerned with the protection of territorial statehood. Statist-individualist constitutionalism is premised on the rise and triumph of the two entities: the sovereign territorial state exercising a monopoly over centralised political power, and the abstract individual with universal equal *human* rights.[7]

The rise of statist-individualist constitutionalism did not coincide with the emergence of the territorial state. Statist-individualist constitutionalism emerged hundred and fifty to two hundred years later in the days of the French and American revolutions.[8]

Although recent times saw a slight relaxation of the dominance of the territorial state in the practice and discourse of constitutional law and constitutionalism,[9] contemporary constitutionalism is primarily still distinctively statist. The themes of the discourse of constitutionalism are still determined by the need for safeguarding the present territorial statist order.

---

3   The term nation state incorrectly suggests some cultural commonality among the citizenry of the modern state. The state is rather a sovereign political organisation within a defined territory regardless of the degree of homogeneity or heterogeneity of the population. The only commonality among the populace is their abstract legal relationship with the state and the fact that they permanently live within the boundaries of the same territory. For this very reason the term territorial state is more descriptive. It is also used by the English historian Holdsworth, 1937:310; Falk, 1988:26; Strange, 1995:70; Figgis, 1960:72; Habermas, 1988:260; Bozeman, 1976:131 and Kymlicka, 1991:239 who calls it the multination state instead of the nation state and Walzer, 1995:140 refers to the modern state as the putative national state.

4   Buttleritchie, 2004:40.

5   Malan, 2012a:1-2 and 99-116.

6   Preuss, 2007:23-46 at 23.

7   Thus Loughlin, 2007:61 states that present processes of constitutionalisation (in terms of statist constitutionalism) are not concerned with decentralisation, diversity and tension between competing political values and centres of power. On the contrary: "Constitutionalism expresses a centralising philosophy: it both proclaims basic rights as trump card in the political game and maintained that the nature, scope and status of these rights must be determined by a small cadre of judges either in the rarefied atmosphere of supreme courts or, in the international arena, through a variety of tribunals of uncertain status."

8   This is borne out by the fact that the commencing period of modern constitutions is precisely round about this period. See for example the often quoted work by Elkins, 2004.

9   Venter, 2010:11. Constitutional law and constitutionalism are undergoing processes of supranationalisation, internationalisation or just simply globalisation.

Since its advent, the territorial state set the context for what might best be described as the statist paradigm[10] in political philosophy and constitutional law. The defining characteristic of the statism, first articulated by Jean Bodin and then elaborately by Thomas Hobbes followed by John Locke,[11] is that it recognises only two entities, namely the state and the individual. The state according to the statist paradigm, is the centralised power apparatus with an almost inherent tendency towards imposing homogenisation. The state guarantees public peace among antagonistic individuals. Individuals are viewed to be atomistic and they have no public identity other than their identity as citizens of the state, that is, other than their statist identity.[12] Correspondingly statism does not recognise or tolerate any identity other than the statist identity, that is, other than the homogenised collection of all inhabitants within the boundaries of the state. It is antagonistic towards any non-statist, specifically cultural/linguistic communities. By the same token, it rejects any apparatus of political authority apart from the centralised authority of the territorial state, specifically intermediate political authorities for specific communities between the individual and the state.

Statism proceeds from the premises of the fundamental absence of any real human community. There is not a variety of communities each with its own tradition passed on from one to the following generation. Essentially, there are only abstract individuals (often perceived to be mutually antagonistic atoms) combined within the state, as the centralised sovereign political force, which has to keep the public peace among the individual atoms. All individuals are considered to be essentially the same; and any differences that might exist between them are held to be superficial and politically of no moment.

Statism requires public identity to be monopolised for the benefit of the state. In consequence, only one community is recognised, namely a statist community comprising of all who happen to find themselves within the (arbitrary drawn) boundaries of the territorial state and regardless of whether there exists any real bonds of culture, language, ethnicity or religion among them.[13] All the citizens, as Bikuh Parekh insightfully describes:

> "(a)re expected to privilege their territorial over their other identities; to consider that they share in common as citizens far more important than what they share with other members of their religious, cultural and other communities; to define themselves and relate to each other as individuals; to abstract away their religious, cultural and other views when conducting themselves as citizens; to relate to the state in an identical manner; and to enjoy an identical basket of rights and obligations. In short, the state expects of all

---

10   On the rise of the statist paradigm see Malan, 2012a:43-50.

11   Malan, 2012b:65-93.

12   Vincent, 1987:186.

13   See in this regard the incisive analysis by Nisbet, 1990:71-187 – the state and community and Malan, 2012a:127-172.

its citizens to subscribe to an identical way of defining themselves and relating to each other and the state. This shared political self-understanding is its constitutive principle and necessary presupposition. It can tolerate differences on all other matters, but not this one, and uses educational, cultural, coercive and other means to secure that all its citizens share it."[14]

Thus viewed, the statist community is no real community at all. On the contrary, it is but a mass, any aggregate of persons or, in the words of John Locke,[15] *any number of men*. In pursuance of statism there is an inherent and often a stringent intolerance against any non-statist community, that is, any community of a cultural, linguistic, ethnic or religious nature which claims public recognition – its own publicly recognised institutions with public authority over the community concerned. Rights therefore exist only on two levels, namely the level of the individual and that of the state. The state is the sole collective entity in which rights and public authority vest.[16] In terms of a raft of programmes of homogenisation such communities are liquidated into a single uniform statist mass-society. These programmes are often called programmes of nation building – a misnomer because such programmes build neither nations nor national, cultural, ethnic or language communities. On the contrary, they are, in the words of Walker Connor, "programmes of nation destruction, not nation building."[17] Members of all communities are required to be remade in the image of the statist Leviathan, the mortal god, as Hobbes dramatically described the state. Statism might tolerate individuals with particular cultural or language affinities. However, such affinities are only for the private sphere. They should not be expressed publicly. Cultural and language communities are denied any public recognition. In the final analysis the operative concepts of statist identity are homogenisation and uniformity – voluntarily if it can and forcibly if it must.[18]

Since statism recognises but a single centralised power apparatus, no power should be vested in any institution other than the power apparatus of the centralised state. Political pluralism, federalism, dispersal/diffusion of power or devolution of power to non-statist (cultural, language or other) communities or mechanisms that could dilute the centralisation of power are dismissed.[19] Modes of federalism, which were still potent in the thinking of, for example Johannes Althusius,[20]

---

14   Parekh, 2000:185.

15   Locke, 1992:89. See the insightful comments on this by Van Dyke, 1976-1977:343-369 and Van Dyke, 1974:725-741.

16   Van Dyke, 1974:726.

17   Connor, 1971-1972:336.

18   It is significant to note that the onslaught on non-dominant communities prevails over the entire ideological spectrum – left right and centre (liberal) as it were. The common denominator of all these anti community trends is statism. See in this regard Malan, 2014b:462-480.

19   This was dominant in the thinking of Rousseau and exponents of other trends of thinking in pre-revolutionary France. See the discussion by De Tocqueville, 2011:158-168 and Malan, 2012a:231-242.

20   As set out in Althusius, 1994 discussed in Malan, 2017a:1-27 and Malan, 2017b:1-35.

just prior to the victory of the territorial state, were until recently completely marginalised and regained new interest only fairly recently.[21] To the extent that mechanisms of pluralism were in existence, they embodied a fairly weak anomalous contra-tradition in opposition to statism.

Statism is no monolith, however. Over time it has been playing out on a continuum, with an individualist approach on the one extreme and a collectivist approach on the other. Still the homogenising territorial state remains essential all over the continuum, encompassing the full spectrum of important ideological currents – left, right and liberal.[22] For that reason the designations preferred here are not merely *individualistic* or *collectivist* but specifically *statist-individualistic* and *statist-collectivist,* thus underscoring the homogenising territorial state as the defining common factor.

Alongside the state, *statist-individualism* posits the abstract individual (basically the same as and equal to all other individuals) and able to make free choices on their personal identity and life style. The abstract individual of the statist paradigm, as the comprehensive discussion in Chapter 8 will show, is not a timeless given. On the contrary, there is much truth in the assertion that it is a modernist discovery.[23] The abstract individual has been abstracted from the multitude of specific people in specific settings and with a multitude of specific communal identities. The cultivation and enforcement of a homogenous statist public identity is less overt and more tacit and subtle in statist-individualist statism. The statist-individualist current is alive to the risks of absolute political power and seeks to fend that off with constitutional strategies for the protection of individual rights. It is in this context that modern statist-individualist constitutionalism, enunciated in the next part of this chapter, comes into the picture.

The opposite – the statist-collectivist approach – dispenses with the subtleties of statist-individualism. Any concern for the free individual is absent or at least much less pronounced. In contrast to statist-individualism, statist-collectivism is distinctively more overt and often brutal in forging a homogeneous statist nation.

The state-nation is the collective agent for the sake of which all particular communities have to dissolve and individuals have to change their identities in order to be remade in the image of the homogenous statist nation. Ordinarily

---

21   See De Benoist, 2000:26.

22   Malan, 2014b:462-480. See also McRae, 1979:675-688 at 681-682.

23   Macintyre, 1981:73. Arguably the most important figures metaphorical to the rise of the individual are Luther in theology (the individual's direct relation with God instead of an indirect relationship through ecclesiastical authorities); Descartes, who found in individual doubt the sole but a certain foundation for knowledge, but whose individual doubt also constituted the radical break of the subject from the object and the radical divorce of all individuals from one another (in a society without any community) and Hobbes, whose politics and constitutionalism were based in radical individualism comprising individual atoms engaged in a perpetual *bellum omnia contra omnes.*

the mould of the state-nation is provided by the dominant faction of the state's population into which all non-dominant communities have to be assimilated.

In terms of statist-individualism, the state – the Leviathan or mortal god in Hobbes' words – is aloof. It is authoritarian but not totalitarian. It insists on obedience of its subjects and enforces the public peace. However, it does not insist on a flock (a statist nation) to be created in its image. In statist-collectivism, however, Leviathan adopts a totalitarian (though not necessarily absolutist) character. This mortal god, historically a later outgrowth of an older and more aloof one, is much more caring and much more jealous. It insists on a flock in its own image, and tolerates no apostasy – membership of and public allegiance to a different community. When such non-statist apostasy occurs, punishment is sure to follow because no community other than the statist flock forged in the image of the state is tolerated.[24]

Between statist-individualism and statist-collectivism there is an array of variations. Statist-individualism, for which John Locke was arguably the prototypical protagonist,[25] places the emphasis on individual rights to be acknowledged and guaranteed by the state. The contemporary liberal and social democratic states of Western Europe and North America may be viewed as the prime examples of statist-individualism. However, in view of the varying state-sponsored statist identities and wide-ranging social and economic interventions of the state, none of these states will be found on the extreme end of statist individualism.

The collectivist extreme of statism (statist-collectivism) drew inspiration from and found justification in two trends of thinking: the trend provided by the work of Jean Jacques Rousseau, and the other one by utilitarianism incepted by Jeremy Bentham. Endeavouring to establish a totalitarian republicanism in which the most intimate of bonds between a close-knit monolithic citizenry and their state should be forged, Rousseau could tolerate neither a multitude of communal identities, nor individualism, which to him was no genuine expression of freedom but rather a dreadful aberration of freedom. People have to be rescued from their wrong ways and "forced to be free,"[26] that is, forced to be assimilated into a state-prescribed identity and way of life. That identity usually emanated from the dominant, usually the majority community within the state which provided the mould within which all others – communities and individuals – have to be cast. Modern totalitarianism, most notably that of the Jacobins in revolutionary France, Bolshevism in Soviet Russia and Maoism in China, all drew inspiration from this mode of usually majoritarian-driven politics.[27] The spirit of Rousseau can also be detected in right-wing totalitarianism – Fascism and National-socialism.[28]

---

24   See Malan, 2012a:Chapters 6 and 9.

25   As set out in the second treatise of Locke J, *Of civil government*.

26   Rousseau, 1968:64.

27   See the lucid exposition of Nisbet, 1990:Chapter 7. See in this regard also Hueglin, 1999:170.

28   See the remarks by Hueglin, 1999:2.

On close analysis utilitarianism, as for example conceived by Bentham, provides the other original impetus for statist collectivism. In the name of what is (mis)perceived to best serve the interest of the majority (which is identified with the public good) utilitarianism also disregards deviant communities and (the rights of) individuals and enforces on all[29] that which the majority would perceive to be most feasible.

There are vast differences between statist-individualism and statist-collectivism. The former may claim to have a concern for the dignity and the rights of individuals against majority infractions, in contrast to the latter that would be much more inclined to sacrifice individual integrity on the altar of the perceived *Volente Générale* as inspired by Rousseau,[30] or the perceived predominant interest of the majority of people as conceived by utilitarianism. Moreover, these differences are underscored by the fact that the individualist and the collectivist currents provide the premise for the two great ideological struggles of the twentieth century, namely first, between liberal democracy and fascism and subsequently, the struggle between liberal democracy and communism in the guises of Bolshevism and Maoism.

Yet, although opposing one another on account of their respective individualism and collectivism, statist-individualism and statist-collectivism share fundamental assumptions. They are currents within statism, united in a common premise, rendering them opposing forces *within* the common statist tradition of political and constitutional theory.[31]

The statist tradition is distinctively positivist in that the existing territorial states have set the paradigm within which political and constitutional thinking have taken place over the centuries since the dawn of the territorial state.[32] In consequence, the dominant concepts and themes of reflection in the field of constitutional law and political philosophy as well as in political practice are all statist in nature, that is, conditioned by and safeguarded for the territorial state. The accepted meaning of these concepts serves the specific needs of the territorial state.

Thus, citizenship is citizenship of the *state*; democracy is *statist* democracy, that is, democracy made safe for the territorial state – democracy converted from the unruly and incoherent master to the docile and dependable servant.[33] Human rights also presuppose the indispensability of the *state*. Dependent individuals now have no option but to resort to the state for protection since communal bonds have

---

29   Lucidly explained by Nisbet, 1990:156-160.

30   Rousseau, 1968:69 and further. For a concise discussion of the relevant aspects of Rousseau's political thinking see Malan, 2012a:131-142.

31   This evidenced by the fact that all these trends have this in common that they act against small languages and cultures in the states in which these ideologies have gained the upper-hand. See Malan, 2014b:462-480.

32   This is one of the main themes of Robert Nisbet's discussion in his 1990 *The quest for community: a study in the ethics of order and freedom.*

33   Dunn, 1993:248.

disappeared, leaving individuals with no choice but to seek protection from the state[34] in the form of human rights *guaranteed* by the state and thus reinforcing individual dependence on the indispensable state. By making itself indispensable in this way, the state arguably draws more benefit from this than individuals.[35] Nationhood also presupposes the state to such an extent that the terms "state" and "nation" are increasingly identified with one another.[36] Citizenship is also identified with the state. Even though the term *citizen* and its counterparts in many languages – for example Bürger in German, citoyen in French, citidanos in Spanish and burger in Afrikaans suggest association with a smaller and closer knit unit, more specifically the city, or burg,[37] citizenship has since the advent of the territorial state exclusively been identified with and monopolised for the state. In terms of the statist paradigm, self-determination is basically exercised by the state and not by any particularist community.[38]

These examples, among many others, show how our (academic) theorising and practical conduct have become statist, that is, absorbed and conditioned by the statist paradigm and directed towards safeguarding and reinforcing the existing territorial state. In Chapter 8, I will focus in more detail on the rise of the abstract individual with universal human rights together with the territorial state, forming the other party to the consortium of statist-individualist constitutionalism.

2.3

The establishment of statist-individualist constitutionalism

Statist-individualist constitutionalism arose within the political framework of the fully established centralised territorial state,[39] and the academic hegemony of the statist paradigm in political theorising and legal academia. Statist-individualist constitutionalism is the embodiment of statist-individualism within the discourse of constitutionalism.

Statist-individualist constitutionalism has largely monopolised the notion of constitutionalism. That is why the apparatus of the present territorial state and individual rights are presented as the sole incarnation of the idea of justice and of a constitution based on an apt system of division (separation), balance and control of power. Premised on the same statist basis the territorial state (and

---

34 Diamond, 1971:115-144 at 124.

35 Malan, 2012a:215-222; 233-236.

36 Seton-Watson, 1977:1.

37 See Malan, 2012a:309 and note 18.

38 It is only recently that self-determination for communities is also recognised in the form of internal self-determination.

39 Grimm, 2007:3-22 at 11.

the abstract individual) takes centre stage in thinking on constitutionalism and constitutional law to such an extent that constitutional law has become *law of the state* as the names, Staatsrecht, staatsregt and staatsreg for this discipline in the German, Dutch and Afrikaans languages, respectively, expressly denote.[40] In step with the basic assumptions of statism as outlined above, (statist) constitutionalism is fixated on the state and the individual, thus ignoring, and often justifying even pernicious programmes for the destruction of cultural and linguistic communities.[41] By the same token, political science has also become the *study or science of the state* (*staatsleer/Staatslehre* – as often described in German, Dutch and Afrikaans).

According to the individualist current of statist-individualist constitutionalism, constitutionalism is premised on the doctrine of abstract individual with so-called inalienable universal equal rights.[42] Hence, the very notion of a constitution is identified with the individual rights, in the absence of which there is in fact no constitution at all.[43] During the French and American revolutions, the notion of natural individual rights, already prominent in the crass individual atomism of Hobbes, blossomed into inalienable, inborn individual human rights in the work of the leading theoretical exponents of the revolutions and in various defining documents of these revolutions. The writings of Thomas Paine are particularly pertinent in this context. Among the official revolutionary documents the French Declaration of the Rights of Man and the Citizen of 1789 was the most prominent.[44] Statist-individualist constitutionalism has come to full fruition after World War II, being expressed in numerous contemporary constitutions as well as in international legal instruments.[45]

Since these rights were regarded inborn and inalienable[46] they had to be defined in writing in emphatic terms. Moreover, there was an absolute need to insulate these rights against political forces. Hence, they had to be sanctified in an unchangeable – rigid and permanent – Constitution. They are defined during a flawless constitution-making moment after which no political process shall ever change them since they have become *guaranteed* constitutional-rights. Hence, the Constitution, specifically the constitutional-rights, are inherently pre- and a-political.

---

40 The English *constitutional law* and the French *droit constitutionnel* are more preferable in the sense that they are open to conceiving of constitutional law outside the confines of the (territorial) state. On the other hand, however, these terms are also somehow deceiving in the sense that they obscure the fact that present-day constitutional law has in fact largely been monopolised by statist.

41 Van Dyke, 1974.

42 Compare article 1 and 2 of the French 1789 Declaration of the Rights of Man and of the Citizen.

43 Thus article 16 of the French Declaration of Rights of man and the Citizen provides: "Any society in which the guarantee of rights is not assured, nor the separation of powers determined, has no Constitution."

44 The first article reads: "Men are born and remain free and equal in rights."

45 Most notably in the sweeping terms of the 1948 Universal Declaration of Human Rights of the United Nations (UN).

46 Jung Friedrich, 1974:87 observes that these rights are not natural at all. If so there would have been no need to protect them in a constitutional document.

This development, which is a crucial aspect of statist-individualist constitutionalism, can best be understood when contrasted with the classical view of a constitution dating back to ancient political thinking and practice. McIlwain explains how the classical view of constitutionalism was articulated by Bolingbroke in 1733 and by Edmund Burke at the advent of the French revolution. According to this view, the constitution is not a document setting out how government and the citizenry ought to behave. On the contrary, the constitution exists in the *actual condition* – the actual state of affairs – of the polity. This includes the actual functioning arrangements relating to the division and control of power, the actual conduct of political authorities and the citizenry, and the content of the norms that are actually prevalent in the polity. The conduct of the inhabitants, more specifically of political authorities in terms of this view of the constitution is not regarded as constitutional or unconstitutional, measured against the yardstick of a constitutional document, simply because there is no such document existing outside the actual state of the polity. Bad things are simply wrong and reprehensible and indicative of the bad shape of the constitution. Bad behaviour is not judged as unconstitutional, but it is rather seen as a scenario calling for improvement by political actors and for better political practice. By the same token, a good constitution would be a condition in the polity in which people, including political authorities generally act commendably. The constitution is therefore not pre-political, but political. It exists and is reflected in the actual state of the polity. The constitution is constituted and re-constituted by the political (and other) actors and forces on a continuing basis.[47] Accordingly Leo Strauss gives the following succinct explanation of this view of the constitution (*politeia*):

> The politea is rather the factual distribution of power within the community than what constitutional law stipulates in regard to political power. The politea may be defined by laws, but it need not be. The laws regarding the politea may be deceptive, unintentionally and even intentionally, as to the true character of the politea. No law, and hence no constitution, can be the fundamental political fact, because all laws depend on human beings. Laws have to be adopted, preserved, and administered by men. The human beings making up a political community may be 'arranged' in greatly different ways in regard to the control of communal affairs. It is primarily the factual 'arrangement' of human beings in regard to political power that is meant by politea.[48]

This outlook on the constitution resonates clearly in classical works of political philosophy. Aristotle states for example that the constitution of a city is really the way it lives.[49] It is for that reason that the constitution also changes, as Aristotle says, owing to custom and upbringing.[50]

---

47   McIlwain, 2007:2-3 and generally 1-38.

48   Strauss, 1953:136.

49   Aristotle, 1962:Chapter 11, 171.

50   Aristotle, 1962:Chapter 5, 160-161.

The statist-individualist constitution is something entirely different, existing not in the actual condition of the polity, but in a document that is separate from the actual conditions. This document is *The Constitution,* which is a supreme law. It seeks to lay down and enforce norms of appropriate (constitutional) conduct in conformity with what the Constitution as a normative document requires; and any rule or conduct of whatever nature which does not conform with the document is invalid and void. This Constitution is contained in a supreme document and is consisting of a set of norm-formulations. The first letter of its name is a capital letter 'C' to distinguish it from its classical predecessor, which was not of similar supremacy. It is (primarily) a written instrument.

In its formative stages this view of the Constitution was formulated by Thomas Paine and Arthur Young.[51] The Constitution – the constitutional document to be precise – is constituted by virtue of an act of popular sovereignty. This represents the flawless constitution-making moment mentioned above. During this moment the only agent we now view to be vested with legitimate constitution-making authority, namely the People – *We the People* – as the preambles of many modern Constitutions solemnly proclaim,[52] lay down the Constitution and constitutionalise the norm-formulations that claim to provide for inalienable, inborn, individual human rights. This is the only moment of the exercise of popular sovereignty. Once that responsibility is discharged, popular sovereignty is a spent force for all posterity. In due course popular sovereignty permanently falls by the wayside to be replaced with constitutional supremacy.[53]

The Constitution therefore assumes a static-formal character. It exists exclusively in the norm-formulations of the Constitution, and it may only be amended in terms of its own strict amendment provisions. It is harnessed against forces – political and social forces – outside the Constitution and they cannot change the Constitution, thus making the Constitution itself the supreme and unchallengeable force in the existence of the state.

The discussion now proceeds to define the essential characteristics of statist-individualist constitutionalism.

---

51 McIlwain, 2007:141 and 147.

52 The preambles of the Constitution of the United States of America and the Constitution of the Republic of South Africa serve as examples. This resonates with the view of Paine, 1996:141, 149.

53 Modern theories of justice such as that of John Rawls as set out in his *Theory of justice* do away with popular sovereignty as a flawless constitution-making and rights proclaiming moment and replace it with a rationalised theory under ideal circumstances, in the case of Rawls, in the original position in which a veil of ignorance covers all those that have to agree on the constitution and who will be living under it.

24

The nine essential beliefs of statist-individualist constitutionalism

The essence of the doctrine of statist-individualist constitutionalism is encapsulated in the following nine closely intertwined and mutually reinforcing beliefs, namely that:

1. the positive law emanating from the designated law-making and law-interpreting bodies of the state as defined in the legal norm-formulations of positive law, more specifically the Constitution, is omnipresent;

2. the Constitution is rigid and actually supreme; being actually supreme, it claims to be descriptive of the actual state of affairs in the polity; it is also prognostic in that it claims to have the authority to determine that the future state of affairs in the polity would be in conformity with the norm-formulations of the Constitution;

3. the actual condition of the polity is formulation-driven, which entails that the actual state of affairs of the polity is determined by the norm-formulations of the Constitution. The actual state of the constitution also has a formal-static nature: it remains as it is (static) until such time as a norm-formulation of the Constitution is amended;

4. the Constitution is written (document-based) which implies extraordinary faith in written language and the concomitant importance of constitutional interpretation;

5. the Constitution is pre-political;

6. the Constitution is power-structured on the basis of the trias politica (the threefold separation of governmental power), supported by additional so-called independent and impartial institutions, among which there is a system of mutual checks and balances, believed to limit power adequately and to secure justice;

7. the constitutional discourse is largely preoccupied with micro-theory, forthcoming from judicial pronouncements and based upon a deductive (orthodox) view of interpretation;

8. the Constitution is premised on the exclusive twosome consortium of the territorial state with undivided sovereignty and the abstract individual with universal individual human rights – the latter purporting to be the embodiment of justice;

9. the Constitution is anti-communitarian and anti-pluralist.

The doctrine of statist-individualist constitutionalism is bolstered by its own distinctive magic-like and gospel-like language, (the doctrine's language), which inculcates the trust in statist-individualist constitutionalism. The doctrine's language pretends that words have an autonomous ability to create factual realities and to prevent materialisation of potential counter realities. It is gospel-like and redeeming as it inculcates the faith in the Constitution's unwavering supremacy and ability to secure justice. The doctrine's language will be alluded to in Chapter 3 on statist-individualist constitutionalism in post 1994 South Africa, and dealt with in fuller detail in Chapter 4 in which statist-individualist constitutionalism's claims to rigidity and supremacy are critiqued.

In the ensuing chapters in which the statist-individualist constitutionalism is critiqued, it will be shown that these beliefs are untenable and unfounded.

I proceed now to discuss these nine beliefs and the doctrine's accompanying language.

2.4.1 State-based positive law, more specifically the formulations of the Constitution, is omnipresent

Law, more in particular positive law, captured in the relevant norm-formulations, is viewed as an omnipresent system of legal precepts in terms of which human behaviour in all spheres of life is prescribed, measured, controlled and remedied. The view is specifically state-centred since the conviction is that the state institutions, as designated by the norm-formulations of the Constitution as law-making bodies (mainly the legislature), and to a limited extent the executive (through subordinate legislation and administrative-rule making) and the courts (through judicial interpretation) entirely exhaust the function of making and amending law. Beyond that, the belief is not only that no law may be made or amended but that no law is in fact made or changed. Yes, the norm-formulations are interpreted by the designated interpreters but that gives meaning to what is imminent in the text; it obviously does not replace the formulations.

This belief accords with the generally avowed premise upon which present-day constitutional states are based. This premise is so firmly inculcated that it tends to be generally assumed without reflection. Occasionally, however, it is explicitly articulated. Ronald Dworkin's exposition of law provides arguably the purist and most well-known exposition of the omnipresence of positive law. Dworkin proposes that law consists of principles alongside rules that enable law to maintain such a lacuna-free omnipresence that the need for exercising discretion to fill gaps never arises. There are in all cases principles capable of providing a legally-based correct solution for all legal questions.[54] Aharon Barak's view of law is similar. The legal universe is full of fundamental principles and there is no corner of our lives not controlled by them.[55] Barak further declares that every dispute is normatively justiciable and then elaborates as follows:

> Every legal problem has criteria for its resolution. There is no 'legal vacuum.' According to my outlook law fills the whole world. There is no sphere containing no law and no legal criteria. Every human act is encompassed in the world of law. Every act can be 'imprisoned' in the framework of the law. Even actions of a clearly political nature – such

---

54 Dworkin, 1977:Chapters 4 and 7.

55 Barak, 2002-2003:84-85.

as waging of war – can be examined with legal criteria, as evidenced by the laws of war in international law. The mere fact that an issue is 'political' – that is, (seemingly) predominantly political or could have far-reaching political consequences – does not mean that it cannot be resolved by a court of law. Everything can be resolved by a court in the sense that law can take a view as to its legality.[56]

2.4.2 The Constitution is rigid and actually supreme

The norm-formulations of the Constitution regulate, command and standardise all conduct of those under its jurisdiction, including the conduct of the agencies of the state. The norm-formulations of the Constitution are themselves the supreme social reality. The supreme Constitution is believed to be actively regulating not only the law outside the Constitution. It is, moreover, also viewed to be in command of these realities. This highlights three intertwined dimensions of the norm-formulations of (positive) law, specifically those of the Constitution, namely its constitutive, descriptive (truth) and prognostic dimensions.

The norm-formulations are regarded as a reliable reflection of the actual state of the law. In its turn the law, mirror-imaged in the formulations, is the supreme social reality that actually regulates these realities. Conditioned by the doctrine of statist-individualist constitutionalism, as embodied in the belief in the actual supremacy of the Constitution, norm-formulations that are prescriptive (contained in prescriptive formulations), undergo an epistemological metamorphosis and become descriptive, that is, formulations that (pretend to) describe social realities (truths). Hence, the norm-formulations are believed to describe social realities, or as Karl Llewellyn said: "... that the verbal formulations of the oughts describe precisely the is-es of practice."[57] Once again in the words of Llewellyn, the paper rules of the oughts are assumed to govern people's conduct.[58] As the more detailed discussion in Chapter 4 will show, the written legal norm-formulations, more specifically those of the supreme Constitution, are particularly highly valued – supremely valued. These formulations essentially describe a reliable prognosis of future social realities.[59]

By virtue of the Constitution, having proclaimed its own supremacy, Dutch jurist, Van der Hoeven,[60] observes that lawyers are strongly inclined to believe the bold claim of the supreme Constitution, namely to subject political power effectively to the norm-formulations of the Constitution and to make the Constitution impervious

---

56   Ibid, p.98. Barak's views resonate those of Dworkin on principles. These views are all at the root of the dominant doctrine on the rule of law and constitutional supremacy. These, more particularly those of Dworkin, have drawn sharp criticism from Hart who in my view quite aptly described Dworkin as *"the most noble dreamer of them all* for his (Dworkin's) belief that the norm complex of law was sufficient to provide a right answer for all legal questions, thus avoiding the need ever to resort to discretion." See Hart:179.

57   Llewellyn, 2008:17.

58   Ibid.

59   Van der Hoeven, 1958:251; 248.

60   Van der Hoeven, 1976:504.

to political power. Even in the face of strong evidence to the contrary, namely that the "supreme" Constitution has been overcome by political forces which are stronger than the Constitution, they still adhere to the belief in the supreme law as encapsulated in the norm-formulations of the Constitution. The conviction is that the norm-formulations of the Constitution are actually ruling and will keep on doing so in future. Van der Hoeven observes:

> The constitutionalists seek to achieve their objectives on account of a very high value that is placed upon written law. They are convinced that human conduct, including conduct by government can be regulated by legal norms.[61] (Own translation).

With reference to the position in the United States of America, Griffin further elaborates:

> Lawyers tend to regard the Constitution as a set of ultimate normative standards appropriate for judging any political practice. The Constitution occupies so much normative space that it is hard to see anything else. The Constitution is "a machine that (goes) of itself" and policy disasters and even constitutional crises are not evidence of a failure of the document, but only that Americans have failed its high expectations.[62]

To the extent that the realities are incongruent with the norm-formulations, the effect of the supreme Constitution would be to change such realities in order to conform with the formulations. Hence, to the extent that norm-formulations are as yet not describing the social realities, they would at least be correcting and (re)constituting these realities so as to bring them into step with the norm-formulations. Legal norm-formulations that do not describe social realities would therefore at least reliably predict future realities.

The doctrine of statist-individualist constitutionalism is hard-pressed (in principle as a matter of fact) not to make the following concessions that would unsettle the doctrine.

Firstly, any concession that law's norm-formulations are not omnipresent. Such concession would imply that certain areas of human life were not regulated by law and therefore not under the rule of law.

Secondly, any concession that the law (and the Constitution) is not formulation-driven. Any such concession would allow for the possibility that law could lapse into non-existence and be replaced with new law, through events other than formal amendments of the law as prescribed by the acknowledged norm-formulations of positive law, more specifically those of the Constitution. Such concession would further surrender the determination of the content of the law and the Constitution to the unpredictable quirks of social and political forces. That would amount to a concession that the norm-formulations, perceived to be signifying the actual state

---

61 Van der Hoeven:496. The original Dutch reads: *"De constitutionalisten trachten hun doelstellenigen te verwerklijken, gelijk wij zagen, vanuit een zeer hogere waardering voor het geschreven recht. Zij menen het menselijk handelen ook op het terrein van gezag en gezachsoefening door rechtsnormen te kunnen regeren."*

62 Griffin:43-44.

of the law, were in fact not the supreme social reality as the doctrine would have it. The belief system of the doctrine of statist-individualist constitutionalism is forced to reserve the privilege of calling something "law" exclusively to the institutions of the Constitution. Van den Bergh thus states:

> In the legal ideology of the liberal constitutional state the privilege to call something "law" is strictly reserved for designated institutions. Freedom means the supreme rule of law and only of the law. Custom is no autonomous but at most a derivative source of law.[63] (Own translation)

Not to do so would, on close analysis, allow people to take the law into their own hands[64] and for law to be made, undone or replaced by the actors other than those bodies designated by the Constitution to make, change and interpret the law.

It should therefore be obvious that any concession enabling sectors of the public or state agencies, acting outside their official mandates to make binding law, would be out of the question.

Thirdly, any concession that law (more specifically the Constitution) is not the supreme social and political force but one among many others. Such concession would surrender the (belief in the actual) supremacy of the Constitution to the uncertain vagaries brought about by other social forces and even to the domination of one or more such forces. In that way the belief in the actual supremacy of the Constitution would make a self-defeating concession to legal realism and to unbridled politics beyond the control of the norm-formulations of the Constitution, thus surrendering the principle of the rule of law and the supremacy of the Constitution to the volatility of socio-political forces.[65]

2.4.3 The Constitution is formulation-driven and has a formal-static character

The law and the Constitution, captured in written legal norm-formulations, are contained in their own sovereign corpus, clearly distinguishable from other modes of social control and independent of social and political forces.[66] In terms of this view, which in Western legal culture has its roots in the papal revolution in the eleventh century,[67] law essentially assumes a formal-static character.

By *formal* is meant that since law, captured in the legal norm-formulations, may only be amended in terms of the relevant precepts of positive law, ordinarily provided for in the amendment provisions of the Constitution, changes in the law can occur

---

63 Van den Bergh:44. The original Dutch reads: "In de rechsideologie van de liberale burgerstaat is het privilegie om iets 'recht' te noemen streng voorbehouden aan welomschreven instellingen. Vrijheid betekent heerschappij van de wet en de wet alleen. De gewoonte is geen autonome, hoogstens nog een afgeleide bron van recht."

64 Van den Bergh:46.

65 Van den Bergh:6.

66 Malan, 2012:276-280. See also in general Berman, 1983.

67 Berman, 1983:99 et seq.

only in strict compliance with such amendment provisions. Using the terms of H.L.A. Hart, these would be called rules of change.[68] By *static* is meant that the law and the Constitution remain unchanged until a norm-formulation is amended or repealed (and replaced) in terms of the prescribed amendment provisions (which are obviously also legal norm-formulations) of the Constitution.

In consequence, law and the Constitution captured in the legal norm-formulations, have an integrity making them impervious to social and political forces. These forces cannot change the law and the Constitution, at least not directly,[69] (that is automatically) in ways other than those prescribed by the amendment provisions of the Constitution. The law, as noted, may – and can – only be changed in accordance with the prescribed amendment procedures of the law (and the Constitution). These procedures must be duly signified in the relevant norm-formulations and the bodies authorised in these formulations to execute the function of amendment must strictly comply with them. The corpus of law *(the totality of all legal norm-formulations)* has its own sovereign existence and grows in terms of its own rules and independent of any forces outside the corpus of law.

In terms of this formulation-driven view of the law, law and the Constitution come into existence and are changed solely on account of the law-making and amending activities of the law-makers (legislatures and constitutional-making bodies) combined with the interpretive activities of the courts. Full knowledge of the law and the Constitution can in principle be acquired solely by consulting the norm-formulations of the acknowledged sources of positive law emanating from these bodies and from the bodies designated by the Constitution to interpret the formulations. The legal norm-formulations of the positive law, including the Constitution, are therefore perceived to provide the full and reliable picture of the law. In consequence, every legal activity, is document-based and a matter of interpretation. Lawyers, being prisoners of language, in the words of Aarnio,[70] have to identify the relevant authoritative documents containing legal norm-formulations which they must then interpret. When new law is to be created, the services of lawyers are enlisted and once again their activities are document-centred: the lawyers have to draft new documents containing new authoritative legal norm-formulations. The meaning of the law and the Constitution is not to be found beyond these legal norm-formulations. More in particular, it does not require social inquiry in order to establish what the law and the Constitution factually entail since the legal norm-formulations are perceived to provide the full answer to all questions on the content of the law. By the same token, the curricula of legal education are

---

68 Hart outlined his system of secondary rules (alongside primary rules in order to constitute an actual legal order) in 1994:89 et seq.

69 If conceded that the populace or forceful sections of the populace could change the law directly, the opposing principle of constitutional supremacy, namely popular sovereignty (or merely to unbound political force) and thus the rule of law succumbs to socio-political forces that trump the law. For the tension between constitutional supremacy and popular sovereignty see Malan, 2015b:248-268.

70 Aarnio, 2011:131.

also equally formulation-conditioned. The exclusive focus is on establishing the relevant norm-formulations and on the interpretation of the formulations.

2.4.4 The supreme value that is placed on the formulations – the written words of the constitutional Document

In step with the Enlightenment trust in the written constitution,[71] the Constitution is a written instrument – a document.[72] Written format (writtenness) is inherent in statist-individualist constitutionalism. The terms of its supremacy are captured in the written text of the Constitution. It is there and nowhere else that the Constitution is located and it is the written norm-formulations with perceived clear, accurate, certain, stable meanings that constitute the supreme Constitution. The written Constitution is the creator and regulator of the political order. The Constitution is specifically not to be found in something outside the text of the written (supreme) Constitution. The crucial importance of documentary essence of the Constitution (encapsulated in a single written instrument) goes back particularly to Thomas Paine, in whose view England, in contrast to the United States of America and France, does not have a constitution at all since there is no single written (and legally supreme) constitutional Document.[73] In terms of this view, there is no source of constitutional law outside the constitutional Document – the written constitutional instrument.[74] The Constitution as a written instrument contains the Constitution and is the embodiment of constitutionalism.

The textual nature of the Constitution also entails that finding the meaning of the text is distinctively important. This highlights the importance of interpretation (of the constitutional Document) in terms of statist-individualist constitutionalism. Since the written text is so important, interpretation of the text is at the very centre of the activities of constitutional jurists in terms of the doctrine of statist-individualist constitutionalism. In fact, in terms of statist-individualist constitutionalism basically all activity is (text-based) interpretation.

Trust in the written word of the Constitution causes what Van der Hoeven aptly highlighted, namely that (under statist-individualist constitutionalism) "the constitutionalists," as he puts it, seek to realise their objectives from the perspective of a very high regard for written law. They assume that human action in the sphere of the execution of political power can also be subjected to legal regulation.[75]

---

71   Ackerman, 1997:772.

72   See Murphy, 1993:10 et seq.

73   Paine, 1996:141-163.

74   Or in that which the constitution expressly prescribes, such as legislation to be adopted in terms of specific provisions of the constitution, which would also fall within the broader defined constitution. Examples in South African law are the Promotion of Equality and Prohibition of Unfair Discrimination Act, 2 of 2000, the Promotion of Access to Information Act, 4 of 2000 and the Promotion of Administrative Justice Act, 3 of 2000, adopted in terms of sections 9, 32 and 33 respectively.

75   Van der Hoeven, 1976:496 states: *"De constitutionalisten trachten hun doelstellenigen te verwerklijken, gelijk wij zagen, vanuit een zeer hogere waardering voor het geschreven recht. Zij menen het menselijk handelen ook op het terrein van gezag en gezachsoefening door rechtsnormen te kunnen regeren."*

2.4.5 Pre-political

A clear distinction between what is regarded as political in contrast to what is pre-political is crucial for statist-individualist constitutionalism. Whatever is included in the Constitution is agreed to pre-politically, that is, before actual (normal) politics come into play. Specifically *individual human rights* are agreed to pre-politically. Politics starts only when the Constitution (with individual human rights) have been agreed to, and since such politics have to be executed strictly within the framework of the supreme Constitution, it is restricted to the legal administration in accordance with the written formulations of the Constitution. The pre-politically agreed Constitution may not be amended,[76] or if amendment is permitted, then only in accordance with and within the confines of the Constitution.[77] For that very reason the Constitution is described – praised – as an entrenched Constitution: entrenched and safeguarded against and impregnable to political forces. Specifically the constitutional rights are regarded as firmly entrenched against the vagaries of politics. That is why they are generally viewed as *guaranteed* and *enshrined* in the Constitution, thus affording an almost sacred status to them, in contrast to the often so non-sacred and profane ways of politics. Politics – in terms of statist-individualist constitutionalism reduced to mere legal administration – takes place within the boundaries allowed in terms of the Constitution. Tampering with the Constitution falls outside the terrain of politics. The Constitution, after all is pre-political.

These first five beliefs of statist-individualist constitutionalism are embodied in a set of constitutional mechanisms, concisely described in the last part of this chapter, namely mechanisms that purport to entrench the (written, rigid and supreme) Constitution, accompanied and strengthened with *conformity provisions* and provisions that seek to safeguard the Constitution against political forces.

2.4.6 The trias politica and the independence, impartiality and effectiveness of the judiciary

Under the statist-individualist doctrine of constitutionalism governmental power is distributed within the framework of undivided state sovereignty in accordance with the doctrine of the trias politica – the trite threefold separation of powers between the legislature, the executive and judiciary. To that is added a number of "independent" and "impartial" state institutions such as the ombud or Public Protector, Auditor-General, Human Rights Commission, prosecutorial authority and other similar "independent" and "impartial" bodies, all of which are organs of state. This framework represents statist-individualist constitutionalism's version,

---

76   As for example under the doctrine of the basic structure as developed Indian constitutional law, in the judgment of the *Indian Supreme Court in Kesavananda Bharti v Union of India* 1973(4) SCC 225 and absolute prohibitions against the amendment of the German in sections 19(1)-(3) of the German constitution of 1949.

77   Such as article V of the Constitution of the United States of America and section 73 of the Constitution of the Republic of South Africa.

which as will be shown in the latter chapters, is an inordinately restricted state-departmentalised version, of the notion of the mixed constitution.

In terms of the doctrine of statist-individualist constitutionalism the judiciary, more specifically the highest court, occupies an august and often hallowed position. The fate of the Constitution, the direction of constitutional law and the content and enjoyment of rights are perceived as dependent on the courts. The courts are believed to be truly independent and impartial. They are the supreme patrons of the Constitution, the guardians of the bill of rights and the protector of justice by upholding individual rights. They are further believed to adjudicate cases on the basis of the applicable law and objective legal reasoning. As independent and impartial institutions of the law, they are not politically driven and do not reach decisions informed by any non-legal (specifically political) considerations. All can rest assured that their rights will be protected. The courts are the final guarantee of that. This doctrine invests tremendous trust in the independence and impartiality of the judiciary. As will be shown in the last part of this chapter, this belief is embodied in mechanisms for the threefold separation of power, judicial independence and mechanisms of checks and balances between the three branches of governmental power.

2.4.7 The preoccupation – fixation – with micro theory (and the statist-individualist approach to interpretation)

The importance of the courts to adjudicate, in particular with regard to the protection of individual rights, causes the doctrine of statist constitutionalism to be fixated with micro theories of constitutionalism. This implies a preoccupation with judicial reasoning on the assumption that court judgments are the pivot of constitutional law and constitutionalism. In consequence, judicial reasoning captured in such judgments is meticulously studied. Approaches to interpretation of individual rights – purposive, generous, systematic, contextual, comparative, historical, transformative, originalist and a raft of others – are intensely debated, and so are theories of judicial reasoning – proportionality, fairness, rationality and others. Questions regarding the balanced constitution (the allocation and balance of power and checks on power) which are the central focus of macro constitutional theory, are pushed to the periphery on the assumption that macro-constitutional questions have been clarified adequately. As a result of its preoccupation with the judicial interpretation of the written text of the Constitution combined with the micro theory, the judiciary is always brightly under the spotlight of the doctrine of statist-individualist constitutionalism, to such an extent that constitutional jurists are primarily preoccupied with judicial interpretation almost as if the doctrine of statist-individualist constitutionalism is only about judicial interpretation. That also explains the exceptionally august status of the judges in terms of the doctrine of statist-individualist constitutionalism. They are the *legal kings*[78] of statist constitutionalism, privy to knowledge, insight and wisdom other people are deprived of. They are clothed with a distinctive almost sacred status and they sometimes even describe themselves as a secular priesthood.[79]

Believing in the actual supremacy of the written Constitution, statist-individualist constitutionalism subscribes to a deductive (orthodox) view of judicial interpretation. This deductive view is particularly pertinent, as will be shown in Chapter 7. Hence, the written Constitution is essentially a done deal. Its provisions have essentially fixed meanings. Through judicial interpretation these meanings are deduced and applied to practical situations. Interpretation thus viewed naturally does not make up and change the Constitution with every new act of interpretation, because that would defeat the very notion of the supremacy of the written Constitution. Interpretation merely brings the meanings inherent in the Constitution, to light. To argue otherwise – to say that the Constitution is changing all along through interpretation – amounts to acknowledging that supremacy vests in the interpreters instead of the Constitution and this to hollow out the very notion of constitutional supremacy or to sacrifice it altogether.

2.4.8 The twosome consortium of the state and the individual – state sovereignty and abstract universal, individual human rights

As highlighted above, the statist-individualist doctrine of constitutionalism basically recognises only two entities: the state and the individual. The state is clothed with undivided sovereignty. It is a monist institution that monopolises all political power. Sovereignty vests in the *nation* and law is an expression of the single general will of the nation,[80] as expressed by the majority of the populace. The individual is abstract and universalist and essentially the same as all other individuals, which under the doctrine of *abstract universal, individual human rights* have basically the same rights as all other individuals.[81] (Next to individuals with inalienable equal human rights there are individual-like institutions with legal personality which are also capable of enjoying rights in a similar way as individuals). The recognition of the individual person is ordinarily embodied in a catalogue of basic rights (a bill of rights) which occupies a hallowed position in statist-individualist constitutionalism. It captures a tremendous amount of attention and is generally viewed as the backbone of the Constitution. The bill of rights is viewed as the very embodiment of the Constitution's commitment to justice.

---

78 See Labuschagne, 1988:330. The idea of legal kings resonates with Ronald Dworkin's use of the concept Law's Empire.

79 See for example *Zuma v National Director of Public Prosecutions* 2009(1) BCLR 62(N) para 161.

80 See in this regard the seminal formulations articles 3 and 6 of the French 1789 Declaration of the Rights of Man and of the Citizen.

81 Thus articles 1 and 2 of the seminal of the French 1789 Declaration of the Rights of Man and of the Citizen provide, amongst others: Men are born and remain free and equal in rights. Social distinctions can be founded only on the common good (Article 1). The goal of any political association is the conservation of the natural and imprescriptible rights of man (Article 2).

Federalism has always been a qualification – arguably even a counter movement – within the doctrine of statist-individualist constitutionalism. The rise of the notion of rights and powers for cultural and linguistic communities (and not only for individuals) together with constitutional mechanisms in terms of which legislative and executive powers are allocated to corporate (non-territorial) governing organs for such communities are exceptions within statist-individualist constitutionalism. These constitutional mechanisms, depending on their strength, may even be expected to supersede or transcend statist-individualist constitutionalism.

2.4.9 The state is anti-communitarian and anti-pluralist

Cultural and linguistic communities, and generally political pluralism are particularly anathema in the eyes of statist-individualist constitutionalism.[82] Cultural communities are comprehensive wholes with organic characters. They are capable of sustaining themselves and upholding their own traditions (specifically those embodied in their languages) which they received from previous generations to be passed on to posterity and thus perpetuating themselves as it were. For this very reason these communities attract the animosity from statist-individualist constitutionalism because such communities often strive towards the achievement of self-determination, thereby challenging the exclusive twosome consortium of the state and the individual inherent in the doctrine of statist-individualist constitutionalism. The latter's response is to dismiss communities as fictions[83] worthy of no real existence. It equally rejects political pluralism, which allows political power to vest in a multitude of centres established within communities, instead of solely within the structures of a single centralised state government. To the extent that communities and power for communities might enjoy some recognition it is perceived as anomalous and exceptional in terms of statist-individualist constitutionalism.

2.5

Statist-individualist constitutionalism's three key mechanisms

The belief system of statist-individualist constitutionalism set out above is embodied in a trite set of three constitutional mechanisms exemplifying modern-day statist-individualist Constitutions, namely:

σ   Supremacy proclamations, entrenchment and conformity mechanisms and strict amendment requirements;

---

82   See for example Du Plessis, 1988:Chapter 7.

83   This view goes back to the very beginnings of statism in the radical individualism of Thomas Hobbes. Later on Bentham, 1967:Chapter 1 iv articulated this radical individualism and rejection of community with the following terse remark: "The community is a fictitious body, composed of the individual persons who are considered as constituting as it were its members. The interest of the community then – is what? The sum of the several interests of the members who composed it."

σ   the separation of powers and the independence and impartiality of the judiciary; and

σ   bills of individual rights.

These three mechanisms are now discussed.

2.5.1 Supremacy proclamations, entrenchment and conformity mechanisms, and strict amendment requirements

Supremacy proclamations and mechanisms for the entrenchment of the Constitution are the backbone of statist-individualist Constitutions. These proclamations and mechanisms are accompanied by conformity provisions and provisions to safeguard the Constitution against political forces.

Supremacy provisions proclaim the supremacy of the Constitution within the state concerned over all law outside the Constitution and over all social and political forces within the constitutional dispensation concerned. Conformity provisions, which are logically incidental to the supremacy provisions, proclaim that whatever is done within the constitutional dispensation concerned which does not conform to the (supreme) Constitution, is invalid/void and therefore of no consequence.

Strict amendment requirements and procedures seek to safeguard the integrity of the Constitution by (purporting to) make it impervious to any eventualities that might change, disrupt or dismantle the Constitution, and in so doing cause the Constitution to lose its supremacy. This is done through mechanisms that altogether prohibit the amendment of the Constitution and/or lay down strict requirements for constitutional amendments. Through these mechanisms, the formal-static nature of the Constitution is believed to be safeguarded. At the same time the integrity and supreme reign of the Constitution are believed to be placed beyond the reach of disruptive social and political forces that might pose a challenge to the Constitution's supremacy. Such forces are put under the control of the Constitution.

Supremacy proclamations, conformity provisions and strict amendment requirements give expression to and are the embodiment of the first five beliefs of statist constitutionalism described in the previous section, namely the belief or faith in: the omnipresence of the Constitution and positive law; the Constitution's rigidity and actual supremacy; the Constitution's formal-static nature; written language; and the pre-political nature of the Constitution.

Article V of the Constitution of the United States of America, which in many respects is the ground-breaking statist-individualist Constitution, set the tone for entrenchment and strict amendment procedures. In terms of article V loaded, instead of simple majorities (involving Congress, as well as the states), are required for amendment of the Constitution.[84] The example of the United States of America has been followed on numerous occasions, especially in entrenchment, conformity and strict amendment provisions in the vast number of Constitutions adopted after World War II, in Europe, the Americas, Africa and Asia. The underlying belief was that the written formulations in the entrenched Constitution would ensure its full protection against politics.[85]

In some cases mechanisms of constitutional entrenchment have gone so far that they not only make amendment of the Constitution difficult but outlaw it altogether. Article 79(3) of the German Constitution, for example, forbids, amongst other things, any amendment of the Basic Law (the Constitution) of the country that would affect the structure of the Federation and the *Länder* and amendments to the provisions of article 1 (human dignity and the commitment to the inviolable and inalienable human rights and their legally binding force) and the provisions of article 20 (the nature of the German state as a democratic, social federal republic).[86]

An overwhelming majority or even full-fledged consensus on amendments would therefore not suffice in effecting a constitutional amendment if such amendment relates to any of the subject matters listed in section 79(3).

Indian constitutional law has gone another route to achieve a similar end, namely through the judicially created doctrine of the *basic structure of the constitution*. According to this doctrine conceived by the Indian Supreme Court in *Kesavananda Bharti v Union of India*[87] certain amendments to the Indian constitution, namely those that would change the basic structure of the constitution are invalid and of no consequence. Hence, even though the power of amendment under article 368 does allow amendments to the Constitution, that does not include the power to abrogate the Constitution, or the power to alter the basic structure or framework of the Constitution.[88]

---

84 Article V of the Constitution of the United States of America provides as follows: The Congress, whenever two thirds of both houses shall deem it necessary, shall propose amendments to this Constitution, or, on the application of the legislatures of two thirds of the several states, shall call a convention for proposing amendments, which, in either case, shall be valid to all intents and purposes, as part of this Constitution, when ratified by the legislatures of three fourths of the several states, or by conventions in three fourths thereof, as the one or the other mode of ratification may be proposed by the Congress; provided that no amendment which may be made prior to the year one thousand eight hundred and eight shall in any manner affect the first and fourth clauses in the ninth section of the first article; and that no state, without its consent, shall be deprived of its equal suffrage in the Senate.

85 Section 2 read with 255-257 of the Kenyan constitution of 2010 serve as a good recent example of mechanisms of this kind in a recent African constitution.

86 The original German texts of section 79(3) of the German Constitution of 1949 reads: "*Eine Änderung dieses Grundgesetzes, durch welche die Gliederung des Bundes in Länder, die grundsätzliche Mitwirkung der Länder bei der Gesetzgebung oder die in den Artikeln 1 und 20 niedergelegten Grundsätze berührt werden, ist unzulässig.*"

87 1973(4) SCC 225.

88 Article 368 provides that: "An amendment of this Constitution may be initiated only by the introduction of a Bill for the purpose in either House of Parliament, and when the Bill is passed in each House by a majority of the total membership of that House and by a majority of not less than two-thirds of the members of that House present and voting, it shall be presented to the President who shall give his assent to the Bill and thereupon the Constitution ..."

The effect of the Indian basic structure doctrine is essentially the same as that of article 79 of the German Basic Law, namely to prohibit some amendments altogether no matter how strong the support for such amendments may be. According to these strategies, those aspects of the Constitution that may never be amended are therefore believed to be unchangeable for all posterity. Prohibition of amendment therefore does not only stabilise the Constitution, but eternalise it. In Chapter 4, I will show that these supremacy proclamations and mechanisms that seek to prohibit amendment or to subject it to strict requirements and procedures, are not as effective as they pretend to be. They fail to account for the factual dimension of law as explained in Chapter 4. Chapter 5 will demonstrate this with reference to the practical experience in South Africa since the beginning of the country's constitutional transition in 1994. It will be shown that although entrenchment mechanisms and strict amendment requirements may be successful in prohibiting *amendments to the text* of the Constitution as a written instrument (*grondwet* in Afrikaans/Dutch; *Grundgesetz* in German), they cannot prevent changes – even profound changes – to the (actual) constitution. Constitutional changes do not only take place by way of amendment of the text effected by the legislature in accordance with the amendment provisions of the Constitution, but also, and often very profoundly so, by way of the social and political forces for which the norm-formulations of the text of the Constitution are simply no match. Such social and political forces simply cause existing law, including constitutional law, to lapse and in some cases to be substituted by new law, even without any amendment to the text itself. The belief underlying supremacy proclamations, entrenchment and conformity provisions and strict amendment requirements is therefore unfounded. Those proclamations, provisions and requirements cannot secure the eternal existence of any aspect of the Constitution. Often they cannot even stabilise the Constitution. Potent social and political forces are often simply too strong for the *supreme* Constitution to hold sway.

2.5.2 The trias politica, checks and balances and the independence and impartiality of the judiciary

The second trite (set of) mechanisms is statist-individualist Constitutions' typical power structures, namely the separation of powers between the legislature, the executive and the judiciary and the independence and impartiality of the courts. The trias politica may be viewed as statist-individualist constitutionalism's version of the classical notion of the mixed and balanced constitution referred to in Chapter 1. As indicated in the previous part of this chapter, the judiciary, more specifically a constitutional court is viewed as the most important institution that guard against abuse of power. The courts are believed to be the supreme patron of the Constitution, the guardians of the bill of rights and the protector of justice – in the guise of individual rights. As will be shown in Chapter 6, the tremendous trust that is invested in the courts' independence and impartiality and their ability to secure justice is greatly exaggerated.

2.5.3   Bills of individual rights

The bill of rights as interpreted in the final analysis by the courts is the crown jewel of statist-individualist constitutionalism. The bill of rights is the embodiment of the last beliefs discussed in the previous section, namely the belief that the Constitution is premised on undivided state sovereignty and individual rights; that the bill of rights is the fundamental expression of justice; and that the Constitution is anti-communitarian and anti-pluralist, accompanied by the preoccupation of the constitutional discourse with micro-theory, forthcoming for judicial pronouncements.

The bill of rights is so important that it is often almost completely identified with the Constitution and generally with constitutional law. It is the one sector of the Constitution that mostly features in constitutional litigation and also attracts most public attention.

Bills of rights are identified with the broad concept of (individual) human rights. Originally bills of rights only include so-called first generation civil and political rights. In due course, however, new interests were accommodated within the ever broadening framework of human rights. In fact human rights are almost like a sponge, which appears to absorb almost every conceivable human interest.[89] In consequence, bills of rights nowadays also include second generation social and economic rights and a vaguely and ever broadening category of third generation of rights.

There are two reasons why bills of rights stand out as a specifically statist-individualist mechanism of constitutionalism. The first is that the emphasis is placed on the rights of individuals. In consequence, it is accompanied by an express or implied rejection to accommodate the claims of communities, more specifically cultural and linguistic communities. The second reason is its emphasis on the state. The state is the guarantor of the individual rights. As a result of that, individual human rights engender a culture of individual dependence on the state. With each new right that is recognised and included in a bill of rights the individual's dependence expands further; the role of the benign Leviathan in the life of individuals expands and a life without the ever present Leviathan gets less and less conceivable.[90]

Pluralist political thinking allowing room for forms of federalism, for the diffusion of political power and for institutions for autonomous communities can break this stranglehold of the centralist state. As indicated at the beginning of this chapter, such thinking has always been there as a challenge to the doctrine and practice of statist-individualist constitutionalism. The last decades have in fact witnessed the increasing strength of these trends which are posing a mounting challenge to statist-individualist constitutionalism.

---

89   Szabo, 1982:35-36 and Donnelly, 1982:303-316 at 315.

90   See Malan, 2012a:Chapter 8.

*　　　*　　　*

Statist-individualist constitutionalism expanded with consecutive waves of constitution-making since the late 1940s. It began with Constitutions for the erstwhile colonised territories in Asia and Africa. This was followed in the middle of the 1970s with new Constitutions in post fascist Portugal and Spain and in the early 1990s with Constitutions for the previous communist states of Eastern and central Europe.[91] The 1990s saw a new wave of statist-individualist constitutionalism in a number of African states, accompanied by considerable academic interest in these African developments.[92] The present South African Constitution which entered into force in 1997 has been hailed as a shining example, if not the singular zenith of statist-individualist constitutionalism. The next chapter explains why the South African Constitution embodies a distinctive example of the doctrine of statist-individualist constitutionalism and how for that reason it has earned such high accolades.

---

91   See Huntington, 1991.

92   See for example Fombad & Murray, 2010.

Statist-Individualist Constitutionalism in Post 1994 South Africa

3.1

Introduction

The South African Constitution is a glowing embodiment of the triad of constitutional mechanisms that exemplifies statist-individualist constitutions, as explained in Chapter 2. It is precisely for that reason that it is one of the most vaunted legal documents of the past decades. Constitutional jurists (locally and abroad), politicians and the public media have poured acclaim on the Constitution. The Constitution has been hailed as one of the best Constitutions, if not the best in the world. It is submitted that this acclaim is primarily based on the fact that the Constitution categorically subscribes to all the essentials of statist-individualist constitutionalism.

The present South African constitutional order first saw the light of day in April 1994 when the interim Constitution[1] took effect. The interim Constitution embodied the political settlement that brought the protracted struggle against white minority rule in South Africa to a close. At the same time, it replaced the dismantled Westminster-like order that was premised on parliamentary sovereignty. All this happened amidst an atmosphere of almost unbridled exuberance both locally and internationally. Soon thereafter in 1997, the present South African Constitution, generally referred to as the *final* Constitution,[2] came into force. The final Constitution emphatically affirmed and rounded off the foundations of statist-individualist constitutionalism in South Africa.

---

1   Constitution of the Republic of South Africa, Act 200 of 1993.

2   Constitution of the Republic of South Africa, 1996 (hereafter *the Constitution*).

This chapter starts off in part 3.2 with a discussion of the three mechanisms that embody the belief system of statist-individualist constitutionalism as encapsulated in the final Constitution. The constitutional and political discourse kindled by South Africa's new constitutional order assumed a very extraordinary character. In this discourse the belief in statist-individualist constitutionalism reached an unprecedented zenith. The South African brand of statist-individualist constitutionalism was praised as nothing short of a miracle. It was eulogised in enchanting terms and with gleeful astonishment. The praises assumed the character of a gospel, expressed in the faith-strengthening language of statist-individualist constitutionalism. This gospel had free rein at the time. Doubts about the validity of the devout claims of statist-individualist constitutionalism as encapsulated in the South African Constitution could in this atmosphere only be raised at the risk of being pilloried for insolent constitutional apostasy. The faith-strengthening language of statist-individualist constitutionalism is of necessity intertwined with the discussion of the three mechanisms of statist-individualist constitutionalism in the South African Constitution. Key aspects of this faith-strengthening discourse are discussed in the third part of the chapter.

3.2

The key mechanisms of statist-individualist constitutionalism in the South African constitutional order

3.2.1 Supremacy proclamation, entrenchment and conformity mechanisms and strict amendment requirements

The first five beliefs of the doctrine of statist-individualist constitutionalism (beliefs 1 to 5) as outlined in the fourth part of Chapter 2 constitute the basis for the first (set of) mechanisms/strategies of statist-individualist constitutionalism, namely supremacy proclamations, entrenchment and conformity mechanisms, and strict amendment requirements. In consequence the Constitution is believed to be all-powerful: none of what is laid down in its written formulations can be undone by any countervailing force.

The entrenchment and conformity mechanisms of the South African Constitution are emphatic. Hence, constitutional supremacy is the most definitive feature of the present South African Constitution.[3] The supremacy of the Constitution is encapsulated in the text of the Constitution, not only as the basic enforceable principle in terms of section 2, but also in terms of section 1(c), as one of the Constitution's fundamental values. Section 2 provides:

> This Constitution is the supreme law of the Republic; law or conduct inconsistent with it is invalid, and the obligations imposed by it must be fulfilled.

---

3   See for example the observations made by De Vos, 2014:54-55.

In keeping with these trite strategies of statist-individualism constitutionalism, the supremacy provision is shored up by strict amendment requirements and procedures which in the case of the South African Constitution are provided for in section 74. In essence section 74 requires that the Constitution may only be amended by a Bill passed by the National Assembly, with a supporting vote of at least two thirds of its members; and by the National Council of Provinces, with the support of a minimum of least six of the nine provincial delegations. In the case of proposed amendments to section 1 of the Constitution – the foundational values – the requirements are even stricter in that the amending Bill must carry the support of at least 75% of the members of the National Assembly.[4]

By these mechanisms the South African Constitution, in keeping with the general belief system of statist-individualist constitutionalism, purports to safeguard the formal-static nature of the Constitution. In doing so, it is believed to guarantee the reign of the Constitution over all political forces and also guarantees that the Constitution is insulated from any social and political forces that might pose a challenge to it.

On account of these mechanisms, the so-called finality of the (1996) Constitution is considered to be guaranteed. Save for the minor textual amendments to the Constitution that have been passed since that time, and save for any further amendments to the text that may in future be passed in accordance with section 74, (and allowing for the limited effect of evolvement of the Constitution through judicial interpretation), the Constitution has still remained the same Constitution, guaranteed to stay the same stable and final Constitution for (all) posterity.[5] Hence, in essence nothing else, but the text – the formulations – of the Constitution need to be consulted in order to determine the authentic content and meaning of the Constitution.

The message of constitutional supremacy contained in section 2 is self-assured and faith-strengthening. Thanks to its supreme potency everyone can rest assure that the Constitution is stable; it is not delivered to any forces that could destabilise it; that it is the actively constituting driving force in the constitutional-political dispensation; and that it is capable to fulfil the benevolent pledges, articulated amongst others, in its values and its exhaustive list of rights dealt with in the next section.

On close analysis the principle of constitutional supremacy is based on two claims. The first claim is intra-legal. It pertains to the relation between the Constitution and law outside the Constitution. This claim (expressed in a number of constitutional

---

4   Section 74(2) of *the Constitution*. Section 74 also lays down a number of other procedural requirements for amendment to the Constitution.

5   The amendment of section 25 of *the Constitution* (under consideration at the time of the writing of this book) in order to provide for so-called expropriation without compensation does not detract from the validity of this assertion since there is general consensus that non-compensation for expropriation has all along been permissible under section 25.

provisions, including sections 2, 8 and 39(2)),[6] denotes a hierarchical relationship between the Constitution and other bodies of law in terms of which the latter must conform with and be developed in terms of the values outlined in the Constitution. The scope of this claim is fairly limited and arguably not that difficult to sustain. It is primarily directed to organs of state and the courts which are responsible for administering the law through law-making, execution and adjudication. In whatever they do, they have to comply with the formulations of the Constitution.

The second claim is that the Constitution is actually supreme and therefore the actual driving force of politics – of socio-political realities in the broadest sense of the word. Hence, the Constitution is not only at the apex of the corpus of law; it is at the apex of all socio-political forces and all socio-political conduct. All such conduct must live up to the formulations of the Constitution. This claim falls into an entirely different dimension. It is much more far-reaching and is much more difficult to realise.

The premises of this claim holds that there is no point in having a hierarchical system of bodies of law with the Constitution at the apex (the first claim), yet with the law and the Constitution not fortified against and in active control over all the socio-political forces in the political order over which the Constitution has jurisdiction – that is, over the actions of all political actors, including organs of state under the jurisdiction of the Constitution. For that very reason the principle of constitutional supremacy must obviously imply this second sweeping assertion. Accordingly, the Constitution is also in command of the social and political spheres, that is, of all conduct, specifically governmental conduct, and the actions of all political forces regardless how potent these forces might be. In terms of the notion of constitutional supremacy, whatever is happening in the sphere of politics must conform to the norm-formulations of the Constitution, failing which such non-conforming conduct would be invalid and of no consequence. This is precisely what the Constitution purports to provide for in the supremacy clause. Section 2, having laid down the supremacy principle, asserts that all *conduct* (apart from law) inconsistent with it (with its norm-formulations) is invalid.[7]

---

6   Section 2 declares that *law* inconsistent with *the Constitution* is invalid and according to section 8 the Bill of Rights applies to all *law*. In its turn section 39 secures the reach of *the Constitution* (more in particular of the Bill of Rights) in all *law* outside *the Constitution* stating that whenever legislation is interpreted, or the common law or customary law are dealt with, it must be developed so as to promote the spirit, purport and objects of the Bill of Rights. This may be called the intra-legal notion of supremacy in that it pertains only the relationship between *the Constitution* and other legal sources.

7   This claim is by implication repeated in a number of other sections. Section 7(2) enjoins the state to respect, protect, promote and fulfil the rights in the Bill of Rights. Compliance with this provision would obviously also require conforming conduct and not only conforming law. In similar vein section 8(1) provides that the Bill of Rights applies to all law, and binds the legislature, the executive, the judiciary and all organs of state. Giving effect to this provision would once again require not only law that conforms to *the Constitution* but also conforming conduct. The same applies for section 8(2) which provides for conditional application of the Bill of Rights to juristic and natural persons.

The very notion of constitutional supremacy (and the pre-political nature of the Constitution) would lose all significance if this assertion is not made because the doctrine of statist-individualist constitutionalism dare not countenance social and political forces more powerful than the norm-formulations of the Constitution. Besides, the very rationale for a Constitution cast in the mould of statist-individualist constitutionalism, is to place political conduct under the control of the written Constitution and therefore to provide legal protection and security against the peril of arbitrary conduct in general and the potential tyranny of the lawless and arbitrary wielding of political power in particular. What the logic of constitutional supremacy in terms of the premises of statist-individualist constitutionalism therefore does, is to assert that the Constitution is in actual command of politics – in actual control of political power.[8]

But here is the rub. Because unlike constitutional supremacy's first assertion which is fairly easy to sustain and is therefore a relatively plausible claim, the second assertion, that claims that the Constitution is so potent that it is in control of all political and social realities is way more difficult to realise, if at all. It is so intrepid an assertion that believing in it requires a giant leap of faith. Yet, the South African brand of statist-individualist constitutionalism does not disappoint. On the contrary, it radiates confidence that there are compelling grounds for trusting in the truthfulness of this second assertion. The first ground for this trust – in keeping with the doctrine of statist-individualist constitutionalism – is the unequivocal faith that is invested in written law.[9]

The time-honoured strategy of faith-strengthening language (referred to in Chapter 2 and more fully discussed in Chapter 4) is once again enlisted to inculcate faith in this gallant claim. The supremacy clause intimates that conduct – including conduct of the most powerful political actors – which is inconsistent with the Constitution is of no consequence. The clause does not assert that such conduct *ought not* be valid; it simply proclaims that it *is invalid*. Section 1 – the foundational clause – is even more gallant in enlisting this strategy when it states that "The *Republic of South Africa is ... founded* on the values as set out in that section, including human dignity, the achievement of equality and the advancement of human

---

8   Thus Van der Hoeven explains that constitutionalism "...wilden de grote stap doen naar beheersing van de macht door het recht. Zij stonden daartoe voor de noodzaak om onder het recht een fundament te leggen, dat voor de macht onaantasbaar zou zijn." Own translation: " ... takes the bold leap to subject politics to law. They (the constitutionalists) seek to entrench law so firmly that it would be impregnable to power." (Van der Hoeven, 1976:504).

9   As Van der Hoeven, 1976:496 states: "De constitutionalisten trachten hun doelstellenigen te verwerklijken, gelijk wij zagen, vanuit een zeer hogere waardering voor het geschreven recht. Zij menen het menselijk handelen ook op het terrein van gezag en gezachsoefening door rechtsnormen te kunnen regeren." Own translation: The constitutionalists seek to realise their objectives from the perspective of a very high regard for written law. They assume that human action in the sphere of the execution of political power can also be subjected to legal regulation.

rights and freedoms."[10] Had it stated that the Constitution (and not the Republic of South Africa) is founded on the values listed in the section, it would have been a norm formulation, because the Constitution itself is at root a normative instrument – a complex of norm-formulations. But this is clearly not what section 1 does. It refers to the *Republic of South Africa* as a state (a real entity, in contrast to the Constitution which is essentially a normative entity) which it then proclaims, using the word, *is,* as being founded on the values outlined in the provision. Solely on account of the wording of these provisions, that is, solely on account of the Constitution's (verbal) proclamation of its own supremacy over the social and political spheres, and entirely dispensing with corroborating of social and political evidence extraneous to the text, the Constitution is presented as being fully in command of these spheres. This is an extraordinary bold descriptive statement, something which, without evidence extraneous to the document, clearly does not warrant such description. What we encounter here is that the legal language in the Constitution is perceived to possess the intrinsic and autonomous ability to create actual realities – actual social conditions – independent of the empirical world outside it, and is then enlisted to create and maintain such realities. The awesome fact-creating and fact-maintaining faculty of the language of the Constitution is inherent in statist-individualist constitutionalism in general. However, in the South African constitutional discourse these gospel-like and magic qualities reach an unprecedented culmination point, thus inculcating faith in the power of the formulations of the Constitution to control social and political forces.

This forms part of a widely used accompanying vocabulary that inculcates faith in the Constitution. Phrases of this vocabulary that spring to mind prominently are that *rights* are *guaranteed, entrenched* or *enshrined* in the Constitution and that rights are referred to as constitutional *guarantees.* The *Constitution* itself is described as *entrenched,* even *enshrined.* All this contributes towards inculcating faith in the actual supreme power of the Constitution and in the justice bestowed by its individual rights. The genre enfolding here is not (only) a legal one; it is a distinctively religious-like redemptive genre, representing the zenith of the belief system of statist-individualist constitutionalism. This genre is rounded off (as noted above) by describing the present South African Constitution as final – *the final Constitution.* The designation 'final' is technically sensible in that it distinguishes the 1996 Constitution from its predecessor, the interim Constitution. However, the detailed terms of the interim Constitution have lost all practical significance. The practical need for distinguishing the 1996 from the interim Constitution and for referring to the present Constitution as final has therefore fallen away. Yet, the designation 'final' has stuck. Habit is one explanation for that but there is also another, more plausible

---

10   Section 1 reads: The Republic of South Africa is one, sovereign, democratic state founded on the following values: (a) Human dignity, the achievement of equality and the advancement of human rights and freedoms. (b) Non-racialism and non-sexism. (c) Supremacy of the constitution and the rule of law. (d) Universal adult suffrage, a national common voter's roll, regular elections and a multi-party system of democratic government, to ensure accountability, responsiveness and openness.

explanation and one that confirms and extends this faith-strengthening genre of the South African version of the doctrine of statist-individualist constitutionalism. The point is that the *finality* of the Constitution might be regarded as the temporal element of its supremacy, which, as shown in Chapter 2, is part and parcel of the statist-individualist doctrine of constitutionalism. Supremacy, which denotes that the Constitution is in command of the social and political spheres must obtain not only with regard to the present time but for all posterity. The gospel of salvation is after all of no significance if it is but of fleeting duration. Hence, the Constitution and its accompanying salvation must be permanent, that is, it must be final. Nothing shall unsettle or destabilise it, neither now, nor in future. To the (final) Constitution is also attributed a life of its own. The Constitution is a *living document*.[11] It is an organism which is alive and growing and it has its own intelligence. It is to remain in good health so as to retain its supreme strength against whatever challenges it might have to face and retain its ability to bestow justice. The notion that the Constitution is a growing entity has long been recognised and it should therefore be ensured that it retains its relevance and agility[12] and not be allowed to degenerate into a liability.[13] It must remain stable and coherent so as to keep on relating the same story,[14] bestowing the same justice and ensuring the continued faithful support of the people.

3.2.2 Trias politica, checks and balances and the independence and impartiality of the judiciary

According to the sixth belief of statist-individualist constitutionalism (as described in Chapter 2.4) the South African Constitution is also power-structured on the basis of the trias politica and an accompanying system of mutual checks and balances, which is believed to limit power adequately and to secure justice.[15] The separation applies structurally, functionally and in terms of personnel. Especially between the legislature and the executive on the one hand and the judiciary on the other, strict separation is maintained.[16] Over and above the trias politica the Constitution also provides for a number of so-called state institutions to strengthen constitutional democracy (the so-called Chapter IX institutions, namely the Public Protector;

---

11   See for example the observations made in the following judgments: *Qozeleni v Minister of Law and Order and Another* 1994(1) BCLR 75(E) at 84; *Bangindawo & others v Head of the Nyanda Regional Authority; Hlantlalala v Head of the Western Tembuland Regional Authority & others* 1998(2) All SA 85(Tk) at 101.

12   See the observation by Sachs J in *Minister of Home Affairs v Fourie* 2006(1) SA 524(CC) at para 102.

13   See the observation by Sachs J in *Minister of Home Affairs v Fourie* 2006(1) SA 524(CC) at para 102.

14   Ronald Dworkin's metaphor of the chain novelist encapsulates the belief in a single coherent constitutional narration.

15   The phrase, *separation of powers* or *trias politica* is nowhere used in as many words in the Constitution. It is, however, clearly implied in a number of provisions, for example in the provisions that allocate power to the various branches, namely sections 43 and 44 with respect to the legislative authority; section 85 with respect to the national executive authority and section 165(1) with respect to judicial authority.

16   See for example *South African Association of Personal Injury Lawyers v Heath and Others* 2001(1) SA 883; 2001(1) BCLR 77(CC).

the South African Human Rights Commission; the Commission for the Promotion and Protection of the Rights of Cultural, Religious and Linguistic Communities; the Commission for Gender Equality; the Auditor-General and the Electoral Commission).

The Constitution is viewed to provide for a system of multiple mutual checks and balances, most prominent of which are: the check available to the national legislature to exercise control over the national executive; the check of the Chapter IX bodies to exercise over the executive; and the check of the judiciary over all organs of state, including the national executive and the national legislature. The review powers of the courts in relation to the actions of all organs of state are particularly sweeping, thus strengthening the judiciary's powers of checks and balances.[17]

The Constitution seems to go out of its way to strengthen the position of the judiciary vis-à-vis all organs of state, and particularly to the politically potent national legislature and executive.

The Constitution provides that the courts are independent and subject only to the Constitution and the law, which they must apply impartially and without fear, favour or prejudice; that no person or organ of state may interfere with the functioning of the courts; that organs of state, through legislative and other measures, must assist and protect the courts to ensure the independence, impartiality, dignity, accessibility and effectiveness of the courts; and that orders or decisions issued by a court are binding on all persons to whom, and organs of state to which they apply.[18]

A variety of other constitutional provisions are believed to provide the architecture for guaranteeing the independence, impartiality and effectiveness of the judiciary. The Constitution provides for the Judicial Service Commission (JSC)[19] which is independent from the executive, the legislature (and the ruling party). The Commission plays an important part in the appointment and discipline of judges. It seeks to guard the judiciary against the power and influence of political forces, more specifically, the legislature, the executive and the ruling party. The JSC is cited as an institution that safeguards the judiciary more effectively than in many other jurisdictions, even jurisdictions that are famous for the strength of their judiciaries.[20]

---

17   See the discussion of O'Regan, 2005:1-30.

18   Sections 165(2)-(5) of *the Constitution*. Sections 181(2)-(5) provides similarly in relation to Chapter IX institutions.

19   Section 178 of *the Constitution*.

20   Chief Justice Mogoeng is quoted (Mogoeng, 2015): "I dare say, there are very few constitutional democracies that have gone out of their way to have a body that recommends judges for appointment constituted in the way the South African body is"; "Go to America, go to Germany, go to Russia, go to the UK, it is a politician's work, so the question of political influence does not even feature."

3.2.3 The (justiciable) Bill of Rights

Typical of statist-individualist constitutionalism (more specifically the eighth belief of statist-individualist constitutionalism as outlined in Chapter 2) the Bill of Rights, is also the crown jewel of the South African Constitution. It has been inspiring a tremendous amount of pride in the South African constitutional discourse and is one of the primary reasons for extolling the Constitution as (one of) the best in the world. The Bill of Rights is wide-ranging, encompassing all three generations of rights, thus catering for and satisfying all legitimate human needs and interests. Moreover, it does not only provide for existing interest in the form of individual rights but also provides the basis for what is often described as transformative constitutionalism – transformationism.[21] This serves as the foundation for a wide long-term and wide-ranging programme of social change with a view to the accomplishment of an egalitarian and essentially homogenous society.[22]

The Bill of Rights must be considered in conjunction with the wide-ranging powers of South Africa's independent and impartial judiciary (something to be critiqued in Chapters 6 and 7). Accordingly, the rights contained in the Bill of Rights are justiciable. Whenever a right is infringed or under threat, a competent court can be approached for appropriate relief. Thanks to the wide ranging powers of the courts in relation to constitutional-rights, the Bill of Rights can be trusted as a fool-proof safeguard for all protectable human interests.

The Constitution's commitment to justice is primarily defined in the values it avows in the foundational clause[23] and of course in the encompassing Bill of Rights. The Bill of Rights is believed to *guarantee* the full materialisation of a new benevolent dispensation of justice by way of the individual rights it *enshrines*.

The magnificence of the Constitution, more specifically of the Bill of Rights was proclaimed by Karl Klare, a member of the leftist Critical Legal Studies School who was awestruck by the marvellous South African Constitution. Klare produced a gospel-like and one of the most celebrated articles – scriptures – in the South African

---

21 See for example De Vos, 2014:319.

22 See Klare, 1998:150. See further the academic commentary referred to by Liebenberg, 2010:25; For just one of many judicial pronouncement committing the country to egalitarianism, see *Minister of Constitutional Development and Another v South African Restructuring and Insolvency Practitioners Association and Others* 2018(5) SA 349(CC); 2018(9) BCLR 1099(CC) para 1(1102 A).

23 Section 1 of *the Constitution*, the foundation provision, provides that the Republic of South Africa is one, sovereign, democratic state founded on the values of (a) Human dignity, the achievement of equality and the advancement of human rights and freedoms; (b) Non-racialism and non-sexism; (c) Supremacy of the constitution and the rule of law; (d) Universal adult suffrage, a national common voters roll, regular elections and a multi-party system of democratic government, to ensure accountability, responsiveness and openness; Section 36(1) proclaims the values of reasonableness and justifiability in an open and democratic society based on human dignity, equality and freedom within the context of the limitation of rights; Section 39(1) (a) proclaims the values that underlie an open and democratic society based on human dignity, equality and freedom within the context of the interpretation of the Bill of Rights. There are also additional provisions in *the Constitution* dealing with values such as those contained in sections 41(1) and 195.

constitutional discourse over the past decades[24] in which the praises of the Constitution was lavished. Klare was enthralled by the Constitution's so-called post-liberalism as attested to, amongst others things, in its socio-economic rights (over and above the traditional civil and political rights);[25] by the substantive conception of equality;[26] the numerous affirmative duties that the state owes to the bearers of rights to enhance an array of social conditions;[27] the horizontality of the Bill of Rights[28] which would enable the democratic values and norms of the Constitution to permeate into the private sphere; participatory decentralised governance, (multi-)culturalism, including the protection of language and cultural diversity.[29] The praises that have befallen the Bill of Rights have made it the most hallowed part of South Africa's vaunted Constitution.

The emphatic commitment of the Constitution to a number of values further reinforces the benevolent nature of the dispensation that it has ushered in. Noteworthy in this context are in the first place the values outlined in the foundational clause, the limitation clause and the interpretation clause.[30] Foremost among these are human dignity, the achievement of equality and the advancement of human rights and freedoms, non-racialism and non-sexism in section 1 (the foundational clause of the Constitution);[31] the values of an open and democratic society based on human dignity, equality and freedom, featuring in the limitation clause (section 36(1));[32] and the values that proclaim to underlie an open and democratic society based on human dignity, equality and freedom that have, in accordance to section 39(1)(a) to be given effect to when the Bills of Rights is interpreted.[33] Of great importance for underscoring the Constitution's commitment to justice is the value of ubuntu, which has inspired tremendous excitement among

---

24   Klare, 1998:151.

25   Such as the right to property, which specifically also refers to the "nation's commitment to land reform, and reforms to bring about equitable access to all South Africa's natural resources (section 25(4)(a)) and that the state must take reasonable legislative and other measures, within its available resources, to foster conditions which enable citizens to gain access to land on an equitable basis. Section 25(5); the right to housing (section 26); the right to health care services, including reproductive health care (section 27); the right to education (section 29)."

26   Sections 9(1) and (2) of *the Constitution.*

27   Sections 9(2) of *the Constitution.*

28   Sections 8(3), (3) and 9(4) of *the Constitution* within the context of the right to equality.

29   Klare, 1998:152-156.

30   Sections1, 36 and 39 of *the Constitution* respectively.

31   Section 1 of *the Constitution* amongst other things provides as follows: The Republic of South Africa is one, sovereign, democratic state founded on the following values: (a) Human dignity, the achievement of equality and the advancement of human rights and freedoms. (b) Non-racialism and non-sexism.

32   Section 36(1) provides as follows: The rights in the Bill of Rights may be limited only in terms of law of general application to the extent that the limitation is reasonable and justifiable in an open and democratic society based on human dignity, equality and freedom …

33   Section 39(1)(a) provides as follows: When interpreting the Bill of Rights, a court, tribunal or forum – (a) must promote the values that underlie an open and democratic society based on human dignity, equality and freedom.

a number of South African commentators[34] and once again among American commentators.[35] Ubuntu is associated with, among other things, the notions of humaneness, human dignity, reconciliation, group solidarity, compassion and restorative justice, all which could further contribute towards Constitution's singularly enhanced commitment to justice.[36]

The evidence attesting to the Constitution's commitment to individual rights is overwhelming, thus qualifying as a leading example of statist-individualist constitutionalism's commitment to justice through individual rights.

The Bill of Rights is specifically a bill of individual rights. Accordingly, the South African Constitution, in keeping with the doctrine of statist-individualist constitutionalism is premised on undivided state sovereignty and individual rights (as encapsulated in the Bill of Rights). Individual rights are believed to be the full-fledged embodiment of justice. Rights or powers for communities are accordingly not countenanced. There is an emphatic denunciation of the notions of (multi-)communitarianism and pluralism, and accompanying constitutional strategies such as federalism, forms of cultural, territorial and corporate self-government, subsidiarity and devolution of power. Even the one constitutional body, that is seemingly mandated to protect and promote the rights of (cultural, linguistic and religious) communities, namely the Commission for the Protection of the Rights of Cultural, Linguistic and Religious Communities has lived up to the anti-communitarian beliefs of statist-individualist constitutionalism by failing to execute the mandate it purports to be dedicated to.

3.3

The statist-individualist belief system in the South African constitutional discourse

The praises for the South African Constitution have gone far beyond the triad of mechanisms of statist-individualist constitutionalism that we dealt with above.

---

34 See for example Mokgoro, 1998:15-26; Cornell, 2009:43-58 and See also the incisive critique by Keevy, 2009.

35 Most notably Cornell, 2004.

36 The value of Ubunu has featured in numerous cases. For the most prominent among them see S v Makwanyane and Another 1995(3) SA 391; 1995(6) BCLR 665(CC); Port Elizabeth Municipality v Various Occupiers 2005(1) SA 517; 2004(12) BCLR 1258(CC); Dikoko v Mokhatla 2006(6) SA 235; 2007(1) BCLR 1(CC); Masethla v President of the RSA 2008(1) SA 566; 2008(1) BCLR 1(CC); Union of Refugee Women v Private Security Industry Regulatory Authority 2007(4) SA 395; 2007(4) BCLR 339(CC); See also for example Hoffmann v South African Airways 2001(1) SA 1; 2000(11) BCLR 1211(CC) para 38; Barkhuizen v Napier 2007(5) SA 323; 2007(7); BCLR 691(CC) par 50; 2011(3) SA 274(CC); 2011(6) BCLR 577(CC) para 200 ; 2011(3) SA 274(CC); 2011(6) BCLR 577(CC) para 200 Bhe and Others v Magistrate, Khayelitsha, and Others 2005(1) SA 580; 2005(1) BCLR 1(CC) paras 45 & 163; The Citizen 1978 (Pty) Ltd and Others v McBride (Johnstone and Others, Amici Curiae) 2011(4) SA 191(CC); 2011(8) BCLR 816(CC) paras 164-165, 168, 210 & paras 216-218; Joseph and Others v City of Johannesburg and Others 19 and Koyabe and Others v Minister for Home Affairs and Others (Lawyers for Human Rights as Amicus Curiae) 2010(4) SA 327(CC); 2009(12) BCLR 1192(CC) para 62. See in general about Ubuntu the comprehensive discussion by Bennet, 2018.

Generally, the South African brand of statist-individualist constitutionalism has been praised as nothing short of a miracle. In the South African constitutional discourse the redeeming gospel-like language of statist-individualist constitutionalism has reached a charismatic zenith. These gospel-like praises inculcated faith in the Constitution and in the doctrine of statist-individualist constitutionalism. We cannot deal with statist-individualist constitutionalism without referring to that.

The solemn phrases of the postscript to the 1993-Constitution, under the heading *National Unity and Reconciliation* mark the official birth of the South African version of the redeeming nature of statist-individualist constitutionalism. The postscript proclaims that with the adoption of the Constitution the people of South Africa opened a new chapter in the history of their country. The first paragraph of the postscript proclaims:

> This Constitution provides a historic bridge between the past of a deeply divided society characterised by strife, conflict, untold suffering and injustice, and a future founded on the recognition of human rights, democracy and peaceful co-existence and development of opportunities for all South Africans, irrespective of colour, race, belief or sex.

It continues as follows in the third paragraph:

> The adoption of the Constitution lays the secure foundation for the people of South Africa to transcend the divisions and strife of the past, which generated gross violations of human rights, the transgression of humanitarian principles in violent conflicts and a legacy of hatred, fear, guilt and revenge.[37]

In the ringing phrases of salvation the postscript interprets, proclaims and prophesises. It interprets South African history as entirely a history of dread and evil: of deep division, strife, conflict, untold suffering, injustice, gross violations of human rights, violent conflicts marked by the transgression of humanitarian principles, a history of hatred, fear, guilt and revenge. This vision of the horrible past bears a striking resemblance with Thomas Hobbes' vision of a dismal state of nature in which there was perpetual war of all against all (*bellum omnia contra omnes*), in which there was no community but only continuous fear and danger of violent death and where life was solitary, poor, nasty, brutish and short.[38]

Up to the moment of the adoption of the interim Constitution there was nothing good or even neutral to report according to this sombre Hobbesian state-of-nature-like vision of South African history. It was a history of complete dread and evil. From that dreadful condition the tormented inhabitants of South Africa coveted to be delivered. There was a desperate cry for a redemptive mortal god.

---

37 The Preamble to the 1996 Constitution carries on in the same vein. In it the injustices of the past are recognised and a commitment is made to heal the divisions of the past and to establish a society based on democratic values, social justice and fundamental human rights and that lay the foundations for a democratic and open society in which government is based on the will of the people and every citizen is equally protected by law; that improve the quality of life of all citizens and free the potential of each person.

38 Hobbes, 1985:186.

Then mercifully came the interim Constitution and three years later the *final* Constitution, which decisively responded to this craving for redemption. The interim Constitution self-assuredly proclaimed that the miserable past is now beaten off to be replaced by a harmoniously bright future which is now dawning. It is marked by human rights, democracy, peaceful co-existence and development of opportunities for all South Africans, irrespective of colour, race, belief or sex, the transcendence of the horrible divisions and strife, gross violations of human rights, hatred, fear, guilt and revenge.

Yet, bolder than prophesising for the future, the Constitution proclaims present factual realities. It states that it – this Constitution – provides the bridge between the woeful past and the bright future and that with the adoption of the Constitution the foundation is laid for overcoming the evil past.[39]

The redeeming message of the postscript feeds on the faith-strengthening and magic-like faculty of the language of the doctrine of statist-individualist constitutionalism, that we have referred to above. The language of the doctrine is believed to possess the autonomous, intrinsic power to create new and change existing social and political realities. Faith in the doctrine of statist-individualist constitutionalism is inculcated by the seemingly magical quality of the doctrine's (of statist-individualist constitutionalism) language.

Obviously the doctrine's language in fact does not have this magical quality. However, more often than not it assumes the deceiving character, namely to convincingly represent something which on proper analysis is nothing more than a *norm formulation* (an ideal) as if such formulation describes an undeniable concrete reality. This phenomenon of the descriptive deceit of the doctrine's language (which is discussed in more detail in Chapter 4), is particularly relevant in the discourse of the South African species of statist-individualist constitutionalism. By virtue of this descriptive deceit norm-formulations are dressed up in descriptive garb, thus deceitfully spinning formulations into social realities – *oughts* into *isses*. This means that something which on close analysis is an ideal statement or a norm formulation, is phrased in such a way that it self-assuredly pretends to describe an actually existing (material-like) fact. What are therefore essentially (nothing more than) normative formulations which may or may not be obeyed, are misrepresented as irrefutable facts. Norm-formulations are inherently tenuous. If they are met with disobedience, they are nothing more than unfulfilled wishes. The effect of this parading of normative formulations as if they have the character of real facts is to disguise this inherent fragility of norm-formulations. More specifically in the context of the constitutional discourse, descriptive deceit obscures this tenuousness – this precariousness – of constitutional norm-formulations and

---

39   The metaphor of the bridge inspired tremendous excitement among some academics. Apart from the
      often quoted article by Mureinik, 1994, see also White, 1998:390-405; Bray & Joubert, 2007:49-59;
      Du Plessis, 2015:1332-1365; Langa, 2006:351 and Fourie, 2016.

affords to them the quality of undisputed factuality (reality) that normative formulations by their very nature simply do not have. Though deceitful this may be argued to be a benevolent deceit because it inculcates trust in the delightful formulations of the Constitution. However, the downside of this deceit is that of misrepresenting the actual condition of the constitutional order. Regardless of whether one views this to be a good or bad deceit, the bottom-line is that this descriptive deceit is a potent faith-enhancing rhetorical stratagem that inculcates the belief that what is stated in the Constitution's norm-formulations are in fact (tantamount to) actual real facts of life. Once the Constitution is dressed up in the compelling descriptive garb of undeniably real facts of life instead of coming to us in the tenuous form or norm-formulations there remains hardly any ground for doubt and mistrust. In consequence, any suspicion that the factual realities proclaimed by the provisions – the formulations – of the Constitution might indeed be out of step with the pleasing picture sketched by these misleading formulations is fended off. Hence, this (magical) faculty of the language of the doctrine of statist-individualist constitutionalism is mobilised as a means by which tenuous *ought*-formulations, such as rights are attributed a real, almost tangible character. It seeks to transform the super-natural objects of law such as rights and obligations into real-life objects,[40] thus rendering these super-natural entities the quality of incontestable real truths.

Thus the language of statist-individualist constitutionalism was perceived to be capable of calling the required effects into existence solely on account of the proclamation of these effects by using the prescribed legal phrases. Karl Olivecrona commented on the compelling effect which the term *law* itself has, observing that the use of the word *law* is sufficient to trigger the belief in the mind of many people that they are under the obligation to act in a prescribed way: Olivecrona stated:

> The texts reach them under the official appellation of law and that is enough. The appellation of law, when presumed to be correctly applied, carries with it the implication that the rules of conduct contained in the text are binding on everybody.[41]

In consequence, as Olivecrona continues to explain, in the ideal world of law, often encapsulated in the deceitful descriptive formulations of legal language, more specifically in this case the doctrine's language: "(t)he effects take place according to the law with infallible regularity."[42] This phenomenon of the descriptive deceit of the doctrine's language acts as the rampart of the doctrine of statist-individualist constitutionalism.

---

40   Olivecrona, 1971:223.

41   Olivecrona, 1971:131.

42   Olivecrona, 1971:252-253. This resonates in the often used phrase that *the law takes its course*. This also reflects and inculcates trust in the law as a personified being with an autonomous intelligence. That is in spite of the fact that in "(t)he empirical world of facts, the effects of legal rules, transactions between individuals, the attitudes of people in general, etc. are varied and more or less uncertain." (Olivecrona, 1971:252-253).

The solemn postscript reveals the redemptive power that the doctrine's language as encapsulated in the script of the Constitution is perceived to command. The power of the constitutional text is perceived to be so compelling that it can create real facts of life. Thus the Constitution does not state in normative terms that the Constitution "shall," "ought to" or "must" provide a historic bridge but declares in bold descriptive terms as a *fait accompli* that the "(C)onstitution provides a historic bridge ..." By the same token, the text dispenses with the juridical phraseology such as that it (the Constitution) *shall, must* or *ought to* lay the foundation for overcoming a bad past and asserts instead once again in descriptive terms as a *fait accompli* that the adoption of the Constitution does lay that secure foundation.

The faith-enhancing oratory of the constitutional script is enlisted here to inculcate the belief that assertions in the postscript, are already accomplished facts or at least facts that are ineluctably certain soon to come about and thereafter to be everlasting.

The vision of the unbearably horrible past, the redeeming Constitution and the bright present and future became a chant that has been echoing in legislation,[43] judicial pronouncements, beginning with a number of dicta of the Constitutional Court in *S v Makwanyane*,[44] and thereafter regurgitated in numerous judgments in academic commentary and handbooks,[45] as well as in the popular media ever since. Hence, the message of salvation from the evil past and the creation the everlasting benevolent new dispensation proclaimed by the interim Constitution has been perceived in a distinctively matter of fact way. It is therefore not only a self-assured prophecy of an order destined to arrive but also a proclamation of something that through the proclamation of the Constitution has already been established.[46]

---

43 See for example *Preamble of the Promotion of National and Reconciliation Act* 34 of 1995; *Preamble of the Repeal of the Black Administration Act and Amendment of Certain laws* Act 28 of 2005; *Preamble and section 2 of the Promotion of Equality and Prevention of Unfair Discrimination* Act 4 of 2000; *Preamble of the Commission for the Promotion and Protection of the Rights of Cultural, religious and linguistic Communities* Act 19 of 2002; *Preamble of the national Health* Act 61 of 2003.

44 Beginning with the dictum by Mohammed J in *S v Makwanyane* 1995 6 BCLR 665(CC) para 262 who states the Constitution: (r)epresents a decisive break from, and a ringing rejection of, that part of the past which is disgracefully racist, authoritarian, insular, and repressive and a vigorous identification of and commitment to a democratic, universalistic, caring and aspirationally egalitarian ethos, expressly articulated in the Constitution. The contrast between the past which it repudiates and the future to which it seeks to commit the nation is stark and dramatic. The past institutionalized and legitimized racism ... The past was redolent with statutes which assaulted the human dignity of persons on the grounds of race and colour alone; ... The past accepted, permitted, perpetuated and institutionalized pervasive and manifestly unfair discrimination against women and persons of colour ... The past permitted detention without trial ...The past permitted degrading treatment of persons ... The past arbitrarily repressed the freedoms of expression, assembly, association and movement ... The past limited the right to vote to a minority ... The past ... "

45 See for example *Shabalala and Others v Attorney-General, Transvaal, and Another* 995(12) BCLR 1593; 1996(1) SA 725(CC) at para 26; *Dawood and Another v Minister of Home Affairs and Others; Shalabi and Another v Minister of Home Affairs and Others; Thomas and Another v Minister of Home Affairs and Others* 2000(3) SA 936(CC) at para 35; and *Minister of Home Affairs v Fourie and Others* 2005(10) BPLR 807(CC) paras 59-61.

46 This is a striking paradox: the redemption is completely here, still though, it is still to come. This kind of paradox of the godly redemption that is here, yet not fully here, is not unknown in religious doctrine. See Tarnas, 2010:96-97.

This encapsulates the three key mechanisms of statist-individualist constitutionalism in the present South African constitutional order faithfully though deceitfully strengthened by the gospel-like redeeming language of statist-individualist constitutionalism.

*　　　*　　　*

The next five chapters critique statist-individualist constitutionalism. Chapter 4 focuses on the first mechanism of statist-individualist constitutionalism which is rooted in the first five beliefs of the doctrine. It will be shown that the claim of supremacy of the written Constitution is ill-founded and that strict amendment procedures that seek to safeguard the integrity, stability and permanency of the Constitution are ineffectual. Supremacy provisions and strict amendment procedures are no match for potent socio-political forces that create, recreate and change the (actual) constitution, which is a function of the changing balance of socio-political forces in the state concerned.

Chapter 5 builds on Chapter 4 and makes the insights of Chapter 4 applicable to the South African experience. The claim of section 2 of the Constitution that it is supreme will be debunked. It is in fact not supreme and as the examples discussed there show, it has in fact been profoundly changed by potent socio-political forces that have been operative in South Africa over the last decades.

Chapter 6 turns to the second mechanism of statist-individualist constitutionalism, namely the separation of powers, checks and balances and specifically the exceptionally high trust that it invests in the *independent* and *impartial* judiciary. With reference to the South African experience over the last decades it will be shown that separation of powers and the concomitant doctrines of judicial independence and impartiality are largely metaphorical. The courts are in an important sense dependent rather than independent and their impartiality is relative in that it is conditioned by the ideological commitments and objectives of the dominant elite of which the courts are an integral part. The courts are impartial only *within* the limited ideological assumptions of the dominant elite.

Chapter 7 also deals with the judiciary but from another angle, namely from the vantage point of judicial interpretation and its effect on the claim that individual rights secure a system of justice. It is shown that there is no interpretive theory that guarantees objective, predictable and impartial judgments. With reference to the South African experience it is also demonstrated that the highest courts fully subscribe to the ideological convictions of the dominant political elite of which they are an integral and cooperating element and that they interpret rights in such a way that they justify action that flows from these commitments, and at the same time, deny the interests – and violate the rights – of sectors in society that challenge the ideological convictions of the dominant elite.

Chapter 8 focuses exclusively on the individualist side of statist-individualist constitutionalism and the accompanying third mechanism of statist-individualist constitutionalism, namely that of the individual rights. It is shown that individual rights are often not truly individualistic and that the protection of so-called individual interests are community-based. It is also shown that a system of separation – more specifically diffusion – of power is not sustainable in the absence of a (multi-)communitarian constitutional structure that goes beyond mere individual rights protection.

Chapter 9 goes back to the basic tenets of constitutionalism set out in Chapter 1. That chapter contains ideas as to how an improved constitutionalism could be brought about, a constitutionalism giving expression to the classical notion of the mixed and balanced constitution in a fashion which is more reliable and therefore more suitable for securing justice. The argumentation in this chapter builds on notions first raised in Chapter 10 of *Politocracy – an assessment of the coercive logic of the territorial state and ideas around a response to it.*

THERE IS NO SUPREME CONSTITUTION

4.1

Introduction

This is the first of five chapters in which the fundamentals of statist-individualist constitutionalism are critiqued. The first mechanism is rooted in the first five beliefs of statist-individualist constitutionalism discussed in Chapter 2[1] and provides for the supremacy of the Constitution combined with conformity and strict amendment requirements. It will be shown that the claim of supremacy of the written Constitution is ill-founded and that stringent conformity requirements and amendment procedures that seek to safeguard the integrity, stability and permanency of the constitution are ineffectual. These mechanisms are no match for potent socio-political forces that create, recreate and change the (actual) constitution. In the next chapter this point will be demonstrated with reference to the South African experience of the last decades.

In debunking the belief in and mechanisms for the supremacy of the Constitution, conformity mechanisms and strict amendment procedures, the five beliefs on which these mechanisms are based will also be exposed as unfounded. Hence, state-based positive law and the Constitution are in fact not omnipresent (not encapsulated in

---

1   Where it is submitted that positive law emanating from the designated law-making bodies of the state, which is indicative of the omnipresence of positive law, more specifically the document-based Constitution, is omnipresent; that the document-based Constitution is rigid, and actually supreme, from which follows that it is prognostic and by implication claims to be descriptive; that this Constitution is formulation-driven and that it therefore has a formal-static nature; that the Constitution is written, which implies extraordinary faith in written language; and that the document-based constitution is pre-political.

the norm-formulations of the document-based Constitution and the law in general). Law, including constitutional law, may in fact lapse or be replaced, and does in fact lapse and is replaced by forces outside the framework of the norm-formulations of the law and the written Constitution. Hence, the constitution, that is, the actual constitution – not the written Constitution – is in fact often not as formulation-driven and as formal-static as the doctrine of statist-individualist constitutionalism would suggest. In the result, the constitution – that is, the real or actual constitution – is in fact made and remade by political forces. The constitution is therefore not really pre-political and to a lesser or larger extent, not located and reflected in the text of the Constitution but in commanding and ever-changing political forces. Supremacy provisions and strict amendment procedures cannot guard against changes of the actual constitution, which is a function of the changing balance of socio-political forces in the state concerned. Hence, the impression that the doctrine of statist-individualist constitutionalism seeks to inculcate the idea that the written Constitution is really supreme and is the foundation of a stable constitutional order with guaranteed protection of all interests, though soothing and reassuring, is simply false.

The central reason why the protagonists of the doctrine of statist-individualist constitutionalism can make all their unfounded claims and put so much trust in supremacy and conformity provisions and strict amendment procedures is their disregard of the fundamental two-dimensional nature of positive law, more specifically its second dimension, namely law's factual dimension.

Law, as will be shown in this chapter, is in fact two-dimensional. It has an ideal and a factual dimension. In keeping with the discussion in Chapter 1, the ideal dimension of law relates to the quest for justice. Law has a justice, moral or critical dimension (and requisite). On the other hand, law also has an essential real or factual dimension (and requisite). Both of these dimensions are essential for an individual norm to qualify as a norm of positive law, including a norm of the constitution. The belief in the supremacy of the Constitution and the effectiveness of conformity and strict amendment requirements, prevalent in contemporary constitutional states is premised on a failure to account for the factual dimension. In consequence, it also obscures a clear insight into the factual dimension of law and therefore of a clear understanding of the nature and content of (positive) law, including the constitution.

In part 4.2 of the present chapter, law's two essential dimensions are expounded in brief with the specific purpose of elucidating the essential nature of the factual dimension. In part 4.3 important conceptual instruments in support of the arguments developed in this chapter are clarified. Thereafter, part 4.4 concisely posits, without any detailed discussion, the basic thesis on the factual dimension of law. Part 4.5 discusses the faith-strengthening language of the doctrine of statist-individualist constitutionalism. The magic-like and gospel-like nature of the language that bolsters the doctrine of statist-individualist constitutionalism is referred to in Chapter 2. This faith-strengthening language features prominently in the present context, being enlisted as a means of strengthening the claim that the Constitution is stable and supreme, and at the same time obscuring insight into the factual dimension of law. Part 4.6 develops in more detail the thesis of the factual dimension of law, and further presents a critique on the trite doctrine of statist-individualist constitutionalism, more specifically on the belief in the supremacy of the Constitution and the effectiveness of strict amendment provisions. Part 4.7 concludes with some final remarks.

4.2

Law's dual dimensionality

The insight that law is essentially dual-dimensional has a long history. The basic contours of such dual-dimensional understanding of law might be as ancient as legal reflection itself.

In the first place, as explained in Chapter 1, it must be pointed out that any conception of law without the notion of justice would be impossible. At the very beginning of the Digest (of Justinian's *Corpus Iuris Civilis*) the essential connection between law and justice (*ius* and *iustitia*) is proclaimed, with reference to the view of the classical jurist, Celsus, that the law is the art of goodness and fairness.[2]

Ideas on justice (and morality) as shown in Chapter 1 have either been laid down as normative standards for rules to qualify as (positive) law or as a moral yardstick to evaluate the quality of positive law.

In the second place, it is necessary to cast light on the factual dimension of law. This dimension relates to the factor of effectiveness, the essential importance of which has been highlighted all along as an equally fundamental dimension of, and prerequisite for, positive law (including constitutional law).

There is a widely held view that the proclamation of norms (more correctly norm-formulations, in terms of the views developed in the discussion in part 4.3 of this chapter) by political authorities on their own is not sufficient to establish new law or to change existing law. This view goes back to at least the twelfth century Benedictine monk, Gratian, the author of the *Concordantia Discordantium Canonum* (c. 1140), which formed the basis of the *Corpus Iuris Canonici*. In the beginning of the Concordantia it is stated that: "Laws are established through promulgation and validated when they are approved by the acceptance of the people."[3] Hence,

---

2   Mommsen & Krueger P, 1985:1 Latin English translation edited by Allan Watson 1.1.

3   Pennington, 1988:424; Carlyle, 1928, *A History of Medieval Political Theory in the West*:3: *Political Theory from the Tenth Century to the Thirteenth Century*, 3:48; *Political Theory from the Thirteenth Century*, 5:82.

promulgation of a rule as law alone, was not sufficient to turn it into law. It first had to be approved through acceptance by those destined to be affected by it. As long as it remains unaccepted, it does not assume the status as a law. The Glossator, Azo (d. 1220) echoed the same view when he stated that custom arising after a written law had been established could abrogate such written law. Commenting on Digesta 1.3.32,[4] the Glossator jurist from Bologna, Odofredus (d. 1265) maintained that the Roman people could still make law, and that their customs could therefore still annul existing law.[5] In this regard it is of particular importance to note what Thomas of Aquinas had to say in 'Treatise on Law' which is part of his magnum opus, Summa Theologiae. Thomas expanded on the work of the Civilian jurists since the beginnings of the Glossator school. According to him, custom could and did create, abolish (change) and interpret law.[6] To Thomas it was of particular importance that law could be created and changed (or abolished) fundamentally in two ways: firstly, by words and secondly, by action. In the first case, law is laid down by the express promulgation thereof by a designated political authority who formulated new law (in words). In the second case, law could be lived by those to whom the law applies by consistently acting in a particular way.[7] Specifically with regard to the changing of law, quite obviously including the changing of written law through consistent action, Thomas stated:

> Wherefore it is sometimes possible to act beside the law; namely, in a case where the law fails, yet the act will not be evil. And when such cases are multiplied, by reason of some change in man, the custom shows that the law is no longer useful: just as it might be declared by the verbal promulgation of a law to the contrary.[8]

Such customary action contrary to officially promulgated existing written law, does not amount to unlawful action but rather marks the fact that the officially existing law is no longer fitting. Instead of being unlawful (gauged against the yardstick

---

4   Digesta 1.3.32 reads as follows: "Age-entrusted custom is not undeservedly cherished as having almost statutory force, and this is to be the kind of law which is said to be established by use and wont. For given that statutes themselves are binding upon us for no other reason than that they have been accepted by the judgment of the populace, certainly it is fitting that what the populace has approved without any writing shall be binding upon everyone. What does it matter whether the populace declares its will by voting or by the very substance of its actions? Accordingly, it is absolutely right to accept the point that statutes may be replaced not only by vote of the legislature but also by the silent agreement of everyone expressed through desuetude." Mommsen & Krueger, 1985:13.

5   Carlyle, 1928:49.

6   Van Drunen, 2003:37; See also Carlyle, 1928 5:47.

7   Thus he declared as follows in Summa Theologiae 1.2.97.3: "Now all law proceeds from the reason and will of the lawgiver ... Now just as human reason and will, in practical matters, may be made manifest by speech, so it might be made known by deeds: since seemingly a man chooses as good that which he carries into execution. But it is evident that by human speech, law can be both changed and expounded, in so far as it manifests the interior movement and thought of human reason. Wherefore by actions also, especially if they are repeated, so as to make a custom, law can be changed and expounded; and also something can be established which obtains force of law, in so far as by repeated external actions, the inward movement of the will, and concepts of reason are most effectively declared, for when a thing is done again and again, it seems to proceed from a deliberate judgment of reason. Accordingly, custom has the force of law, abolishes law and is the interpreter of law" (quoted by Van Drunen, 2003:37-38).

8   Van Drunen, 2003:39, quoted from the same passage in Summa Theologiae.

of the officially existing formulations of the norms of law) the new customary action constitutes, supersedes and abolishes the officially existing written law and creates new law in its place.[9] This obviously happens tacitly and is not overtly articulated as in the case of changes by way of written formulation. This, however, does not detract from the fact that it has the same consequence as amendments of written formulations.[10]

For Jacques Cujas (1522-1590), the great French Civilian jurist from the Humanist school, the determining requirement for the manifestation of law was actual conduct. No law was binding unless it was received by custom. Custom was decisive for law, and written laws were not binding unless they had been accepted by the judgment of the people, that is, unless they had been approved – affirmed – by custom.[11] Commenting on the famous definition of Papinian of the concept of lex in Digesta 1.3.1, Cujas stated that laws were binding for no other reason that they have been accepted by the populus and approved by custom.[12] These views also resonated strongly in the Roman-Dutch legal tradition in a work no less famous than the *Commentarius ad Pandectas* of the author of equal fame, Johannes Voet (1647-1713). Voet argued, with reference to applicable Roman law texts, that it would be patently impossible for legal rules to prevent spontaneous change of the law through custom. Thus Voet stated:

> It flows as just as much from what we have said that an earlier may not be abrogated only by a later law, but also by custom. It made no difference whether the people declared its wish by vote or by its very acts and doings. It has therefore very rightly been recognised that laws might be done away with or changed not only by the vote of the lawgiving power but also through disuse with the silent consent of everybody. It follows that this cannot be prevented by the clause not infrequently found, especially in municipal laws – 'Custom to the contrary notwithstanding'. These words must be taken as applying merely to past customs, and not to others to be brought in later. No private person can make a law for himself in his testament so as to disable himself from changing his earlier will. And owing to the constant change of times and manners, laws do not forever remain praiseworthy by reason of benefit like that with which they were originally brought into force. Thus it would clearly be incongruous to want to secure by a law that it should not be reshaped for the better whether by new laws or new customs such as right reason might recommend.[13]

---

9   Van Drunen, 2003:40.

10   Insights resonating and expanding on that of Thomas of Aquinas were repeatedly articulated afterward. Nicolas Vigelius (1529-1600) in a work of 1568 stated with reference to various passages in the *Codex* and the *Digest* (amongst others D 1. 32. 3), that laws were abrogated not only by the will of the legislator, but also with the tacit consent of the populus. He eventually concluded that if custom was subsequent to written law, it prevailed over the written law. See Carlyle, 1936:306-307.

11   Carlyle, 1936:314.

12   Car Carlyle, 1936:314. Digesta 1.3.1 includes in the definition of statute *a communal covenant of the state*. The whole definition reads: A statute is a communal directive, a resolution of the wise men, a forcible reaction to offences committed either voluntarily or in ignorance or a communal covenant of the state.

13   Voet, 1955:37.

Many contemporary conceptions of law also in some way or the other, subscribe to this two-dimensionality.[14] Hence, the assertion by the prominent contemporary legal theorists, Robert Alexy that law, more specifically positive law, is essentially of a dual nature,[15] on close examination falls within a well-established tradition of thinking on the fundamental nature of law. Alexy explains that law comprises, on the one hand, a real or factual dimension and, on the other hand, an ideal or critical (justice) dimension. Both these dimensions must be present for law to be in existence. According to Alexy the central element of the real dimension of law is coercion or force. As argued in Chapter 1, and further elaborated in part 4.6 of this chapter, I differ in this respect from Alexy in that on close analysis, the real dimension is sustained primarily by consensus-based voluntary conduct while coercive enforcement, imposed by agencies of the state plays but a secondary part, namely in the exceptional cases where voluntary obedience does not occur. On the other hand, the ideal or critical dimension always includes a claim of moral correctness, which if violated, implies legal defectiveness, and in extreme cases invalidity.[16]

In accounting for the real element, Alexy maintains that law must be marked by the characteristic of effectiveness in order to qualify as law. However, by insisting on the ideal dimension alongside the real dimension as essential for positive law, Alexy avoids a crude or extreme positivist risk of reducing law to purely a matter of the exertion of sovereign power. Alexy's view of positive law therefore (unwittingly) amounts to a compromise between an extreme notion of natural law and (crude) positivism. To my mind, the crucial merits of this view, as well as its antecedents referred to above are, however, not this compromise as such, but rather, the fact

---

14   In line also with the distinction between norms and norm-formulations. For scholars drawing this distinction see for example Aarnio *Essays on the doctrinal study of law* (as referred to in this article); Niiniluoto "Truth and legal norms" in MacCormick et al., *World Congress on philosophy of law and sociology Conditions of validity and cognition in modern legal thought* Stuttgart Steiner:168-190 and Neumann, 1986:29.

15   Alexy, 2004:156-166; Alexy, 2008:281-299.

16   Alexy, 2008:290. In this regard Alexy endorses the view of Gustav Radbruch that state-made law based on due enactment and enforcing state power does constitute law even if the rule is unjust and contrary to the general welfare, unless, however, the violation of justice is of such an intolerable degree that the rule becomes in effect 'lawless' for its failure to meet the minimum standard of justice. Alexy refers here to Radbruch, 2006:7. This thesis is sometimes referred to as the extreme injustice hypothesis. See for example Aarnio, 2011:55. Alexy's explanation of the dual nature of (positive) law to accommodate both the real and the ideal dimensions, clarifies two important issues. Firstly, Alexy integrates a requisite minimum natural law element, that is, the element of justice or moral correctness, in the definition of positive law. (This view somehow also resonates with the view of Ronald Dworkin, positing that in addition to rules there are also deep-seated principles that encapsulate the broad political philosophy of the institutional history of the legal order that serves as a the comprehensive and coherent (contradiction-free single collective moral agent and as such the most important source of law, that enables principle-based decisions that give effect to the rights of legal subjects (involved in disputes) and that makes the exercise of discretion completely redundant.) Dworkin, 1977:81-130; Dworkin, 1986:188. For Dworkin's distinction between principles (directed towards giving effect to rights in contrast to policies which are *statistically defined* and directed toward the achievement of broad public goals). See Dworkin, 1986:223; 243. Hence, in terms of this perspective one need not depart from the positive law discourse into the realm of moral philosophy or natural law in order to engage with questions of justice since the justice question is an indispensable element of positive law itself. This view resonates with the Digest's identification of ius with iustitia as noted above.

that it provides the basis for a reliable ontology of law in tune with the long-standing tradition as briefly outlined above. The dual nature of law suggests two interrelated yet distinguishable themes of reflection on, and research into the essential nature of positive law, one pertaining to the ideal or justice dimension and the other to the real dimension. As noted above, the present discussion in which I shall try to clarify the factual requisite of law is focussed mainly on the factual or real dimension.

The ideal dimension of law finds expression in the extent of tolerance for injustice which the law will endure. In determining such tolerance typical questions that arise are: How unjust must a specific rule of "law" be before it would forfeit its claim to be law in terms of the ideal standards of law? On a comprehensive or systemic scale, the question is how unjust must a "legal order" be before it would forfeit its claim to be a legal order in terms of the ideal standards of law. This question may also be worded as follows: What are the consequences if a specific "legal rule/norm" or "legal system" in general, should forfeit its status as a rule/norm or system to be recognised as "legal"? In other words, when will a specific norm or a legal system in general, owing to a grave deficiency in justice, no longer qualify as *legal*; and what would it be replaced with? All these questions are somehow ontological in nature. They involve the essential qualities of law. However, ordinarily they might incline to arise in an effective state, that is, a political order with well-functioning, more specifically effective institutions, capable of not only creating law but more particularly, also meticulously enforcing the law in each instance,[17] regardless of the justness of such law and specifically in spite of the fact that such law might arguably be gravely unjust.

The focus here is, however, on the factual dimension of law, since a clear understanding of that will cast light on the tenability of the doctrine of statist-individualist constitutionalism, more specifically on the first five beliefs of the doctrine and on the doctrine of the supremacy of the Constitution. The typical questions that arise in this inquiry are: Does an individual legal rule or a Constitution in general remain law regardless of its level of compliance and effectiveness, or does it pass into non-existence once a certain level of non-compliance of the rule or ineffectiveness of the constitutional dispensation is reached? If the answer is in the affirmative, the ensuing question focuses on the degree of non-compliance or ineffectiveness. Hence, how weak must the level of voluntary compliance or enforcement be before a specific legal rule or a Constitution in general lapses into non-existence? Stated differently, which level must disobedience of law reach before such disobedience would render the law concerned no longer part of positive law? What are the consequences of such lapse? What replaces the relevant lapsed rule or Constitution? Since the factual or real dimension is also an indispensable

---

17   Tthis assertion draws on the distinction by Mac Cormick, 1974:102-129; 104-110 between legal *institutions* in contrast to institutions no longer disregarded as legal institutions. In such situations the adage *ubi ius ibi remediem* would effectively be in place. However, if there are no remedies for infringement of rights the continued existence of such rights at positive law is called into question.

dimension of law, these questions are also philosophical in nature because they involve general ontological questions concerning law. However, like the questions on the ideal dimension cited above, they will arguably be inclined to arise in specific social conditions, namely in conditions of a faltering state, that is, a state lacking high levels of law enforcement and/or lacking levels of voluntary compliance. Such state may have good legal formulations, radiating justice and apparently meeting the ideal element of law, yet severely lacking compliance with the norm-formulations in consequence of which it might forfeit the claim to be recognised as a legal system.

4.3

Conceptual clarification: *legal norms* and *legal norm-formulations*

The terms *legal norm/s* in contrast to *legal norm-formulation/s* are crucial for the present discussion.[18] They are not the same and it is important that their meaning and the distinction between them be clarified.[19] Legal norm-formulations are primarily a question of language. They constitute a distinctive mode of language, namely normative language which essentially seeks to articulate norms even though they are not necessarily expressly phrased in normative terms. Typical of sentences that articulate such normative language is that they are susceptible to expressions in typical normative terms, such as the words "ought," "must," "may," "is required," "obligatory," "right," "permit to," "forbidden to," etc.[20] These words all have the same function in common, namely the function of a normative operator.[21] The crucial point for the present discussion is that these norm-formulations are prescriptive but not descriptive in nature. They differ in their epistemological character from descriptive sentences in that, unlike descriptive sentences, they do not assert facts. They are not true or false depending on whether or not they correspond with the social facts to which they refer, but rather valid or invalid,[22] depending on whether they are authorised by preceding and more comprehensive norms within the legal order.[23] They are imperatives without truth values.[24]

---

18 Legal norms and legal norm-formulation/s are used here in encompassing terms and cover rules, principles, institutions of law, prohibitions, directives, permissions more specifically norms and norm-formulations of constitutional law.

19 Various scholars, though not necessarily using the words draw a similar distinction. See for example Aarnio, 2011; A similar distinction is immanent in Mac Cormick, 1974:103-106 who distinguishes between "institutions" and "instances"; Koller, 2014:157-159; Niiniluoto, 1985:168-190.

20 Niiniluotu, 1985:175. "Deontic logic is the name of the study of sentences containing normative expressions such as these words".

21 Koller, 2014:157.

22 Koller, 2014:157-158.

23 As explained for example in the systems of both Kelsen and Hart.

24 Niiniluoto, 1985:175; A norm-formulation can also be viewed as something that, depending on whether or not it is adhered to, may be true or false. Niiniluoto, 1985:175; true, when it is followed and thus describing the actual state of social reality, and false, when it is not followed, and thus not representing social reality.

Legal norm-formulation is a prescriptive legal sentence consigned to writing and contained in an acknowledged source of positive law including the constitution, legislation and case law that enunciate norms of the common law. Legal norm-formulations relate to the ideal or critical dimension in Alexy's terms. They are, paraphrasing Lawrence Boulle,[25] prescriptive and not descriptive in nature, indicating how people ought to act but not necessarily how they might actually behave in practice. Hence, a legal norm-formulation does not necessarily imply that the norm which the formulation seeks to enunciate is effective, that is, that it is actually obeyed and/or enforced. On a sliding scale the level of obedience and/or enforcement may vary from complete obedience and/or enforcement, on the one extreme, to complete disobedience and/or absence of enforcement, on the opposite extreme.

A legal norm in contrast to a legal norm-formulation is by definition effective. Hence, it is usually obeyed and/or enforced. Unlike a legal norm-formulation, which by definition does not reveal anything about the actual effectiveness of the norm signified in such formulation, a norm has a distinctive descriptive property and truth value. It describes a social reality in that in the normal course of events people, either voluntarily or under coercion by the relevant authorities, actually act in compliance with the norm.[26]

Legal norms as conceived in this discussion are, however, not dependent on express formulation. Actual legal norms sometimes do appear in linguistic form, but often they do not. They can exist without ever having been formulated in linguistic terms.[27] It must, in principle, be possible, however, to express them in the form of linguistic utterances which can be represented through prescriptive or norm-expressive sentences.[28] Hence, a legal norm, including a norm of the constitution, may be in existence in the absence of express formulation. As long as the members of a community habitually act in a particular way (*usus*) in the belief that they are legally bound to do so, (*opnio iuris*) a legal norm, more in particular a norm of customary law, is in existence. Legal norms of this customary kind distinctively account for the descriptive (factual) property of law since legal norms owe their existence to actual social conduct without the formal (linguistic) stamp of a preceding legal formation.

---

25 Boulle, 1989:20.

26 The term "legal norm" therefore largely resembles what Alexy calls the real or factual dimension (and not only ideal or critical dimension) of law.

27 Niiniluoto, 1985:180.

28 Koller, 2014:157.

44

The basic thesis of the factual requisite (or dimension) of law

Given that legal norms as conceived above have an essential factual element (and accompanying descriptive quality), knowledge on the actual content of law, cannot be obtained solely with reference to legal norm-formulations. This applies also to the actually existing constitution (in contrast to the document-based Constitution as conceived by the doctrine of statist-individualist constitutionalism). Reliable knowledge on and an accompanying reliable description of the actual constitution can also not be obtained only with reference to the formulations of the written Constitution. In order to grasp the actual content of law and the functioning of the constitution social research and political observation is necessary[29] in order to establish:

σ   to what extent actual behaviour corresponds with the legal norm-formulations; and

σ   whether there is regular conduct that deviates from the legal norm-formulations, yet regarded as binding by those who deviate.

The results of such research may reveal the following scenarios:

a.   The actual behaviour closely corresponds with the legal norm-formulations, including the norm-formulations of the (document-based) Constitution. Transgressing behaviour is an exception to the rule and it is effectively remedied by measures of enforcement as described in the norm-formulations of the law in general and the written Constitution in particular. Such norm-formulations are in fact actual (effective) norms. They provide a reliable description of the actual state of law and the constitution as articulated in the legal norm-formulations concerned. The transgressing behaviour is actually unlawful in terms of the existing norm-formulations and they are remedied by effective enforcement mechanisms.

.   In this kind of scenario the socio-political forces essentially correspond with the norm-formulations of the law in general and with that of the constitutional document. This gives rise to the impression that the written Constitution embodied in its norm-formulations, is supreme.

b.   The second scenario entails large scale transgression of norm-formulation(s), including transgression of (a) norm-formulation(s) of the Constitution. The transgressors' flouting of the norm-formulations is accompanied by regular and consistent deviating behaviour (*usus*) and the deviators, moreover, regard

---

29   Any social research that could cast light on the degree of compliance or non-compliance with law could be relevant. This includes the sociological political-science research, as well as the observations of sharp and experienced political commentators and journalists. In the final analysis jurists have on close analysis a dual part to play in research of this kind: first to identify law (legal norm-formulations) that are suspect for their non-compliance, which will then further call for the attention of the mentioned experts; secondly, to consider, on the basis of the results of such research whether or not a norm is in fact in place (i.e. taking into account the level of compliance) or has been replaced by new substituting law, or has simply fallen by the wayside as explained below.

themselves legally bound to act in the way they are acting (*opinio iuris*). In that case, such behaviour constitutes a new substituting norm and therefore new substituting law, including constitutional law. In a scenario of this kind the norm-formulations concerned do not signify actual norms. They are mere formulations that fail to describe the actual state of the law and the actual constitution. They are mere legal norm-formulations that do not reliably signify actual legal norms (existing positive law) anymore. The norm will then lapse because its requisite factual dimension has fallen away and is moreover, replaced by new, substituting law (including constitutional law).

.   Scenarios of this kind bring to light that the whole belief system of statist-individualist constitutionalism is fallacious and the accompanying mechanisms of the so-called supreme Constitution and accompanying conformity provisions and strict amendment requirements are ineffectual. These scenarios reveal that the so-called supreme Constitution is *not* supreme; that it is *not* formulation-driven; that it is *not* located in (and reflected by) the formulations of the Constitution; and that the (written) Constitution is *not* pre-political because it is made and continuously remade by potent socio-political forces. In consequence, the premise that underpins supremacy provisions, namely that everything which is at variance with the written Constitution is invalid, is wrong, because potent socio-political forces as explained in this scenario are continuously changing the constitution. Strict amendment requirements cannot prevent these changes. Potent socio-political forces simply automatically change the Constitution outside the parameters of formal amendment. The changing of the constitution – the real and actual constitution – is the function of these forces. If these forces are tumultuous, the actual constitution is equally turbulent and if the socio-political forces are stable the actual constitution, is equally stable.

c. In the third scenario, (a) norm-formulation(s), including (a) norm-formulation(s) of the document-based Constitution, are transgressed on a large scale. However, unlike the second scenario the transgression is not accompanied by consistent and regular deviating conduct and/or the deviators do not believe that they are legally bound to act in the various deviating ways in which they are in fact acting. Still, unlike the first scenario, enforcement might be haphazard, thus allowing deviators to get away with their transgressions. Unlike the first scenario, the purported norm (law), including a (purported) norm of the so-called supreme Constitution, encapsulated in the norm-formulations, is in part unsettled but unlike the second scenario, no new norm and therefore no new law (including constitutional law) has come into being. In this scenario there is legal uncertainty. A legal *lacuna*, or *non liquet*, that is, an area not regulated by an existing legal norm of positive law, which includes constitutional law – a legal no-man's land – is opening up.

.   Similar to the second scenarios, the scenarios of this (third) kind also debunk the belief system of statist-individualist constitutionalism and reveal that the accompanying mechanisms of the so-called supreme Constitution are ineffectual.

Somewhat different from the second scenario, the third scenario reveals that conduct at variance with the written Constitution simply causes existing norms of the constitution to be undone, that is, to lapse (without necessarily constituting new constitutional law as in the second scenario). Once again strict amendment requirements cannot prevent these norms of the law and the Constitution to be undone by potent socio-political forces which simply occur automatically outside the parameters of formal amendment of the text of the Constitution. Over and above all of these peculiar characteristics exposed by this scenario it further belies the validity of the first belief of statist-individualist constitutionalism, namely that positive law, including the written Constitution emanating from the designated law-making bodies of the state, is omnipresent.

It should now be apparent that a clear understanding of the factual dimension of law, as enunciated above, belies the first five beliefs of the statist-individualist constitutionalism and refutes the belief in the effectiveness of supremacy provisions and the strict amendment procedures that seek to safeguard the integrity, stability and permanency of the so-called supreme Constitution. As the discussion of the thesis of the factual requisite further proceeds, the outlines of the tension between the factual dimension of law and the doctrine of statist-individualist constitutionalism will get more pronounced. It will be shown that the doctrine of statist-individualist constitutionalism is inappropriate because it impairs, instead of promotes insight into the nature of law as such and, more specifically, because it obscures a reliable insight into the actual state of the law and the constitution at any given time, and on the stability of law, including constitutional law and on how it changes.

Moreover, clear insight into the doctrine of statist-individualist constitutionalism also functions as a soothing, yet, deceiving device in terms of which it is proclaimed that whatever is pronounced in the formulations of the law and the *supreme* (document-based) Constitution is a reliable reflection of the actual state of the law, while that is in fact often not the case. Another – the real – constitution, the function of the ever changing balance of forces in the state concerned might already be in place.

I now proceed to discuss in some more detail something that was alluded to but not thoroughly dealt with in Chapters 2 and 3, namely the linguistic strategy of the language of the doctrine of statist-individualist constitutionalism. This is important because it is enlisted to inculcate trust in the doctrine and faith in its beliefs.

4.5

The doctrine's faith-strengthening language

Belief in the supremacy of the document-based Constitution is bolstered by the doctrine of statist-individualist constitutionalism's own magic-like and gospel-like faith strengthening language.

Being formulations, legal norm-formulations essentially exist in language. Legal norm-formulations constitute the language of law, which is put into use by the doctrine of statist-individualist constitutionalism. It consists of ought-formulations, that is, prescriptive formulations that set out ideal types of conduct on how those under the jurisdiction of the supreme Constitution concerned should be acting and correspondingly ideal situations that would be in existence if they would be acting as required in the norm-formulations. Legal language on close analysis is specifically not a complex of descriptive formulations. Thus Karl Olivecrona aptly observes that legal language is not a descriptive but a directive, influential language.[30] As already pointed out in part 4 above, norm-formulations are not descriptive. They are not true or false (depending on whether or not they correspond with the social facts they refer to), but rather valid or invalid.[31] In step with this, specifically in the field of constitutional law, Lawrence Boulle remarks that constitutionalism – the doctrine of statist-individualist constitutionalism in the terminology used here – is a prescriptive and not a descriptive doctrine that indicates how governmental power should be exercised and not how it is actually exercised in practice.[32]

However, in spite of its essential normative character, legal language, more specifically the language of the doctrine of statist-individualist constitutionalism, has a distinctive propensity for misrepresenting that which is normative as if they were describing social realities, that is, as if they were facts. What happens, is that normative sentences take on a descriptive mode, namely that it is written and read as social realities. Niiniluoto explains this phenomenon and gives appropriate examples.[33] One can for instance say that a person has the right (in descriptive mode as a social truth) instead of (more correctly) that people ought to act in a particular way towards other people. Olivecrona is also aware of this phenomenon of prescriptive or ideal formulations often being draped in the phraseology of factual rather than normative sentences,[34] thus pretending to be descriptive while masquerading the contents of such sentences as social facts. In his turn Llewellyn points out that normative legal sentences quite regularly have a descriptive appearance,[35] and that they thus purport that whatever is required in the norm-formulations is actually happening and thus constituting an actual reality. He states:

> I think that such precept-on-the-books ... tacitly contains an element of pseudo description along with its statement of what officials ought to do; a tacit statement that officials do act according to the tenor of the rule; a tacit prediction that officials will act according to its tenor.[36]

---

30   Olivecrona, 1971:253.

31   Koller, 2014:158.

32   Boulle, 1989:20.

33   Niiniluoto, 1985:176, 177, 179. Such sentences are often referred to normative propositions.

34   Olivecrona, 1971:217.

35   Llewellyn, 1962:23.

36   Llewellyn, 1962:23.

Hans Kelsen also recognises this deceptive feature of norm-formulations to assume the guise of factual descriptions.[37]

As noted, a statement that someone has a right to something has the appearance of a factual statement that purports to describe a factual situation. When for example a Constitution or human rights instrument states that everyone has the right to equality, human dignity, life or freedom of movement, etc. such statements are seemingly not normative. They do not indicate how (normatively) action ought to be taken, and thus leaving open the question of how people do in fact act. On the contrary, such formulations have a misleadingly descriptive quality[38] as though the relevant legal interests that the norm-formulations purport to protect – equal treatment, human dignity, life and free movement, etc. – are in fact fixed and consistent social realities. Conditions that ought to be but are not necessarily in existence are represented as factual realities – actual truths. Legal, and more specifically norm-formulations of the Constitution so consistently and definitely convincingly communicate this deceiving factual message that those exposed to them tend to trust the credibility of the message and to believe in the actual existence of such factually represented conditions. These formulations act as a means by which (abstract) norm-formulations (ideals) are assigned an almost tangible (factual) existence. In consequence, as Olivecrona argues, the formulations may be regarded as transposing agents between the real (or factual) world in which there are no supreme Constitutions, rights and duties, and a super-tangible world where these things are called – phrased – chanted – into existence.[39] Norm-formulations therefore have the propensity of purporting to describe a pleasingly salutary law-abiding reality, something which these formulations are obviously not capable of achieving regardless of whatever rhetorical strategies might be employed in seeking to achieve it. As Llewellyn quite bluntly, yet not without merit asserts:

> 'Rights' adds nothing to descriptive power. But it gives a specious appearance of substance to prescriptive rules. They seem to be about something.[40]

The faith-strengthening language of the doctrine pretends to transpose what is stated in the norm-formulations into actual realities in the form of the conduct required in such formulations. In so doing this language acts as faith-strengthening rhetoric convincing the reader that the norm-formulations are describing factual truths,[41] that is, that they create and sustain actual realities of whatever is articulated

---

37   Kelsen, 1967.

38   See in this regard Niiniluoto, 1985:175-180.

39   Olivecrona, 1971:223.

40   Llewellyn, 1962:13.

41   Olivecrona, 1971:222.

in such formulations. Hence, the doctrine's language is premised on the (tacit) belief that it has the ability to create effects merely by articulating such (desired) effects.[42]

This distinctive faith-strengthening trait of the doctrine's language is the mainstay of the doctrine of statist-individualist constitutionalism.[43] By disregarding the indispensable ideal (or critical) dimension of law and representing law instead as definitive facts, the doctrine's language inculcates faith in the doctrine of statist-individualist constitutionalism. Stated in the terms of the conceptual framework proposed in part 3 above, this means that the doctrine's language represents legal norm-formulations as if they were actual, fully-fledged norms, that is, as if the norm-formulations were effective and therefore actually obeyed and/or enforced. On a systemic scale involving the whole constitutional order, the effect of the doctrine's language is similar, yet more comprehensive. The doctrine's language represents the document-based Constitution as though it was a factually incontestable reality as if the entire complex of norm-formulations of the written Constitution were fully-fledged norms, actually effective and supreme, that is, actually obeyed and/or enforced.[44]

4.6

Exposition of the factual requisite of law and critique of the doctrine

In consequence of the insight into the factual requisite of law, the answer to questions as to what the law, including the constitution, entails and to what extent it has remained stable and/or has changed, cannot as the doctrine statist-individualist constitutionalism claims, conclusively be answered solely with reference to the legal norm-formulations of the sources of positive law. These norm-formulations, regardless of how bold and dapper they are phrased, provide but the (first) prima facie indication of what the law and the constitution entail. For example:

σ   There might be formulations suggesting the existence of rights, but no effective remedies in the event of any violation of a right, and if there is no remedy for an infringed right, the "right" in those un-remedied circumstances can arguably be said not to have been in existence at all;

---

42   The magical quality of language – its ability to create realities – is possibly as old as law itself. Olivecrona referring to practices in Roman law explained how formal legal language accompanied by rituals was regarded as capable of creating new realities. Olivecrona, 1971:222. "Thus legal language was perceived as capable of calling the required effects into existence solely on account of the proclamation of these effects using the prescribed legal phrases. The term, *law*, has itself compelling effect. What comes under the official appellation of law, Olivecrona notes carries with it the implication that the rules of conduct contained in the text are binding on everybody." Olivecrona, 1971:133.

43   The constitutional discourse specifically also in South Africa is permeated with such faith-strengthening language widely used among lawyers and the general public such as *rights* that are *guaranteed*, *entrenched* or *enshrined* in the Constitution and that rights are referred to as constitutional guarantees. The Constitution itself is described as *entrenched* or *enshrined*.

44   Ironically the effect of norms being portrayed as facts is to expose the trite doctrine of the rule and law and supremacy of the constitution to the same classical criticism that has always been levelled against natural law, namely to confuse the *is-es* with the *oughts* and to portray the latter as if they were the former.

σ   There might be formulations attesting to the existence of legal institutions, yet wide-spread instances where there are no binding legal consequences flowing from these institutions;

σ   There might be formulations relating the tale of the Constitution's magnificent supremacy, yet widespread deviating conduct belying that tale;

σ   There might be formulations attesting to the foundational values of the supreme Constitution. Yet the actual state of affairs might attest to the absence of such values and/or to new values that have superseded those that feature in the written text of the Constitution; and

σ   There might be formulations allocating power to defined institutions and purporting to regulate the relationship between these institutions, whilst in reality these relationships might be at variance with these formulations, so that such power is in fact exercised by institutions other than those designated by the formulations.

In conclusion, there might be words speaking of the existence of law, yet not (sufficient) corresponding action – deeds – for these formulations to have real consequences in the lives of people.

In order to acquire a reliable indication of the actual content of the law and the constitution, the socio-political realities have to be studied. Hence, the actual behaviour of politicians, the state administration and the public in general have to be assessed. The extent of actual compliance or deviation from the norm-formulations, and not the legal norm-formulations as such, will reveal the actual changing content of the law and the constitution at any given time. Therefore I agree with Llewellyn that:

> ... the most significant aspects of the relations of law and society lie in the field of behaviour, and that words take on importance either because and insofar as they are behaviour, or because and insofar as they demonstrably reflect or influence other behaviour.[45]

In consequence, the field of study of law and the constitution should go way beyond the legal norm-formulations of the acknowledged sources of the positive law. Bingham thus noted in rather blunt terms that the field of study of law should be "... far wider and more complex than an imaginary system of promulgated or developed stereotyped rules and principles."[46] This resonates the warning of classical legal sociologist, Eugen Ehrlich against a reductionist theory of legal sources in terms of which the boundaries of the law are confined to the formulations in the (seemingly authoritative) sources of the law and the document-based Constitution laid down by the designated agencies of the state. A more realistic and expanded approach to legal sources would be to look for the actual prevalent norms of the law beyond the acknowledged sources, namely also in the socio-political forces, which

---

45   Llewellyn, 1962:16. See also Bingham, 1912:105 et seq.

46   Bingham, 1913:11.

in the final analysis constitute the law.[47] If one suspects that the norm-formulations will not reveal a reliable picture of the totality of the law (including the document-based so-called supreme Constitution) and that such complete picture will only be revealed once the socio-political forces are also explored, and if one then nevertheless proceeded to limit oneself to the formulations as if they were the only sources, legal science would descend into mere dogma or doctrine.[48] Any scholarly endeavour undertaken on such basis would prohibit instead of pursue knowledge and insight. Thus, Ehrlich is of the view that the methods employed by modern legal science cause substantial parts of the law to become unknown (or obscured).[49]

In the field of constitutional law, Griffin warns that the disregard of non-textual changes to the constitution could weaken one's insight into the actual functioning of the constitutional dispensation.[50] The studies of Bruce Ackermann underscore this warning.[51]

Both Ehrlich and Griffin emphasise the importance of heeding socio-political factors in order to gain knowledge about what the law and the constitution really entail. Whether the legal norm-formulations signify true norms, namely actual, effective positive law (including the actual constitution) will therefore depend on forces outside and not necessarily recorded in the norm-formulations, including those of the document-based Constitution. These forces determine the level of compliance with norm-formulations; the degree of effectiveness of the law and the Constitution, purported to be signified in the norm-formulations; and finally, the extent to which such formulations reflect the actual state of positive law, including the constitution. On close analysis, these forces are basically twofold: firstly, the level of consistent voluntary adherence to the law (the norms signified in the norm-formulations) by the public and the state itself; and secondly, coercive action taken by the designated agencies of the state to address any lack of voluntary compliance.

Franz Neumann, focussing on the latter, states that the question whether legal norm-formulations really denote actual effective law, or in his words, whether law is in fact sociologically valid, depends on:

> ... whether the coercive machinery 'state' provides for coercion on behalf of those legal norms, and whether it has such a power that on the average it can be expected that the legal norm will be fulfilled.[52]

---

47   Ehrlich, 1936:84; 501-502.

48   Ibid, p.41.

49   Ibid, p.489.

50   Griffin, 1995:56.

51   See for example Ackermann, 2007. See in this regard also the ground-breaking study by Van der Hoeven, 1958; Tushnet, 2009:239-279; and various authors in Mclouglin & Walker, 2007.

52   Neumann, 1986:12.

Important as coercion might be for law's effectiveness and for its factual dimension, it is wrong to overemphasise coercive measures of agencies of the state as if they are the primary factors for securing the effectiveness of law and thus for sustaining law's factual dimension. Edgar Bodenheimer levelled criticism against the approach, which he referred to as an academic preoccupation with sanctions which leads to a false view of the law.[53] The overemphasis on coercion by state agencies stems from a view of the law, including the constitution, in terms of which too much is ascribed to the state, not only in regard to the making of law but also in regard to law's effectiveness. In this respect I am in agreement with Peter Koller who is of the opinion that the factual dimension is based on widespread acceptance and voluntary behaviour,[54] and that this is the basis of the rule of law. I am also in agreement with Edgar Bodenheimer in whose opinion coercion is meaningless and the threat of coercion impotent if vast sections of the populace are unwilling to obey the law.[55] Bodenheimer, in keeping with insights of the authors referred to in part 4.2 above, maintains that the primary guarantee for the efficacy of a legal order is the acceptance by the community while compulsory sanctions are merely a secondary and auxiliary requirement. In this regard he states as follows:

> A reasonable and satisfactory system of law will be obeyed by most members of the community ... Compulsion is used against a non-cooperative minority; in any normal and effectively working commonwealth the number of lawbreakers against whom sanctions must be employed is much smaller than the number of law-abiding citizens.[56]

Voluntariness and consensus are the backbone of a well-functioning legal order. Thus Bodenheimer is spot on in stating:

> We are justified, therefore, in taking the position that the necessity for primary reliance on government force as a means for carrying out the mandates of law indicates a malfunctioning of the legal system rather than an affirmation of its validity and efficacy. Since we should not define a legal system in terms of its pathological manifestations, we should not see the essence of law in the use of compulsion.[57]

If, on close analysis of the socio-political realities, it is established that a legal norm-form formulation is not factually effective, either because of a lack of voluntary abiding behaviour or because of major glitches in the relevant coercive apparatus, or of both, the conclusion should be that there is in fact no norm and therefore no positive law on the issue that is articulated in the norm-formulation in question. In that scenario, law is devoid of its factual dimension which is the one indispensable half of law's dual wholeness. There is but a half-reality, because it represents only the ideal or critical side which comprises the norm-formulations,

---

53   Bodenheimer, 1974:274. In this respect Bodenheimer aligns himself with the views of George Paton.

54   Koller, 2014:163.

55   Bodenheimer, 1974:273.

56   Bodenheimer, 1974:273; Also see Malan, 2004:474-479.

57   Bodenheimer, 1974:274.

while the factual or real side, containing the actual effective norms, is absent. Since the simultaneous presence of both dimensions is required to constitute law, there is no law at all.

In analysing the socio-political realities, two points of focus can be distinguished. In the first place, the spotlight is on the behaviour of public office-bearers, in other words the government and the public administration. In the second place, the spotlight is cast on the conduct of (segments of) the public in general vis-à-vis the norm-formulations of the officially recognised sources of positive law, including the constitution. In both cases, the level of consistent voluntary adherence and the level of effective law enforcement by the relevant coercive agencies are decisive. These two points of focus are now discussed with reference to four scenarios. These scenarios will now be dealt with under four headings and in various combinations of lapsed, substituted and/or substituting and still-born law.

4.6.1 Substituting law arising from the behaviour of public office-bearers

In scenarios of this kind, the conduct of public office-bearers, more in particular officials who are part of the state administration, shows a pattern of deviation in conflict with legal norm-formulations, including the Constitution. The deviating conduct assumes a fixed pattern, a pattern, either not provided for, or clearly disallowed by the legal norm-formulations, including that of the Constitution. In pursuing the new practice, office-bearers bona fide consider themselves to be legally bound to follow that pattern, namely to behave in a particular manner because they ought to do so. Hence, their actual behaviour – *usus* – is accompanied by *opinio iuris*. Once that occurs, new substituting law comprising both the factual and the ideal components of law's dual structure is quite obviously in the process of being created. Its establishment can only be prevented if effective measures to enforce the law articulated in the legal norm-formations (and which is now under pressure of the new substituting practice) can still be taken. However, if the relevant state agencies are not able to do that, or if they are acquiescent to such behaviour, thus tacitly consenting thereto (*tacitus consensus superioris*),[58] the disobeyed norm lapses into non-existence. In the latter case, the new law replaces the old one with government as a passive, participating party. The old law ceases to exist as part of positive law and is replaced by the new law that has resulted from consistent deviating conduct. If the old norm was part of the constitution, it ceases to be part of it, and is, by the same token, replaced by new constitutional law that has arisen from consistent deviating conduct. The replaced law may be called substituted law and the new law substituting law, which includes substituted constitutional law and substituting constitutional law. This substitution occurs in spite of the fact that the norm-formulation that purports to signify an effective norm of positive law is still intact. It also occurs in spite of asserting the written Constitution's so-called

---

58 Insightfully explained by Van den Bergh, 1982:39.

supremacy and stability that forbids constitutional amendments or allows for constitutional amendments only on compliance of strict amendment procedures. The norm-formulation in this scenario is misleading because it is a misrepresentation of the law (including constitutional law) that is actually in existence. The substitution that has taken place is not reflected in the legal norm-formulations that still have the appearance of the substituted instead of the substituting law. What has occurred in this scenario is that the law and the constitution changed, without the legal-formulation (the text) reflecting such change.

4.6.2 Lapsed law resulting from the behaviour of public office-bearers

In this scenario, public office-bearers transgress the norms articulated in legal norm-formulation on a large scale without, as in the first scenario, engaging in consistent deviating behaviour. Or there may be consistency in their deviating behaviour, yet without the bona fide belief that they are legally bound to act in that way. There is *usus* but no accompanying *opinio iuris*. In this scenario, the existing law (which might include constitutional law) lapses without having been replaced by new law and a legal vacuum, that is, a field not governed by any positive law – a *non liquet* – is opening up. Since government – here meant to include the legislature, the executive and the administration – might be acquiescent to such behaviour and thus be consenting to it, there is *consensus superioris*, which means that government is passively a party to such law, which may include "supreme" constitutional law which has lapsed into non-existence.

4.6.3 Substituting or lapsed law arising from the behaviour of (segments of) the public

What occurs in this scenario is not different in principle from the previous two, yet arguably even more incongruent with the trite doctrine of statist-individualist constitutionalism. In this case the collective agent that creates substituting law or causes existing law to lapse is not agencies of the state but segments of the public. Hence, the substitution or lapsing of law does not emanate from the law-making, law-changing or law-interpreting institutions of the state but from sectors of the public. The latter's conduct may deviate so substantially from (what appears to be) the positive law (as articulated in the legal norm-formulations) and the state's failure to effectively enlist its coercive apparatus (if any) to remedy such deviations may be so far-reaching that the positive law simply lapses. Depending on the actual socio-political realities, this may occur for longer or shorter periods and over smaller or larger territorial areas within a particular state. On condition that the *usus* and *opinio iuris* requirements for substituting (customary) law are complied with such deviating behaviour could also give rise to substituting law, however, in practice less readily than in cases where the agencies of the state are the changing agents.

4.6.4 Still-born law, including still-born constitutional law

There is also a fourth scenario, namely that of still-born law, including still-born constitutional law. In this scenario new norm-formulations are promulgated by the law-giver (in the case of the Constitution, by a Constitution-making body). However, the norm-formulations never take effect because, in keeping with the argumentation of Jacques Cujas and others discussed in part 4.2 above, the promulgated norm-formulations never become positive law (including actual constitutional law) because the relevant norm-formulations are never affirmed - accepted - through corresponding custom. Hence, the norm-formulations never progress beyond the status of a norm-formulation so as to become actual real norms of the law and the constitution. The ideal element of law is present, but the essential real or factual element in law's dual dimensionality never arises. The law in this case is still-born since the confirmatory custom never transforms the norm-formulation into effective law - an actual norm of law. Judged by the formulation, there appears to be law, yet owing to the absence of confirmatory conduct it has never really become law. It is still-born.

Conduct deviating from law is a typical characteristic of even the most smoothly functioning constitutional dispensation. It should be clear therefore that not all transgressions or deviating conduct would cause the existing law to lapse or to be substituted with new law. It is a matter of degree of non-compliance or ineffectiveness, not ineffectiveness or non-compliance as such. For that very reason, as indicated at the outset in part 4.2, questions surrounding the factual dimension will tend not to arise in smoothly functioning dispensations where there are low levels of non-compliance, but rather in weak ones where there are rapidly changing social and political conditions, and therefore low levels of voluntary obedience of law where law enforcement institutions are faltering and weak.[59]

The need for considering the above scenarios can be traced back to the insightful observations of Georg Jellinek who states that *the factual* continuously breeds new law.[60] Hence, a realistic assessment of the actual prevailing law requires scrutiny of the factual, that is, an assessment of what really occurs in terms of the actual conduct of government and the public. This would avoid the risk to be misled by the norm-formulations of the formally recognised sources of the law, on the actual prevailing condition of the law, especially when these formulations are

---

59 This view of the fate of law invokes the perspective that positive law and a well-functioning constitutional state presuppose a "perfect" imbalance between the forces of existing positive law on the one hand and those that rather transgress, without necessarily trying to replace, the existing law (e.g. criminal law) or forces that expressly seek to replace the existing law (forces that seek to destabilise the government and/or the state). Once the challenging forces grow stronger, and compliance of the existing law gets less consistent resulting from less voluntary adherence and/or weaker enforcement by state agencies, the required imbalance gets unsettled which causes the gradual lapse of the "existing" law or, depending on the strength and success of the challenging forces, constitute a new imbalance and therefore new (substituting) law. See Malan, 2004:474-479.

60 Jellinek, 1919:340; 368; See also Ehrlich, 1936:86.

in the misleading guise of descriptive, truth-asserting sentences referred to in part 4.5 above. A distinction has to be drawn between what one might call the constitution of the formulations – the document-based Constitution – in contrast to the actual constitution. The latter, which is an expression of the actual relations of power, might be independent from the formal legal position.[61] In keeping with this approach the Dutch jurist H. Hijmans, quoted by Van den Bergh, declares that the most important source of the law is not the recognised sources of legislation, custom, case law and secondary legal science, but the living reality which carries its own law within itself.[62] It follows that many norms in terms of which action takes place fall outside the documentary framework and the complex of the formally recognised law and the Constitution. A reliable reflection of the actual constitution must therefore account for these non-formally recognised practices.[63]

It is significant that in spite of his pure theory of law that limits the analysis of positive law to the norms validly ordained by designated organs of state to make and amend law, Hans Kelsen expressly acknowledges the operation of the factual dimension in his analysis of the positive law. It might even be more apt to say that Kelsen in spite of his pure theory of law cannot in the final analysis escape the law-creating and law-substituting force of the factual dimension when he acknowledged that the validity of norms depend in part on their effectivity so that there has to be at least a minimum degree of obedience of the law for the law to remain valid.[64] Hence, a norm that is never obeyed is no longer valid[65] and therefore ceases to be a norm of positive law. It is possible, according to Kelsen, that a norm may forfeit its validity due to consistent disobedience. Kelsen declares:

> If effectiveness in the developed sense is the condition for validity not only for the legal order as a whole but also for a single legal norm, then the law creating function of custom cannot be excluded by statutory law, at least not as far as the negative function of desuetude is concerned.[66]

The same is true for Hart who formulates:

> (t)wo minimum conditions necessary and sufficient for the existence of a legal system. On the one hand those rules of behaviour which are valid according to the system's ultimate criteria of validity must be generally obeyed, and, on the other hand, its rules of recognition specifying the criteria of legal validity and its rules of change and adjudication must be effectively accepted as common public standards of official behaviour by its officials.[67]

---

61   Jellinek, 1919:341.

62   The original Dutch text reads: "Ik zou mijn meening bij voorkeur aldus willen uitdrukken dat de voornaamste rechtsbron niet is de wet noch de gewoonte en evenmin de rechtswetenschap of de rechspraak, ... maar de levende werklijkheid zelf. Deze draagt haar recht in zich, en de rechtsorde is één haarer zijde" Van den Bergh:93. Van den Bergh does not state which work of Hijmans he quoted from.

63   See further the discussion of Andrew, 1968:21-22.

64   Kelsen, 1967:11, 211-212; Kelsen, 1961:119.

65   Kelsen, 1967:213.

66   Kelsen, 1967:213.

67   Hart, 1994:113.

JAG Griffith is specifically alive to the operation of the force of the factual dimension. He maintains that everything done in the belief that legally it ought to be done (that is, with the necessary *opinio iuris*) which has a binding effect on people is (included in) the constitution, regardless of what the text – the norm-formulations of the statutory instrument – that goes by the name Constitution provides. The ever altering constitution undergoes consistent changes as the constitution is finally that which is actually happening.[68] Thus Griffith bluntly declares, to my mind not without merit: "Everything that happens is constitutional. And if nothing happens that would be constitutional also."[69]

What emerges clearly from this exposition is that a reliable grasp of the actual state of the positive law, including the constitution, at any given time requires that the behaviour of state agencies and the public continuously be considered. That may show that some ostensible rules of positive law are merely paper-rules as Llewellyn called them.[70] This means that some apparent norms are in fact no more than formulations (words and sentences), yet not actual norms and on that score not actual positive law. On the one extreme, in the smoothly functioning dispensation with stable socio-political conditions, the norms are largely voluntarily obeyed, and enforced by state agencies in the exceptional cases where they are not obeyed. Thereafter, however, follows a sliding scale of increased disregard of the norms up to the point where conforming conduct is so haphazard that only the norm-formulations – the paper rules – remain. Once a certain level of disregard is reached, the norm lapses and only the formulation remains. A norm-formulation gets increasingly misleading as the actual deviating behaviour increases. It reaches the zenith of its deception when deviating conduct is at its worst. In spite of the fact that the dominating socio-political forces, which have once produced conforming conduct, have lapsed in favour of new forces and accompanying deviating conduct, the norm-formulation still falsely pretends that the lapsed norm – the substituted law – is in existence. It might be quite difficult to reliably determine whether the norm-formulation reflects the actually existing law, or whether, under the cloak of these formulations, the (old) law has already lapsed or has been substituted by new law. The reason for this difficulty is that these changes occur largely tacitly. Unlike formal amendments (of the text of the Constitution or legislation), they are not reflected in the changed text of the law, although they may in fact be much more profound than those that are recorded in the text. Thus Steven Griffin states:

> One need not believe in rule-of-law constitutionalism to think that the changes in the role of the national government in the regulation of the economy proposed by President Roosevelt were so fundamental that they should have been authorized through appropriate constitutional amendments. The New Deal changes were likely the most

---

68 Griffith, 1979:19.

69 Griffith, 1979:19.

70 Llewellyn, 1962:21 et seq.

significant changes in the constitutional system made in the twentieth century, yet one cannot tell from the text of the Constitution that any changes occurred at all.[71]

Hence, new law, including new constitutional law, may long be in existence in place of the substituted law, before it is actually realised that the change has in fact taken place.[72]

In a state in which the leading socio-political forces underpin the legal norm-formulations of positive law (including the Constitution) the behaviour of the inhabitants and public office-bearers will largely correspond with these formulations. The norm-formulations will therefore largely be a reliable reflection of the actually prevailing law in such state. In such scenario, we have what in trite terms could be described as a well-functioning constitutional state. In the event of an inquiry into what the law in such situation entails, it will suffice to consult the norm-formulation of the acknowledged sources of positive law. By the same token, a reliable image of the constitution could then be acquired solely with reference to the formulation of the statutory instrument(s), more in particular the Constitution (the written Constitution) and its interpretation by the relevant authoritative bodies – primarily the courts. Knowledge of the law and the constitution could in that case be acquired solely by consulting the legal norm-formulations of the acknowledged sources of positive law. On the basis of the assumption that the sources of law are fully constituted by the whole collection of norm-formulations of positive law, legal education consists entirely in systematically acquainting law students with such formulations.

But here is the rub – the first one: At the moment of their promulgation, the legal norm-formulations of the written Constitution might correctly reflect social behaviour. However, from the time of their promulgation there might be discrepancies between dominant socio-political forces and the accompanying behaviour by office-bearers and segments of the public, the latter being underpinned by dominant socio-political forces in the politico-constitutional dispensation concerned, but not reflected in the norm-formulations. In that case, the legal norm-formulations might reflect a misrepresentation of the law, including the constitution, from the moment of their promulgation. This is a case of still-born law explained above.

Here one has to be alive to the fact that although the legal norm-formulations at the time of their promulgation might reliably record the actual socio-political forces and accompanying behaviour, that does not mean that the formulations will remain such a reliable recording in future because legal norm-formulations are directive and influential, as Olivecrona reminded us (and as we have seen in

---

71   Griffin, 1995:51.

72   Van den Bergh, 1982:42.

parts 4 and 5),[73] yet not able to arrest and rigidify existing socio-political forces and social behaviour.[74] The law, more specifically the constitution, operating in the domain of politics, is particularly prone to changing power relations and social behaviour. For that reason it might reliably record the power relations of the immediate past,[75] yet unable to predict the future. Norm-formulations might be promulgated in highly fluctuating social conditions in which socio-political forces and the accompanying behaviour would soon be at variance – possibly patently at variance – with the norm-formulations, and this could cause a swift lapse or substitution of the "law" signified in formulations.

In both these scenarios actual behaviour will first have to be assessed in order to establish the degree of equivalence (or discrepancy) between the norm-formulations and such behaviour. Until that enquiry is concluded, no decisive conclusion can be reached on what the law and the constitution actually entail. By the same token, a sound constitutional state cannot be proclaimed to be in existence solely with reference to the norm-formulations of the Constitution's text (and the interpretations thereof by the designated agencies of the state). The norm-formulations (the ideal dimension) of the law and the constitution must, as it were, be verified with reference to the actual socio-political forces and accompanying behaviour before reliable conclusions may be reached on what the law and the constitution really entail. The norm-formulations are therefore just the first prima facie indications of what the law entails. The outcome of the inquiries into the actual behaviour of the public and office-bearers underscores the fact that the law and the constitution, irrespective of the imposing omnipresence of the law and supremacy of the Constitution, might in fact not necessarily be as omnipresent and supreme as the doctrine of the supremacy of the Constitution, would suggest. In the final analysis, it might be argued that although constitution-making and law-making bodies are capable of defining and controlling legal norm-formulations, the actual (content of) law and the constitution is determined by a raft of socio-political forces (alongside the formulations) as manifested in accompanying behaviour.[76] Thus, Stephen Griffin remarks, with respect to the constitutional order of the United States of America, that more constitutional truth can be obtained by examining the way government operates than by reading the document.[77]

Here we encounter the second rub: that jurists are clearly not well-placed to conduct the kind of socio-political inquiry which is necessary to acquire insight into actual social behaviour. In fact, the weakness of jurists in this field has been commented on in rather forthright terms by Karl Llewellyn, a renowned jurist

---

73   Olivecrona:253.

74   Van der Hoeven, 1976:41.

75   Röling, 1962:x.

76   See in this regard, the observations by Jacob:36, concerning the criminal justice system.

77   Griffin, 1995:56.

himself, when he noted that lawyers are admirable in word techniques and on the facts of a particular case but helpless and even childish when it comes to broad social facts in their social bearings. The reason for this is that the activities of jurists are text-based, that is, formulation-conditioned. Their attention is directed to the text, which they interpret; not to the socio-political forces outside the text, which are the terrain of social scientists and astute political observers. Jurists work with legal norm-formulations which they assume to embody the law. They are not required to assess the actual sociological validity of the text (the actual effectiveness of law) and also not schooled to undertake such assessment. They simply interpret the text to the best of their ability, assuming that it signifies actual law, regardless of whether deviating behaviour has reduced it to mere formulations instead of actual norms. Whereas lawyers are well-positioned to pronounce on the meaning of the legal norm-formulations, that is, on law's ideal dimension, they are particularly ill-positioned and untrained to pronounce on the factual or real dimension of law. And since the factual dimension is crucial for determining the actual state of the law and the constitution, it is rather ironic that jurists might often not be as sufficiently equipped, as might generally be assumed, to say what the law really entails. The truth of this startling statement will obviously apply in situations where there are material discrepancies between norm-formulations (the ideal dimension) and the actual norms (the factual dimension). Such situations might be common and wide ranging.

4.7

Conclusion

In this chapter the two-dimensional nature of law is clarified and its factual dimension is explained. The reality is uncovered that legal norm-formulations – the ideal dimension of law – cannot be relied upon to access reliable knowledge of the actual state of the law and the actual constitution. Insight into the factual dimension casts a long shadow over the tenability of the first five beliefs of statist-individualist constitutionalism. It specifically shows that supremacy provisions in the written Constitution and strict conformity and amendment requirements might be ineffective to prevent changes to the law and the Constitution.

The balance of social and political forces determines the actual and ever-changing content of the law and the (actual) constitution. In the final analysis there is no such thing as a supreme Constitution in spite of whatever convincing terms the written and so-called supreme Constitution might mobilise to proclaim its own supremacy. The constitution is in fact continuously made and remade – constituted and reconstituted – by potent socio-political forces. Potent socio-political forces simply automatically change the constitution outside the parameters of formal amendment of the text of the Constitution. The constitution – the real and actual constitution – is the function of these forces. If these forces are tumultuous, the actual constitution is equally turbulent and if the socio-political forces are stable, the actual constitution, is equally stable. To the extent that anything might be supreme, these socio-political forces are supreme, not the written Constitution.

There is therefore a clear need for continuous social observation and inquiry in order to reliably fathom the trends in social behaviour and thus the actual state of the law and the constitution. If we fail to do that, we run the risk of misleading ourselves with acquiring "knowledge" of façade law and a façade Constitution that differs from the actual constitution and fails to provide reliable insight into the actual state of the constitution.[78]

Using this theoretical insight into the factual dimension of law, the focus of the next chapter will be practical. It shifts to the South African constitutional order in the first decades after the commencement of the constitutional order in 1994. It will be shown that in spite of its high claims of supremacy, its conformity provisions and its strict amendment requirements, the South African Constitution, is not supreme and that there is a real and changing South African constitution resulting from the ever-changing balance of socio-political forces. With reference to a number of examples it will be illustrated that the actual behaviour of organs of state as well as non-statist actors, have profoundly changed the (actual) constitution, resulting in important aspects of the provisions of the written Constitutions being effectively replaced by new constitutional law and in other cases simply being caused to lapse.

---

78   Sartori, 1962:861.

THE CONSTITUTION OF THE REPUBLIC OF SOUTH AFRICA IS NOT SUPREME AND ITS RIGHTS NOT ENTRENCHED

The Changing South African Constitution

5.1

Introduction

In Chapter 4 it was demonstrated that the claim of supremacy of the written and so-called supreme Constitution is theoretically ill-founded and that strict conformity requirements and amendment procedures are ineffectual. I will in this chapter reinforce the argumentation presented in Chapter 4 with reference to the practical South African experience of the last decades since the establishment of the present constitutional order in 1994. The South African Constitution, notwithstanding its vaunted supremacy, its conformity requirements and strict amendment procedures, is in fact not really as supreme as the doctrine of statist-individualist constitutionalism claims.

The Constitution has in fact undergone profound changes, not as a result of formal amendments in accordance with its *entrenched* amendment provisions, but as a result of the following phenomena outlined in Chapter 4: In some cases the Constitution has changed because certain provisions have been *substituted* by *substituting* constitutional law arising either from the behaviour of public office-bearers or from the behaviour of (segments of the) public. In other cases provisions of the Constitution simply lapsed, once again either as a result of the behaviour of public office-bearers or from the behaviour of segments of the public. Further informal changes of the constitution were brought about by the so-called still-born provisions, namely those that never really entered into force because they were either never given effect to by conforming conduct or by combinations and mutations of all of the phenomena now under discussion. In all these cases the text of the Constitution – the Constitution as conceived by the doctrine of statist-individualist constitutionalism – still remains unchanged. The provisions are, however, not accompanied by actual conforming conduct. Such provisions, as explained in Chapter 4, are not real norms; they are mere norm-formulations which do not constitute actually existing constitutional law. The trite mechanisms of statist-individualist constitutionalism – supremacy and entrenchment provisions, conformity requirements and strict amendment procedures – are no match for potent socio-political forces that create, recreate and change the (actual) constitution.

As indicated in the previous chapter, an inquiry as to the actual state of the constitution cannot be limited to a study of the text of the Constitution. Aside from consulting and interpreting the text, the actual socio-political conditions will have to be assessed in order to establish the actual – and changing – state of the constitution – the true and real constitution.

5.2

The actual changes to the South African constitutional dispensation

I now proceed to discuss a selection of the most important changes to the South African constitution. Even though all the changes are somehow entwined, the various items of change are divided as follows: The first two have to do with the changing locus of governmental power. The third deals with so-called cadre deployment in the public sector. The forth change pertains to the fact that the South African public have to a considerable extent accepted responsibility for their (own) physical safety and for combating crime in general. The fifth, sixth and seventh phenomenon all relate to the value basis of the Constitution. The eighth has to do with the wholesale change of the written Constitution's dispensation regarding the official languages.

The first two items under the spotlight pertain to the shift of the centres of political (more specifically governmental) power in South Africa. The first involves the shifting of power between organs of state, the three levels (spheres) of governmental power – national, provincial and local. This is a phenomenon that can be explained with reference to the conceptual tools of constitutional law, such as federalism and unitarism. This will be the focus in part 5.2.1 immediately below. The second form of power shift is much more profound. In this case power migrates to bodies other than those that are recognised by the written Constitution, which then in full or in part become the new centres of governmental power in place of the ones described in the written Constitution. The trite concepts and terminology of constitutional law do not lend themselves to explaining this phenomenon. Political concepts and concepts of political science must be invoked instead to explain this phenomenon. The concept of hybrid government and ancillary concepts must be utilised to clarify what is occurring in this case. This will be dealt with in part 5.2.2 in this chapter.

5.2.1 The centres of governmental power (1) (quasi-federalism)

In view of the Constitution's allocation of governmental authority among the various spheres of government, South Africa may be described as a quasi-federal state. It is at least in part federal in that: the legislative powers of the various provinces originate directly from the Constitution itself instead of deriving from legislation of the national legislature;[1] the second house of the national legislature (the National Council of Provinces (NCoP)), in keeping with the tenets of federal constitutional dispensations, represents the various provinces (the federating units);[2] and the Constitutional Court, in typical federal vein, also has the jurisdiction to adjudicate disputes between the national and provincial spheres of government.[3]

Notwithstanding all this, right from the time that the Constitution took effect, three socio-political forces have been undermining the quasi-federal nature of the state envisaged by the Constitution and replacing it with a different state form.

The first of these forces were those that practically changed the quasi-federal form of the state into a centralised, unitary state.[4] These forces have emanated from the following:

In the first place, the ANC is the ruling party in eight of the nine provinces, apart from being dominant on the national level. Hence, save for the one province (the Western Cape) where the ANC does not form the government, there is no incentive in any of these provinces to pursue its own distinctive character. Distinctive own identities for each of the federating units, which identities they desire to protect and for which they require a notable degree of self-government,[5] is generally a prerequisite for sustaining a federal constitution. As a result of the domination of the ANC, that federal factor is wanting in South Africa.

In the second place, the ANC itself is strongly centralised. In consequence, all but one of the nine provinces as well as the national government are ruled from a single party centre.[6] Strategic political risk analyst, Heinrich Matthee, comments as follows on this:

---

1   Compare sections 43 and 104 read with Schedule 4 and 5 of the Constitution. Heuglin & Fenna, 2015:9 refers to the constitutional dispensation provided for by the South African Constitution as a "federal system in all but name."

2   Section 42(4) of the *Constitution of the Republic of South Africa*, 1996 (hereafter *the Constitution*).

3   Section 67(4)(a) of *the Constitution*. It is typical of federations that the judiciary has jurisdiction to decide cases of this kind. Compare for example De Villiers, 2004:212-213.

4   Shortly after the Constitution took effect, these centralising tendencies came to the fore. See for example Simeon & Murray, 2001:65-92. See also the observations by De Villiers, 2004:230. In order to establish the true and changing nature of a (federal) state, it is not sufficient to consider the constitutional provisions on the allocation of legislative and executive powers among the various levels of government. To that end the dynamic political forces operating in the state should continuously be analysed. That is so because the true nature of the form of state (and hence of the constitution) may significantly be altered by these political forces.

5   See in this regard the observations made by Friedrich, 1963:585, as well as Kriek, 1983:174.

6   Steytler, 2001:240-254 et seq; Welsh, 2004:5-21.

The ANC has adopted 'democratic centralism' as a central policy: this means that the making of all policy decisions is concentrated in the National Executive Council (NEC), the ANC's highest decision-making body. This policy is not only indifferent to the federal structure and multiple centres of policy-making envisaged by the South African Constitution. In its execution, it is corroding the democratic checks and balances built into the Constitution.[7]

Another political analyst, William Gumede, further explains:

All too often, democratic centralism, or 'vanguardism' – which the ANC has adopted as its operational model – serves only to perpetuate the notion of a small group of people operating in the name of democracy, but in fact taking decisions and enforcing them without a mandate from the electorate.[8]

The third factor giving rise to the forces referred to above bears upon the fact that provincial administrations are generally weak with the effect that national guidance and even interventions are constantly required;[9] that local government are in ruins in many places; and that provincial as well as national intervention are therefore required. The cumulative effect of these political forces is that the quasi-federal nature of the state as envisaged in the Constitution has changed notwithstanding the fact that this turn-about was never authorised by any amendments to the Constitution.

In contrast to the above, during the last years of the presidency of former President Zuma which came to an end in February, 2018 strong centrifugal forces have drawn the constitution into the opposite – a non-centralised – direction. Three forces are relevant here:

σ   The Democratic Alliance (DA) which, at least until the end of 2017, proved to be an increasingly rising opposition party, took over the reins of power in the Western Cape province in 2009 where it has been governing with a fair amount of success in contrast to the nature of the ANC government in the rest of the country. The success with which DA has governed in the Cape Province has provided a distinctive character to that province. This constitutes a federalist rather than a unitary force and is promoting a form of asymmetric federalism in contrast to the unitary character of the constitutional order in the rest of the country.

σ   Intense internal strife within the ruling ANC is another aspect of asymmetry. The strong support base of the previous president, Jacob Zuma in the province of KwaZulu-Natal (KZN), at least until the first quarter of 2018, is the strongest case in point. What differentiates KZN from the other provinces is the extensive influence exerted by the Zulu kingdom within that province. These factors give a distinctive

---

7   Matthee, 2014:7. Available: http://bit.ly/33jjQMp

8   Gumede, 2005:305.

9   Simeon & Murray, 2001:65-92. Various provincial departments in the Limpopo and North West provinces have been placed under national control and numerous municipal councils have been placed under administration owing to incompetence.

definition to KZN requiring government and the ANC leadership [10] to treat it with great sensitivity.

σ   In the third place, it is important to mention the co-operation (albeit seemingly precarious) of the opposition parties in the municipal sphere of government (in several cases the DA supported by the Economic Freedom Fighters – EFF) resulting in seizing control over several of the country's largest local governments – first Cape Town by the DA on its own in 2011 and then the metropolises of Tshwane (Pretoria and environs), Johannesburg and Port Elizabeth (Nelson Mandela-Bay) by the DA with the support of the EFF and smaller parties.[11]

It is of great significance that in all these developments the actual constitution has undergone significant changes without any amendments to the text of the written Constitution. These changes occurred in direct consequence of the dynamics of political events, without any formal amendment to the text of the Constitution.[12]

5.2.2   The centres where governmental power is exercised (2) (Hybrid governmental power)

In accordance with the principle of legality, the Constitution contains detailed provisions allocating every aspect of governmental power – legislative, executive, judicial, administrative, policing, military, monetary, etc. – to designated organs of state. All the organs of state together are therefore vested with the totality of all governmental powers. Hence, no part of governmental power vests in any other formation of power (private, civil, business or any other institution of power of whatever nature) other than in the relevant organs of state. In other words, all aspects of governmental power originate from the (written) Constitution and from no other source.

South Africa has nevertheless since 1994 experienced the development of what in political science is known as a hybrid system of political power.[13] This signifies in a nutshell that power migrates from the relevant organs designated by the Constitution to other power formations without the required constitutional mandate. According to Matthee, this is precisely what happened in South Africa. Matthee declared: "The locus of politics has shifted from accountable democratic institutions to a field

---

10   In the last years of the presidency of former president Jacob Zuma, the Gauteng province developed a form of asymmetry due to the ANC leadership of that province being a strong opponent of Zuma.

11   At the time of the writing of this there are signs that this development may change since the EFF is considering new alliance options after the leadership change of the ANC late in 2017.

12   Pertaining specifically to its federal nature the Canadian constitution, that Constitution also did not undergo any textual amendments. Yet, as a result of the operation of political forces the insistence of Quebec to be more self-governing, Canada changed from a centralised federation into a much looser one. In India, political events also changed the structure of the constitution without any preceding constitutional amendments. See for example Simeon, 1998:46 and De Villiers, 2004:227.

13   See in general about this Matthee, 2015, *Zuma's hybrid regime and the rise of a new political order*. Available: http://bit.ly/2MLJyU5

of power in which weak democratic institutions and non-democratic institutions interact."[14] In consequence, to a significant extent the relevant organs of state have become mere fronts behind which the actual wielders of power are hiding and operating without any sanction of the formal Constitution.

At this stage it is important to note, in the first place, that the ANC's own leadership structures, more specifically the National Executive Committee (NEC), the National Working Committee (NWC) and the six central leadership figures (the so-called big six – the president, deputy president, the secretary-general, the deputy secretary general, the national chair and the treasury-general of the organisation) – more often than not act as the actual government of the state, thus sideling the constitutionally designated bodies, namely the national executive (cabinet) and Parliament. Crucial governmental decisions are taken by these party structures instead of by the designated constitutional structures.[15]

Matthee[16] explains:

> The ANC NEC has tremendous power over elected MPs. The system of closed-list proportional representation assigns legislative seats to candidates based on their relative position on a party list, and the NEC draws up the ANC's party list. Even elected MPs can be redeployed by the ANC NEC and replaced by another ANC cadre. The non-parliamentary wing of the ANC dominates the parliamentary wing. Unelected party functionaries thus set the national government's policy priorities. The public officials subject to electoral accountability tend to be subordinated to the unelected party functionaries. Politics are pulled out of the elected legislature into the party and into processes that lie outside Parliament, and do not need to comply with the same norms of transparency, participation and accountability.[17]

Secondly, during the Zuma presidency that ended in February 2018 there has been the growing concentration of power in cabinet around the person of the president, seemingly in close cooperation with sectors of the security forces (the security cluster). Cadre deployment, which is discussed in the next section, that is, the appointment, of loyalists of the governing party (or factions of the governing party) plays an important part in this.[18] Important governmental decisions are taken by these formations, instead of by cabinet, Parliament or other relevant organs of state. One of the consequences of this is that cabinet's accountability to the legislature is

---

14 Matthee, 2015:31.

15 Matthee, 2013:10. Available: http://bit.ly/31oYzPO Explains: Strict enforcement of ANC party discipline against ANC MPs has weakened national legislative oversight of the executive. Formally, legislative authority is vested in Parliament, but in practice its role has been reduced to approving bills drafted by the ANC-led executive. Behind the formal structures and processes, cadre deployment and the party rules.

16 Matthee, 2013:Report 11.

17 See further Choudry, 2010:17-18, 33-35. Available: http://bit.ly/2M8tRac

18 On this Matthee, 2015:7 states: "Patronage has turned cadre deployment into a policy that does not only ensure control on the party's behalf, but has also morphed into a means to ensure the unfettered power of the presidency."

weakened, simply because executive decisions are taken by the informal structures rather than by the executive itself. As a result, the provisions of the Constitution relating to accountability and transparency are hollowed out.[19]

Thirdly, and most importantly, the ANC and the governing tripartite alliance (the ANC, the South African Communist Party – the SACP – and the Congress of South African Trade Unions – (COSATU)[20] are marred by persistent feuds and power struggles. These struggles have been raging on for many years. They first came to the fore in the run up to the fifth-yearly ANC's national congress in December 2007 in the acrimonious struggle between the Zuma and the Mbeki factions. Factions within the ANC have been maintaining close ties with private formations, especially in business in order to promote their own (the factions') position whilst these business formations cashed in on their ties with these factions to further their (financial) interests. In consequence, crucial governmental decisions were essentially being made jointly between the faction and the business ventures concerned. These decisions related to senior appointments in the public service, state-owned companies SOE's), and the corrupt awarding of lucrative state contracts to business ventures under the control of individuals with close contacts with the relevant faction in the ANC. The close ties between the former president of the ANC and of the country, Jacob Zuma, his family and his faction, with leading members of the prominent Gupta-business family serve as the most telling example of this phenomenon which has been referred to as state capture.

There is strong evidence that state capture in South Africa has caused the transmutation of the government into a hybrid dispensation to such an extent that governmental functions were not shouldered by the constitutionally designated institutions, but by a mixture of organs of state in cahoots with a collections of business and other private formations. The Public Protector's *State of the capture*-report of October 2016[21] brought this phenomenon prominently into the open.

---

19 Provisions on this feature in a variety of contexts in *the Constitution* for example in sections 1, 41(1)(c), 57(1)(b), 70(1)(b), 116(1)(b), 152(1)(a), 181(5), 195(1)(f), 196(5), 199(8) and 215(1).

20 These three bodies have been in alliance since before the beginning of the constitutional transition in 1994. Senior members of the COSATU, and especially the SACP, ordinarily play an important part in the actual governing of the country. Especially the SACP, with a fairly small membership, has consistently maintained a very important position in the central executive. The close alliance between the ANC and the SACP goes back to the early 1960s.

21 See Report No:6 of 2016/2017 of the Public Protector on an investigation into alleged improper and unethical conduct by the President and other state functionaries relating to alleged improper relationships and involvement of the Gupta family in the removal and appointment of Ministers and Directors of the State-Owned Enterprises resulting in improper and possibly corrupt award of state contracts and benefits to the Gupta family's businesses.: Available: http://bit.ly/31rqWNq [Accessed, 20 May 2017].

The extent to which South Africa has descended into a hybrid regime was further elucidated by a report of May 2017 of a research team consisting of academics of four universities.[22] According to the report a silent coup took place in South Africa, "(t)hat has removed the ANC from its place as the primary force for transformation in society."[23] Hence, next to the state there is what the team called a shadow state. What South Africa was confronted with was not merely large scale individual cases of corruption but:

> (a) political project at work to repurpose state institutions to suit a constellation of rent-seeking networks that have been constructed and now span the symbiotic relationship between the constitutional and shadow state. This is akin to a silent coup.[24]

Hence, there is a symbiotic relationship between the state as provided for by the Constitution and a shadow state, the latter having in part captured the state to pursue its own private segmental project. Cabinet, which in terms of the Constitution is supposed to be at the centre of the national executive, is side-lined. Instead executive authority is located in a number of other centres:

> There is evidence that Zuma tends to govern via a set of 'kitchen cabinets' comprising selected groups from different networks. Kitchen cabinets are small informal reference groups that are convened on an as-needed basis. They can also be shell structures that are activated when needed ... they have been known to be drawn from the state security establishment, Gupta networks, SOE sector, sub-groups of cabinet ministers and deputy ministers, family networks, international networks (e.g. Angola, Russian intelligence), key black business groups, the ANC (in particular the Premier League and Magashule), and selected loyalists in the public service (usually loyal directors generals).[25]

In the place of the system of government ordained by the Constitution a new and entirely different kind of government – the product of socio-political forces, not warranted by the Constitution – was established in its stead.

The common denominator of all three cases just discussed is that organs of state – the president, cabinet, state departments – which derive their power in pursuance of provisions of the Constitution, surrendered these powers in favour of a variety of structures of the ANC, factions of the ANC, private individuals and business ventures. Formations next to the bodies allocated by the Constitution usurped power from the constitutional bodies. The exercising of governmental power became hybrid and diffused. This means that one cannot count on the relevant provisions of the Constitution in order to establish where governmental power really vests.

22　"Betrayal of a promise: how South Africa is being stolen. State capacity research project." Available: http://bit.ly/2MNu2qY [Accessed, 25 May 2017].

23　Bhorat, 2017:1. Available: http://bit.ly/2MNu2qY [Accessed, 25 May 2017].

24　Ibid.

25　Ibid. Also see Chapter 3 of the report.

Viewed from what has just been described the provisions of the Constitution lost its descriptive faculty in that it is not capable as argued in Chapter 4, to provide a reliable reflection of the actual loci of governmental power. This held increasingly true for the last part of the Zuma presidency. It remained to be seen if and to what extent this change of the constitutional order into a hybrid state will be effectively arrested under the new leadership of the ANC since the end of 2017 and more specifically, since President Ramaphosa took office in February 2018.

Cadre deployment and the accompanying patronage state in South Africa are closely intermingled with the hybrid nature of government in the country. This will now be discussed.

5.2.3 Cadre deployment and the patronage state

According to the Constitution the public sector which includes the public service, must be impartial and professional. Consequently, the forming of relationships of patronage, that is, appointments, promotions, delivery of services and the awarding of contracts on account of the involvement in and/or in exchange for loyalty to the ruling party or any of its factions is unambiguously impermissible and unconstitutional. This is spelt out in detail in section 195 of the Constitution that sets out the basic values and principles governing public administration.[26] This is particularly evident from the following values and principles: A high standard of professional ethics must be promoted and maintained; Efficient, economic and effective use of resources must be promoted; Services must be provided impartially, fairly, equitably and without bias; People's needs must be responded to, and the public must be encouraged to participate in policy-making; Public administration must be accountable; Transparency must be fostered by providing the public with timely, accessible and accurate information; Good human-resource management and career-development practices, to maximise human potential, must be cultivated.

There are several other provisions that also deal with the functioning of organs of state and the courts and which also underscore the principles of professionalism, impartiality, service to the public in general instead of only one part of it, namely section 165(2) which relates to the judiciary,[27] section 179(4) which relates to the

---

26 Section 195(1) provides: (1) Public administration must be governed by the democratic values and principles enshrined in the Constitution, including the following principles: (a) A high standard of professional ethics must be promoted and maintained; (b) Efficient, economic and effective use of resources must be promoted; (c) Public administration must be development-oriented; (d) Services must be provided impartially, fairly, equitably and without bias; (e) People's needs must be responded to, and the public must be encouraged to participate in policy-making; (f) Public administration must be accountable; (g) Transparency must be fostered by providing the public with timely, accessible and accurate information; (h) Good human-resource management and career-development practices, to maximise human potential, must be cultivated; (i) Public administration must be broadly representative of the South African people, with employment and personnel management practices based on ability, objectivity, fairness, and the need to redress the imbalances of the past to achieve broad representation.

27 Section 165(2) reads: The courts are independent and subject only to the Constitution and the law, which they must apply impartially and without fear, favour or prejudice.

functioning of the Public Prosecutorial Authority;[28] and various other provisions in section 193 that relate to appointments to the bodies instituted in terms of Chapter 9 of the Constitution.[29]

The individual and cumulative effect of all these values, principles and other provisions is that politically partial appointments and promotions on account of association with and loyalty or service to only a part of the populace – a party, leader, or faction of a party, etc. – instead of the whole, is constitutionally repugnant. It is clear that the Constitution is unequivocal in its rejection of any form of patronage, that is, of the *neo-patrimonial state* as it is described in the language of political science. The patrimonial state is the opposite of the modern administrative state. Typical of the administrative state is its impersonal nature. Unlike the erstwhile dynastic state,[30] in which the state was closely interwoven with the person of the monarch and his family, the modern state is by definition impersonal. Hence, in the modern administrative state there is a clear distinction between the head of state and government, his/her family and party on the one hand and the impersonal state on the other. The state is not governed for the benefit of the head of state/government or his/her family and party, but for the benefit of the whole of the citizenry. In consequence, public appointments are also not made on account of personal friendships, party bonds or business links, but on the basis of relevant merit and expertise.[31]

Since the Constitution took effect potent forces have exerted themselves which marginalised these values and principles and at least in part substituted them for new ones. In consequence, contrary to what the Constitution envisages, South Africa has assumed the character of a patrimonial state. The most prominent force that led to this was the ANC's own totalitarian ideological drive as consistently spelt out in its policy documents, to impose party control on all levers of power and all spheres of society. This totalitarian project is encapsulated in the umbrella term "transformation" or transformationism as it is referred to in this book (discussed in Chapter 7) which in the decades since the Constitution took effect became the master concept of the South African constitutional order. A synonym

---

28 Section 179(4) reads: National legislation must ensure that the prosecuting authority exercises its functions without fear, favour or prejudice.

29 Section 193 amongst others reads: (1) The Public Protector and the members of any Commission established by this Chapter must be women or men who – (b) are fit and proper persons to hold the particular office; and (c) comply with any other requirements prescribed by national legislation.
(3) The Auditor-General must be a woman or a man who is a South African citizen and a fit and proper person to hold that office. Specialised knowledge of, or experience in, auditing, state finances and public administration must be given due regard in appointing the Auditor-General.

30 Compare for example on this, amongst others, Malan, 2012a:42-50 and the sources quoted there.

31 Fukuyama, 2014:26-27. (Fukuyama's two volumes, of which this is the second (the first is *The origins of political order* which was published in 2011), is essentially dedicated to the theme of the emergence of the modern impersonal administrative state.)

for this, according to the ANC's own partly Leninist inspired terminology,[32] is the
so-called national democratic revolution. The strategy that is enlisted in order to
achieve this goal, named in part after the erstwhile communist nomenclature in
the Soviet Union, is known as democratic centralism. According to this strategy
all key centres of power must be placed under the control of the ANC – more
specifically the central decision-making bodies of the ANC. In consequence, the
ANC has over the years repeatedly committed itself to placing all centres of power
under the national liberation movement as embodied in the ANC. Included in these
centres are the armed forces, the police, public service, intelligence agencies, the
judiciary, state-owned enterprises, regulatory bodies, the public broadcaster and
the central bank. Later on the private sector was also added.[33] It is on the basis of
these totalitarian objectives that the ANC appoints its own supporters – "*deploys
its cadres*" in standard ANC nomenclature – in all these spheres, sometimes under
the legitimate guise of constitutionally legitimate affirmative action and black
economic empowerment.

This totalitarian drive provides the main explanation for cadre deployment in
South Africa. It is not merely some fleeting error soon to disappear. It occupies a
central place in the ANC's ideological project.

Even though Constitutions, including the South African Constitution, do not
expressly so recognise, it is not inordinate for leaders and parties to appoint their
own supporters in senior positions in the public service. Moreover, this is quite
acceptable since the governing leadership can hardly be expected to count on its
opponents to execute its policies, especially when such policies are ideologically
strictly demarcated. There is an essential qualification, however, that appointees,
even if they are supporters, must be fit and proper professional persons for the
positions to which they are appointed. This is particularly true when appointments
are made to positions that require specialised knowledge and experience. Cadre
deployment may in these circumstances be acceptable, but only if the "cadre" in
question is suitable for the position in question, more specifically if he/she is one of
the most professionally suitable persons for the position. This is precisely what the
quoted constitutional provisions directly or indirectly require; and precisely this
demarcates the distinction between a patrimonial state and an administrative state.

Following cadre deployment the patrimonial South African state has over the
past decades been established deeply. This is borne out by the bloated and hardly
affordable public sector. The number of officials in the broader public sector has

---

32   See on this the observation by Du Toit, 2016:114.

33   Matthee, 2015:42 states: "The ANC pursues democratic centralism through a policy of cadre deployment.
     This policy entails placing party loyalists in "key centres" of power. The ANC conference in 1997 identified
     these centres of power as "the army," the police, the bureaucracy, intelligence structures, *the judiciary*
     [my emphasis], parastatals, and agencies such as regulatory bodies, the public broadcaster, the central bank
     and so on. The 2007 ANC Polokwane conference, during which Jacob Zuma was elected as president of the
     ANC, added the 'private sector'."

over the years since 1994 soared to more than three million. Approximately 12% of the national GDP is spent on the public service. This compares very negatively with many other states in which expenditure on the public service is considerably lower, for example Russia (3,7%), Brazil (4,4%), Nigeria (4%) and Egypt (6,9%).[34] The South African public service had not undergone a steady, planned expansion to serve the public's needs, but was experiencing (the execution of a policy) of jobs for pals, obscene salaries, expensive cars, lavish travel (allowances) and extravagant bonuses.[35]

Moreover, public service salaries have increased at a rate which exceeded that of inflation. In essence the tax payers are compelled to contribute towards the running of the ANC's growing cadre-based patronage machine[36] at the expense of a struggling private sector. Furthermore, salaries in the public sector are now substantially higher than those in the private sector,[37] something that was previously unheard of in South Africa. What emerged from this cadre-fed patrimonial state, is what political commentator, R.W. Johnson, quite aptly refers to as South Africa's *predatory burocratic bourgeoisie.*

South Africa has developed a crippling shortage of suitable, qualified public officials with the required specialised knowledge and know-how to sustain a functioning public sector. Although cadres may be loyal to the party (leadership), they are generally not suitable for the institutions to which they are deployed, often to occupy most senior positions. In addition, the public sector is marred by chronic and wide-ranging corruption. This is not unknown to the ANC's leadership. On the contrary, the poor performance of senior ANC functionaries portrays a dark picture of inefficiency in the public sector.[38]

What we are witnessing here is an inherent and debilitating contradiction in the ANC's own ideological make-up. Its goal, by virtue of its policy of transformationism, is to establish a full-fledged totalitarian state. To that end it requires a properly functioning state. However, cadre deployment is an obstruction because cadres are often not appropriately competent to properly discharge the duties required of professional state functionaries. Hence, the totalitarian state cannot really be established because incompetent cadres cannot sustain a functioning state.

Cadre deployment with the accompanying deployment of incompetent staff is clearly one of the foremost causes for the widespread collapse of municipal government, the deterioration of provincial departments and national state

---

34   Matthee, 2013:6-7.

35   Matthee, 2013:6.

36   Matthee, 2015:31 and the sources there referred to.

37   Johnson, 2015:114-115.

38   See Plaut & Holden, 2012:288.

departments, the malfunctioning of the police (which is discussed in more detail in the next section), the serious problems that have now for almost a decade been damaging the prosecutorial authority, the spectacular failure of state-owned companies such as Eskom (the state-owned national electricity supplier), Transnet, South African Airways, the South African Broadcasting Corporation, to mention but a few, accompanied by large-scale wasting of public funds. The decreasing ability of organs of state to provide basic services is widely ascribed to cadre deployment.

With respect to state departments, the Management Performance Assessment Tool (MPAT) of 2012/2013, released in September 2013 by the then minister in the President's office, paints a dark picture of state malfunctioning.[39]

With respect to the intelligence agencies, Ronnie Kasrils, a founding member of the ANC's armed wing, *UmKhonto we Siswe* (MK), and Intelligence minister from 2004-2008, declared that the State Intelligence Service had descended into an instrument of the ruling party and that its officials were working for the ANC rather than for the state. On this issue Kasrils submitted a report to the ANC leadership in 2008. However, no remedying action followed.

During the acrimonious leadership battle in the ANC in 2007 about the removal of former president Mbeki, the Intelligence Services were enlisted against each other by the two factions. It was apparent that the State Security Agency (SSA) under president Zuma had become entirely politicised and beyond control.[40]

Owing to cadre deployment's ruinous effect on the state administration and its depressing effect on the quality of the public services, it has often been subjected to criticism. The courts have expressed concern about inappropriate appointments (without necessarily referring to cadre deployment).[41] However, judicial intervention is happenstance. It can only be effective if it addresses individual breaches of the law, but judicial intervention cannot remedy systemic cadre deployment, playing out in terms of the general governmental policy of transformationism. Furthermore, the composition of the judiciary itself is to a considerable extent determined by cadre-deployment-like policies and practices (See Chapter 6). This is obvious from the fact that the Judicial Service Commission, which plays an important role in the

---

39 80% were non-compliant with regard to service delivery improvement requirements; 76% were non-compliant in ensuring that they had policies and systems in place for promoting professional ethics; 64% were non-compliant with the legal requirements for fraud prevention; 74% were non-compliant with the Department of Public Service and Administration directive that their organisational structure should reflect funded posts only; 88% were non-compliant with human resource planning; and 60% did not have processes in place for detecting and preventing unauthorised expenditure, addressing audit findings and communicating findings to responsible officials. See Matthee, 2013:6-7.

40 Jordan, 2015. Available: http://bit.ly/2TlaNWY [Accessed, 14 May 2017]. Compare also Sole. Available: http://bit.ly/2ZG6Ezh [Accessed, 14 May 2017].

41 Probably the most notorious case is that of Menzi Simelane. He was appointed as the director of the national prosecutorial authority in spite of a finding of a commission of inquiry that he was not fit for public office. Compare *Democratic Alliance v President of the RSA* 2012(12) BCLR 1297(CC).

appointment of judges in South Africa, has always been adamant that aspirant judges need to be transformationism-minded in order to be suitable for appointment.[42] A statement by Chief Justice Mogoeng that the best candidates need not necessarily be appointed to the bench (see Chapter 6) can obviously be associated with the phenomenon of cadre deployment.

There is no indication that the ANC will part with cadre deployment. On the contrary, the former secretary-general of the party, Gwede Mantache (since December 2017 the national chair of the ANC), repeatedly, for instance in September 2011 and in June 2014, emphatically rejected criticism against cadre deployment.[43] Since the ANC came to power in 1994, cadre deployment has been one of the primary methods through which the system of patronage has over decades been established. In pursuance of this system the ANC (or the leading faction within the ANC) is rewarding its supporters in exchange for their loyal service and support.[44]

Cadre deployment, an incidence of the ANC's project of transformationism, has developed into a decisive constitutional principle – substituting constitutional law and superseding the relevant provisions of the Constitution. Hence, a crucial constitutional change in the form of substituting constitutional law has once again occurred, without it having been approved in terms of the Constitution's amendment provisions. Once again the actual constitution has acquired a content which is different from what the text of the written Constitution suggests.

5.2.4 The responsibility for safety and security

The state is premised on a qualified cession agreement in terms of which every inhabitant in the state concerned has ceded to government his/her (natural) right of personal defence, which entails protection against any unlawful attack on life, body or property. By virtue of this cession, government (through its relevant agencies) is under the obligation to continually and effectively provide the protection concerned.[45] The state's responsibility to be effective in its execution of this power is obviously conditional. If the state should fail to effectively exercise its power, the right of personal self-defence would automatically revert back to every affected individual in need of the protection which is not provided by the

---

42 See Chapter 6 for a detailed discussion on separation of powers and the independence and impartiality of the judiciary; Moerane, 2003:713, as well as the pronouncements of ANC MP and erstwhile deputy minister of justice, Johnnie de Lange Hansard (2003-02-17) at 128-124.

43 Staff reporter, 2011, *Mantashe defends ANC cadre deployment.* Available: http://bit.ly/2TdUfQu and Seale, 2014, *Cadre deployment is not a swear word.* Available: http://bit.ly/2yLJGeq [Accessed, 13 May 2017].

44 Comprehensively discussed in Johnson, 2015.

45 Malan, 2007:642-654.

state.[46] It is against this backdrop that the constitutional provisions – also those of the present South African Constitution, which are referred to below – should be understood. These provisions define government's obligation to acquit its protection responsibility on behalf of and to the benefit of the inhabitants of the state.

Violations of the rights to life, body and property occur in all constitutional dispensations. As long as such occurrences are the exception and criminal justice agencies effectively prosecute these cases when they do occur, the integrity of the constitutional order remains intact. However, when crime assumes wide-ranging proportions and/or the relevant organs of state fail in their responsibility to effectively prosecute crime, the constitutional order itself falters. Then follows a steep rise in the instances of reverse cession from the state back to the public, who in consequence reassume the right to fend for themselves. As the extent of reverse cession increases the basis of the constitutional order gets proportionately dislodged. The relevant constitutional provisions purporting to regulate government's responsibility to provide safety and security then simply forfeit their practical significance. To the extent that the citizenry increasingly assumes the responsibility of self-protection, new, substituting constitutional law arises in place of, or alongside the practically lapsed provisions of the Constitution.

Various provisions of the South African Constitution are pertinent to the present matter. Section 198 posits the governing principles of national security. The forth principle in section 198(d) provides that: "(d) National security is subject to the authority of Parliament and the national executive." According to section 199(1) the security services of the Republic consist of a single defence force, a single police service and any intelligence services established in terms of the Constitution. According to section 199(3) armed organisations or services other than the security services established in terms of the Constitution, may be established only in terms of national legislation. Section 205, which pertains specifically to the police in sub-section (3) provides that the objects of the police are to prevent, combat and investigate crime, to maintain public order, to protect and secure the inhabitants of the Republic and their property, and to uphold and enforce the law.

These provisions are supposed to give effect to the constitutional right to be free from all forms of violence (and other constitutional rights relating to the protection of life, body and property). This right which, is provided for in section 12(1)(c) of the Constitution imposes the duty to protect inhabitants of the state and is the embodiment of the underpinning operative rule that the state is (in principle) the entity authorised to exercise lawful violence to protect those inhabitants.

---

46 Thus, criminal law jurist Snyman, 2002:102 aptly declared as follows: "The rules relating to private defence presuppose that the police authorities, whose task it is to protect the citizens from unlawful attack, function reasonably adequately. What is the position if the functioning of the police and other state security services in a given state has deteriorated to such an extent that their capacity to protect citizens adequately from unlawful attack from criminals is seriously reduced? It is submitted that in such an event the field of application of private defence should be broadened, affording private citizens greater scope to protect themselves from unlawful attack compared to the scope of the rules which apply in a society in which police protection of its citizens is up to standard."

Owing to persistent crime, more specifically violent crime, combined with the inability of relevant organs of state, more specifically the police, to discharge its protection responsibility, the general public of necessity has increasingly assumed responsibility for self-protection. Cadre deployment is also pertinent in the present context. This is one of the factors that hampers the state in efficiently fulfilling its protection responsibility, thus causing – essentially compelling – the public to take over this responsibility. South Africa suffers from violent crime. Murder, attempted murder, aggravated robbery (including robberies at private residences, businesses and when committing motor vehicle hijackings), rape and serious assault have now been wreaking havoc among the South African population for more than two decades.[47] The high incidence of violent crime makes South Africa one of the most dangerous countries in the world.[48] Especially some communities, such as the agricultural community, and the communities of the Cape Flats are prey to exorbitant violence, which is quite often combined with torture.[49] Government has responded to the brutal crimes, that members of these communities (including farm workers) have been subjected to, with an unsettling degree of carelessness. It could even be argued that government is in part complicit in the commission of this violent crime.[50] The murder rate in the farming community is per capita one of the highest in the world. However, crime is not limited to rural South Africa. City dwellers are also prone to high levels of violent crime. After repeatedly announced strategies to combat violent crime, it simply carries on unabatedly.

Politically inspired crime, which is linked, among other things, to the factional struggles within the ANC, have also become an ingredient of the toxic mix of prevalent crime in South Africa. Many political murders have been committed especially in the KwaZulu-Natal and the Mpumalanga provinces. Very senior political office bearers, including the deputy president and former premier of Mpumalanga, David Mabuza, are implicated in alleged political murders in Mpumalanga.[51] Relevant in this context are also a series of house-breakings into the offices of the Chief Justice, the director of public prosecutions, the police's special investigation unit as well as the offices of various non-governmental organisations such as the Helen Suzman Foundation, which is often locked in litigation with organs of state.[52]

---

47 Full statistics on this is contained in South African Institute of Race Relations, 2017:823-830. Compare also South African Police Services (SAPS) Annual crime report. Available: http://bit.ly/33uqNKW [Accessed, 2 June 2017].

48 In comparison with most other places in the world. See for example World Bank, *Intentional homicides (per 100,000 people)*. Available: http://bit.ly/2Z2hXR3 [Accessed, 8 June 2017]. South Africa is number 6 on the list.

49 South African Institute of Race Relations, 2017:818.

50 See the comprehensive discussion by Roets, 2018.

51 See for example Tolsi, 2017. Available: file:///C:/Users/u04186516/Downloads/DD_%20 Tactical%20genius%20or%20Dark%20Lord_%20_%20News%20_%20Politics%20_%20M&G.pdf [Accessed, 31 August 2018].; Gerber, 2018.

52 Compare about political murders Matthee, 2017 *The rise of political murder*. Available: http://bit.ly/2KANKmS [Accessed, 13 August 2017].

The South African Police Service (SAPS) is marred by poor leadership and lack of professionalism at the highest level. The services of three consecutive commissioners (national heads) of the SAPS have been terminated owing to corruption, crime and incompetence in which cadre deployment clearly played an important part. All three were political appointments and none of them had any previous police experience.[53]

The Police's maladies go beyond that of bad leadership. There is severe incompetence and absence of basic skills and laxity is running deep. There is a lack of discipline. There is inadequate infrastructure, a shortage of vehicles and poorly equipped offices.[54]

Unprofessional conduct leads to civil claims of huge amounts against the police, based mainly on unlawful arrests and malicious damage to property. The 2012 *National Victims of Crime Survey* showed that the police was the second most corrupt organ of state in the country.[55] The perceptions of members of the SAPS themselves are also that the police is an exceptionally corrupt institution.

There is an unsettling level of involvement of police officers in crime. In this regard a former Gauteng premier, Nomvula Mokonyane, stated in September 2013:

> A worrisome statistic shows that 18 out of 50 provincial policing precincts were reported as crime-infested dens that recorded police collusion and outright corruption. The Johannesburg central police precinct tops the list with approximately 13,000 criminal cases that were perpetrated by officers in uniform.[56]

In August 2013 the parliamentary portfolio committee for the police was informed that one general-major, ten brigadiers, 21 colonels, 43 lieutenant colonels, ten majors, 163 captains and 706 warrant officers were convicted of serious crimes including murder, attempted murder, culpable homicide, rape, abetting escape, theft, house-breaking, drug trafficking, abduction, robbery and intentional damage of property.[57] According to Gareth Newham of the Institute for Security Studies

---

53 One of them, Jackie Selebi was convicted of corruption in 2011 and sentenced to fifteen years imprisonment. His successor, Bheki Cele had his services terminated in 2012 after allegations of corruption. He later became a deputy minister and in February 2018 he was appointed minister of safety and security. His successor as national commissioner, Riah Phiyega, was found by the Farlam commission of inquiry to be incompetent and was dismissed. The commission undertook an inquiry into the mine worker massacre near Marikana on 16 Augustus 2012.

54 For example, as long ago as in 2007 it was set out in a report of the *Police Advisory Council* on state of policing in the period November 2006 to October 2007. The advisory board was appointed in terms of section 34(1)(l) of the South African Police Services Act by the national commissioner to advice on the levels of service delivery in the SAPS. The Council consisted of fifteen retired senior police officers under the chairmanship of deputy national commissioner M. Chetty.

55 Newham, 2013, *The South African police service once again finds itself in the spotlight over abuse.* Available: http://bit.ly/2M6H575 [Accessed, 15 May 2017].

56 Maromo, 2013, *Gauteng cop corruption worrier premier.* Available: http://bit.ly/2MRw9Kp [Accessed, 15 May 2017].

57 Ibid. Smith, 2013, *Nearly 1500 members of the police were exposed as convicted criminals.* Available: http://bit.ly/2KzNHYE [Accessed, 17 May 2017]. Compare further Institute of Race Relations (IRR), 2015:6-8.

(ISS), the professional ethos of lower ranking members of SAPS has disappeared.[58] Research published in the last quarter of 2018 shows this crisis of the police's involvement in specifically violent crime has deepened further.[59]

The socio-political environment in which members of the police have to do their work is also unfavourable. Poor border control caused the unhindered, unlawful inflow of millions of people into the country. That obviously places tremendous pressure on police resources.

So-called service delivery protests have assumed endemic proportions in modern-day South Africa. The protests are usually against unsatisfying or the complete lack of municipal services. Protests are not only wide-ranging and persistent; they are also violent,[60] thus draining the ability of the police to attend to common crime[61] as a result of which members of the public have to fend for themselves. More often than not, these protests are caused by rivalry among local ANC politicians.[62] Due to the increase of this and other forms of violence sociologist, Karl von Holdt is of the view that South Africa is in the midst of a transition into a violent democracy.

Various other forms of public violence must also be brought into calculation, all of which are straining police resources at multiple levels. Violence against foreign nationals – especially small businessmen – is part of the South African scene since 2008. During 2016 serious violence erupted on the country's university campuses causing huge damage, yet without impunity.[63]

On 30 October 2018 the National Commissioner of the SAPS, Khehla Sithole, appearing before the Parliamentary Committee on Safety and Security made the startling statement that the Police is unable to discharge its (constitutional) mandate.[64]

Against this backdrop private citizens are increasingly faced with the option to resort to self-protection. South Africa's private security industry has expanded to such an extent that it is believed to be one of the largest in the world. A few years ago South Africa had the fourth largest per capita number of private security officers

---

58 Quoted by Matthee, 2013:31.

59 Roodt, 2018.

60 Statistics on public violence is available in South African Institute of Race Relations, 2017:823. Compare further Lancaster, 2016, *At the heart of discontent – measuring public violence in South Africa*. Available: http://bit.ly/2YzvnZg [Accessed, 20 June 2017].

61 On average the police have to deal with 40 demonstrations daily, which requires considerable resources and time ISS paper, 2016:292. Available: http://bit.ly/2YzvnZg [Accessed, 20 June 2017].

62 Von Holdt, 2013:589-604. Available: http://bit.ly/2YRizNI [Accessed, 15 May 2017].

63 Boonzaaiser, 2018, *#Fees Must fall: Miljoene se skade, 1 betoger in tronk*. Available: http://bit.ly/31opACX [Accessed, 8 November 2018].

64 Jalinous & Reynolds, *Police and MPs blame immigrants, unemployment, gangs, and each other for crime*. Available: http://bit.ly/2KAB2EB [Accessed, 8 November 2018]. Sithole, 2018, *Police are overstretched*. Available: http://bit.ly/2ZHxebb [Accessed, 8 November 2018].

globally (after Guatemala, Panama and Honduras).[65] It has approximately nine thousand private security companies with 450 000 active security officers. There are 2,57 private security officers for each police man in South Africa.[66] Moreover, the general public is involved in numerous local private security activities such as neighbourhood watches. Civil rights organisation, Afriforum, has recently introduced its own expanded neighbour watch system.[67]

It is clear that the responsibility for securing safety and security in South Africa is increasingly moving away from the state to various private institutions such as those run by civil society. This is highly significant because it represents an institutional failure to uphold one of the most important foundations of a successful state.

Vigilante activities are the order of the day, especially in many townships. Although these activities must fill the void left by the absence of the police, they frequently descend into new patterns of vigilante crime, especially violent crime, often occurring with impunity.[68]

On close analysis – and that is the crux of the matter – this is once again an example of tacit change of the constitution. The relevant provisions of the Constitution, referred to above, are simply suggesting a deceiving picture of reality. In practical terms, the security function which is supposed to be shouldered by the police is clearly no longer, as envisaged by the Constitution, subject to the authority of Parliament and the national executive. On local level, the responsibility to ensure safety and security has in many places slipped into the hands of private bodies which autonomously exercise authority to perform this function. Moreover, although the Constitution stipulates that the security services of the Republic consist of a single defence force, a single police service and any intelligence services established in terms of the Constitution, the truth is that a plethora of private and civil safety and security institutions are operating next to those mentioned in the Constitution. The police now have to share the responsibility imposed upon them in terms of section 205 of the Constitution, "to prevent, combat and investigate crime, to maintain public order, to protect and secure the inhabitants of the Republic and their property, and to uphold and enforce the law." To the extent that the Constitution seeks to describe a (typical statist) dispensation in which organs of the state such as the police have the monopoly to perform these functions, it is a patent misrepresentation. These provisions have been overtaken and new substituting law has silently established itself next to the partially substituted provisions of

---

65   http://bit.ly/2OHFZkr [Accessed, 27 April 2017].

66   Wikipedia, 2017, *Private security industry in South Africa.* Available: http://bit.ly/2GV6xs7 [Accessed, 27 April 2017].

67   Afrikaans civic organisation, Afriforum, is currently expanding its system of neighbourhood watches. Compare, amongst others, the organisations, so-called 'Projek Nehema' Afriforum, 2017. *Projek Nehemia.* Available: http://bit.ly/2yMQOSI [Accessed, 22 June 2017].

68   Compare on this for example Institute of Race Relations (Institute for Security Studies (ISS)), 2016:21-24.

the Constitution. The actual constitution is markedly different from what the text of the Constitution proclaims. Practical events propelled by socio-political forces once again brought about significant change to the actual constitution, without any preceding amendment in terms of section 74.

5.2.5-5.2.8 The value basis and the official language dispensation in terms of the Constitution

The discussion now shifts to the changes of the value basis of the Constitution as set out in section 1 and affirmed elsewhere in the constitutional text. Socio-political forces caused this value basis to be superseded and in part replaced by new law – the new and the actual values. In some cases these forces substituted the values that the Constitution solemnly proclaims. Pertinent in this case is the re-racialisation, which has replaced non-racialism as well as the multilingual language dispensation which has been replaced by a unilingual English dispensation. It might also be argued that the value of non-racialism has never formed part of the value basis of the Constitution in that it might have been still-born. In another case a new value, not provided for in this part or elsewhere in the Constitution, was added as a constitutional value. Pertinent in this case is the value of ubuntu, which, as will be shown, is often not compatible with the value of the rule of law, which is also part of the value basis proclaimed by section 1. Lastly, there is the principle of representation (*representivity*), which has burgeoned into a comprehensive constitutional value and principle. Representivity is tightly interwoven with re-racialisation. It will be shown that representivity also renders official multilingualism impossible, thus making it a potent factor in favour of official English unilingualism.

The primary force behind all these value changes is the ANC's own ideological commitments articulated on numerous occasions in its policy documents. The two concepts, already referred to above are the (ideology of) transformationism, also known as the national democratic revolution. The objective of transformationism (which is discussed in more detail in Chapter 7) is to establish a centrally imposed so-called national democratic society, which is homogenised and socialist, and is premised on the basis of (black) majoritarian hegemony.

The first three items of constitutional change now to be discussed relate to the changes of the value basis defined in section 1 of the Constitution. The fourth is the official language dispensation. That does not feature in section 1, but in section 6, which like the value basis of section 1, is still part of Chapter 1 and is closely related to the value basis as articulated in section 1.

Under the heading *Founding provisions*, section 1 defines the value basis of the Constitution in the following terms:

The Republic of South Africa is one, sovereign, democratic state founded on the following values:

a.   Human dignity, the achievement of equality and the advancement of human rights and freedoms.

b.   Non-racialism and non-sexism.

c.   Supremacy of the constitution and the rule of law.

d.   Universal adult suffrage, a national common voters roll, regular elections and a multi-party system of democratic government, to ensure accountability, responsiveness and openness.

5.2.5   Founding values: (1) (Re)racialilastion substituting non-racialism (and consequences for freedom of expression)

Non-racialism, which goes back to several provisions of the *Freedom Charter* adopted under the auspices of the ANC in 1955,[69] is the cornerstone of the dispensation imported by the Constitutions of 1993 and 1996. Non-racialism epitomises the essential difference of the present Constitution in contrast to its pre-1994 predecessor. The constitutional order before 1994 was premised on racial, differentiation (and hierarchy). Non-racialism purports to part decisively with the racially based foundation on which erstwhile white minority rule was based. The new order, now based on the 1996 Constitution, is premised on equal individual citizenship, in which a person's racial identity (to the extent that the concept of race is recognised at all and not rejected altogether) is of no legal or social moment anymore,[70] also because racial identity is basically viewed as a fiction. Non-racialism proclaims everybody to be essentially individuals in spite of the false illusion of racial (group) identity. The individualist value of non-racialism differs distinctly from multi-racialism, which recognises the variety of racial groups and racial identities as a given reality and which therefore concerns itself with (sound) relations among racial (and other) groupings. In contrast to non-racialism, multi-racialism is not individualist-homogenous but group- or (multi-)communal-based.

It might be argued that there is no clear evidence showing that non-racialism has ever established itself as an actual norm (instead of a mere norm-formulation) of the constitution, marked by wide-spread behaviour among the South African public, and that is was therefore only embodied in still-born law. However, if non-racialism has ever established itself, it has disappeared in the period since the adoption of the Constitution. South Africa has starkly been re-racialised. Race is a predominant factor in the public discourse, whilst the individualism of non-racialism has retreated to the distant background. It goes further than this. At the time of writing there is a rising tide of racially inflammatory discourse in which senior politicians

---

69   Historical Papers Research Archive, 2013, *The freedom charter.* Available: http://bit.ly/31pCDE2 [Accessed, 20 July 2017].

70   *The Constitution,* as the courts have said on many occasions, is aimed at the establishment of a non-racial society, non-racial democracy, non-racial education, non-racial personal identification, a non-racial unitary state and non-racial local government.

both in government and opposition parties take the lead. Specifically minority communities are harshly targeted and there seems to be hardly any regard for the fact that this egregious discourse might cause segments of various racial groups to be pitted antagonistically against each other. This has caused South Africa to be a society which is sharply divided along racial boundaries and is showing ominous signs of rising racial tension.

Legislation

It is ironic that one of the first factors that ushered in (or reinforced) the present re-racialisation of South Africa is a series of legislation that was passed to overcome the effects of previous racial discrimination. Three sets of legislation are relevant. The first is remedial or corrective, that is, affirmative action legislation of which the Employment Equity Act[71] is the most important. The second is legislation directed towards black economic empowerment, namely the Broad Based Black Empowerment Act,[72] which is the source of a plethora of codes and charters, which are applicable in various sectors of the economy. Thirdly, there is a vast number of statutes, based on the principle of racial representativeness (representivity), which is discussed under the next rubric of this chapter.

In order to achieve the aims of correction, empowerment and representivity (and equality) which this legislation purports to achieve, it necessarily has to be premised on racial definitions and racial classification.[73] The ironic consequence is that racial identity, which is incongruous with the individualistic nature and aim of non-racialism, is underscored. Scores of the disputes emanating from the application of this legislation, especially disputes relating to affirmative action, in accordance with the Employment Equity Act revolve around race and cause people of different racial groups to join issue in litigation. Albie Sachs in his capacity as a justice of the Constitutional Court already at an early stage expressed concern that commitment to non-racialism might be defeated as a result of affirmative action.[74]

"Race war"

The exuberant public discourse referred to in Chapter 3 that accompanied South Africa's constitutional transition in and immediately after 1994 and which included a tremendous amount of non-racial romanticism and gleeful clamours about the rainbow nation has also changed dramatically. The observations of political

---

71   Act 55 of 1998 and many other schemes adopted in accordance with the Act.

72   Act 53 of 2003.

73   For example section 1 of the Employment Equity Act, 55 of 1998 and section 1(b) of the Broad Based Black Empowerment Act, 53 of 2003.

74   He stated as follows in *Minister of Finance v Van Heerden* 2004(6) SA 121(CC) para 137: "At the same time it is important to ensure that the process of achieving equity is conducted in such a way that the baby of non-racialism is not thrown out with the bath-water of remedial action."

journalist, Ferrial Haffajee, accurately summarises the effect of re-racialisation on the South African society. According to her, South Africa has undergone a *generational shift* away from non-racialism.[75] Haffajee explains that the meaning and objects of non-racialism have vanished over the past two decades "(a)nd has congealed into a nasty race consciousness."[76] New thinking about race has become prevalent in South Africa. A generational shift occurred with new radicalised black opinion makers who dispute the foundations of non-racialism gaining prominence.[77]

Various minorities are targets in this growing re-racialisation and inflammatory racial rhetoric in South Africa, namely whites (and Afrikaners), coloureds, Indians and foreign nationals.

Whites

A substantive part of the new black intelligentsia is irritated because they regard the black government under the leadership of the ANC to be in office but not in power. Government, according to them is suffering under the hegemonic so-called *Ideology of Whiteness*. Accordingly, there is but a single standard for cultural, economic and political achievement, namely a Western (white) standard. Black people, this intelligentsia claims, are persistently subjected to subordination and humiliation in accordance with the criteria of this Ideology of Whiteness. This view is the order of the day notwithstanding the emergence of a strong black middle class. The perception prevalent among the ranks of this new intelligentsia, Haffajee describes as follows:

> The shade that whiteness and white supremacy narrative takes in South Africa is inevitably backward focussed. It is an anger and a reckoning with the past by a generation that is free (and born free) and completely unarmoured with my generation's rainbow naivety and nostalgia. It is the unfinished business of apartheid being taken up by a generation free of the uhuru gratitude that I reflect.[78]

This new generation is adamant to wage a race war against this so-called *Ideology of Whiteness*. This view has trumped and replaced the notion of non-racialism.[79]

There are numerous cases of senior political leaders who expressed themselves in racially hostile terms. Often it goes as far as incitement to violence. Two cases are emblematic. In January 2015, the previous president of the country, Jacob Zuma, declared as follows about Jan van Riebeeck who in 1652 set foot in the Cape to lay the foundation of what later gave rise to the formation of the Afrikaner people:

---

75   Haffajee, 2015:49.

76   Ibid, p.17.

77   Ibid, p.33.

78   Ibid, p.43.

79   Ibid, p.66.

> A man with the name of Jan van Riebeeck arrived in the Cape on 6 April 1652 ... What followed were numerous struggles and wars and deaths and the seizure of land and the deprivation of the indigenous peoples' political and economic power.[80]

He added: "The arrival of Van Riebeeck disrupted South Africa's social cohesion, repressed people and caused wars." The statement is clearly aimed at Afrikaners in particular and whites in general. It caused much distress among Afrikaners.[81] The repeated *original sin rhetoric* of Zuma's successor, Cyril Ramaphosa, has given further impetus to this anti-White discourse – a discourse that expressly criminalises whites as land thieves and robbers.[82] The parliamentary debate of 27 April 2018 that led to the resolution that the confiscation of white-owned property without compensation should be considered (and that the amendment of the Constitution be considered towards that end), was permeated with inflammatory statements against the white population.

Chief Justice Mogoeng added his voice to this racially divisive discourse. According to him,[83] basing his view on a quote that turned out to be an Internet forgery,[84] South Africa and Africa in general was in a paradisiacal state that was only uprooted by the terrifying arrival of white colonialists, who are still wreaking havoc in South Africa, yet now using devious stratagems.

Julius Malema, leader of the Economic Freedom Fighters (EFF) and a former leader of the ANC Youth League, is notorious for his incitement to racial violence and racially based hate speech against whites in general and Afrikaners in particular and increasingly also against South Africans of Indian origin. (See below.) In November 2016 Malema exclaimed:

> We are not calling for the slaughter of white people, at least for now ... The rightful owners of the land are black people. No white person is a rightful owner of the land here in South African and the whole of the African continent.[85]

Malema is also notorious for his chant "Shoot the Boer", which was held by the court to constitute hate speech.[86] Kill the Boer, kill the farmer was also chanted at Overvaal High School in Vereeniging, Gauteng province, during February 2018. This occurred amidst the campaign of the MEC for education of Gauteng, Phanyaza Lesufi, to crush Afrikaans schools. The campaign came against the backdrop of the Gauteng education department having lost a court case against the school just weeks before.

Incitement and revulsion against whites are often channelled through chants that whites stole the land (as noted above), the so-called *"Ideology of Whiteness,"* which ascribes a feeling of racial superiority to whites and *"white monopoly capital,"* which comes down to an innuendo that whites have unlawfully usurped the riches of the land. This kind of criminalisation of whites is the order of the day, amongst others, in certain sectors of the mainstream media. In fact the criminalisation of whites has developed into an official South African historiography – the master narrative of South African history.[87] The white minority is portrayed as a collective criminal, which is guilty of colonialism, racism, apartheid, the Ideology of Whiteness, theft of the land and other collective crimes.[88]

Symbols associated with whites and Western culture – statues and paintings of historical figures, art, buildings, monuments, etc. – have become close to anathema in the present South African situation. Such symbols are damaged or destroyed or otherwise it is insisted that they be removed from public spaces. In numerous cases the Constitutional Court has also weighed in on this by providing its own anti-white and anti-Afrikaner historiography and to vehemently denying the cultural-rights claims of Afrikaners.[89]

During the student protest in 2016 at and in the immediate vicinity of South African university campuses the drive against Western culture culminated in campus violence as part of the so-called Fallist movement aimed at Africanisation, de-Westernisation (including a sharp rejection of *Western science*), nativism and autochthonism. This represents the direct opposite of the clear world-openness of the text of the Constitution as encapsulated, for example, in the provisions on the relationship between South African domestic law and international and foreign law.[90]

Re-racialisation assumes even more serious proportions given the fact that racial rhetoric and racial tensions are not only an anti-White and anti-Western matter. There are also incidents of inflammatory speech against other non-white citizens of South Africa, such as people from Indian descend and coloureds, as well as violence against black people from elsewhere in Africa residing in South Africa.

Indians and coloureds

Indians and coloureds are also in the firing line of the re-racialisation of South African society and the accompanying hostile rhetoric. In his discussion of re-racialisation Ismail Lagardien observes that there is a significant anti-Indian sentiment in KwaZulu-Natal, the province which is home to the majority of members of the country's Indian community. He states that this group is stripped of authority in the provincial bureaucracy and increasingly find themselves marginalised while their work is shoved aside.[91]

---

87   This culminated in the South African National Assembly's decision on 27 April 2018 to set a process in motion for the attachment – expropriation without compensation – of white-owned property.

88   The Constitutional Court also participates in this, more specifically in relation to the land question. See for example *Daniels v Scribante and Another* 2017(8) BCLR 949(CC).

89   See for example *City of Tshwane Metropolitan Municipality v Afriforum and Another* 2016(9) BCLR 1133(CC) discussed in detail Chapter 7.

90   More specifically sections 232 and 233, as well as sections 39(1)(a) and (b) of *the Constitution*.

91   Lagardien, 27 April 2015, "The re-racializing and tribalization of politics: Where will we end up?" *Daily Maverick*. Available: http://bit.ly/2KDWrwG [Accessed, 19 May 2017].

June 2018 saw an acrimonious outburst of fury against the South African Indian population, mostly from the ranks of the EFF. It began with an utterance by Floyd Shivambu, deputy leader of the EFF, during proceedings of a parliamentary committee. Shivambu accused the deputy director-general of the treasury, Ismail Mononiat, who is of Indian descend, of being "un-African," apparently for no other reason than that Mononiat was often representing the director-general at parliamentary committee hearings.[92] This lead to an indignant outcry among sectors of the public – also members of the ANC – many of whom are also Indian. Shivambu, however, was backed, by his EFF colleagues. A week later, EFF leader, Julius Malema, accused Indians – at least the majority of South African Indians as he said – of being racist and hating black people.[93]

In the Western Cape, that houses the bulk of the country's coloured population, the racial factor also prominently exerted itself. This is caused, among other things, by government's ideology of homogenisation, through the means of the policy of *representivity* (which is dealt with under the next heading). It is in the Western Cape, Lagardien said: "(w)here 'coloured' workers – professionals like nurses and librarians – are losing their jobs because 'there are too many coloureds' in the province. The official policy is that the province should reflect that 'national' population/racial demographics."[94] It is in this respect that re-racialisation and "representivity" which go hand in hand, have emerged as values of the constitutional order. The official policy of government is that the national population profile in terms of race must be reflected in the labour force of all employers and at all points of services delivery (offices, etc.). This requires a comprehensive project of social engineering, which is premised on racial classification and racialisation.[95]

Foreigners

Since 2008 violence against foreigners, more specifically black foreigners from other African countries (and people from the Indian subcontinent) has become an established feature of the South Africa's domestic scene. This includes damage to property, assault, arson and murder of which especially foreign business people, are the victims. The sentiment against black foreigners is running deep and wide[96]

---

92 http://bit.ly/2KACzdP [Accessed, 8 June 2018].

93 http://bit.ly/2M79CcC [Accessed, 20 June 2018].

94 Lagardien, 2015.

95 Jimmy Manyai, prominent ANC ideologue and a former director-general of the department of labour stated: This over-consecration of coloureds in the Western Cape is not working for them "... They should spread in the rest of the country ... they must stop this over-concentration situation because they are in over-supply where they are so you must look in the country and see where you can meet the supply." SAPA & AFP Reporter, 2011. *Manyi 'Over-supply' of coloureds in the Western Cape.* Available: http://bit.ly/2KoN7hz [Accessed, 21 May 2017].

96 Adam & Moodley, 2015, *Mob violence sets SA xenophobia apart.* Available: http://bit.ly/2M6C92h [Accessed, 18 May 2017].

and the situation is exacerbated by inflammatory grandstanding against black foreigners. by senior political figures, including senior office bearers in government and the ANC.

The former secretary general and at the time of writing, the national chair of the ANC, minister Gwede Mantashe, expressed his disapproval of foreign businessmen (usually small business people doing business in black townships) and added that government was considering measures to restrict their business activities. Amongst other things he said:

> If you go to Soweto, corner shops have been taken over by foreigners. We must do something about it. If you see all the malls here, who is in those malls? Who owns shops there? Why can't our people pull their resources together and own business opportunities in their backyards?[97]

According to minister Lindiwe Zulu, small foreign business men had to meet certain conditions if they want to do business and live in South Africa. If they want to live free from disruption in South Africa and carry on with their business ventures, they must share their business practices with the local people, the minister stated.[98]

In March 2015 the Zulu king, Goodwill Zwelithini, called upon foreigners to leave the country. He stated that it was unfair that locals had to compete with foreigners and reproached government for not placing a halt on the influx of foreigners.[99] Members of government were loath to go against the king.[100] and the king did get the backing of Edward Zuma, son of the former president.[101]

Incitement of racial hatred

Section 16 of South Africa's Constitution, which deals with freedom of expression, is pertinent in the present context. Section 16(1) is generous in its allowance for freedom of expression. However, in keeping with contemporary international law,[102] it also excludes certain species of expressions from constitutional protection. According to section 16(2), the right to freedom of expression does not extend, amongst other things, to the incitement of imminent violence or the advocacy

---

97 Author not indicated, 2014, *South Africa's ANC to restrict foreign business.* Available: http://bit.ly/33maXSw [Accessed, 18 May 2017].

98 Pilane, 2015, *Small business minister wants spaza-shop trade secrets.* Available: http://bit.ly/2KyGvfh [Accessed, 18 May 2017].

99 Ndou, 2015, *Foreigners must go home – king Zwelithini.* Available: http://bit.ly/2Kyzew6 [Accessed, 18 May 2017].

100 Author not indicated, 2015, *More trouble than they are worth.* Available: https://econ.st/2YuN2l3 [Accessed, 18 May 2017].

101 Khoza, 2015, *Zuma's son wants foreigners out of the country.* Available: http://bit.ly/2KnSwW7 [Accessed, 18 May 2017].

102 See for example article 19 and 20 of the International Covenant on Civil and Political Rights (ICCPR) of 1966.

of hatred that is based on race, ethnicity, gender or religion, and that constitutes incitement to cause harm.[103]

Judged by the discussion above, the prohibition of hate speech on the basis of race against whites, Indians, coloureds and foreign nationals, and even the incitement of violence against (sectors within) these communities, have gained the status of constitutionally protected expressions, thus no more to be excluded from protection under section 16(1). Conduct, mostly forthcoming from the ranks of the ANC and the EFF, have caused this change to the (actual) constitution. Section 16(2) has in part simply lapsed and is not part of the actual constitution anymore.

The re-racialisation of South African society must be considered together with the emergence of an acrimonious form of divisive identity politics in South Africa. It manifests in movements for the so-called decolonisation and Africanisation which go way beyond political and constitutional independence. It also includes psychological, intellectual, spiritual, economic and various other forms of *decolonisation*. The transformation of the academic curriculum represents most probably the most thorough-going expression of the decolonisation and Africanisation drive. It is aimed at the dismantling of the much impugned *Western colonised science* and to replace that with a (re)discovered African-based science. This represents a very intensified form of identity politics and is the precise opposite of the universalism and individualism of section 1 of the Constitution.

Identity politics, albeit identity politics with a constructive flavour, have also manifested itself among the coloured community, especially in the Western Cape. There is a seemingly mounting movement among coloured people in the province claiming that the coloured people, being the decedents of the Khoi and the San, are the true first nations (indigenous population) of South Africa who had been living at the southern tip of Africa millennia before the black newcomers migrated into the region only recently. Black people are accused of being engaged in undue competition with coloureds, such as taking the jobs of coloured people in the Western Cape. This coloured movement strongly rejects the naming of the airport in Cape Town after a black person and wants it to be called Krotoa airport, after a historically famous Khoi woman. By the same token, they also want the airport in the Eastern Cape (Port Elizabeth) to be named after another famous Khoi historical figure (Dawid Stuurman).[104]

---

103 Section 16 provides as follows:
(1) Everyone has the right to freedom of expression, which includes – (a) freedom of the press and other media; (b) freedom to receive or impart information or ideas; (c) freedom of artistic creativity; and (d) academic freedom and freedom of scientific research.
(2) The right in sub-section (1) does not extend to – (a) propaganda for war; (b) incitement of imminent violence; or (c) advocacy of hatred that is based on race, ethnicity, gender or religion, and that constitutes incitement to cause harm.

104 Sain, 2018, *Khoisan tribes demand airport to be renamed after David Stuurman.* Available: http://bit.ly/2KxKZmv [Accessed, 8 June 2018].

There is nothing inherently untoward about identity politics. In fact, it can be very constructive to affirm one's own identity which can serve as the basis for communal self-respect and sound inter-communal relations to promote the establishment of mutual respect. However, against the backdrop of the egregious forms of re-racialisation and inflammatory rhetoric against minorities, it can exacerbate the already ominous tensions among some sections of South Africa's heterogeneous society.

Conclusion

Political commentator, RW Johnson relates the heated racial rhetoric with the late phase of the nationalist movement in Africa. In this phase the nationalists are deeply frustrated with their own mal-performance and lack of achievement and in desperation is taking resort to all kinds of almost magical formulas as solutions for their predicament, such as ridding the country of foreigners, confiscating farms and nationalising assets.[105] Matthee also associates re-racialisation with the growing failure of the ANC government. He states:

> After twenty years of underperforming one-party dominant rule, there is an undercurrent of volatile scapegoat politics in South Africa. Foreign Africans are excluded, marginalized or not recognized in the nativist discourse. So are indigenous Western and Asian Africans.[106]

All these trends suggest that non-racialism as envisaged in the vaunted *strongly entrenched* foundational provision of the Constitution can no longer be regarded as a founding value of the present South African constitution. On the contrary, it is more correct to state that South Africa's constitutional order has become a racially accentuated and racially polarised constitution. As Haffajee stated: "Non-racialism is, to all intents and purposes, dead."[107]

5.2.6 Founding values: (2) Homogenisation and racial representation (representivity)

In a number of provisions the Constitution requires the national racial (and gender) composition of South Africa to be considered as one of various factors when appointments are made in the public sector: the courts, Chapter 9 bodies[108] and the

---

105 Johnson, 2015.

106 Matthee, 2015:20.

107 Haffajee, 2015:49.

108 Or as they are referred to in the text of *the Constitution* "state institutions for supporting constitutional democracy," namely the Public Protector, the Human Rights Commission, the Commission for the Promotion and Protection and Promotion of the Rights of Cultural, Religious and Linguistic Communities, the Commission for Gender Equality, the Auditor-General and the Independent Electoral Commission.

public service.[109] Broadly speaking, the national population profile in terms of race, has to be reflected in the personnel composition of these institutions. It must be emphasised that this is but one of a variety of factors to be taken into account when appointments are made.

However, a very strict interpretation of racial representation (or racial representivity as it has become known in South African jargon) has over the past decades grown into a new and full-fledged foundational principle of the actual South African constitution. According to this principle the personnel composition of all public and private institutions on each level of seniority, has to square with the national racial population composition.[110] The effect of this principle, is that the racial profile of all public and private institutions is required to be exact replicas of one another. The strict enforcement of racial representivity provides the mechanisms for enforcing the comprehensive homogenisation of South African society. No room is left for diversity. In practical terms in view of the country's population profile, all institutions will be predominantly black and under black control.

As explained in more detail in 5.2.8 below, the application of the racial representivity principle also has profound linguistic implications. Institutions and organised spheres that meet the representivity standard will only be able to function in a language that more or less everybody is conversant with and in which they can communicate with one another. In South Africa that language would generally be English. However, there are many areas in the country that are populated by large numbers of speakers of the same indigenous language. In such areas the dominant regional language in question would naturally be the rational and suitable choice for the institutions in question. Accordingly isiZulu would clearly be the choice for the largest part of the KwaZulu-Natal province where isiZulu is predominantly used. By the same token, isiXhosa would be the appropriate choice for most of the Eastern Cape, Afrikaans in the Northern Cape and Setswana in the North West province, etc. However, as the discussion on the changing of the constitution's multilingual dispensation in 5.2.8 below shows, various governmental institutions have enforced English also in areas in which English has virtually no footprint. The parallel linguistic effect of the principle of representivity over and above that of black control is therefore one of Anglicisation.

Representivity therefore entails a comprehensive project of social engineering for the achievement – the enforcement – of homogenisation. Homogenisation, which is enforced through the strategy of representivity, allows no minority spaces, because

---

109 Section 174(2) relates to appointments to the bench of the superior courts; section 193(2) relates to appointments to the Chapter 9 institutions and section 195(1)(i) relates to appointments to the public administration. Section 174(2) provides: "The need for the judiciary to reflect broadly the racial and gender composition of South Africa must be considered when judicial officers are appointed." This provision, however, has to be considered alongside section 174(1) that reads: "Any appropriately qualified woman or man who is a fit and proper person may be appointed as a judicial officer. Any person to be appointed to the Constitutional Court must also be a South African citizen."

110 For a detailed discussion see Malan, 2008a:427.

minorities by reason of their unique and therefore inherently *unrepresentative* racial and linguistic composition, are not and cannot be representative of the national population profile unless they dissolve in order to become something entirely different from what they have always been. On proper analysis, it is clear that representivity constitutes a wide-ranging project for the liquidation of minorities and for forcing them to be absorbed into a single national homogenous identity.[111] Racial representivity prevents any national minority to organise itself either geographically or on a corporate basis. At the same time, it ensures that the black majority in pursuance of their vast numbers are everywhere – territorially and corporately – placed in a position of control in accordance with their numerical weight.

The Employment Equity Act that dates back to 1998 and has been referred to under the previous heading was the first legislative instrument that introduced this principle on a comprehensive scale. General racial representivity is the organising principle on which the Act is based.[112] Since that time a comprehensive collection of legislation has been passed that gave further expression to this principle and which reinforces the homogenisation ideology.[113] The Courts, more specifically the Constitutional Court, has also thrown its weight behind the principle.[114] In spite of profound criticism racial representivity is identified with the substantive equality in South African jurisprudence[115] and with the broader ideology of transformationism (discussed in Chapter 7).

The representivity principle has assumed omnipresent proportions. It has expanded to fields hardly foreseen before. Parallel medium education is one such case in point. Whilst parallel medium education that provides for tuition in Afrikaans and English has for a long time been regarded as entirely uncontroversial, it has recently become constitutionally repugnant, because Afrikaans classes are mostly white, that is, not black enough and therefore in conflict with the representivity principle.[116]

In the general public discourse, representivity has assumed the status of a supreme value. Former Constitutional Court Justice Kriegler is of the view that representivity has grown into the *be all land all* principle in South Africa.[117] Chief Justice Mogoeng,

---

111 Malan, 2010:438-448.

112 Brassey, 1998:1363.

113 Compare the comprehensive list in Malan, 2010:428-429. A count done in March 2017 shows a further increase of ten laws since 2010.

114 See on this *Solidarity and Others v Department of Correctional Services and Others* 2016(5) SA 594(CC) para 40. *South African Police Service v Solidarity obo Barnard* 2014(6) SA 123(CC); 2014(10) BCLR 1195(CC).

115 Compare for example Louw, 2015, 593-667, (Part I); 668-733(Part II); Rautenbach, 2015:431-443.

116 See the judgment of the Constitutional Court in *Afriforum and Another v University of the Free State* 2018(4) BCLR 387(CC) in which basically followed the similar argumentation of the Supreme Court of Appeal in *University of the Free State v Afriforum and Another* 2017(4) SA 283(SCA) paras 25-28.

117 Kriegler, 2009.

expressing himself in support of representivity on the bench, went so far as to state that there was no need to appoint the *best of the best* candidates as judges.[118]

The representivity principle has now gained so much traction as a foundational value and principle of the South African constitutional order, that no other principle or value can match it. The principle of racial representivity provides a graphic example of a major constitutional change that has come about without any textual amendment. The constitution has undergone a profound change through the sheer force of politics.

5.2.7 Founding values: (3) Ubuntu and its uncomfortable co-existence with the rule of law

Ubuntu was one of the constitutional values expressly acknowledged in the text of the interim Constitution.[119] However, it does not feature anywhere in the text of the 1996 Constitution. In spite of that it has emerged prominently as a constitutional value. The courts, amongst others, subscribed to ubuntu in various legal sectors, for instance in the law of delict and in constitutional law.[120] In fact it came to occupy such a prominent place that TW Bennet quite justifiably concluded that ubuntu has developed into one of the core values of the present constitutional order.[121]

Ubuntu was defined as follows with reference to relevant jurisprudence:

> Ubuntu is contrasted to vengeance; dictates that a high value be placed on the life of human beings; is inextricably linked to the values dignity, compassion, humaneness and respect for the humanity on which it places a high premium; dictates a shift from confrontation to mediation and conciliation; dictates good neighbourliness and shared concern; favours the re-establishment of harmony in the relationship between parties in that such harmony should restore the dignity of the plaintiff without ruining the defendant; favours restorative rather than retributive justice; operates in the direction of reconciliation and not estrangement of disputants; works towards sensitizing a disputant or a defendant in litigation to the hurtful impact of his actions to the other party and on changing of such conduct accordingly rather than merely punishing the disputant; promotes mutual understanding rather than punishment; favours face-to-face encounters of disputants with a view to facilitating differences being resolved rather than conflict and victory for the most powerful; ubuntu favours civility and civilized dialogue premised on mutual tolerance. [122]

---

118 Anonymous, 2017, *Advocate under fire over JSC*. Available: http://bit.ly/2Tk4SkP [Accessed, 28 May 2017].

119 Contained in the postamble to the interim *Constitution of the Republic of South Africa* 200 of 1993 under the heading *National unity and reconciliation*.

120 Compare the list of judgment in Malan, 2014c:234.

121 Bennett, Munrie & Jacobs, 2018:29-60.

122 *Afriforum and Another v Malema and Others*, 2011(6) SA 240; 2011(12) BCLR 1289(EqC) para 19.

Various academic commentaries provide definitions of ubuntu.[123] Although the exact meaning of ubuntu is arguably still not sufficiently precise, there is no doubt, as Bennett submitted, that its emergence has exacted a change in the value basis of the constitution. The change that it has brought to the constitution is nominal (terminological) as well as substantive, that is, in name and in content.

The term as such, has gained so much traction that it enjoys preference above other value related terms in the Constitution or is at least dealt with on par with those that are acknowledged in the text. However, the substitution is not only nominal. Judged by the quotation above, as well as the academic commentary, it is also substantive.

Ubuntu represents a change in the constitution to the extent that it is an add-on to the existing text of the Constitution. However, apart from an add-on, it may be argued that it is also in part substituting law provided for in the text with which ubuntu is incongruent. The relevant constitutional value which ubuntu is incompatible with is the rule of law (in section 1 of the Constitution).

The rule of law is marked, amongst others things, by the following five interrelated characteristics: it is based in a sovereign corpus of law; it has a literary (scriptural) foundation; it is impersonal and abstract; it is characterised by and functions on account of the authority of the past; it is marked by the temporal distance between the legal norm and the (legal) decision.[124]

The rule of law is premised on the existence of a corpus of law (legal rules, principles and precedents) which is clearly distinguishable from non-law. Legal decision-making under the rule of law is determined by the relevant norms in the corpus, which are clearly distinguishable from and independent of non-law, such as considerations of morality, religion, feasibility, etc. All these other considerations might be very important. For legal decision-making they are irrelevant, however. For such non-legal considerations to play any part in legal decision-making they must first be converted into law – into legal norms.[125] Only then can such rules, now forming part of the corpus, be taken into account in legal decision-making. Legal decision-makers must always go back to the corpus of law that serves as the sole authoritative basis for legal decision-making. They must always remind themselves of the past – of the corpus of law that has already been in existence. They must consult the literature in which the law has been recorded over the ages and apply it to the facts of a matter.[126] There must necessarily be a temporal distance between

---

123 English, 1996:641-648; Keevy, 2009:19-58; Mokgoro, 1998a:15-23; Mokgoro, 1998b:15-26; Cornell, 2009:43-58; Cornell, 2004:666-675; Bilchitz, 2010:45-78.

124 See Malan, 2012b:276-280 in relation to the rule salient characteristics of the rule of law.

125 This argumentation is in line with H.L.A Hart's exposition of the rules of recognition in widely read *Concept of Law*, first published by Clarendon Press, London in 1961.

126 Through the art of artificial reason of the law as Edward Coke once reminded King James I. Quoted by Sabine, 1973:65.

the adoption of a legal rule that authorises a decision and the decision itself. The norm must necessarily precede the decision. The proclamation of the norm and the decision in terms of which it is taken cannot occur simultaneously. If that were so, the norm would not predetermine the decision simply because it did not predate it. The rule of law is also inherently impersonal, general and abstract, that is, not personal and specific.[127] The impersonality, generality and abstractness of law ensure its application without regard to person. If a legal rule is applied to a defined category of persons, it is applied without exception. The specific person in relation to whom the rule will be applied in a specific case, does not determine the (legal) decision, that is, the specific individual is not relevant to the legal decision about to be taken; the decision is determined by the operation of the relevant legal rules themselves.

Ubuntu is different on all these scores. It is not based on a distinguishable corpus of law. It is also not abstract and impersonal but personal, inter-personal (relational) and concrete. Its core concern is the cultivation and maintenance of warm personal relations, more specifically cosy relationships marked by friendship and on processes for promoting such relationships and processes that could mend such relationships to the extent that they might have gone astray. Unlike the rule of law, ubuntu is not concerned about the consistent application of the relevant norms of the corpus of law. It does not look back at those norms that have been adopted in the past – and then apply them. On the contrary, ubuntu is exclusively present-centred: concerned with present interpersonal relations and present decisions not determined – hampered – by the corpus of law. Ubuntu places so much emphasis on the cultivation of good interpersonal relations that it allows the typical impersonal and abstract application of legal rules, which lies at the core of the rule of law, to be disregarded for the sake of such relations.[128]

It is clear that the emergence of ubuntu represents a change in the value substance of the Constitution: it relegated the section 1 value of the *rule of law* and in part substituted that with a different value content, namely one which is identified with the notion of ubuntu.

Ubuntu side-lined – and substituted – the rule of law. Owing to ubuntu's indifference and disregard towards the impersonal and consistent application of the abstract rules of positive law, it causes legal rules to no longer being applied and enforced with the degree of fidelity and consistency that the value of the rule of law requires.

---

127 It may be argued that law is by definition abstract and impersonal and that the abstractness and impersonality of law distinguishes it from other forms of control of human behaviour. There is a long history, dating back to the Roman legal tradition that can be drawn upon as authority for this. See for example the references of Jolowicz, 1954:25; Cicero De Legibus Part III 19 (English translation by Keyes (1966)); D 138 (translation by Watson (1985)).

128 Compare Malan, 2012b:272-305 especially 276-280 in relation to foundation of the rule of law, as well as in general Malan, 2014:231-257.

At the same time, it can be argued convincingly that ubuntu has caused the legal rules that govern the execution of a public function to be relaxed in the name of the sentiments associated with ubuntu, such as compassion, humaneness, the need to protect human dignity, an inclination towards reconciliation and mediation rather than confrontation, the need for restoring and maintaining broken personal relationships, forgiveness rather than confrontation and various other notions associated with ubuntu. Instead of allowing decisions to be taken in accordance with the applicable norms of positive law, sentiments that are identified with ubuntu are allowed to reign. Not the applicable norms of law, but the best individual decision viewed through the prism of ubuntu is allowed to be decisive.[129] Once again, it is noteworthy that this change has come about without any amendment to the text of the Constitution.

5.2.8 The substitution of the multilingual official language dispensation

The constitutional provisions on the official languages are not part of the Constitution's foundational values of the South African state. The provisions about languages are contained in section 6. However, section 6 gives further expression to the foundational values in that it afford official status to the mother tongues of the vast majority of the South African population and seems to commit the Constitution to the protection and promotion of all these languages. As such it gives expression to the values of inclusiveness and the promotion of the indigenous cultural assets of the inhabitants of the country. Due to the value content of these provisions it is apt to discuss them in this context.

Section 6 provides for eleven official languages. Section 6 enjoins the state to take practical and positive measures to elevate the status and advance the use of indigenous official languages and requires that the official languages enjoy parity of esteem and be treated equitably.[130] Various other provisions that relate to language and culture have in common that they affirm inclusivity of all the country's linguistic and cultural communities and the cultural and linguistic assets associated with these communities. Sections 9(3) and (4) prohibit unfair discrimination, on grounds of language (and many other grounds). Section 29(2) conditionally provides for mother tongue education. Sections 30 and 31 provide for rights pertaining to language and culture. In pursuance of section 185 of the Constitution the

---

130 The most important provisions of section 6 are contained in sub-sections (1) to (4) which provide as follows:
(1) The official languages of the Republic are Sepedi, Sesotho, Setswana, siSwati, Tshivenda, Xitsonga, Afrikaans, English, isiNdebele, isiXhosa and isiZulu. (2) Recognising the historically diminished use and status of the indigenous languages of our people, the state must take practical and positive measures to elevate the status and advance the use of these languages. (3) (a) The national government and provincial governments may use any particular official languages for the purposes of government, taking into account usage, practicality, expense, regional circumstances and the balance of the needs and preferences of the population as a whole or in the province concerned; but the national government and each provincial government must use at least two official languages. (b) Municipalities must take into account the language usage and preferences of their residents. (4) The national government and provincial governments, by legislative and other measures, must regulate and monitor their use of official languages. Without detracting from the provisions of sub-section (2), all official languages must enjoy parity of esteem and must be treated equitably.

Commission for the Promotion and Protection of the Rights of Cultural, Religious and Linguistic Communities has been established. Lastly, section 235 conditionally provides for self-determination.[131]

Recent jurisprudential developments show that official status should not merely be a matter of symbolism. Official status denotes a minimum obligation upon the state to actually use official languages for official purposes. There are trends to that effect in both European and African jurisprudence.[132] Moreover, the discretionary character of the language clause (section 6) allows considerable space for state organs in South Africa to afford practical content to the language provisions.[133]

The language clause as well as all the other provisions sited above, together attest to an emphatic commitment to actual linguistic and cultural diversity.

In spite of this, South Africa has over the past decades developed into a constitutional dispensation distinctively marked by official English unilingualism. The evidence to that effect is overwhelming: national legislation is consistently only available in English, whilst the other official languages are only randomly used; it is reported that the Chief Justice, usurping legislative power, issued a controversial decree providing for English to be the sole language of record in South Africa's superior courts; official services, more specifically official documentation, is very often only available in English; advertisements for positions in the public sector are generally only in English; higher education has almost completely been Anglicised with support of the Constitutional Court; in school education the position of Afrikaans has deteriorated considerably, while the other (African) official languages have made no progress.[134] The bottom line is that English has for all practical purposes become the sole official language of the South African state.[135]

---

131 Section 29(2) allows for mother tongue education, including single medium educational institutions. It reads: Everyone has the right to receive education in the official language or languages of their choice in public educational institutions where that education is reasonably practicable. In order to ensure the effective access to, and implementation of this right, the state must consider all reasonable educational alternatives, including single medium institutions, taking into account-equity; (b) practicability; and (c) the need to redress the results of past racially discriminatory laws and practices. Section 30 provides: Everyone has the right to use the language and to participate in the cultural life of their choice, but no one exercising these rights may do so in a manner inconsistent with any provision of the Bill of Rights. Section 31 provides: (1) Persons belonging to a cultural, religious or linguistic community may not be denied the right, with other members of that community– (a) to enjoy their culture, practise their religion and use their language; and (b) to form, join and maintain cultural, religious and linguistic associations and other organs of civil society. (2) The rights in sub-section (1) may not be exercised in a manner inconsistent with any provision of the Bill of Rights.

132 Mentzen alias Mencena v Latvia 2004 *application no 71074/01, admissibility decision of 7 December 2004*. Available: http://bit.ly/1pxGhTR [Accessed, 13 March 2014] and African Human Rights Case Law Analyser, 2009, *Kevin Mgwanga Gumme et al. v Cameroon African Commission on Human and Peoples' Rights, Communication 266/2003*. Available: http://bit.ly/1otpofD [Accessed, 13 March 2014]. See generally Malan, 2015a, 116-120.

133 Malan, 2011:381-407.

134 See, amongst others, Malan, 2008b:59-76 and Malan, 2009:141-155.

135 Compare Johnson *South Africa's brave new world: The beloved country since the end of apartheid*, 2009:370.

The most important reason for official unilingualism is that the ANC as the dominant force in South African politics has all along been opposed to official multilingualism. Right from the outset the ANC was committed to establishing a unilingual English dispensation.[136] The ANC's point of view and actions in this regard closely correspond with that of a variety of other governments in sub-Sahara-Africa over the past five decades.[137] This force – the ANC's own view on language – was the foremost cause for South Africa's official unilingualism.

These changes are, however, not to be traced in the text of the Constitution. None of the provisions that pertain to language has been amended. When one therefore only refers to the constitutional text, the impression would be that South Africa does actually have a dispensation of a multitude of official languages, that is, that the official languages are in fact used to a significant extent for governmental functions.

The establishment of official unilingualism is closely intertwined with the second value change that has been elucidated above, namely that of racial representivity. A dispensation in which all the official languages are actually used for governmental purposes would require that appointments in the public sector be made in a way that responds to the demographic composition and preferences of the communities to which appointments are made. In that way it can be ensured that public functionaries would be able to communicate with and to serve the public in the language/s that they prefer. However, the principle of racial representivity to which the ANC so strictly subscribes, does not allow for this. The principle of racial representivity dictates that the national population profile pertaining to race must be reflected at each and every point of service delivery, regardless of the language preferences of the communities where these functionaries are deployed and regardless of the language proficiency of the functionaries concerned.

In consequence it is quite common that these functionaries and the public are not able to communicate with each other in the language/s of the communities concerned and that they necessarily have to resort to English just to more or less find their way. In this way racial representivity is a potent force that promotes official English unilingualism. These two factors – English unilingualism and racial representivity – both emanating from the ANC's ideological arsenal – are strong mutually reinforcing forces that have caused major changes to the value basis of the actual constitution.[138]

---

136 Johnson, 2009:370 explains that the policy of eleven official languages has been an ANC stratagem right from the outset. The ANC new that a policy of eleven official languages was not practically feasible.

137 See Malan, 2012c:55-78.

138 It might be argued that official multilingualism as envisaged in section 6 was in fact never established and that there was no change from multi- to unilingualism and that we here rather have a case of still-born law as explained in Chapter 4.

5.3

Conclusion

The constitution – also the constitution of South Africa in the period after 1994 – is continuously changing in keeping with the changing socio-political forces in the country. This cannot be prevented by the principle of constitutional supremacy, conformity requirements and strict amendment procedures of the Constitution. In the final analysis, the conclusion reached in Chapter 4 that the so-called supreme Constitution is in fact not supreme, not conformed with and continuously subject to change, is also true for South Africa. This also shows that the first five beliefs of statist-individualist constitutionalism on which the South African Constitution is based, are not supported by reality and that they lack credibility.

The Unity of Powers and the Dependence and Partiality of the Judiciary

6.1

Introduction

The present chapter shifts the focus to the second of the three mechanisms of statist-individualist constitutionalism outlined in Chapter 2.5, namely the mechanism of the threefold separation of powers and the independence and impartiality of the judiciary. This mechanism is premised on the sixth belief of statist-individualist constitutionalism.

According to the sixth belief, a Constitution which is power-structured on the basis of the threefold separation of governmental power between the legislature, executive and the judiciary (supported by additional so-called independent and impartial institutions), among which there is believed to be an adequate system of mutual checks and balances, is viewed by statist-individualist constitutionalism to constitute a basically foolproof system of power limitation and a guarantee for justice. These arrangements, as indicated in Chapter 2, may be regarded as the statist-individualist doctrine's version of the mixed and balanced constitution.

However, the judiciary, highly aggrandised in terms of statist-individualist constitutionalism, takes centre stage in the power structure and the checks and balance belief system of statist-individualist constitutionalism. The focus of the discussion of this chapter will therefore be on the judiciary. It will be shown that the judiciary is in fact not as independent and as impartial as the doctrine of statist constitutionalism proclaims and that the doctrine engages in unfounded myth-making of the threefold separation of powers and mutual checks and balances between these centres for the control of power. Ordinarily there is in fact an actual unity of the three powers and not the doctrine-proclaimed separation. The three powers are separated in terms of institutions, personnel and functions but ordinarily firmly unified in one single power elite: integral segments of one and the same dominant political leadership, informed by the same ideological assumptions, committed to achieving the same goals, yet organised on the basis of a division of labour performed in separate branches.

Chapter 7 which deals with constitutional interpretation, will corroborate this conclusion from a different point of view, namely the point of view of interpretive theory. The discussion will show that the courts are only impartial within the bounds of ideological assumptions and commitments of the dominant elite of which they form an integral part, and that they are the juridical apologists of the ideology of the dominant elite.

In step with its status as a prime example of statist-individualist constitutionalism, much has been made of the magnificence of the system of checks and balances of the South African constitutional order. Ironically, however, it has turned out to be a telling demonstration of exactly how tenuous the statist-individualist system of separation of powers and checks and balances in fact are. Parliamentary control over the executive – the first of the checks and balances – has proven to be haphazard and generally ineffectual. This is in part a consequence of South Africa's one party dominant system where at the time of the writing of this, the ANC is in its twenty fifth year as the ruling party in South Africa. It dominates both the national legislature and the national executive. The national executive is also to a considerable extent the senior leadership of the party. The career prospects for the ANC members of the national legislature depend on decisions of the president and generally of the party leadership. In these circumstances it is hardly conceivable that Parliament, dominated by the ANC, can really serve as an effective check on their own leadership which dominates the executive. In these circumstances parliamentary control over the executive is hardly more than a constitutional paper tiger. Parliament is a rubber stamp of executive decisions rather than a check on it. Had political parties been more loosely organised, such as in the United States of America, where there is not such strict party discipline and where members belonging to the same party as the president, may withhold their support to the president, there could be effective legislative control over the executive. In South Africa, however, that is well-nigh impossible. Members of Parliament may severely criticise state departments, but real control over the higher echelons of the executive, which is the real test stone for parliamentary control over the executive, is largely out of the question.

In South Africa under the present Constitution there is a raft of independent and impartial constitutional institutions that each in its own way have to exercise control over the executive (and to a lesser extent over the legislature). These are the so-called institutions that have to promote constitutional democracy.[1]

All these institutions suffer from structural defects that severely hamper their ability to apply effective checks and balances over the executive. Most prominent among these defects is the fact that the power to appoint the incumbents of these institutions is finally in the hands of the executive, specifically the president, one of the institutions over which these independent institutions are supposed to exercise control. Moreover, the financing of these institutions are in the hands of the ruling party in the legislature and finally, the national executive also fall under the control of the ruling party.

Important as the above checks and balances might be, they are by far not as important as the judiciary in the belief system of statist-individualist constitutionalism. The judiciary is viewed to be truly potent, almost as powerful, if not more powerful than the legislature and the executive, and therefore sufficiently capable of executing effective checks and balances in respect of the executive, the legislature and finally the ruling party. This is particularly true for South Africa where, as indicated in Chapter 3, the judiciary is held in extraordinary high regard. The Constitutional Court in particular occupies an august position. The courts are believed to adjudicate cases by the application of the relevant law through objective legal reasoning in reaching their decisions. As independent and impartial institutions, they are not politically disposed and therefore do not reach their decisions on account of any considerations other than purely legal ones. All can rest assured that all their rights will be protected. The courts are the final guarantee of that.

---

1   Also known as the Chapter 9 institutions since they are provided for in Chapter 9 of the Constitution. namely the Public Protector, Human Rights Commission, Commission for the Promotion and Protection of the Rights of Cultural, Religious and Linguistic Communities, the Commission for Gender Equality, the Auditor-General and the Electoral Commission. According to the Constitution, these institutions are independent, and subject only to the Constitution and the law, and they must be impartial and must exercise their powers and perform their functions without fear, favour or prejudice. Moreover, they are accountable to the National Assembly, and must report on their activities and the performance of their functions to the Assembly at least once a year. Statist constitutionalism nowadays also allocates forms of public power to specialised bodies, which have to exercise these powers *independently, impartially* and free from executive (or legislative) interference for example the prosecuting authority (Sections 179(2) and (4) of the *Constitution of the Republic of South Africa,* 1996 (The Constitution), respectively.) The South African National Prosecutorial Authority (NPA) has, however, fallen prey to heavy political interference and abuse in the struggle among various factions within the ruling ANC. The NPA has been subjected to acrimonious infighting for many years, to such an extent that the reputation of this independent and impartial institution has severely been tarnished. See Institute for Security Studies (ISS), crime hub 22 June 2016, *Can the NPA's credibility be rebuilt?* Available: http://bit.ly/31rKykl [Accessed, 31 December 2016]. See also Matthee, 2016, 57-65. *Political turbulence and business risks in the ANC's hybrid regime, South African Monitor Report.* Available: http://bit.ly/33j2hMH [Accessed, 31 December 2016]. The Reserve Bank is also a specialised institution that has the duty to protect the value of the currency in the interest of balanced and sustainable economic growth in the Republic. In terms of section 224 of the Constitution it must also perform its functions independently and without fear, favour or prejudice, but there must be regular consultation between the Bank and the Cabinet member responsible for national financial matters. The South African Reserve Bank is functioning quite satisfactorily.

I will show that the doctrine of statist-individualist constitutionalism's trust in the judiciary as an effective power check is vastly over-rated; that instead of being independent and impartial, it is in fact part and parcel of the same unified dominant elite together with the legislature and the executive (and the ruling party), all within the broader ideological framework of the dominant elite. More fundamental than the largely superficial, if not putative independence and impartiality of the judiciary, is its actual dependence and partiality. Separation of powers is putative – metaphorical – rather than real.

The starting point of the present discussion is the acrimonious dispute between the so-called liberals and the transformationists which finally came to head in 2013. This dispute serves as a telling case study that debunks the ardent belief in judicial independence and impartiality and the actual content of separation of powers.

The South African Constitution provides for a strikingly wide purview of judicial review which is one of the important reasons why it is held in such high esteem.[2] The courts in South Africa are assigned powers to review and to declare administrative and executive conduct, as well as legislation, in all spheres of government, unconstitutional and invalid. Such extensive powers should make them more powerful than the judiciaries in most other jurisdictions. The Constitutional Court is the apex court and in a number of constitutional issues it exercises exclusive jurisdiction. Since 2012 it may also exercise appeal jurisdiction in relation to matters not constitutional in nature, on the grounds that such matters could relate to points of law of general public importance. Except for this particular power, the Supreme Court of Appeal (SCA) is the highest court in all matters not of a constitutional nature and also has sweeping jurisdiction in constitutional matters, with a few exceptions which fall within the exclusive jurisdiction of the Constitutional Court. The High Courts are not courts of final instance, but in all other respects the subject matter of their jurisdiction is essentially the same as that of the SCA.[3] That fact, together with the justiciable Bill of Rights in the Constitution, has rendered the South African Constitution a splendid example of statist-individualist constitutionalism. The constitutionally endowed strength of the courts underscores the importance of judicial appointments, which is a particularly sensitive and often controversial issue in which all political actors and notably the ruling party and legislature and the executive (the political branches of government) have an important stake.

The drafters of the Constitution were at great pains to secure the integrity of the judiciary. Hence, section 165(2) provides that the courts are subject only to the Constitution and the law, which they are required to apply impartially and without

---

2   See for example Fombad, 2011:1007-1108, stating at 1105: "South Africa's Constitution clearly stands out as an exemplar of modern constitutionalism and provides a rich source from which many African countries can learn."

3   The jurisdiction of these superior courts is provided for in ss 167-169 of the Constitution as amended by the *Constitution Seventeenth Amendment Act* of 2012, which has amended S 167 of the Constitution by adding sub-section 167(3)(b)(ii).

fear, favour or prejudice. Section 165(4) requires organs of state,[4] through legislative and other measures, to assist and protect the courts to ensure their independence, impartiality, dignity, accessibility and effectiveness.[5]

In the run-up to the South African constitutional transition of the mid 1990s and in subsequent years, this confidence in the capacity of the judiciary assumed the status of a basic credo which is underpinning the present constitutional order. Hence, the general truism put forward by statist-individualist constitutionalism was that a Bill of Rights such as the one contained in Chapter 2 of the Constitution, which provides for a wide variety of civil, political and socio-economic rights, together with a truly powerful judiciary, would safeguard and promoting all legitimate interests. All of these projections must of course be based on the assumption that the judiciary will be sufficiently capable to perform its functions in a fully independent and impartial manner and in accordance with the imagery of statist-individualist constitutionalism.[6]

The South African Judicial Service Commission (JSC) is the most important body for assisting and protecting the independence, impartiality, dignity, accessibility and effectiveness of the courts. Its role in the appointment (as well as the disciplining and removal) of judges[7] is at the centre of its mandate. The JSC is formally independent from the executive.

The JSC is without a doubt one of the most crucial bodies for securing the claims of statist-individualist constitutionalism.[8] It makes recommendations to the President for judicial appointments to the benches of the country's superior courts (the Constitutional Court, the SCA and the High Courts and other specialised courts, such as the Labour Courts and the Labour Appeal Court). To that end it conducts public hearings of candidates for such appointments.[9] Due to its composition and broad responsibilities in relation to the structure of the judiciary and because it arguably neutralises executive control over judicial appointments, the JSC is regarded as exemplary for similar organs in states which are premised on the

---

4   In terms of S 239 of the Constitution, an organ of state (is): (a) any department of state or administration in the national, provincial or local sphere of government; or (b) any other functionary or institution (i) exercising a power or performing a function in terms of the Constitution or a provincial constitution; or (ii) exercising a public power or performing a public function in terms of any legislation, but does not include a court or a judicial officer.

5   In prominent non-South African, notably North American, scholarship, some of which will be referred to below, insistence on these qualities is found to be less pronounced, if not absent. Hence, it is found that where scholars would seemingly be dealing with independence, they are on closer analysis actually dealing with the related quality of judicial impartiality.

6   Other constitutional strategies, such as the protection of communities through their own (self-governing) institutions, devolution of power and certain levels of federalism might not necessarily be entirely out of kilter with the basic assumptions of liberal constitutionalism. (Sometimes they are in fact regarded as superfluous or out of step with the principles embodied in such constitutionalism.)

7   ss 174 and 177 of the Constitution and the *Judicial Service Commission Act* 9 of 1994.

8   On paper the JSC is a fine example of modern democracy at work, Calland, 2013:280.

9   In terms of the JSC's own procedures, the creation of which is authorised by S 178(6) of *the Constitution*.

belief system of statist-individualist constitutionalism.[10] Although the JSC is not part of the executive, the way in which it is composed would ordinarily secure a dominant position for the ruling party in that body. This once again attests to the political nature of the JSC. In compliance with the Constitution, the majority of at least twelve of its twenty-three members will be politicians from the ranks of the majority party in the national legislature.[11]

In view of the sweeping nature of judicial review in South Africa, the mandate of the JSC lies at the very heart of the present South African constitutional order. It follows that the JSC's role in the discharge of its responsibility (interviewing and recommending suitable candidates for judicial appointment) is of pivotal importance for the well-being of the constitutional order based on the belief system of statist-individualist constitutionalism in general.

Tension about the way in which the JSC discharges its responsibilities surfaced fairly soon after the Constitution took effect in 1997. The JSC was criticised on a number of occasions for not recommending for appointment to the bench, candidates with so-called impeccable liberal credentials and a history of participation in the struggle of the ruling party, the ANC, against white minority rule.[12] In April 2013, as South Africa entered the twentieth year of its celebrated constitutional democracy, this tension, which is discussed in part 3 below, erupted into a full-scale public wrangle. In the one camp of this clash were those who could be referred to as the transformationists, and in the other camp, the liberals. The transformationists are by and large (regarded as) part of the post-1994 dominant elite under the leadership of the ANC. They are staunch exponents of the ideology of transformationism referred to in more detail below (in this chapter, as well as in Chapters 3 and 7). They include the majority of the members of the JSC, including the present Chief Justice (and ex officio chairman of the JSC), Mogoeng. Their supporters are insisting on the preference of "transformation" and "representivity" as deciding criteria for judicial appointments.

Transformationism is the master concept of the ANC's ideological project and of the present South African politico-constitutional order. In terms of this project, at times as the discussion in Chapter 5 shows, also referred to as the national democratic revolution, all structures of power must be placed under control of the ruling

---

10 See for example the assertions of Chief Justice Mogoeng, referred to in note 26.

11 Namely: the cabinet member responsible for the administration of justice, or an alternate designated by that Cabinet member; three of the six persons designated by the National Assembly from its members; four permanent delegates to the NCoP designated together by the Council with a supporting vote of at least six provinces; and four persons designated by the President as head of the national executive, after consulting the leaders of all the parties in the National Assembly. (Respectively S 178(1)(d),(h),(i) and (j)).

12 See for example Rickard, 2002:16 and Rickard, 2004:16 (this view was rejected by Ntsebeza, 2004:19). Also see Gordon & Bruce, 2007:32-33, 47-49.

party.[13] The transformationism drive also expands to the judiciary. In that context (as explained in more detail in 4.1) it entails that, firstly, the composition of the judiciary must reflect the national population profile (that is, in typical present-day South African parlance, it must satisfy the representivity principle),[14] and, secondly, that individual judges must subscribe to and pursue the same ideological goals as the ruling party. The liberals include the critics of the (majority of the) JSC. They cannot subscribe to this definition of transformationism as that would obviously amount to a full-scale contradiction of the notion of a powerful (independent and impartial) judiciary. They argue, among other points, that the professional competence of candidates for judicial appointment must be the deciding factor in judicial appointments. The liberals reproach the JSC for its alleged preference for recommending less competent but pliant pro-government candidates. They have misgivings about the JSC's propensity against liberal and independent-minded candidates, who are regarded as the foremost subscribers to the values underpinning the South African Constitution[15] but who are at the same time prepared to make rulings against government and in so doing to uphold these values.

In part 2 the seemingly clear constitutional criteria and the JSC's own criteria for judicial appointments are dealt with. It is important to discuss these criteria because the conflict between the liberals and transformationists pivots largely around the interpretation of these criteria. In part 6.3 the views of the parties to the dispute are presented and the question arises as to how such a bitter quarrel could have erupted on an issue which was thought to have been clearly settled, namely the interpretation and application of the said criteria. This question is canvassed in part 6.4, where it is pointed out that the two camps differ fundamentally on the meaning and consequences of the two foundational notions of the present constitutional order, namely on judicial independence (as an incidence of the separation of powers) and on judicial impartiality and legally principled judicial reasoning. In part 6.4.1 the doctrine of judicial independence (and separation of powers) is discussed, and in part 6.4.2 judicial impartiality (and legal reasoning) receive attention. The liberal view of the powerful judiciary, a product of judicial independence and impartiality, which basically amounts to the trite articulation of statist-individualist constitutionalism is subjected to critical assessment. A similar assessment of the transformationist views on the judiciary is contained in part 6.4.3. Part 6.5 concludes with a number of conclusions.

---

13   Stated on numerous occasions in ANC, 1998, *The State, Property Relations and Social Transformation*. Available: http://bit.ly/2TiCsHR [Accessed, 3 September 2013].

14   This means in a nutshell that all bodies, institutions and organised spheres are required to reflect that national population profile. On the issue of representivity see the discussion by Malan, 2010:427-449.

15   These are the values provided for in ss 1, 36 and 39 of *the Constitution*. S 1 provides, among other matters, for the following founding values: (a) human dignity, the achievement of equality and the advancement of human rights and freedoms; (b) non-racialism and non-sexism; (c) the supremacy of the Constitution and the rule of law; (d) and universal adult suffrage, a national common voters roll, regular elections and a multi-party system of democratic government, to ensure accountability, responsiveness and openness. Both ss 36(1) and section 39(1) provide for the values of openness and a democratic society based on human dignity, equality and freedom.

6.2

Criteria for judicial appointments

Sections 174(1) and (2) of the Constitution prescribes the criteria for judicial appointments. The JSC has also set its own further criteria, giving more detailed content to the constitutional provisions.

Sections 174(1) and (2) reads as follows:

1. Any appropriately qualified woman or man who is a fit and proper person may be appointed as a judicial officer. Any person to be appointed to the Constitutional Court must also be a South African citizen.

2. The need for the judiciary to reflect broadly the racial and gender composition of South Africa must be considered when judicial officers are appointed.

The JSC's further criteria for judicial appointments were adopted in 1998.[16] They are in close conformity with those set out in the Constitution quoted above.[17]

All these provisions must be read with section 165(4) of the Constitution in terms of which the JSC (like all other organs of state) is entrusted with the responsibility to assist and protect the independence, impartiality, dignity, accessibility and effectiveness of the courts.

6.3

The falling-out of April 2013

As mentioned above, the falling-out of April 2013 was preceded by a gradually mounting tension amongst members of the JSC. Only a few years after the

16 Judicial Service Commission, 2010, *Summary of the Criteria Used by the Judicial Services Commission when Considering Candidates for Judicial Appointments.* Available: http://bit.ly/2OLzNrl [Accessed, 19 November 2014]. According to the JSC, the decision to publish the criteria was in keeping with its principle that the process of judicial appointments should be open and transparent to the public so as to enhance public trust in the judiciary.

17 The criteria are:
    1. Is the particular applicant an appropriately qualified person?
    2. Is he or she a fit and proper person, and
    3. Would his or her appointment help to reflect the racial and gender composition of South Africa?
It then proceeds with the following list of so-called "Supplementary Criteria" namely:
    1. Is the proposed appointee a person of integrity?
    2. Is the proposed appointee a person with the necessary energy and motivation?
    3. Is the proposed appointee a competent person?
      a) Technically competent
      b) Capacity to give expression to the values of the Constitution
    4. Is the proposed appointee an experienced person?
      a) Technically experienced
      b) Experienced in regard to values and needs of the community
    5. Does the proposed appointee possess appropriate potential?
Symbolism. What message is given to the community at large by a particular appointment?

Constitution had come into operation it was becoming clear that neither sections 174(1) and (2) nor the JSC's additional criteria had succeeded in forging consensus on important issues amongst members of the JSC. The tension resulted from differences of opinion with regard to the interpretation of the relevant criteria for the appointment of judges, the nature and content of the hearings for judicial appointments, and the recommendations made for the appointment of candidates. The JSC was repeatedly criticised for its failure to recommend exceptionally suitable candidates, specifically highly esteemed and experienced senior counsel with impeccable records as human rights lawyers for judicial appointments. For many years while the reviled white minority was governing the country in the period before 1994, some of these candidates had zealously participated in the litigation struggle against that government. Their commitment to the values of the Constitution was entirely beyond reproach.[18]

The JSC is also condemned for grilling these independent-minded human rights committed applicants during its interviews with irrelevant politically charged questions, such as the applicants' commitment to transformation (transformationism) instead of focussing on what is really pertinent, namely the candidates' professional competence and suitability for a judicial position in accordance with the criteria stated earlier. Moreover, some candidates, especially those viewed as strongly independent-minded (more often than not white males) were subjected to prolonged and gruelling examinations in contrast to the purportedly pliable and conformist candidates, whose interviews tended to be brief, cordial and rather affable.[19]

In April 2013 the simmering criticism against the JSC boiled over and resulted in a full-scale, acrimonious public clash when one of the commissioners, Izak Smuts (a senior counsel, white male and exponent of the liberal camp) released a document in which the JSC's application of its appointment criteria was challenged.[20] The document (the Smuts memorandum) caused battle lines to be drawn openly and the JSC's conduct to be debated in the media. Smuts eventually decided to resign from the JSC, stating that his understanding of the role and duties of the JSC and even of basic rights, such as human dignity and freedom of speech, was so different from that of the majority of the JSC that he could no longer play an effective role in it.[21]

---

18 Most notably among them is Geoff Budlender, a stalwart in the anti-apartheid struggle. Budlender appeared before the JSC on several occasions but it consistently declined to recommend him for appointment. The list also included Willem van der Linde, Torquil Paterson, Jeremy Gauntlett and, Judge Clive Plasket. The name of Supreme Court of Appeal, Judge Azhar Cachalia, can also be mentioned in this regard. He was not recommended for appointment to the bench of the Constitutional Court, allegedly for his independent-mindedness.

19 For criticism of alleged failure to appoint suitable candidates, see for example Rickard, 2012; Rickard, 2004:16; Rickard, 2002:16; and Calland, 2013.

20 Smuts, 2013b (copy obtained from the JSC on file with author).

21 Rabkin, 2013.

All the matters raised in the Smuts memorandum basically revolve around the criteria for judicial appointments. Smuts took issue with the JSC, firstly, for allowing its determination of the suitability of a candidate to be informed by considerations of "transformation" which, according to Smuts, is neither constitutionally nor legislatively mandated (the term does in fact not feature anywhere in the text of the Constitution); and secondly, for the undue value that the JSC attaches to representivity which, under section 174(2), is but a secondary factor to be borne in mind when judicial appointments are considered. In his view "transformation" introduces a purely subjective element to which any meaning that would suit the fancy of the person favouring that meaning could be attached.[22]

As to representivity, Smuts cautions against appointments being made simply to ensure racial and gender quota representation. He points out that the imperative of section 174(1) requires the JSC to establish that a candidate for judicial appointment is appropriately qualified and a fit and proper person. On the other hand, he suggests that section 174(2) is not a constitutional imperative which enjoins the JSC to promote the appointment of black and female candidates as a matter of course. According to Smuts, section 174(2) merely requires that "the need for the judiciary to reflect broadly the racial and gender composition of South Africa must be considered when judicial officers are appointed". In his view the JSC would fail in its duty if it considered only the need for such representivity without also considering other vital issues pertaining to a candidate's suitability and propriety. Issues such as the existing experience of judicial officers on the particular bench under consideration, the needs in terms of special expertise of that bench, the mean age of judges on that bench, and the likelihood of the retirement of experienced judges in the near future.

Smuts was of the view that the currency of transformation and representivity as factors to be considered by the JSC has established a perception that the JSC has in general taken a principled stance against the appointment of white male judges, unless exceptional circumstances should dictate otherwise. If the majority of the JSC is of the view that for the foreseeable future, white male candidates are to be considered for appointment only in exceptional circumstances – an approach that Smuts considers unlawful and unconstitutional, it must openly say so.

Smuts' memorandum led to discord within the JSC and unleashed an acrimonious public wrangle in which the Chief Justice, judges and retired judges representing either the transformationist or the liberal camps took hard and apparently irreconcilable stances against one another. Smuts was attacked by, among others, the member and the spokesperson of JSC, advocate Dumisa Ntsebeza SC, and the then

---

22   See, however, Chapter 5 where it is shown that the constitution has undergone tacit though profound changes in that transformationism has effectively replaced the values of section 1 and those that feature in chapter 2 of the Constitution.

deputy president of the Black Lawyers' Association (BLA),[23] Kathleen Dlepu. Chief Justice Mogoeng, as chair of the JSC,[24] took the opportunity to make plain his and the majority of the JSC's views on the criteria for judicial appointments. Mogoeng is clearly of the opinion that the two considerations mentioned in sections 174(1) and (2) respectively are equally important and that the need for racial (and gender) representivity in section 174(2) (the consideration of transformation) may in given circumstances override the fit and proper criterion under 174(1). To Chief Justice Mogoeng the appointment of judges was "not all about merit".[25] According to the Chief Justice, echoing the new value base of the Constitution as shown in Chapter 5: "(t)ransformation is just as important"; and the Constitution did not require that the "best of the best" be appointed as judges. He denied that the JSC was pursuing a political agenda and maintained that there were very few constitutional democracies that have a body (similar to the South African JSC) making recommendations for the appointment of judges.[26]

The then deputy president of the BLA, Kathleen Dlepu, supporting Ntsebeza, said that the real reason why Smuts resigned was that he did not support transformation. Dlepu added that the BLA did not see anything wrong with the JSC and that the body was only fulfilling its constitutional mandate, namely to bring about transformation, which was highest on the agenda.[27]

Smuts' views resonated with those expressed by retired Constitutional Court judge Johan Kriegler,[28] Professor Richard Calland,[29] retired judge of the Appellate Division (the predecessor of the SCA), J.J.F. Hefer,[30] and Advocate Paul Hoffman.[31]

Calland criticised the JSC for its uneven handling of candidates appearing before it and for the unjustifiable recommendations for judicial appointments after the hearings of April 2013. He referred to the severe cross-examination of Judge Plasket as a candidate for the SCA. Plasket, who is widely respected in the legal profession, was cross-examined by the JSC for almost an hour and a half on the question of the transformation of the judiciary instead of on his suitability as a

---

23　The Black Lawyers' Association (BLA) describes itself as a voluntary association of black lawyers in South Africa. Black Lawyers Association, 2013, *Home Page*. Available: http://bit.ly/2YP9ekX [Accessed, 3 September 2013].

24　S 178(1)(a) of *the Constitution*.

25　Du Plessis, 2013.

26　Mogoeng stated: "Go to America, go to Germany, go to Russia, go to the UK, it is a politician's work, so the question of political influence does not even feature." JSC spokesman Ntsebeza, a senior advocate and vocal champion of the transformationist camp waged a vicious media attack on Smuts in which the latter's *bona fides* were questioned. Sunday Independent, 2013. Available: http://bit.ly/2Tk4SkP

27　Sunday Independent, 2013. Available: http://bit.ly/2Tk4SkP

28　Kriegler, 2013:5.

29　Calland, 2013.

30　Hefer, 2013.

31　Hoffman, 2013.

judge of the SCA, where Plasket had served with distinction as an acting judge of appeal.[32] He was not recommended for appointment. Another candidate for the SCA was Judge Halima Sandulkar, an Indian woman. She also had acted on the bench of the SCA. When her interview started, she was informed that her colleagues on the SCA bench did not regard her as suitable for appointment – something that had also been conveyed to her by the president of the SCA, Judge Lex Mpati,[33] a few days prior to her interview. Nevertheless, the JSC, after what Calland[34] described as a bland and uneventful interview, recommended her appointment to the SCA bench. The third candidate, Judge Nigel Willis, was cordially received by the JSC and treated in a way that was exactly the opposite to the way in which Plasket had been treated. JSC member Ntsebeza, who had severely cross-examined Plasket about his interpretation of section 174(2) of the Constitution, for example, did not ask Willis a single question. After the fairly short and relaxed interview, Willis was recommended for appointment. He was viewed by Calland as much less suitable than Plasket for appointment on the SCA bench, and had, unlike Plasket, not acted in that capacity.[35] Calland's[36] explanation for the different approaches presents an opportunity to introduce the last charge which, for the purposes of this discussion, was levelled against the JSC. This charge in part accounts for the description of the struggle around judicial appointments as a clash of transformationists versus liberals. Calland[37] maintains that there is a dominant ANC caucus that forms the majority of the JSC which prefers pliant appointees – either black or white – and which is strongly dismissive of liberal-left white men. Calland[38] claims this was the reason why Willis found favour with the JSC and Plasket did not. Calland[39] states:

> These days the ANC wants obedient judges who 'know the limits of judicial power'. It is not being a white man that is a disqualifier for judicial appointment. It is being a white man with a commitment to progressive values of the Constitution and the protection of human rights that will destroy your prospects.

Kriegler's[40] criticism of the JSC's undue emphasis on transformation, and more notably of representivity when deciding on judicial appointments, goes back to 18 August 2009 when he stated:

---

32   See also Du Plessis, 2013.

33   Mpathi is a highly esteemed black judge who was appointed to the bench and eventually as president of the Supreme Court of Appeal after the beginning of the constitutional transition.

34   Calland, 2013.

35   A corroborating and detailed description of the way in which these three candidates for appointment on the SCA were treated by the JSC also appeared in Tolsi, 2013. Available: http://bit.ly/2YP5KTP Also see Du Plessis, 2013 which noted that Plaskett was "grilled" by commissioners Fatima Chohan-Khota, Dumisa Ntsebeza and Ngoako Rawls.

36   Calland, 2013.

37   Ibid.

38   Ibid.

39   Ibid.

40   Kriegler, 2009.

But, from where I look at the judiciary today, and the way I have been watching the Judicial Service Commission this ethnic/gender balance in section 174 of the Constitution has become the be-all and the end-all when the JSC makes its selections. And if it is not the be-all and end-all, at the very least it has been elevated to the overriding fundamental requirement.

Kriegler[41] emphasised experience, technical skills, the ability to quickly grasp and deal with facts and the ability to deal with a broad field of litigation as (some of) the core competencies without which the judicial office cannot properly be discharged. The obvious subtext of Kriegler's argument is that representivity should never trump these crucial criteria of suitability. A similar view was expressed by the late Marinus Wiechers,[42] an often quoted emeritus professor of constitutional law. Contrary to the Chief Justice's view, Wiechers maintained that the best of the best had to be appointed as judges and added that when the quality of the judiciary deteriorated, people would lose respect for the law, which would be fatal. A retired judge of the former Appellate Division, J.J.F. Hefer emphasises that the appointment of candidates as judges other than those who are most suitable, something which is implicitly acceptable to the Chief Justice, is "neutralising" the judiciary. Hefer points out that the appointment of "a second team of judges" instead of the most competent ones, is causing loss of trust in the judiciary. Moreover, it burdens the competent ones with an undue extra workload.[43]

64

Analysis and critique of the statist-individualist doctrine of judicial independence and impartiality

Why are the transformationists and the liberals holding their respective views and why are they at each other's throats? What are the underlying assumptions of their positions pertaining to the institutional position, relationship and role of the judiciary vis-à-vis the executive and the legislature, as well as about the place and role of the judiciary in the broader constitutional order in present-day South Africa and, for that matter, in any constitutional order that subscribes to the belief system of statist-individualist constitutionalism? How valid and realistic are these respective assumptions and positions?

The answer to these questions will reveal the reason for the conflicting views of the respective camps on the role of the JSC, because the mandate of the JSC is intimately related to the core constitutional mechanisms of statist-individualist constitutionalism, namely the separation of powers, the independence and impartiality of the judiciary, and judges' proper discharge of their judicial functions.

---

41 Kriegler, 2013:5.

42 Gerber, 2013.

43 Hefer, 2013.

Both the transformationist and liberal camps with equal solemnity avow the values of the Constitution, and by implication to statist-individualist constitutionalism, the principle of the separation of powers and the pivotal importance of the independence and impartiality of the courts. They obviously have no differences on the principle that the courts are subject only to the Constitution and the law, and that they (the courts) must apply the law impartially and without fear, favour or prejudice. Yet, when it comes to what all this means in practical terms and how the JSC should be discharging its responsibilities, their feelings and reasoning are at odds. On close analysis the camps quarrel about two closely related matters: judicial independence (and by implication the separation of powers and checks and balances) and judicial impartiality and its incidence of legal (more in particular judicial) reasoning.

What now follows is a discussion of what these concepts mean, and what part they may realistically be expected to play within any politico-constitutional order, including that of present-day South Africa. Judicial independence will serve as the starting point of the discussion, and will be followed by a discussion of judicial impartiality. The views of both parties will be critiqued, leading in the final analysis, in the last portion of this chapter, to a critique of the statist-individualist beliefs on separation of powers and judicial independence and impartiality.

Judicial independence is invariably closely intertwined with and in fact an incidence of the doctrine of the separation of powers and checks and balances within the framework of statist-individualist constitutionalism. For that reason an assessment of judicial independence will necessarily imply references to the latter. Hence the subheading *The judiciary - not so separate and independent from the (rest of) the dominant elite* (part 6.4.1). In its turn, the notion of judicial impartiality largely overlaps with and is premised on the basic assumptions of sound legal reasoning, which is aimed at the so-called objective application of the law, free from contamination by any non-legal considerations. For that reason the discussion is conducted under the subheading *The judiciary - not so impartial and not purely legally reasoning* (part 6.4.2).

The discussion in part 6.4.1 and part 6.4.2 provides the basis for the critique on the stance of the liberal camp. The discussion will show that the liberal view is unrealistic and rather mythical. It does not square with actual constitutional realities, even in jurisdictions where judicial independence and impartiality enjoy a high premium. However, from the critique in part 6.4.3 on the views of the transformationists it would be clear that their views are also seriously flawed and can most certainly not be subscribed to. The views of both camps are finally premised on the same unfounded belief of statist-individualist constitutionalism in the courts as truly independent, impartial and on that account, an effective structure in a system of checks and balances which is an integral part of the statist-individualist constitutionalism belief system.

6.4.1 The judiciary – not so separate and independent from the (rest of) the dominant elite

Trias politica, the prerequisite framework for judicial independence, entails a separation of the personnel and a separation of the functions of the legislature, the executive and the judiciary. The three branches must be staffed by different people[44] who may not perform any function in more than one branch.[45] Where this principle in many jurisdictions is often not strictly applied in relation to the executive and the legislature, most notably in Westminster-like constitutional dispensations, it is ordinarily applied with strict consistency in relation to the judiciary.[46]

The meaning and implications of the principle of judicial independence have in recent times featured prominently in South African case law.[47] Encompassing personal, that is, individual as well as institutional or structural independence, judicial independence comprises the independence of individual judges.[48] It covers issues such as their security of tenure and a basic degree of financial security, as well as institutional independence of the court in which the individual judge presides. It implies that the courts must stand in an independent relationship to the legislature and the executive (and the ruling party), and that judges must be in a position to discharge their functions free from interference of whatever nature and from whatever source.[49]

However – and this is crucial – judicial independence does not imply more than that. It would be unrealistic and incorrect as statist-individualist constitutionalism often tends to do, to portray the judiciary as (essentially) the supreme power centre in the constitutional system which the weak legislature and the executive

---

44 The Westminster-like system, such as the present South African constitutional order, provides an exception to this rule as the members of the executive are selected from among the senior politicians in parliament, and therefore occupy positions in both the legislature and the executive.

45 It is conceded that the application of the principle could be complicated because the distinction between these functions is sometimes not all that clear. See for example Marshall, 1971:99.

46 Members of the legislature and the executive shall not occupy positions on the bench or perform judicial functions, and judges shall never perform any function other than a judicial function. A good example demonstrating this in South African jurisprudence is the judgment in *Association of Personal Injury Lawyers v Heath* 2001(1) SA 883(CC).

47 In South African case law this was discussed in detail in *Van Rooyen v The State* 2002(5) SA 246(CC). See also *De Lange v Smuts* 1998(3) SA 785(CC).

48 Volumes have been written on this and the basic principles of judicial independence have also found a place in a number of international, regional and supranational instruments such as the *Commonwealth (Latimer House) Principles on the Three Branches of Government* (2003), and *Basic Principles on the Independence of the Judiciary* (1985) approved by General Assembly of the United Nations on 13 December 1985.

49 See in this regard the observations made by Larkins as well as the sources he refers to in Larkins CM 1996 *Judicial Independence and Democratization: A Theoretical and Conceptual Analysis* 610, and the citations. One should, however, be realistic about the ambit of this facet of independence, since it is common also in jurisdictions that serve as eminent examples of judicial independence for the executive to have the final say in judicial appointments. See in this regard the useful comparative survey in the Constitutional Court judgment in *Van Rooyen v The State* 2002(5) SA 246(CC) para 107. The same applies to South Africa, where the way in which the JSC is composed by virtue of S 178 of the Constitution secures a comfortable majority for the ruling party. See the references in Du Toit, 1999:259-265.

must obey. Judicial independence does not imply a judiciary in the nature of a threatening opposition to the legislature and the executive (and the ruling party).[50] The judiciary, even one with sweeping powers of review such as the present South African judiciary, cannot on its own be an effective mechanism for the protection of individual and communal interests. It falls well short of securing a balanced constitution as briefly outlined in Chapter 1. However, such a mythical image of a supposedly all-powerful judiciary is often presented. This image of the courts is an implied cornerstone of statist-individualist constitutionalism, a notion which enjoys particular support in the United States of America[51] and which is ingrained in South Africa's post-1994 constitutional discourse which, is explained in Chapter 3. This accounts for the aggrandising terms in which the judiciary, and in particular the Constitutional Court in South Africa, is sometimes described.[52] Judicial adjudication of provisions of the Bill of Rights relating to individual interests have been commended as the foolproof package for effectively safeguarding all interests, thus rendering redundant any additional constitutional mechanism for constraining the power of a legislature and executive controlled by an overwhelmingly dominant ruling party.[53] There is no justification for this soothing aggrandisement of the supposedly powerful judiciary. The judiciary is simply just too weak for that. In the final analysis it is appointed and financed by the legislature and the executive, devoid of its own resources and dependent upon the goodwill and cooperation of the legislature, executive, state administration and the public in general to give effect to its rulings. The frailty of the judiciary has also been eloquently acknowledged by eminent scholars of constitutionalism. In this regard Alexander Hamilton[54] in the 78th Federalist Paper contrasting the weak judiciary with the powerful legislature and the executive, stated:

> The judiciary, on the contrary, has no influence over either the sword or the purse; no direction either of the strength or of the wealth of the society; and can take no active resolution whatever. It may truly be said to have neither FORCE nor WILL, but merely judgment; and must ultimately depend upon the aid of the executive arm for the efficacy of its judgments.

Baron de Montesquieu at times rather frankly acknowledged the weakness of the judiciary. Of the three powers, De Montesquieu stated, "the judiciary is in some measure next to nothing."[55] Moreover, the dependence of the courts upon organs of state and on the executive and the legislature is graphically acknowledged by the South African Constitution itself in section 165(4), which enjoins organs of the

---

50   Devenish, 2003:87.

51   Peretti, 2002:122.

52   See for example the remarks by Calland, 2013:280.

53   Mechanisms such as minority rights and minority institutions, territorial and corporal federalism, internal (local) self-determination, etc.

54   Hamilton, Madison & Jay, 1961:465.

55   De Montesquieu, 2002. Mahommed, 1999:855.

state, through legislative and other measures, to assist and protect the courts to ensure their independence, impartiality, dignity, accessibility and effectiveness. That assistance is the crutch without which the judicial function collapses and court orders fade into unfulfilled judicial wishes. The judiciary is in fact nothing less than helpless when politicians refuse to comply with the Constitution or disregard the courts.[56] The very weakness, that is, the fundamental dependence instead of independence of the (South African) judiciary, was clearly demonstrated in the large-scale non-compliance with court orders owing to the laxity, incompetence or spite of the state administration[57] referred to in part 6.4.3.

The inference can hardly be resisted that in order to account for the judiciary's dependence, the courts must always, specifically when dealing with politically charged matters, heed the potential negative reaction of the ruling party in the legislature and the executive, and also of a disagreeing public. The courts must go about such situations very carefully and very tactfully to ensure the goodwill, protection and assistance of the legislature and the executive (and the ruling party). They must also guard against jeopardising their own institutional security and avoid antagonising the legislature and the executive. They cannot afford to forfeit their assistance and support, on which they are so vitally dependent, especially in a constitutional order such as that of South Africa, where the ruling party has since 1994 been overwhelmingly dominant, commanding around two-thirds of popular support.

Taking into account their dependence instead of their assumed independence, the courts must go about matters strategically rather than on a purely legally principled basis. That is why, in the United States of America, federal courts carefully heeding the response of the legislature and the executive often have to play a "separation of powers game" in order to secure the support of Congress.[58] Devoid of the active cooperation of the legislature and the executive, and at least an acquiescent public response, court judgments will have no or little impact and might assume the character of judicial yearnings instead of really binding judgments. Judgments that are regarded as having brought about considerable social change can bring about such change only if they fit into an already existing socio-political trend where they enjoy the support of the legislature and the executive and a sizable percentage of the public.[59]

The same largely holds true for the South African courts. Judgments of the Constitutional Court regarded as ground-breaking could gain effectiveness only with the support of the ruling party and a considerable segment of the public. The

---

56 Grimm, 2009:23.

57 This came to light prominently in *Nyathi v Member of the Executive Council for the Department of Health Gauteng* 2008(9) BCLR 865(CC) and in the academic debate on the solutions for the failure of organs of state to comply with court orders.

58 Peretti, 2002:112-113.

59 See in this regard the incisive analyses by Rosenberg, 2008.

Court's ruling against the death penalty[60] and its decisions in various cases in favour of the equal protection of gay and lesbian persons, including its ruling that it was constitutionally unacceptable for the South African law not to give recognition to same-sex marriages,[61] serve as examples. Moreover, South African courts, having repeatedly borne the brunt of executive wrath[62] in spite of their careful conduct towards the ruling party, have in recent years gained first-hand experience of their precarious position. (The reason for this wrath, resulting from an exceptionally wide definition of transformationism, is discussed in parts 6.4.3 and 6.4.5 below.) In consequence, their judgments in politically charged matters have to a considerable extent been tactically and pragmatically premised in order to maintain their own safety vis-à-vis the legislature and the executive and the ruling party. As will be shown in part 6.4.2 and in Chapter 7, in matters touching on the basic ideological convictions of the ruling party, the Constitutional Court has emphatically ruled in favour of government (and the ruling party).

Terri Peretti,[63] referring to political science research done in the United States of America on the behaviour of the federal courts, observes that the behaviour of the courts has been strategic rather than based upon legal principle. In politically charged matters the courts have carefully heeded the way in which the legislature and the executive would respond to their rulings. Their judgments have ensured the approval and enlist the support of the legislature and the executive as well as the ruling party without the risk of antagonising them.[64] The assumption that independent judges (always) use their freedom to decide impartially and exclusively according to the law, is contradicted by empirical evidence. Political attitudes exert a substantive influence on judicial decisions.[65]

Concerning South Africa, Theunis Roux[66] has conducted insightful studies on the behaviour of the Constitutional Court. Analysing a number of judgments of the Court on politically controversial issues, Roux[67] shows how what he calls pragmatism in

---

60   *S v Makwanyane* 1995(3) SA 391(CC).

61   *Minister of Home Affairs v Fourie* 2006(1) SA 524(CC). See also *National Coalition for Gay and Lesbian Equality v Minister of Justice* 2012(12) BCLR 1517(CC); *National Coalition for Gay and Lesbian Equality v Minister of Home Affairs* 2000(1) BCLR 39(CC); *Satchwell v President of the RSA* 2002(9) BCLR 986(CC).

62   Examples of these are: The annual "8 January statement" of the ANC which in January 2005 castigated the courts to such an extent that even Chief Justice Chaskalson had to intervene. See ANC, 2005. Available: http://bit.ly/2YB63IK The statement basically insisted that the courts should align themselves with the ruling party and the masses of the people. This episode is discussed in Malan, 2005, *The Unity of Powers and the Dependence of the Judiciary*:99-115. In 2011, in a decision, regarded by many as an onslaught against the courts, government decided to audit the judgments of the Constitutional Court and the Supreme Court of Appeal.

63   Peretti, 2002:111-113.

64   Ibid.

65   Ibid, p.111.

66   Roux, 2009a:106-138.

67   Ibid.

judicial conduct rather than legal principle determines the outcome of judicial decisions in politically controversial cases. The Court, through legally convincing reasoning, guards its own legitimacy in the eyes of the legislature and the executive and also takes care of two additional considerations: its own institutional security, and public support.[68] (In the next Chapter which deals with judicial interpretation, I will analyse how the Constitutional Court as an element of the dominant elite meticulously defends and promotes the transformationist ideology against any possible challenges.)

In view of the considerations explained by Roux, the institutional security of the court has been a particularly sensitive issue, arguably the most important of the three factors. This could be ascribed to the dominant position of the ruling ANC. One may assume that the judiciary, especially the Constitutional Court, had to find its way carefully within the context of overwhelming one-party domination. It could not afford to forfeit the trust and support of the ruling party. It could therefore risk handing down judgments that did not enjoy the support of the majority of the public but were in line with the thinking of the ruling party and would enlist the support of the party. By the same token, it also gave judgments that were favourable to government on matters that were ideologically important to the ruling party in spite of the fact that its legal reasoning was jurisprudentially questionable and caused the court to incur severe criticism within the legal community.[69] The risk in terms of the court's institutional security and thus of forfeiting the support of the ANC by ruling against government in these scenarios was markedly higher than the risk of attracting firm, legally premised (theoretical) criticism from among the ranks of a number of (academic) lawyers and from sectors of the media and the opposition parties. The risk from these latter less powerful and less influential sources was much smaller. Roux also demonstrates how the Constitutional Court used political rhetoric in its judgments as a device for aligning itself with the ruling party, thus further shoring up its own institutional security. The gist of Roux's analysis is that the Constitutional Court acted strategically, that is, pragmatically, rather than in a principled manner, both in cases where it used its reasoning skills to avoid confrontation with the ruling party (in the legislature and the executive) and in more routine (politically non-controversial) cases where, in Roux's words, it has developed context-sensitive standards.

The bottom line is that the courts cannot run the risk of arousing the antagonism of the legislature and the executive and the ruling party by taking decisions based solely on the "purity" of impeccable legal reasoning, particularly not when the ruling party is so overwhelmingly potent.

---

68 See in general the instructive discussion by Roux, 2009:106-138. See also the more detailed discussion in Roux's recently published book Roux, 2013.

69 *New National Party of South Africa v Government of the Republic of South Africa* 1999(3) SA 191(CC); *United Democratic Movement v President of the Republic of South Africa* 2003(1) SA 495(CC).

It follows that when the ruling party is particularly strong it would be unrealistic to assume that court decisions are always purely and solely determined by the applicable "objective" law. Although the doctrine of judicial independence in its purest form dictates that courts should be insulated from politics or any other external interference or pressure, the dynamics of the political situation in which courts are required to function, demonstrates that this is impossible. Courts will be alive to the risks of their political situation, to the political wishes and preferences of the legislature, and the executive and the ruling party, and their judgments must respond to these. If they fail to do so and deliver judgments that meet with the outright displeasure of an overwhelmingly strong ruling party and with the accompanying executive rejection or failure to abide, the court is powerless to do anything about it. The law then spoken by the court remains unfulfilled wishes and the effectiveness of the courts, for which the judiciary depends on the executive, falls by the wayside. For a functioning judiciary to be secured within the politico-constitutional situation, courts are left with no option but to compromise on their doctrinal political insularity, that is, on their independence. If the judiciary loses legitimacy with the legislature and the executive and ceases to be a cog in the state machine working in harmony with the other cogs,[70] it runs the risk of losing the support of the legislature and the executive and its own effectiveness.

Viewed against this background there is considerable sound substance in the assertion of the political scientist Francis Fukuyama[71] that in the final analysis the separation of powers between the executive and the judiciary is only metaphorical and the power of the judicial branch as custodians of the law relies only on the legitimacy that it can confer on the rulers and on the popular support it receives as the protector of a broad social consensus. Fukuyama's observation echoes the assertion of Alexander Bickel[72] that the court usually relies on its own mystique and on the skilled exertion of its educational faculty. However, Bickel[73] adds that in an enforcement crisis of any proportions, the judiciary is wholly dependent on the executive.[74] As Owen Fiss[75] reminds us, judges "speak the law" and can only hope that there will be voluntary compliance with what was "ordered". With their power limited to the speaking of the law only and the moral authority they would hope to command, it should be clear that the position of the judiciary is inherently weak and precarious. It is thus rather unrealistic, and in view of its dependence, illogical to think of the judiciary as a powerful institution "competing" on an equal footing with the other two branches and with socio-political forces, such as a powerful political party, when their very ability to "compete" largely depends upon the assistance, protection and support of the "competitors".

---

70   In step with the metaphor used my Moerane, 2003:711.

71   Fukuyama, 2011:282.

72   Bickel, 1962:252.

73   Ibid.

74   Ibid.

75   Fiss, 1993:64.

6.4.2 The judiciary – not so impartial and not purely legally reasoning

Adjudication and impartiality are inextricably linked. Adjudication always requires that a dispute between two or more vying parties must be decided by a neutral third party (the adjudicator) to apply legal norms to a set of facts. The adjudicator is required, in the words of Baron de Montesquieu,[76] to demonstrate a: "certain coolness, an indifference, in some measure, to all manner of affairs." He/she must command the trust of the parties and must have the knowledge, acumen and judgment[77] to adjudicate the dispute in a proper manner without delay, and to make a ruling binding on the parties. The adjudicator must have no stake in the outcome of the case. That the adjudicator must not be the judge in his/her own case – *nemo iudex in sua causa* – lies at the very core of the idea of natural justice. He/she must not even be perceived to take sides or to have a stake in the outcome of the case. Once a reasonable apprehension arises that the adjudicator could be biased, he/she should recuse himself/herself from the matter and be replaced by another.[78] Party detachment remains as crucial when government – a state organ – is one of the parties to a dispute. The adjudicator must not be biased in favour of government (and obviously also not be biased in favour of the adversary).[79]

Genuine adjudication, which attests to the impartiality and party detachment of the adjudicator, will eventually be gauged by the reasons advanced in support of the ruling. The findings, argumentation and conclusions of the courts must be strictly law-based.[80] The adjudicator, properly discharging his/her responsibilities, will decide a case exclusively on the law that applies to the facts of the case.

This brief account of impartial judicial reasoning will show why the notion of legal reasoning should be considered as it is being done here, namely as a logical incidence of judicial impartiality. With the law being the sole determinant of legal reasoning and outcomes, the identity, social, economic and political standing and the power relations of the parties whose dispute is to be decided will be entirely irrelevant, and therefore of no moment to the legal reasoning engaged in by court, and to the conclusions it reaches.

---

76 De Montesquieu, 2002:80.

77 In the context of Classical Greek notions it is submitted that adjudication requires three aspects of legal competence that a lawyer, more particularly a judge, must possess in order to be capable of discharging the responsibility of adjudication. Firstly, the judge must have knowledge (*episteme*) of the applicable legal rules and principles; secondly, skills (*techne*), i.e. he/she *must be conversant with the techniques of adjudication, including truth-seeking through various techniques of examination*, etc. and lastly judgment, (*phronesis*) i.e. the ability to pass fair judgment with patience, moderation and wisdom.

78 There is a rich jurisprudence on this. In South Africa, following English precedents, it is not required for recusal that there must be a real likelihood of bias; a reasonable suspicion will suffice. See for example *BTR Industries South Africa (Pty) Ltd v Metal and Allied Workers Union* 1992(3) SA 673(A).

79 On the notions of the neutrality and party detachment see for example Larkins, 1996:608 and Fiss, 1993:62.

80 Grimm, 2009:26 refers to this as internal independence, requiring the judge to decide on the basis of the applicable positive law and not anything else. As Grimm indicated, his is also a matter of professional ethics.

Pure legal reasoning, uncontaminated by considerations of a non-legal nature, have been asserted and defended by various scholars, some of the most well-known ones being Herbert Wechsler,[81] Robert Bork[82] and Ronald Dworkin.[83] The gist of their views will now be dealt with briefly.

In Wechsler's[84] view all issues, including challenges to legislation duly passed by the legislature, can be decided by courts without entering the political arena. This is done by applying neutral legal principles. Courts are required only to be faithful upholders of the rule of law and to be consistent in their faithfulness to the relevant text of *the Constitution* (and other relevant legal rules and principles). The way in which the best judgment can be ensured is through "reason called law". Elaborating on this reasoning in a manner that is reminiscent of Dworkin's later argumentation on the integrity of law, Wechsler refers to the (general) postulates behind the wording of the Constitution and of the weight of history in the proper interpretation of the constitutional text. Principled decisions are, according to Wechsler, reached through general, neutral, and impersonal legal reasoning, while discounting any non-legal consideration. A decision not arrived at through such reasoning would be a wrong decision.[85]

Robert Bork's[86] argumentation builds on that of Wechsler. A principled judgment based on the applicable law is justifiable because it is based on law and nothing else. Courts deliver law-based judgments, including judgments against the decisions of an elected government. Judges are not undemocratic wielders of power nullifying the wishes of the popularly composed legislature. Judgments are not based on the will of the judges but on their principled reasoning premised on the Constitution and the law.

Ronald Dworkin is arguably the most ardent recent exponent of and firm believer in pure and legally reasoned judicial decision-making. Dworkin's work is also relevant in South Africa and was often quoted during and immediately after South Africa's constitutional transition in the 1990s.

In Dworkin's[87] view, law is a complete, loophole-free system which comprehensively covers all situations so that gaps in the law which may require the exercise of judicial discretion will never arise. Law consists in the first place of a system of rules to be applied by courts when they adjudicate. Where the rules are inadequate – where

---

81   Wechsler, 1959:1-35.

82   Bork, 1971:1-35.

83   Dworkin propounds his views in this regard – on the integrity of law – in many publications, possibly the most relevantly one being in Dworkin, 1977.

84   Wechsler, 1959:16.

85   Ibid. p.17, 19-20.

86   Bork, 1971:1-35.

87   Dworkin, 1977 and Dworkin, 1989.

there is no ready-made rule that regulates the situation on which a decision is required – the court must resort to the application of general principles on which the legal order is based. The need to exercise a discretion, which would be an unjustifiable usurpation of (law-making) power by the judiciary, would never occur.

These and similar accounts of judicial decision-making should not strike one as quaint.[88] They are widely accepted and are for example echoed in the oath taken by judicial officers in South Africa.[89] The Constitution and the law are the sole determining factors in judicial decision-making and the identities, background or power, etc. of the parties involved in a matter will not make any difference. The bottom line is that judges will base their decisions on the applicable law and the relevant facts and not on any predilection, loyalty or bias in favour of one of the parties.[90]

The fact that government is a party to a dispute with political consequences should obviously not make any difference to the way in which the matter is approached. Principled legal reasoning exclusively based on the Constitution and the law will once again follow its (legally based) course.[91]

The courts will in this case have to maintain detachment from government as one of the parties in exactly the same way as they would be detached from the parties in any other case. Impartiality and "neutral reasoning" will in this case require an additional element described by Owen Fiss[92] as *political insularity*. In order to obtain this quality, judges must continue to decide issues on the basis of the relevant facts and the applicable legal principles. This element must not be used as a tool to further the aims of politically powerful organs of state or of a ruling party.[93] It must give expression to the very heart of the judicial function, namely that courts must decide what is just. They must not exercise the choice of the best public policy or the best course of action preferred by the majority of the public. Courts must not adjudicate the (conflicting) rights of the parties on grounds of the feasibility of public policy.[94]

---

88 The existence and the practical value of these principles are not to be denied. However, they can most definitely not fulfil the very far-reaching function that Dworkin claims they can. H.L.A. Hart can be agreed with in his statement that Dworkin's inexorable faith in the comprehensive value of legal principles underpinning the constitutional order to such an extent that no field is not legally regulated makes of Dworkin *the most noble dreamer of them all*. See Hart, 1983:137.

89 In terms of which they undertake to administer justice to all persons alike without fear, favour or prejudice, in accordance with the Constitution and the law. S 6 of Schedule 2 to *the Constitution*.

90 Larkins, 1996:609.

91 The doctrine has its own faith-strengthening mantra captured in phrases such as "the law taking its course," "entrenched rights," "enshrined rights" and many other phrases. The common factor is that these phrases inculcate and inspire faith in the strength and objectivity of the law, the Constitution and the courts to such an extent that what on close analysis is nothing more than normative or rather idealist doctrine is portrayed as undeniable facts of social and political life.

92 Fiss, 1993:59-60. See also Larkins, 1996:609.

93 Fiss, 1993:59-60. See also Larkins, 1996:609.

94 Dworkins work, for example Dworkin, 1977:22; 82; 218; 223; 243; 244; 381; 410 and Dworkin, 1989 abound of arguments in support of this proposition. See also Fiss, 1993:59-60.

This is as far as a "pure," objective doctrine of judicial impartiality and legal reasoning goes. The question, however, is how realistic these notions of pure legal reasoning, impartiality, party detachment and political insularity are. Do these notions really offer a reliable account of what is happening when courts adjudicate, more specifically when the fundamental ideological commitments of the dominant elite come into play? To what extent can courts indeed be expected to and in fact be capable of maintaining full impartiality, specifically in cases involving important political and ideological questions? Are courts really as politically insular? Are courts' reasoning in all cases premised purely and exclusively on the law (on which micro theory places so much emphasis) or are extra-legal considerations such as the political role of the judiciary within the dominant elite rather than legal principle decisive? Finally, how true and valid is statist-individualist constitutionalism's sixth belief as set out in Chapter 2.4 and the concomitant second mechanism of statist-individualist constitutionalism, namely in the potency of the threefold separation of powers and the independence and impartiality of the judiciary? How reliable is the judiciary in exercising power checks and balances and finally as a guarantor of justice on a systemic scale (for an entire constitutional order)?

Contrary to the statist-individualist constitutionalism's claims on judicial independence and impartiality, the singular response to all of these questions, is that the judiciary's impartiality can never be allowed to extend, and does in fact never extend beyond the basic ideological assumptions and ideals of the dominant elite.

This is the reality of the *actual unity of the three (separate) powers* rather than their doctrine-proclaimed separation. The three powers are separated in terms of institutions, personnel and functions, but usually firmly unified in one single power elite: integral segments of one and the same dominant political leadership, informed by the same ideological assumptions, committed to achieving the same goals, yet organised on the basis of a division of labour performed in separate branches. The courts ordinarily play their part as one of the branches within the overarching dominant elite. They do so in close conformity with the rest of the elite and they are incapable of doing anything outside the consensus which is prevalent within that political elite.[95] The analysis of political scientist Robert Dahl of the position of the United States of America Supreme Court is particularly instructive also for South Africa (and certainly for many other constitutional dispensations that assign an important role to an independent judiciary). Dahl observes:

> Except for short-lived transitional periods when the old alliance is disintegrating and the new one is struggling to take control of political institutions, the Supreme Court is inevitably a part of the dominant national alliance. As an element of the political leadership of the dominant alliance, the court of course supports the major policies of the alliance.[96]

---

95   See in this regard the illuminating discussion by Dyzenhaus, 1982:380 et seq., especially 388-389.

96   Dahl, 1957:293.

As an essential part of the dominant political leadership the courts will obviously not disrupt the dominant position of that political leadership. Neither is it capable of doing so, as that would defeat the court's own legitimacy within the dominant elite,[97] apart from the fact that it lacks (as the discussion in the previous section shows) the institutional capacity to do so. The judgments of the courts on politically sensitive issues and more specifically on ideological matters can hardly go beyond or challenge the consensus that prevails within the dominant elite. That is not to say that the views of the courts will always be precisely the same as that of the executive and the legislature, because hermeneutical experience shows that the consensus within the dominant elite will ordinarily offer a limited number of (interpretive) options to the courts. Judgments are therefore the product of a selection from options available within the thinking of the dominant elite. It is against this backdrop that Dahl observes:

> It follows that within the somewhat narrow limits set by the basic policy goals of the dominant alliance, the Court can make national policy. Its discretion, then, is not unlike that of a powerful committee chairman in Congress who cannot, generally speaking, nullify the basic policies substantially agreed on by the rest of the dominant leadership, but who can, within these limits often determine important questions of timing, effectiveness and subordinate policy.[98]

The court may adjudicate on hiccups, differences and aberrations *within* the broad assumptions of the dominant elite. On the one hand – because of its weakness – it will be incapable, and on the other hand – because it is imbedded in a common power elite – it will usually be unwilling to pass judgments that would disrupt the basic ideology or derail the core goals of the dominant elite. It can make corrections within the framework of the ideological assumptions and policy goals of the dominant elite, but it cannot and will not disrupt or frustrate the framework as such. This point will be demonstrated in Chapter 7 from the vantage point of interpretive theory and the interpretive choices made by the courts as reflected in ideologically sensitive issues.

As a product of the constitutional order that took effect in 1994,[99] the Constitutional Court is an integral part of the dominant political elite. Right from the outset the bench of the Constitutional Court and in due course the (majority of) incumbents of all South African courts broadly shared with the legislature, the executive and the ruling party the same ideological assumptions. The Constitutional Court was established because the power elite, under the leadership of the ANC, could not

---

97 Ibid.

98 Ibid, p.294.

99 During the constitutional negotiations in the beginning of the 1990s the ANC strongly favoured a newly created constitutional court and was specifically against the idea of simply making it the existing courts responsible for constitutional matters or for allowing a constitutional court to be a section of the then Appellate Division. See ANC 1992 *Ready to Govern: ANC Policy Guidelines for a Democratic South Africa.* Available: http://bit.ly/2Z3a9yh [Accessed, 23 August 2013].

tolerate an apex court, responsible for adjudicating politically and ideologically controversial (constitutional) matters, being staffed with incumbents who formed part of the pre-1994 political leadership dominated by the erstwhile white power elite under the erstwhile National Party.[100]

The new ANC-centred power elite set out to transform the judiciary (alongside the rest of the South African public order). There is largely consensus among the ANC and academic commentators about what transformation of the judiciary entails. It corresponds with the explanation of the ideology of transformationism advanced in Chapter 5. On 17 February 2003 Mr J.H. de Lange,[101] at the time an articulate and influential ANC MP, the then Chairperson of the Justice Portfolio Committee and later deputy minister of justice (also a former member of the JSC), stated in the National Assembly that the transformation of the judiciary comprised two components: firstly, the realisation of the objective of the equitable representation of blacks and women, described as *diversity, personnel or symbolism transformation*, and, secondly, transformation relating to the ideological approach adopted by judges and magistrates when implementing the letter and spirit of our Constitution – referred to by De Lange as *intellectual content or substantive transformation*. The litmus test, according to De Lange,[102] for intellectual transformation:

> ... would be how individual judges and magistrates will pursue their legitimate and genuine constitutional obligations, without wittingly or unwittingly going out of their way to frustrate or undermine the legitimate and genuine choices and aspirations of the majority of South Africans to create a fully functioning democracy and a socio-economic and ideologically transformed country.[103]

This transformationism drive would ensure that eventually the entire judiciary, comprising all courts, would form and be perceived to form an integral ingredient of the same coherent political leadership, sharing with the ruling party in the legislature and the executive the same ideological convictions. It is an integral part of what in Chapter 5.6 has been shown to be the new constitutional value of representivity forming part of the ideology of transformationism.

---

100 Ss 98 and 101 of the *Interim Constitution* went so far as to completely exclude the Appellate Division (the predecessor of the SCA), which was dominated by judges appointed by the previous power elite under the National Party, from jurisdiction on constitutional matters.

101 Hansard (2003-02-17) 128-124.

102 Hansard (2003-02-17) 128-124.

103 Moerane, (Moerane, 2003:711) a prominent senior advocate and former member of the JSC, added factors such as the enhancement of accessibility to justice and the reorganisation of the courts to the concept of transformation. Nevertheless, although phrased in more subtle terms, he shared the views of De Lange that in its composition the judiciary should eventually reflect South African society, particularly in regard to race (and gender), and that measures should be taken to ensure that the holders of judicial office are persons who espouse and promote the values enshrined as fundamental rights in *the Constitution*.

As Dahl indicated, the judiciary is, except for brief transitional periods, an integral part of the dominant political leadership. In making this observation Dahl[104] echoed what De Montesquieu had said two centuries before. Alexander Bickel also underscored the intimate relationship between the three branches. Referring to United States of America, Chief Justice W.H. Taft (Chief Justice from 1921-1930), Bickel then highlighted the intimacy of the three branches whose functions can often not be rigidly compartmentalised:

> The Court often provokes consideration of the most intricate issues of principle by the other branches, engaging them in dialogues and 'responsive readings'; and there are times also when the conversation starts at the other end and is perhaps less polite. Our government consists of discrete institutions, but the effectiveness of the whole depends on their involvement with one another, on their intimacy, even if it is often the sweaty intimacy of creatures locked in combat.[105]

The pattern of appointment of federal judges in the United States of America confirms this intimacy. Political considerations are the crucial factor in judicial appointments and appointees ordinarily give judgments that are congenial to the views of the administration that made these appointments. Social research on the selection and appointment of federal judges shows that politics dominates the selection of judges despite the myth that judges should be selected strictly on the basis of merit[106] and that political and ideological compatibility outweighs other considerations, even merit.[107] Having regard to the social research done in the United States of America, Peretti therefore states:

> The evidence is overwhelming that politics pervades the judicial selection process. Exhorting presidents and senators to ignore political factors and instead select judges based on their objective qualifications and capacity for independence thus defies the historical pattern. More importantly, it defies logic. Politicians interested in re-election and policy success cannot reasonably be expected to ignore such splendid opportunities to please their constituents, help their party and realise their policy goals. Until the selection process is radically altered, the call for merit and independence as selection criteria is futile; absent fundamental change, it is about as effective as urging the sun not to shine.[108]

As to the South African context, Moerane[109] also highlights the intimacy, and even more so the unity, of the relationship and refers to the judiciary as a cog in the state machine working in harmony with the other cogs.[110]

---

104 Dahl, 1957:293-294.

105 Bickel, 1962:261.

106 Peretti, 2002:105, quoting O'Brien, 1988:35.

107 Peretti, 2002:105, referring to the research of, amongst others, Abraham, 1999:2-3.

108 Peretti, 2002:109.

109 Moerane, 2003:711.

110 Ibid.

Sandra Liebenberg (referred to again in Chapter 7 in the context of transformative interpretation), also called for an euphemistically so-called dialogic conception of adjudication[111] in which there is no room for strict separation of powers and in which the *partiality* of the judiciary, which closely co-operate with the legislature and the executive is recognised and actively propagated.

The bottom line therefore is that judicial impartiality is relative to and conditioned by the ideological commitments of the dominant elite.[112] Drawing upon the detailed social science research on judgments (voting patterns) of judges of the federal courts in the United States of America and upon insightful analyses of the jurisprudence of the South African Constitutional Court, judicial impartiality proves to be an ideal which is rather distanced from the manner in which judicial decisions are actually arrived at, specifically in politically charged cases that involve fundamental ideological convictions of the dominant elite. Hence, judicial reasoning in politically charged matters is political in nature in that considerations of politics play a critical role in the outcome of judgments.

In present-day South Africa, it is rather common to require, in JSC parlance, candidates for judicial appointments to be "transformation candidates," or to require them to be "transformed" candidates,[113] thereby indicating that they must fully subscribe to the values of the Constitution.[114] However, to insist that candidates must subscribe to the values of the Constitution does not say much because these values do not have a single neutral and objective meaning. They are interpreted values, more in particular values interpreted by the dominant interpretive community composed of the dominant elite. (Moreover, as indicated in Chapter 5, the values also change.) In more concrete and realistic terms, candidates are required to subscribe to these values as interpreted by the dominant elite, that is, to the ideology of transformationism. The resultant interpretation will obviously not be an impartial one and will not be at variance with the one subscribed to by the dominant elite. This means that the courts can be impartial only *within* the ideological assumptions of transformationism. Courts therefore do not adjudicate on the ideological preferences of the dominant elite and other competing ideological trends. It follows that impartiality is emphatically not full-scale and encompassing irrespective of whatever possible persuasions and beliefs may be relevant. On the contrary, the court, as an integral part of the dominant elite, is continually and intensely, albeit subtly, engaging with the other components of the dominant elite (in the legislature and the executive, the ruling party and relevant portions of civil society) as well as with the public, and finds its own ever-changing equilibrium and

---

111 Liebenberg, 2010:66-71.

112 Fiss, 1993:60 speaks here of the regime-relativity of judicial independence. It is submitted that notionally it would be more correct to speak of the regime-relativity of judicial impartiality.

113 Moerane, 2003:713.

114 These values are referred to in para 1.

its politically fluctuating "impartiality" within the boundaries of the acceptable (ideological) convictions set by the dominant elite. The judiciary's "impartiality" – a relative impartiality – is always conditioned by this engagement. Bickel[115] puts it as follows with regard to the Supreme Court of the United States of America:

> The court placed itself in a position to engage in a continual colloquy with the political institutions, leaving it to them to tell the Court what expedients of accommodation and compromise they deemed necessary.

Long ago Martin Shapiro,[116] calling for what he referred to as a "political jurisprudence," urged his readers to be alive to the political partiality of the impartial judiciary. Shapiro[117] rejected the trite doctrine that legal reasoning was conducted solely on the basis of neutral legal principles which would ensure the sustainability of a pure form of judicial impartiality. Shapiro[118] argued that:

> (t)he argument that there are neutral principles in-dwelling in the law itself and discoverable by a specifically judicial or lawyer-like mode of thought, is basically an attempt to return jurisprudence to the position of splendid isolation that it enjoyed in the heyday of analytical jurisprudence.

In politically sensitive matters, specifically in cases where the basic ideological convictions of the dominant elite are featuring, courts will therefore assume the character of political actors[119] within the broader power base of the elite.

The insights into the regime-relativity and ideological relativity of judicial impartiality underscore the political role of the judiciary, which plays its part, as pointed out in the previous section, in close conformity with the rest of the power elite of which it forms an integral part.

In the absence of unprofessional conduct on the part of a judge (and the possibility of such conduct is slim) a judge will not easily disclose in a judgment or outside court that a judicial decision was motivated by political considerations such as the desire or need to protect the institutional security of the courts; or a commitment to defend or promote a policy that government regards as important; or to show that the court shares the ideological preferences of the legislature and the executive and the ruling party; and obviously also not that they are in fact committed to the same ideological convictions and objectives. Judges, being senior members of the legal profession and well-versed in the rhetorical and doctrinal strategies of the legal discourse, can avail themselves of many techniques to express themselves convincingly in legal terms, and to sustain the credible impression that their judicial decisions were genuinely and objectively reached and based on the applicable law

---

115 Bickel, 1962:252.

116 Shapiro, 1963-1964:296.

117 Ibid.

118 Ibid, p.302.

119 Ibid, p.296.

and nothing else.[120] Thus viewed, articulated legal reasoning is in itself a redoubtable political strategy for its ability to hide any extra-legal political considerations and motivations that might have been harboured (and promoted) when a politically sensitive decision was made, more specifically when in judicial decisions, courts endorsed, defended and promoted the ideological convictions and objectives of the dominant elite of which they are an integral part. Trapped in their unrelenting belief in (close to) absolute judicial independence and impartiality in terms of the doctrine of statist-individualist constitutionalism, the liberals in the South African controversy can merely respond with indignation when these unfounded beliefs of statist constitutionalism are upset.

6.4.3   The transformationists in the same statist doctrinal trap

In the discussion above, it was shown that the trust that the doctrine of statist-individualist constitutionalism vests in the separation of powers, in particular with regard to judicial independence and judicial impartiality, is unfounded. Separation of powers is not as potent a notion and strategy of constitutionalism as statist-individualist constitutionalism in general and the South African liberal camp (previously discussed) believe it to be. However, the transformationists also have it wrong. Strikingly and quite ironically as the discussion below shows, they have it wrong precisely because they have essentially bought into the liberals' subscription to the beliefs of the doctrine of statist-individualist constitutionalism.

Two sets of judgments will now be considered in order to understand the transformationists' irritation with the way in which the South African courts have dealt with the matters to be discussed. These cases represent notable examples of the transformationists' views on the role of the courts, on judicial independence and impartiality, and on the JSC's conduct with regard the evaluation of aspirant judges. In Chapter 7 the transformationist view of the role of the judiciary is enunciated, from a hermeneutical vantage point, against the backdrop of the encompassing backdrop of the ideology of transformationism.

The first set of judgments discussed here is a collection of high-profile judgments of the Constitutional Court and the SCA that were decided against leading figures of the ANC and in some cases also against the JSC itself. The second set of judgments relates to the competency or otherwise of the state administration under the ANC government. None of these judgments, however, dealt with the dominant elite's ideology of transformationism.

---

120   See in this regard, among others, Kennedy, 1997:1-2, who observed that judges work in an environment "saturated by ideology". However, says Kennedy, "...they always aim to generate a particular rhetorical effect namely that the decisions were necessitated solely by legal considerations without any regard to ideology."

The high-profile judgments

Five high-profile judgments involving ANC leadership figures and the JSC are particularly pertinent. They are *Glenister v President of the RSA*,[121] *Democratic Alliance v President of the RSA*,[122] *Democratic Alliance v Acting National Director of Public Prosecutions*,[123] *Freedom Under Law v Acting Chairperson of the Judicial Service Commission*[124] and *Judicial Service Commission v Cape Bar Council*.[125]

The first three cases, that of *Glenister v President of the RSA*, *Democratic Alliance v President of the RSA* and *Democratic Alliance v Acting National Director of Public Prosecutions* are all acts from the same drama in which, on closer analysis, the interests of former president Jacob Zuma were at stake. All three somehow related to criminal investigations and decisions on the institution of prosecutions.

In June 2005 former president Thabo Mbeki (Mr Zuma's predecessor) relieved Zuma, at that stage the deputy president of South Africa, from his position in the face of criminal charges against him and a statement by the national director of public prosecutions that there was a *prima facie* case against Zuma for various charges of white-collar crime. The investigation of these charges was conducted in the midst of a mounting power struggle at the time in the ruling party between Zuma and Mbeki. At the national conference of the ANC in December 2007, Zuma trumped Mbeki in the election for the leadership of the ANC and in September 2008 Mbeki was recalled by the ANC as president of the country. The path was then clear for Zuma to take over the presidency. However, the obstacle posed by the spectre of criminal prosecutions could defeat that aim.

Two factors would be decisive. The first was the investigation of Zuma by the Scorpions (the common name for the erstwhile Directorate of Special Operations, a crime-fighting unit with the specialised mandate to combat white-collar crime). Allegations were rife that that unit was politically enlisted for using criminal prosecution as a political stratagem against Zuma. The second factor related to the question of whether or not the national director of public prosecutions would prosecute Zuma. The incumbent at that stage and the head of the Scorpions (respectively Bulelani Ngcuka and Leonard McCarthy) were intimately involved in the investigation against Zuma. However, both were (alleged to be) prime Mbeki protégés balefully conniving against Zuma.[126] Eventually, soon after Zuma became the leader of the ANC, both vacated their positions. The position of national director of

---

121 *Glenister v President of the RSA* 2011(3) SA 347(CC).

122 *Democratic Alliance v President of the RSA* 2012(12) BCLR 1297(CC).

123 *Democratic Alliance v Acting National Director of Public Prosecutions* 2012(6) BCLR 613(SCA) followed by *Zuma v DA* (836/2013) 2014 ZASCA 101 (28 August 2014) in which the SCA repeated its initial order.

124 *Freedom under Law v Acting Chairperson of the Judicial Service Commission* 2011(3) SA 549(SCA).

125 *Judicial Service Commission v Cape Bar Council* 2012(11) BCLR 1239(SCA).

126 There was also judicial support for this allegation in *Zuma v National Director of Public Prosecutions* 2009(1) BCLR 62(N).

public prosecutions was temporarily filled by Mokotedi Mpshe. In April 2009 Mpshe, in a highly controversial decision, dropped the charges against Zuma, arguing that the criminal investigation against Zuma had been politically contaminated beyond redemption.[127] Mpshe based his decision on evidence of the Scorpions' alleged machinations against Zuma. The merits of Mpshe's decision could not be judged as Mpshe chose not to make the evidence available to the public. A new national director of public prosecutions, Menzi Simelane, was eventually appointed whilst the Scorpions was disbanded and replaced by a new agency, commonly known as the Hawks. Against this background, the three judgments will now be reflected on.[128]

Glenister

Chapter 6A of the South African Police Service Act,[129] which created the Directorate of Priority Crime Investigation (Hawks), was the subject matter of the Glenister judgment. In a split judgment, then Deputy Chief Justice Moseneke, speaking for a small majority of five against four and referring to relevant international law binding upon South Africa, ruled that Chapter 6A had failed to secure for the Hawks the required measure of independence from executive control, resulting in its lacking the necessary capability to avoid the infringement of constitutional-rights by the perpetrators of white-collar crime.[130]

The judgment was met with criticism from the ranks of government and from the transformationists in general. It was argued that the majority had disregarded the doctrine of the separation of powers and infringed upon the domain of the legislature and the executive. It was further claimed that the majority judgment was premised on untenable reasoning and among other things, cherry-picking from international treaties to suit the conclusion it wanted to motivate. The judgment was further criticised for undermining the rule of law and the court's own legitimacy. In the opinion of Ziyad Motala, one of the most vocal transformationists, the judgment represented a low-water mark in South Africa's constitutional jurisprudence.[131]

Democratic Alliance v President of the RSA

In the judgment of *Democratic Alliance v President of the RSA* the Constitutional Court set aside the appointment of Simelane as national director of public prosecution, an appointment alluded to earlier. Simelane had been appointed despite the Ginwala

---

127   Mpshe, 2009. Available: http://bit.ly/2ZOyipc

128   At the time of finalising this manuscript and after many political battles Zuma is about to stand trial for at least some of these charges.

129   South African Police Service Act 68 of 1995.

130   The minority judgment delivered by Chief Justice Ngcobo was satisfied that in terms of the legislation which provided for its establishment, the Hawks was sufficiently independent from the executive and the legislation could therefore not be ruled unconstitutional.

131   See for example Motala, 2011, *Divination Through a Strange Lens.* Available: http://bit.ly/2YJYAkv [Accessed, 4 April 2011]. Motala is professor of law at Howard Law School in the United States of America and extraordinary professor of law at the University of the Cape.

Commission of Inquiry's finding that he had been dishonest and had lacked integrity in the execution of his duties in his previous capacity as director-general of the Department of Justice.[132] He was appointed merely on the ground that the President acted on the advice of the Minister of Justice, who regarded Simelane as "the right person for the job." The Court found that the decision to appoint Simelane was irrational and hence incompatible with the principle of legality in that evidence showing that Simelane was in fact not fit and proper for the position concerned had bluntly been ignored. In view of the proven evidence against Simelane the Court held that he (Simelane) was not a fit and proper person for appointment as required by section 179 of *the* Constitution. It was clear that Simelane had been the favourite of the governing party as national director of public prosecutions and such support could go a long way to secure his appointment. This was underscored by the fact that the SCA in a unanimous judgment[133] had already made a finding similar to the one contained in the ensuing judgment of the Constitutional Court. Government nevertheless further pursued the matter by way of its failed appeal to the Constitutional Court.

The judgments of the SCA and the Constitutional Court provoked much annoyance from the government and the transformationists in general, as was clearly attested to by the failed attempt to have the SCA judgment overturned by the Constitutional Court. The transformationists' view was that the judgments of the SCA were excessively activist, unduly trespassing on the terrain of the executive, therefore once again flying in the face of the doctrine of the separation of powers and also favouring the opposition DA.[134]

Democratic Alliance v Acting National Director of Public Prosecutions

The decision of the acting *National Director of Public Prosecutions*, Mokotedi Mpshe, to discontinue the criminal prosecution against Mr Zuma, did not sit well with the official opposition, the Democratic Alliance. Clearly suspecting the decision to have been based on considerations other than purely legal ones, the DA wanted to obtain the information on which Mpshe's decision was based, thus seeking to establish whether there were substantive grounds for discontinuing the prosecution against Zuma and also to get to the bottom of what might have been the true political

---

132 Ginwala, 2008, Report of the Inquiry into the Fitness of Advocate VP Pikoli to Hold the Office of National Director of Public Prosecutions Commission of Inquiry. Available: http://bit.ly/2KvXPCZ [Accessed, 19 November 2014].

133 2012(3) BCLR 291(SCA).

134 Ziyad Motala criticising the judgment of the SCA, the reasoning and conclusion of which were confirmed by the Constitutional Court, argued that the court had made the mistake of accepting the findings of the Ginwala Commission of Inquiry without considering that it was not a genuinely independent and impartial (judicial) body. Therefore, according to Motala, "(t)he court in effect performed the role of a political protection agency for the opposition party, which found things in the report to further its political objectives." (The opposition party referred to is the Democratic Alliance, which was the applicant in the litigation.) Motala, 11 December 2011, *SCA: Beware Politics Masquerading as Law* 5.

reasons for letting Zuma off the hook. The DA therefore sued for access to all of the information which allegedly formed the basis of Mpshe's decision, including the recordings of the conversations referred to above. The SCA ruled that at least some of the material, including the recordings referred to above, had to be made available. Once again this decision annoyed the transformationists.

SCA judgments against the JSC

The JSC was also on the receiving end of two high-profile judgments. In 2012 the SCA in *Judicial Service Commission v Cape Bar Council* held unconstitutional the JSC's decision to leave two vacancies on the bench of the Western Cape High Court unfilled instead of appointing clearly suitable and competent white male candidates.[135] The court held that this decision of the JSC, for which it was not capable of providing reasons, was irrational and therefore incompatible with the principle of legality and the rule of law.[136] This decision followed hot on the heels of another judgment of the SCA against the JSC in *Freedom under Law v Acting Chairperson of the Judicial Service Commission.*[137] The case concerned a decision of the JSC not to conduct a formal inquiry into alleged gross misconduct of the Judge President of the Western Cape, Judge John Hlophe, a prominent black judge. The JSC decision was in response to a complaint of the justices of the Constitutional Court that he (Hlophe) had improperly tried to influence their decision in a case, at that stage pending in the Constitutional Court, relating to the prosecutorial access to evidence in a criminal investigation on charges of corruption against Zuma. The SCA ruled that the JSC's decision not to hold a formal inquiry into the alleged misconduct of the judge president and to regard the matter as finalised, was irrational, contrary to the rule of law and for that reason unconstitutional. The JSC was ordered to hold a formal enquiry.

There was another negative transformationist response against this judgment against the JSC, this time from the transformationists within the ranks of the JSC itself,[138] who are reported to have rather aggressively interrogated Plasket about the SCA judgment in *Judicial Service Commission v Cape Bar Council.*

The courts and administrative incompetency under ANC administration

A prominent feature of public governance under the ANC government since the constitutional transition started in 1994 is the relentless deterioration of the public administration and the rising tide of corruption in South Africa, specifically in the public sector.[139] The extent of the corruption in the public sector prompted

---

135   2012(11) BCLR 1239(SCA).

136   2012(11) BCLR 1239(SCA), specifically paras 37-51.

137   2011(3) SA 549(SCA).

138   Calland, 2013.

139   See in this regard the discussion, specifically of cadre deployment in Chapter 5.

Kgalema Motlanthe[140] in his then capacity as general secretary of the ANC to state: "The rot is across the board ... Almost every project is conceived because it offers certain people a chance to make money." A dilapidated state administration results in public service delivery of a dismal quality, especially on municipal level. So-called service delivery protests, one of the consequences of deteriorating public services, have become so common that they at times consume a substantive amount of police resources which have to be enlisted to control and quell these often violent protests.[141]

Numerous court orders are granted against organs of state but these orders are often ignored and never complied with, frequently owing to the laxity and incompetence of the state administration. This question was dealt with by the Constitutional Court in *Nyathi v Member of the Executive Council for the Department of Health Gauteng*[142] in which in a majority judgment the Court ruled section 3 of the *State Liability Act*[143] (which prohibits the attachment of state assets in the execution of judgments) constitutionally invalid. The Court rebuked the state for its failure to comply with a court order, and expressed dissatisfaction with the laxity of public officials and the flawed conduct in the office of the state attorney.[144]

Transformationists' view critiqued

There are three main points of critique against the transformationists' view.

1. The transformationists have erroneously embraced the statist-individualist imagery about the power of the judiciary which the liberals so firmly believe in, thus sharing with the liberals their beliefs in the doctrine of statist-individualist constitutionalism.

2. The transformationists have adopted an excessively wide definition of the ideology of transformation, calling for an inordinately close relationship between the judiciary and the ruling party (and the legislature and the executive). Linked to this is the transformationists' pronounced tendency to protect the ruling party on matters of poor public administration as if these were matters of ideology.

---

140 Quoted by Plaut & Holden, 2012:288. These authors insightfully discuss the corruption problem in South Africa on 266-304 of this book. During the finalisation of the present manuscript the full extent of the deeply-seated culture of corruption as evidence is presented before a number of commissions of inquiry and investigation panels.

141 See for example the discussion by Burger, 2013.

142 2008(9) BCLR 865(CC).

143 State Liability Act 20 of 1957.

144 See for example paras 52, 60 and 63 of *Nyathi v Member of the Executive Council for the Department of Health Gauteng*. In para 60 Madala J, speaking for the majority of the Court, stated: "In more recent years, and in particular the period from 2002 onwards, courts have been inundated with situations where court orders have been flouted by State functionaries, who, on being handed such court orders, have given very flimsy excuses which in the end only point to their dilatoriness. The public officials seem not to understand the integral role that they play in our constitutional State, as the right of access to courts entails a duty, not only on the courts to ensure access, but on the State to bring about the enforceability of court orders."

3. The transformationists have failed to account for the distinctive professional nature of the judiciary.

The first point leads to the two other points. The first point is therefore at the centre of the critique against the transformationists. All three points will now be dealt with in more detail.

As regards the first point: The transformationists have bought into and now share, with their liberal adversaries, the ardent belief of statist-individualist constitutionalism, that the judiciary, as a political force, is as powerful if not more powerful than the legislature, the executive and the ruling party (the ANC). As should be evident from the discussion on judicial independence and judicial impartiality in this chapter, the exaggerated liberal belief, informed by the doctrine of statist-individualist constitutionalism, in the power of the courts is unfounded in view of the inherent frailty of the judiciary. The transformationists in close accord with the liberals nevertheless seem to cling to this unfounded belief. This explains the excessive drive of the transformationists for the appointment of judges who endorse the transformationist agenda, who would pose no threat to frustrate that agenda, and who would in their rulings be inclined to spare the government and the ruling party any embarrassment, even in basically non-ideological cases such as those discussed above. Had the transformationists not deceived themselves into the aggrandised belief in the political power of the judiciary, and had they instead developed a more realistic understanding of the separation of powers and judicial independence, impartiality and judicial reasoning, as explained in parts 6.4.1 and 6.4.2, they would have spared themselves the unnecessary effort to ensure adherence to that belief. Had they realistically grasped the actual political frailty of the judiciary, the judiciary's dependence on legislature and the executive and the regime-relativity of judicial impartiality, they could have proceeded confidently in appointing judges on no other ground but merit.

But do the judgments discussed in this section (part 6.4.3) not lend credence to the belief of statist-individualist constitutionalism that the judiciary is indeed politically powerful and therefore capable of disrupting the ideological programme of the ruling elite?

The answer to this question must be an emphatic negative. A significant feature of the judgments, viewed from the vantage point of judicial independence and impartiality, is that though politically important, none of them was ideologically sensitive, nor could any of them have posed a real threat of hampering the pursuit of the ideology of transformationism. The subject matter of these judgments was good public governance and sound public administration, not political ideology, specifically not transformationism. Broadly speaking, the first set of cases centred on the conduct of the prosecutorial authority in combating white-collar crime, and the second set focuses on the rendering of public services. These cases were at most marginally ideologically related to any ideological preferences of the ruling elite. They did not pertain to the ideology of transformationism. As will be shown in Chapter 7 which deals with the question of interpretation, all cases involving such ideological questions are in fact consistently and quite predictably decided in favour of the dominant elite. The judgments discussed in this chapter were, however, at most examples of the courts using their limited adjudicatory power to correct hiccups, differences and aberrations *within* the broad ideological assumptions of the dominant elite, thus leaving the achievement of the ideological goals of transformationism undisturbed. The power that the judiciary did exercise in these cases was clearly within the typical, narrow preserve of judicial authority. These and similar other judgments provide no basis for the belief that South African courts are capable of exerting sufficient power to be of real political significance. In consequence, there is no reason for the transformationists to anxiously fend off the appointment of competent applicants (who are feared to be less sympathetically disposed towards the ruling party and the executive) and to show them the door in favour of less competent ones.

What the transformationists are in fact doing – and this leads to the second point of critique – is that they confuse matters of good governance with questions of ideology.

Hence, the transformationists define the ideological programme of transform-ationism in such broad terms that questions of good governance and sound public administration, which are ideologically insignificant, are misperceived as important ideological matters. As pointed out in parts 6.4.1 and 6.4.2, judicial impartiality is politically relative and ideologically conditioned. Courts therefore cannot and will not ordinarily take sides against the legislature and the executive and the dominant elite in general on matters relating to the ideological commitments of the dominant elite. Sharing the same commitments as the rest of the dominant elite and interpreting the Constitution in the same way, they will, as the discussion in Chapter 7 shows, judge in favour of the dominant elite. The combating of crime and corruption and the promotion of sound public administration – the kind of matters in the judgments discussed above – are not ideologically sensitive. These are questions on which one would usually expect consensus and not discord among political role players. These questions relate to issues on which courts should be able to decide without the risk of embarking upon a collision course with the ruling party, the legislature or the executive. These issues therefore fall to be dealt with in a category separate from those dealing with matters of ideology and high politics. Courts should be risk-free in dealing with these issues and be able to pass judgment impartially in terms of the relevant law without fear, favour or prejudice. This is what one would expect in the normal course of events. However, this is not the realm within which South African courts operate, as illustrated by the judgments discussed above.

These judgments would in the normal course of events not have been of any real political significance. Yet, since former president Zuma had a real interest in the outcome of these cases, keen political attention was stirred up by questions such as how the courts would approach these cases, who the judges would be and what their attitudes about this non-ideological issue would be.

Furthermore, with rampant corruption, maladministration, poor public services and the pillaging of the fiscus, and high political figures facing criminal prosecution, these issues have become political – even ideological – issues instead of matters of public governance. Where courts would ordinarily be on firm ground when required to deal with issues of this nature, in this context they run the risk of treading on a dangerous political quagmire. Their decisions on questions that seem to be politically neutral could have severe political consequences, among others, consequences detrimental to the ruling party, which is finding it difficult to get these administrative and governance ailments under control. The importance of the selection of judges should therefore be obvious, because, as described in parts 6.4.1 and 6.4.2, judges are required to be part of the dominant elite.

There is an additional – and in South Africa a very crucial – reason why judgments revolving on bad public services and poor public administration are not only politically sensitive, but are experienced to be ideologically dangerous to the ruling party. Many cases relating to the failure to provide public services might result directly from the dominant elite's programme of cadre deployment, discussed in Chapter 5. Political allegiance to the ANC of appointees in the public sector is a crucial factor in staff employment in that sector, especially in senior positions. The aim is to secure party control in all spheres of South African society.[145] Cadres are deployed for their services to the party and not primarily for their experience and competence as public office-bearers. Court judgments critical of poor public services and public governance may be regarded as reproaching the policy of cadre deployment. These judgments are therefore politically and ideologically much more sensitive than one might think, specifically in the perception of the ANC. That is why the transformationists have a direct stake in fending off judicial interference pertaining to bad public services, as that might be perceived as a disguised onslaught on the core components of transformationist ideology, namely affirmative action[146] and cadre deployment.

The extremely broad scope of the transformationist ideology, encompassing also matters of good governance, causes the transformationists to be rather petulant, because they view criticism of poor governance as matters of politics and ideology.

---

145 See for example Wesson & Du Plessis, 2008:193; Budlender, 2005:716 et seq. Transformation in view of the ruling ANC also includes affirmative action, black economic empowerment and cadre deployment, that is, deploying party operatives in the public service, police, army, etc.

146 Affirmative action is allowed in s 9(2) of *the Constitution*. There is a trend, however, to pursue affirmative action in disregard of any other considerations, even if the individual rights of persons are adversely affected by such measures and also when such measures are in disregard of efficient public services. See in this regard the judgment of the SCA in *Solidarity v South African Police Service* 2014(2) SA 1(SCA).

This petulance is also a feature of the transformationist majority in the JSC. In the context of the judiciary the JSC is the crucial forum in which these supposed onslaughts against the ruling elite must be fended off. It is the place where the "right" appointees can be selected to help protect the ruling elite against this challenge.

The first two points of critique against the transformationists can therefore be summed up as follows: the transformationists accept the liberal view, and thus also like the liberals, fully bought into the basic belief system of statist-individualist constitutionalism, that the perceived great power of the courts is almost on a par with that of the other branches. That is why they view having the courts in the *wrong hands* to be a grave threat to the ruling elite organised around the ANC, which defines their ideology in such broad terms that it includes issues of good governance, which have nothing to do with ideology. The most intimate relationship possible must therefore be established between the courts and the rest of the dominant elite so as to ensure the ruling party licence to pursue its ideology and protection against judicial censure in matters of good governance. The effect of all this is the perpetration of an undue assault on even the much less independence and much less impartiality that the analysis of this chapter shows that the courts could realistically be expected to have. The effect of this assault is to place the courts in the position where they will not be able to perform their functions even in terms of the much relativised position in which the present analysis shows them to be.

In this context, the third point of criticism can now be attended to. Believing that the court has vast political powers, defining the ambit of the ideology of transformationism of the dominant elite in particularly broad terms, and fearing that the supposed judicial power could harm the ruling party, the transformationists put an excessively high premium on the need that the courts should be under the control of, and judges be politically sympathetic towards, the ruling party. This is done at the risk of diminishing the professional qualities required on the bench, in all the fields of legal practice, including fields of law in which issues of ideology can hardly play any part. This is a serious mistake. Not only is it wrong to believe that the courts are politically powerful. It is also wrong to underestimate the need for professional competence and experience on the bench.

The judiciary is one of three powers, but it differs significantly from the other two. In contrast to the legislature and the executive it is inherently weak. The judiciary is (or should be) an assemblage of professional senior lawyers at the pinnacle of their legal careers. They must be able to dispense justice with knowledge, wisdom and sympathy. They must be wise and competent enough to deserve public trust and respect as public office-bearers who have the responsibility to take decisions that profoundly impact on the lives of the parties in the cases they adjudicate. To that end their political sympathies are entirely marginal. Judges do have power, more correctly authority. That authority does not include the capacity to make and execute broad policy decisions, which no court should ever be required to do.

Through their legal knowledge, wisdom and reasoned decision-making they earn respect and high esteem and command moral authority. That respect is the source of the courts' *power*.[147] They have *auctoritas*, not real potestas. Without that they have hardly any power at all. That trust, however, is not based on their power but on their knowledge, wisdom and good judgment; that is, as Alexander Hamilton said, not their force or will but merely their judgment.[148]

In the absence of their wise judgment the basis of the trust in them is bound to evaporate and their power to disappear. People will then have to settle their disputes in ways other than through the courts – through laudable means such as arbitration, mediation, negotiation and reconciliation, or less laudable means such as self-help, including violence. Citizens have a critical interest in the maintenance of professional courts where competent judges preside. If this is not realised and political considerations instead of professional competence receive preference in judicial appointments, the bench is bound to fail the public.

The transformationists on the JSC do not seem to have an adequate appreciation for this. They are not only placing an undue value on political considerations and downplaying the need for the professional nature of the judiciary; they are also running the risk of causing the courts to forfeit the essential characteristics of a well-functioning judiciary. In this context, the transformationists have a dangerously serious blind spot. When thinking of the power of the bench they seem to confuse it with the kind of broad policy powers of the legislature and the executive.

The courts are unable to be as independent and impartial as the doctrine of statist-individualist constitutionalism would suggest. Their independence is limited, and their impartiality is regime-relative and ideology-conditioned. This view of the limited extent of the actual (albeit weak) form of independence and impartiality of the judiciary is not shared by the transformationists. They seem to insist on a still weaker form of independence to be brought about by development of such a close relationship between the bench, and the ruling party, the executive and (the ruling party in) the legislature that the bench could be at risk of forfeiting its distinctive, august professional character.

6.5

Conclusion

The debunking of the independence of the judiciary as a rather mythical notion is incompatible with the statist-individualist notion of constitutionalism because the entire constellation of statist-individualist constitutionalism rests on a questionable

---

147 See in this regard Bickel, 1962:252.

148 Hamilton, Madison & Jay, 1961:465.

belief in the actual separation of powers accompanied by the actual independence, full-fledged impartiality, potency and effectiveness of the courts.

The liberal indignation about the JSC's transformationist stance and the critique levelled against the transformationists, as discussed in part 6.3, are based on the liberal camp's deeply-rooted but unrealistic belief in the real independence of the judiciary. This belief must be ascribed to the liberal camp being oblivious to the limited preserve of the separation of powers and judicial independence, and not realising that, though separated in structure, staff and functions, the judiciary, as a rule, forms an integral part of one harmoniously unified power elite. Any lack of fully appreciating this reality would inevitably result in too much reposing in separation of powers and judicial independence as strategies of (statist-individualist) constitutionalism. Precisely this explains the liberal disappointment in the transformationists' unashamed push for often professionally questionable appointments of politically compliant transformationist judges.

The separation of powers and judicial independence are by far not the competent instruments and strategies of statist-individualist constitutionalism which liberals believe them to be, in order to keep the legislature and the executive and finally the ruling party in check. The judiciary is not required and able to challenge or balance the power from outside the dominant political elite, neither in present-day South Africa nor anywhere else.[149]

Traditionally courts are not there to settle disputes surrounding prominent political issues and matters of ideology. Courts are at their best and function most comfortably when their judgments are in the field of private law, commercial disputes, criminal law, etc. where their judgments do not have any notable political and ideological implications. They are at their best in various respects when they are free to give judgments based on legal principles that are least affected by issues of politics and ideology and therefore without the courts having to be wary of possible negative political reactions; and when they have the best chances to ensure voluntary executive participation in the execution of their rulings.

In South Africa, following a very firm belief in the independence, impartiality and power of the courts, the courts have been entrusted with much more power than the power required to deal with these run-of-the-mill legal issues. With their sweeping powers of review on sensitive political and ideological issues, the courts have become important political actors, as a result of which they find themselves in a potentially awkward and uncomfortable relationship with the ruling party. According to the imagery of statist-individualist constitutionalism, the powerful judiciary would obviously be able to stand its ground also on matters of politics and

---

149 The judiciary might be such a competent challenger when there is a split in the power elite and when it takes sides against one section of that elite. However, even in such a case it cannot act on its own. It would still need support; most probably from the strongest group in such a conflict.

ideology on which it would make rulings followed by due compliance by the co-operative legislature and the executive and an obedient ruling party.

From the discussion in this chapter it is clear that the belief in the power, independence and impartiality of the courts has been fundamentally flawed. A realistic insight into the notions of judicial independence and impartiality, as discussed in parts 6.4.1 and 6.4.2, reveals that the high expectations about the part that the courts would play in controlling the ruling party, the executive and (the ruling party in) the legislature in achieving a balanced constitution and meaningful checks and balances were in fact unfounded. Moreover, as described in part 6.4.3, the courts are also confronted with situations typical of South Africa under its present ruling elite: the dreadful state of public administration, senior figures in the ANC being under criminal investigation yet still being supported by the ruling party, and the very broad definition of the ideological programme of transformationism of the dominant elite. The transformationist response to the challenges posed by these situations is to push for sympathetic judges and a deferential judiciary that would give the dominant elite the required leeway, not only to pursue its ideology but also as far as possible to spare the ruling party any embarrassment, even on matters of poor public administration. Most significant is the fact that the transformationists are even prepared, as pointed out above, to compromise on the quality of judges in order to accommodate their transformationist agenda. This is really ominous because it erodes the very basis of judicial power, namely the trust in and high regard for the judiciary. This erosion not only affects the extensive politically related powers which the Constitution optimistically assigns to the courts; it also undermines the trust in the courts in relation to its core functions, namely to skilfully adjudicate the run-of-the-mill disputes that ordinarily require most of the attention of the courts. Devoid of the best that the legal profession can offer, trust in and high esteem for the courts are bound to fall by the wayside, causing distrust of the courts and rendering them unable to discharge their core responsibilities to the public.

This is a bitterly ironic course of events. In pursuance of the belief system of the doctrine of statist-individualist constitutionalism which (as described in Chapter 3) the South African Constitution faithfully subscribes to, an attempt has been made to control the legislature and the executive and to protect basic rights, that is, to allay the fears of the public by giving the courts very broad review powers and in doing so, to turn the judiciary into a seemingly powerful political actor. This has won the South African courts awe and respect and the Constitution high accolades. But more than two decades into the new constitutional order in South Africa those additional powers are under threat. Even more serious is the fact that the insistence not to elevate the best lawyers to the bench, is also eroding not only the additional powers of the bench – the powers that are arguably on the marginal outskirts of judicial authority – but also the traditional core of judicial authority on which everyone depends.

The three powers of the trias politica are presented by the doctrine of statist-individualist constitutionalism as the very backbone of limited government and constitutionalism.

Trias politaca is important but by far not as effective as the doctrine of statist-individualist constitutionalism purports it to be. The three powers are firmly unified in one single power elite. The courts fulfil their role in close conformity with the rest of the elite and they are incapable of doing anything outside the consensus which is prevalent within that political elite.

This also obtains for the present South African constitutional order in which the highest courts and specifically the Constitutional Court, (like the Chapter 9 institutions) are an integral part of the dominant political elite. Since its inception the bench of the Constitutional Court, and in due course most of the incumbents of all South African courts, broadly shared with the legislature, the executive and the ruling party, which dominated these branches, the same ideological assumptions.

It is therefore hopelessly off the mark to conceive of the judiciary, including South Africa's Constitutional Court, as if it is somehow politically insular. It is as erroneous to think of judicial impartiality in anything close to absolute terms. On the contrary, the courts are a specialised political actor functioning in cooperation with the other actors. They play their political role most prominently when the ideological commitments and objectives of the dominant elite are challenged in litigation. In those scenarios they act as defenders, legitimisers and advocates of the ideological objectives of the dominant elite. To that end they use the instrument of their specialisation, namely seemingly objective and authentic *legal reasoning* couched in seemingly neutral legal parlance, to achieve political ends which is to justify, defend and advance the ideological objectives of the dominant elite.

Judicial impartiality is relative. It is conditioned by the ideological commitments and objectives of the dominant elite. The courts are impartial only *within* the limited ideological assumptions of the dominant elite.

In the final analysis the doctrine of separation of powers and the concomitant doctrines of judicial independence and impartiality are to a considerable extent metaphorical rather than real. Together these doctrines function as a threefold strategy that inculcates the notion of a truly balanced constitution. The checks and balances of the system of trias politica are, however, often dangerously misleading, creating the fiction of, rather than an actual balanced constitution. Trias politica is important. So are judicial independence and impartiality. They fall far short, however, of establishing and securing a truly balanced constitution in keeping with the requisites for authentic constitutionalism as set out in Chapter 1.

CONSTITUTIONAL SUPREMACY AND JUDICIAL IMPARTIALITY HERMENEUTICALLY VIEWED

The Fiction of Guaranteed Rights

7.1

Introduction

According to the belief system of statist-individualist constitutionalism, the so-called independent and impartial judiciary does not only stand at the centre of threefold power structure of statist-individualist constitutionalism. It is also the final guarantor of justice in the guise of individual rights. The judiciary discharges this responsibility by interpreting the Constitution, more specifically the Constitution's so-called guaranteed individual rights. Constitutional interpretation (of individual rights) is therefore crucially important. If something goes wrong in the interpretation process and rights are in consequence not interpreted correctly, the guaranteed individual rights are not protected, resulting in statist-individualist constitutionalism reneging on its guarantee of justice through fundamental rights. In the present chapter, as in the previous one, the focus is once again on the judiciary. This time, however, the focus is not in the first place on the claim of judicial independence and impartiality but on the interpretive enterprise of the judiciary. From the vantage point of interpretation we, however, strengthen the conclusions reached in Chapter 6 in which the belief in the independence and impartiality of the judiciary is debunked. At the same time, however, something very important is added, namely the emphasis on the fact that there is no interpretive approach (no micro theory) that can guarantee something in the nature of an objective outcome which is capable of protecting individual rights to safeguard justice. When the courts, especially the highest courts, are interpreting, they do so in keeping with an ideologically inspired interpretive approach, which the judiciary as part of the dominant political elite, shares with the elite.

Statist-individualist constitutionalism, however, does not admit that the courts and the rest of the dominant elite are all sharing the same interpretive approach. It also does not admit that the courts through their interpretive (and adjudicative) activities are promoting the ideological objectives of the dominant elite. On the contrary, as mentioned in Chapter 2, statist-individualist constitutionalism has its own implied interpretation doctrine, which for present purposes can be referred to as the orthodox doctrine of constitutional interpretation. This concomitant doctrine is logically implied in the doctrine of statist-individualist constitutionalism. This doctrine (seeks to) sustain and inculcate the belief system of statist constitutionalism, more specifically in so far as it entails a belief in the supremacy of the Constitution and the guarantee of justice through individual rights. This doctrine has a particular vision as to the nature of the meanings of the language (the formulations) of the supreme Constitution and as to the nature of the interpretation of these formulations, more specifically regarding the manner in which the judiciary does (and should) interpret. The orthodox doctrine holds that: the meanings of the language of the formulations of the Constitution are at core certain, objective, stable and durable; through interpretation, which is essentially acts of logical deduction, these objective meanings are accurately deduced from the text and applied to concrete situations. In consequence, the meanings of the formulations of the Constitution are at core universal and predictable.

Precisely for this reason the Constitution and the individual rights it provides for in its formulations can be described in the typical faith-strengthening language of the doctrine of statist-individualist constitutionalism, as *guaranteed*, *enshrined* and *entrenched* so that everyone can rest assure that all their interests are firmly protected by the compendious catalogue of individual rights formulations in the Constitution.

This orthodox doctrine of interpretation is a crude over-simplification of what is actually happening in the process of interpretation. The doctrine is in fact patently wrong since the meanings of the language of the formulations of the Constitution that are distilled and applied through the process of interpretation are in fact *not* objective, *not* accurate, *not* certain and *not* stable. Many (constitutional) jurists subscribe to more realistic and sophisticated theories of interpretation that acknowledge the inaccuracy, instability, non-objectivity and uncertainty of the meanings of constitutional formulations, yet are still faithfully clinging to the belief in the supremacy of the (written) Constitution. This is a glaring inconsistency because one cannot subscribe to the doctrine of the supremacy of the Constitution and yet at the same time acknowledge the uncertainty, inaccuracy, lack of objectivity and instability of the meanings of the written Constitution.

Through interpretation the meanings of formulations are articulated, concretised and applied to practical situations. This happens with every decision taken by legislatures, executives, administrators and also the courts. The focus of the present discussion will be on the judicial interpretation of the Constitution, more specifically by the highest courts. It will be pointed out that:

σ   the meaning of rights as expressed in the provisions of the Constitution are in fact not clear, objective, certain, stable, durable or predictable; the rights acquire meaning only when they are interpreted;

σ   these meanings might change (even drastically) – in successive acts of interpretation;

σ   the interpretative exercise is distinctively political in that provisions are interpreted in keeping with the pre-understanding of the interpreters of what the Constitution means, which pre-understandings specifically include their ideological commitments, political preferences and prejudices;

σ   in the case of the highest echelons of the judiciary, these ideological commitments and political prejudices and preferences are generally that of the dominant elite of which the judiciary (as shown in Chapter 6) is an integral part, and in consequence, the meanings that the courts will ascribe to constitutional provisions are essentially those of the dominant elite in the legislature, executive, the ruling party and other subsidiaries of the dominant elite;

σ   in given settings, more specifically in politically and ideologically charged litigation, the meanings that will be attached to constitutional provisions are distinctively politically and ideologically biased. The meanings will vindicate and promote the ideological programme of the dominant elite whilst placing the opponents of these ideological commitments in the wrong. The outcome of the interpretation of these constitutional formulations may therefore seriously disappoint the claimants of rights who might discover through the judgments that their reading of constitutional formulations was offensive to the Constitution and that the meanings which they have attached to the formulations are in fact (vastly) different from those which they had expected them to be. In consequence, these formulations might prove not to be the guaranteed safeguards they were believed to be. Interpretive acts in these cases are acts by which the courts exercise biased political power by virtue of which they rule in favour of the dominant elite and against outside groupings who are challenging the dominant elite. Through their interpretive activity the courts (will) uphold the claims and interests which are dear to the dominant elite and at the same time, the courts' interpretation will violate the claims and interests of groupings outside the elite.

In part 7.2 of this chapter the fundamentals of the interpretive doctrine of statist-individualist constitutionalism are explained and rebutted. Part 7.3 turns to purposive interpretation which is a leading manifestation of the interpretive doctrine (also of statist-individualist constitutionalism). Purposive interpretation is proposed as an approach to interpretation that is faithful to the doctrine of the supreme Constitution (yet more realistic and sophisticated than the orthodox doctrine of interpretation). Purposive interpretation is therefore believed to go a long way towards revealing the correct, accurate and authentic meanings of the Constitution.

Purposive interpretation has considerable currency in many jurisdictions and has been subscribed to also in South Africa under its statist-individualist Constitution in the period after 1994.

It will be pointed out below that purposive interpretation, regardless of its merits and the well-meant sentiments on which it is based, is incapable of achieving the intended aims. In the final analysis, purposive interpretation is distinctively political. In terms thereof constitutional formulations are interpreted and given effect to in keeping with the meaning espoused by the dominant elite.

In South Africa the notion of purposive interpretation has been absorbed into what is called transformative interpretation[1] and which owing to its outright ideological proclivity is here called transformationist interpretation. Transformationist interpretation requires that the achievement of the objectives of the ideology of transformationism (transformation) be regarded as the prime purpose for the adoption of the Constitution. That is why the Constitution must be interpreted in order to achieve the society envisaged by the ideology of transformationism. Transformationism is discussed in part 7.4 of this Chapter. In part 7.5 the operation of transformationist interpretation is demonstrated with reference to a selection of judgments of the Constitutional Court. A clear understanding of the nature and effect of interpretation reinforces the conclusion that constitutional supremacy is devoid of any significant content to the effect that the Constitution is *not* supreme. The discussion elucidates and strengthens the propositions that have been discussed in Chapter 6, namely that the courts are in essential respects not as independent and impartial as the trite doctrine of statist-individualist constitutionalism proclaims, and that they are together with the ruling party in the legislature and the executive and other subsidiary formations, unified in one single dominant political leadership (the dominant elite).

It also reinforces the conclusion, this time from the point of view of interpretation theory that the highest courts, including South Africa's Constitutional Court, are not impartial ideological role players in conformity with the rest of the dominant political elite. Lastly, it brings to light that the individual rights in the Bill of Rights are not the guaranteed instruments for the safeguarding of justice which statist-individualist constitutionalism purports them to be; and that as a result of the way in which they are interpreted, they serve as a biased instrument for promoting the dominant elite's ideological commitments.

7.2

Orthodox (deductive) constitutional interpretation

It has for some time fairly generally been acknowledged that it is impossible to distil the original meaning of the Constitution (or the original intention of the law-maker/constitution maker/s). The assumption has therefore taken root that it is impossible to interpret the formulations of the Constitution in keeping with the original meaning of the text of the Constitution (or the original intent of those who drafted/framed the Constitution). Originalist conceptions of constitutional interpretation are therefore generally met with sharp dismissal. As the analysis in this chapter will show, I also do not subscribe to originalism. It is simply fanciful and does not provide any profound insight into the reality of the interpretive exercise. It is impossible to discover the correct and truly objective meaning of the Constitution with reference the so-called original meaning of the text or the intent of the framers.

In spite of the rejection of originalism, the observation has quite correctly been made that legal scholars are nevertheless loath to abandon originalist convictions of interpretation.[2] It is widely believed, particularly among constitutional jurists, that constitutional provisions in the final analysis do have objective (original) meanings. They tend to cling to the idea that language (formulations) essentially denote names of things and that the meaning of words are securely attached to the things they denote.[3] This belief is no coincidence. On the contrary, as argued in part 7.1, when a constitutional jurist believes in the supremacy of the written Constitution, he/she is of necessity bound to believe that written language – in the present case, the formulations of the Constitution – is the repository of inherent and objective meanings – and on that score, also in the objectivity, certainty and basic stability of the meaning of the formulations of the Constitution. The obvious reason for this is that the doctrine of constitutional supremacy necessitates and prescribes its own orthodox interpretive doctrine, namely a doctrine that sustains the notion of the supreme Constitution. In essence this is a deductive doctrine of constitutional interpretation. Accordingly, the Constitution as encapsulated in its written formulations, once adopted and promulgated, is perceived to be basically a done deal: a perfected (ready made) whole entity that has come into being during an identifiable moment in the past. It has basically fixed, certain, objective durable and predictable meanings,[4] which afterwards, through deduction have to be concretised, that is, applied to specific situations.[5] It is relevant in this context to recall Van der Hoeven's observation as reflected in Chapter 2 "that constitutional jurists seek to achieve their objectives on account of an inordinately high value they attach to written law and their conviction that human conduct, including conduct by government, can be regulated by written legal norms."[6] The belief in the certainty, objectivity, accuracy and stability of the meaning of the formulations of the Constitution is implied in this.

Through judicial interpretation these objective, accurate and stable meanings are logically deduced and applied to practical situations. The meaning of constitutional formulations is viewed basically as being directly accessible through "interpretation" in the form of (logical) deduction. This view of constitutional interpretation goes under a variety of designations (sometimes quite descriptive and sometimes with a derogatory undertone) such as positivist, literalist, liberal, conservative, formalist, etc. This belief in the certainty and accuracy of meanings is also the basis for perceiving law in scientific terms – the *legal science*. It is on that score that judgments can be described as *right* or *wrong*; that it can be proclaimed that a case was *correctly* or *incorrectly* decided.

It is anathema in terms of this conception to think that interpretative activity makes up and changes the meaning of the supreme Constitution with every new act of interpretation, because that would defeat the very notion of the supremacy of the written Constitution.

Interpretation in terms of the statist-individualist doctrine merely brings to light the meanings inherent in the Constitution. Interpretation can therefore never be an activity through which interpreters attribute meaning to constitutional provisions or change any prevailing meanings. Interpreters are essentially passive agents who simply discover meaning through deduction. They do not actively create (construe), attribute or change the meaning of the formulations of the Constitution. To argue that interpretation is an active exercise in which meanings are attributed to formulations, through which meanings are created and changed, would amount to giving up on the belief that the Constitution is supreme; and to acknowledging that if there is something like supremacy, such supremacy vests in the interpreters and not in the Constitution itself. Moreover, it would paralyse or sacrifice the very notion of constitutional supremacy.

The orthodox doctrine of interpretation has a strong abstract flavour. Accordingly, it is assumed that everyone (every reasonable person at least) engaged in the interpretation of a particular formulation (and finding themselves in the same circumstances) would attach essentially the same meaning to such formulation.[7] In the final analysis, as Sanford Levinson (resonating Van der Hoeven) correctly

---

6   As discussed in Chapter 2. Van der Hoeven, 1976:496. The original Dutch reads: *"De constitutionalisten trachten hun doelstellenigen te verwerklijken, gelijk wij zagen, vanuit een zeer hogere waardering voor het geschreven recht. Zij menen het menselijk handelen ook op het terrein van gezag en gezachsoefening door rechtsnormen te kunnen regeren."*

7   See in this respect Dallmayr, 1992:12 referring to Franz Neumann. In my opinion even someone like Ronald Dworkin who employed the metaphor of the chain novelist in his explanation of how constitutional interpretation is (or ought to be) conducted falls in this category. In the final analysis interpretation is to Dworkin an unbroken narrative of a single homogeneous and non-pluralist tradition which produces the best (that is one correct) interpretation. See in this regard amongst others, Dworkin, 1992:262-270.

observed, written supreme Constitutions are perceived as mechanism which can freeze time by controlling the future through what is believed to be the "hardness" of language encoded in a monumental document. The purpose of such control is to preserve the particular vision held by the founders of the Constitution and to prevent its overthrow by future generations.[8]

The belief in the objectivity of meanings which are expressed in the provisions of the Constitution is bolstered by two factors. The first one is the psychological impact of the physically observable phrases on paper which inculcate a sense of meaning as something that is objectively (almost tangibly) in existence. As Stanley Fish insightfully observed: "A line of print on a page is so obviously *there* ... that it seems to be the sole repository of whatever value and meaning we associate with it."[9] The observation of Hans-Georg Gadamer underscores the same point. Gadamer noted that the sheer fact that something is written down gives it a special authority. It is not altogether easy, he added, to realise that what is written down can in fact be untrue, invalid or merely seeking to describe something which is in fact not existing. The written word, he stated, has the tangible quality of something that can be demonstrated. That is why it requires a special critical effort to free oneself from the prejudice in favour of what is written down. The second factor, bolstering the belief in the objectivity of the meanings expressed on provisions of the Constitution, is to be found in the supremacy provisions such as section 2 of the South African Constitution and article V of the United States of America Constitution (as discussed in Chapter 2). These are written formulations of the highest order, claiming that the formulations of the Constitution are basically impregnable. Whereas the tangible quality of legislative formulations already makes it difficult to entertain the possibility that they might in fact be invalid, untrue and of no consequence, it requires an even more critical effort to consider the possibility that supremacy provisions might have uncertain or volatile meanings, or might be of no consequence at all.

No matter how much trust the statist-individualist's deductive doctrine of interpretation invests in the belief in the basic certainty, stability, accuracy and objectivity of language, it is unrealistic and deeply erroneous. In the first place, it is important to understand that interpretation, including interpretation of the Constitution, is a distinctively communal activity. Interpreters are operating within the boundaries of a community of interpreters,[10] that is, a particular tradition of interpretation. Each interpretive community is marked by its own pre-understandings, ideological commitments and objectives and they lay down

---

8   Levinson, 1982:376. This resonates the insight by Van der Hoeven as discussed in Chapter 2 that
     Van der Hoeven, concerning the belief in the mighty objective power of written words to control the exercise of
     political power.

9   Fish, 1980:43.

10   De Ville, 2000:8:13.

(expressly or tacitly) their own norms and disciplinary precepts for interpretation. Interpretation is therefore not generally, universally and objectively correct and accurate. It is correct and accurate only within the confines and in terms of the criteria of the accepted convictions, objectives and disciplinary rules of the interpretive community in question.

Each interpretive community has its own prejudices and preferred interests, which guide and at the same time limit the interpretive choices of participant interpreters of the community in question. The community tradition shapes the horizon (the range) of vision, including everything which can be seen in the text from a particular vantage point. Although it is true that the tradition (including the interpretive rules and disciplines) constrains the scope of possible understanding, it is at the same time the very conditio sine qua non without which understanding and interpretation would be impossible. The prejudices of and interests cherished by a particular interpretive community generate specific expectations of what could be found in the text and how it should be applied. Interpretation and application of the text is possible only because the members of a particular interpretive community have shared prejudices and are in favour of certain interests that bind that community together.[11] When interpreting a text the interpreter is already influenced by and acts in pursuance of a particular pre-understanding of the text, which in the case of legal texts determines his/her understanding of the law (and the Constitution).[12] It is important to underscore that these pre-understandings have nothing to do with the text itself. Pre-understandings are extraneous to the text and are to a large extent also political and ideological. They relate to the political and ideological commitments and interests of the community of interpreters. Yet they play a decisive part in the way the text is interpreted, including with regard to the manner in which the meaning is attributed and how it is applied. When we accept that part of the pre-understanding of the text involves the political and ideological convictions of the interpreters, it must also be accepted that interpretation is a distinctively political and ideological matter. It is in fact deeply political[13] – a "(p)olitically predisposed action involving the exercise of choices with implications for mass distribution of power in society."[14] Accordingly Rosemary Coombe aptly states that interpretive disputes are arguments about political theory.[15]

It is therefore clear that the interpreter is not an independent entity – a lonely agent. As Stanley Fish emphasises, the meanings that individual interpreters confer upon the text have their source in the interpretive community within which interpreters operate. The meanings that they attribute to the texts are therefore neither entirely subjective nor generally (or universally) objective. The meanings

---

11   Feldman, 1996:174-176, 187; See also in general Gadamer, 1989:267-377.

12   See for example De Ville, 2000:4 and Du Plessis, 2002:xv.

13   Coombe, 1989:623.

14   Du Plessis, 2002:xv.

15   Coombe, 1989:624.

are not objective because they are the product of a specific point of view and are therefore not simply being "read off" (logically deducted) from the text. Conversely, these meanings are also not subjective because they are informed by the prejudices, expectations and interests held dear in the interpretive community in question, and the norms of interpretation abided by within that community. Stated differently, one can say that meanings are both subjective and objective: subjective because they are inherent in a particular point of view (that of the interpretive community in question); and objective because the point of view is public and conventional (that of the interpretive community in question) and not individual and unique. The strategies, rules and disciplines prevalent within an interpretive community determine which modes of interpretation and meanings are acceptable and which are unacceptable.[16]

Interpretation, more specifically legal interpretation is not an abstract exercise. It always takes place within a practical situation that requires decisions to be taken on the basis of interpretation. Interpretation involves application in concrete situations. According to Francis Mootz, contemporary hermeneutics is defined by the claim that understanding is achieved only through application. There is therefore no free-floating abstract meaning which is only later applied to particular contexts.[17] This holds true particularly for judicial interpretation and decision-making. A formulation, including a formulation in the Constitution, is therefore not understood in itself and thereafter applied in a practical situation; the text is not given to interpreters as something universal that first has to be understood per se and then afterwards used for its practical applications. The opposite holds true: the text can only be understood in relation to the situation it finds itself in.[18] It is interpreted within a practical situation, for example within the scenario of a specific dispute. This further underscores the pivotal importance of the broader context, which is extraneous to the text, as a factor influencing the meaning of the text that is to be interpreted.[19] As pointed out by Gadamer, the text, either the gospel or a legal text, if it is to be understood properly, is to be understood at every moment, in every concrete situation in a new and different way.[20] Interpretation takes place within a specific, concrete situation and the interpreter's outlook (the way in which he/she understands, interprets and finally gives effect to a text) is determined by that situation.[21]

---

16 See the explanation by Fish, 1980:307; 321; 335-336; 347-349. See also Coombe, 1989:604-652. It is precisely because of the "community-conditioned" way in which interpretation is conducted that Fish, 1980:335 can quite appositely observe that the fear of solipsism – of completely unconstrained subjective individual interpretations – is largely unfounded because the individual interpreter acts within the constraints of the interpretation-enabling thinking, seeing and reading of the interpretive community in question.

17 Mootz, 1994:129.

18 Gadamer, 1989:324.

19 De Ville, 2000:7.

20 Gadamer, 1989:309.

21 Gadamer, 1989:314. This Mootz, 1994:125 states that practical interpretive acts are historically defined, that is, in the specific contexts of the present. This is one of the reasons why originalism, even if it is possible to glean an authentic original meaning, is simply without value since that original meaning might simply not find application in the context in question.

Once it is clearly understood that texts are interpreted in specific (historical) contexts and that interpretation, especially constitutional interpretation, is essentially a matter of application of such texts to practical situations, it should be clear that the meaning of one and the same Constitution and one and the same formulation of any part thereof can and does in fact change. When the historical context changes and the text has to be applied to a new situations, new light is cast on the text and a new meaning, previously unnoticed, emerges; and previous meaning might become obsolete. Moreover, historical contexts change consistently (at times slowly and at times rapidly) in keeping with the ebb and flow of ever-changing socio-political realities. The text is therefore consistently approached in new ways; new light from new angles is cast upon the text as a result of which the variety of new and changing meanings attributed to it may be unlimited. The meaning of the text is therefore always a matter of *work in progress*. It is ever-changing; it is never (universally) objective and accurate, never stable, never finally fixed and never fully predictable.[22] These observations obtain with even greater validity to constitutional interpretation, more specifically when the formulations of constitutional rights are interpreted.

These rights are usually widely and indefinitely formulated. The text in this case therefore leaves broad space for the changing of meanings in keeping with the contexts and the situations in which the rights have to be applied. That is why the Constitution is said to be a value-laden text. These values can hardly be expressed in clear and unambiguous language. Moreover, a constitutional text is a durable one and unlike legislation not readily subject to amendment. The Constitution therefore has expansive and inevitably ambiguous formulations that are meant to cater for an "inestimable array" of exigencies over a long period of time.[23] Thus Du Plessis quite correctly declared: "The open-endedness of the constitutional text makes the inevitable role of the (judicial) interpreter's pre-understanding in construing constitutional provisions more visible."[24]

This reveals an important truth that interpretation, specifically the interpretation of the Constitution and constitutional rights, assumes the character not of *construing* meaning but more correctly, of *constructing* of meaning by interpreters. Through interpretive activity interpreters therefore do not infer or deduce meaning from the text as the orthodox doctrine would suggest. On the contrary, interpreters do not *find* meaning they *make* it; they *attribute* and in fact *create* and *produce* meaning. The text does not speak for itself. It is the interpreter who makes the text to speak. The meaning of the text is not an object waiting to be appropriated or discovered

---

22 See for example the explanation by De Ville, 2000:7-8, Du Plessis, 2002:xviii; 12; 145, Feldman, 1991:687 and 693, and Gadamer, 1989:373.

23 Du Plessis, 2002:145.

24 Du Plessis, 2002:145.

by the interpreter. It arises only through the hermeneutic process.[25] Du Plessis, encapsulates the implications of these observations as follows with specific reference to law-texts:

> To determine the meaning of a law-text, such as a statutory or constitutional provision, does not mean to find the meaning of the text (and then to retrieve it), but to attribute meaning to the text or to decide on the meaning of the text (by engaging with the text in interaction with other texts).[26]

More often than not there is more than one interpretive community engaged in the interpretation of the same document, including the same Constitution. This is why, for example, the appointment of judges to the Supreme Court of the United States is so politically charged. Controversies surrounding these appointments are not only about the competency, of the candidates, but about their ideological and political convictions. This is also, as explained in Chapter 6, why the Judicial Service Commission in South Africa is bent on promoting the appointment of *transformation candidates*, namely judges who share with the rest of the dominant political elite (in the legislature, executive, the ruling party and subsidiary institutions) the same transformationist ideological convictions and objectives. Together with the other sectors of the dominant elite, the judiciary form an integral part of the same dominant interpretive community. They view the Constitution through the same prism as the rest of the dominant elite. They share the same pre-understanding and regard the Constitution as an instrument towards the achievement of the same goals as the rest of the dominant elite and finally interpret it in essentially the same way. They deliver judgments that legitimise and defend the ideologically-motivated actions of the dominant elite and in doing so they advance the ideological commitments of such elite.

A homogenous society will tend to have a single homogenous interpretive community. If there are interpretive struggles they will be mild. Usually, however, there are a variety of interpretive communities in one territorial state, all engaged in the interpretation of the same law and Constitution. Deeply divided societies, however, will have deeply divided interpretive communities engaged in acrimonious struggles about the meaning of the Constitution and the law. The boundaries of these interpretive communities (as manifested also on the bench) generally square with the political oppositions in such state. If the political formations are more or less equally strong in numbers, the various interpretive communities, including the judiciary, will also be approximately of equal strength. Usually, however, there is a dominant interpretive community which articulates the interpretive vision of the dominant political elite. There might also be discord on some, more specifically detailed issues within the same interpretive community. However, on broader ideological commitments, there will be consensus within such

---

25   Feldman, 1991:684. See also Fish, 1980:331 and 342 and Coombe, 1989:616.

26   Du Plessis, 2002. (Italics in the original text.)

interpretive community. If there is a profound ideological transition in a state, the previously dominant interpretive community, with sectors in the legislature, the executive, the administration and the judiciary, will also be replaced with a new dominant interpretive community in all these sectors. Especially within the judiciary, as Robert Dahl remarked,[27] such transitional period might take some time because it is generally not feasible to instantly replace all the judges of a previous dominant elite – and a previous interpretive community – with judges who share the commitments of the newly dominant elite and the newly emerging dominant interpretive community.

Each of the interpretive communities who are engaged in the interpretation of the law and the Constitution are bound together by their own common ideological commitments (and/or cultural and other commonalities). Inspired by the ideological commitments of their own, each interpretive community *views* the Constitution differently and *finds* different things – different meanings – in the Constitution. They view the interests to be protected and pursued by the Constitution differently and they accordingly interpret the Constitution differently. They might be liberal, conservative, (multi-)communitarian, or they might have a religious, for example a particular Christian slant. Among them might count excellent counsel and even the best potential judges. Such counsel may advance cogent legal arguments informed, however, by the ideological convictions of an interpretive community differing from the one which is dominant on the bench. Yet, their arguments will be dismissed as bad in law, not because these arguments are inherently unsound, but because they are incongruent with the ideological convictions held by the dominant interpretive community. By the same token, excellent candidates for appointment to the bench will be found unsuitable for no other reason that they do not share the ideological convictions of the dominant elite and are therefore not members of the dominant interpretive community. For this very reason South Africa's Chief Justice, could say, as mentioned in Chapter 6, that the best of the best need not be appointed to the bench.

Viewed from this perspective, there is strictly speaking no such thing as *The Constitution*, but a variety of competing visions of the Constitution. Finally, there are in fact *different constitutions* emanating from divergent interpretations.[28] Judged from an abstract perspective, there is only one Constitution, namely the Constitution of the physically observable text. However, practically, in terms of the variety of concrete and conflicting interpretations, there are many. Only one of these many constitutions is binding and authoritative, namely the one that is located in the interpretation of the dominant interpretive community. In law, more specifically in constitutional law, these are the interpretations in the majority or unanimous judgments of the superior courts, specifically those of the highest court.

27   See part 6.4.1 of Chapter 6.

28   Coombe, 1989:617.

The views of interpretive communities outside the dominant interpretive community (outside the dominant elite) might be reflected in dissenting minority judgments. They feature in the heads of argument of counsel who argue cases for parties from outside the dominant elite, in case discussion and articles, scholarly commentary, the views of political parties, non-governmental organisations outside the dominant elite, editorial commentary from among the same ranks, etc. These interpretations might be cogent, convincing and intellectually appealing. However, they are of no consequence because they are not binding.

These meanings, forthcoming from the interpretive activities of non-dominant interpretive communities are excluded, denied and even oppressed.[29] De Ville asserted that one can say that "(c)oercion, domination, exclusion and other distinctive effects of power are always part of the hermeneutic act."[30] Hence, interpretations (as finally reflected in judgments) always empower some groups in contrast to others that are disempowered and those interpretations – decisions on meanings – are acts of obscured (or concealed) violence.[31]

I do not agree that interpretation always constitutes coercion, domination, exclusion and violence. On the contrary, it often achieves justice. Depending on the consequences of judgments flowing from a particular interpretation, it could certainly constitute coercion, domination, exclusion and obscured acts of violence.

Through constitutional interpretation binding meanings that are attributed to the Constitution are mobilised to further the ideological programme of the dominant elite. This programme is aimed at legitimising the cause of the dominant elite and delegitimising competing claims in terms of which the dominant elite is challenged Accordingly, judgments can be, and often are acts of institutional violence against the interests of groupings outside the dominant elite. It is apposite in this context to recall St Augustine's statements that a kingdom without justice is but great robberies and in the same vein, the following statement by St Thomas of Aquinas: "a human law ... in so far as it deviates from reason, is called an unjust law, and has the nature, not of law but of violence."[32] In the present context of judicial interpretation, it should be emphasised that not only legislators, executives and administrators, but also judges can be, and often are the authors of such violence.

Viewed in this light, the notion of the supreme Constitution is plainly fictitious. The notion is soothing and reassuring but on close analysis the meaning and effect of formulations of the Constitution are dependent on what meanings the dominant elite, through interpretive activity, ascribe to them. These meanings are mobilised to strengthen the dominant elite and to serve as the rampart against challengers

---

29   See the observations made by De Ville, 2000:18 and 21-22.

30   De Ville, 2000:18.

31   See further the discussion by De Ville, 2000:18.

32   For St Agustine's statement and that of St Thomas of Aquinas see Bodenheimer, 1974:22-23.

whose claims are ruled constitutionally illegitimate and bad in law. In the result, so-called entrenched rights, purported to be guaranteed by the Constitution, might and sometimes do in fact fall by the wayside. These rights only exist and have a meaning in accordance with the way in which they are interpreted. Such interpretation, which does not upset the ideological commitments of the dominant elite, might be deeply disappointing to those outside the dominant elite should they discover that their expectations of how the Constitution would safeguard their interests are proven to be without any basis and that they in fact never had the *entrenched* rights they thought they were entitled to.

The courts are generally referred to as the supreme guardian of the Constitution and of constitutional-rights. This is true, but only in part because as the discussion above has shown, the courts are also violators, albeit legitimised violators of interests, namely the interests of those opposing the dominant elite. Viewed from a different angle, the depiction of the highest courts, as the ultimate protector of rights, is at the same time distinctively romantic – and false.

The state, in the accurate analysis of Max Weber, is the holder of the monopoly of legitimate force,[33] which includes violence. The legitimate wielders of force are not only the security agencies of the state, but also, more subtly, the legislature, executive and the state administration, all sharing in the monopoly through the specific kinds of force associated with each branch. Importantly, it also includes the highest courts, specifically the apex court, whose interpretation exerts force in favour of the dominant elite and against its challengers. They also, in co-operation with the other agencies of the state, take part in the monopoly of force when they legitimately convict and punish, interdict and grant damages, and also, with dubious legitimacy, when they rule against the claims of those sectors in society outside the dominant elite and in doing so violate their interests. To the extent that there might be legitimacy in their actions they are only legitimate in terms of the ideological commitments of the dominant elite as articulated in the legal terms used by the apex court.

But are there no interpretive approaches that could at least ensure a minimum degree of objectivity, certainty and accuracy in the interpretation of meanings of the Constitution; interpretive approaches that could in the final analysis safeguard the constitutional rights of all regardless of their communal membership and ideological commitments? Are there no approaches to the interpretation of constitutional rights available that could prevent the Constitution from descending into partiality that result from the kinds of biased interpretation discussed above? Are there no avenues open to interpretation that would protect the integrity of the Constitution and sustain its claims of supremacy instead of delivering it to the biased aberrations of interpretive communities. It is in response to these questions that purposive interpretation presents itself.

---

33   Weber, 1962:309.

7.3

Purposive interpretation

Purposive interpretation, as noted in the introduction, is proffered as an approach to interpretation that vindicates the doctrine of the supreme Constitution. This approach is believed capable of bringing to light with an acceptable degree of accuracy and objectivity the authentic and stable meanings of constitutional provisions. Purposive interpretation has considerable currency in a number of jurisdictions and has repeatedly been subscribed to in South Africa. The two leading judgments of the Constitutional Court in this regard are *S v Zuma* and *S v Makwanyane*.[34] In these judgments, the Constitutional Court stated that provisions of the Bill of Rights have to be interpreted in such a way that their purpose is achieved. The critical question is how to establish the purpose. According to both these judgments, following the lead of the Canadian Supreme Court, the purpose of any provision is to be determined with reference to the interests it seeks to protect.

This must be determined taking into account:

σ   the nature and larger objects of the Bill of Rights;

σ   the language used to articulate the specific provision (right);

σ   the historical origins of the provision or the concept to be interpreted as well as the history and background to the adoption of the Constitution;

σ   the meaning and the purpose of other rights associated with the right in question.

The court added that the meaning should be generous rather than legalistic, and ensure that those entitled to the rights should enjoy the full benefit of the Bill of Rights. Purposive interpretation involves a value judgment which in itself is a controversial matter since a variety of (conflicting) value judgments may be based on one and the same formulation.

No doubt, there is considerable merit in purposive interpretation. Placing the purpose of a provision in the centre of the interpretive exercise is to my mind obviously correct. Moreover, the above-mentioned considerations to be taken into account in determining the purpose of a provision are comprehensive and balanced.

However, on close analysis none of the considerations listed above are either individually or taken together sufficient to establish accurately the correct and objective meanings of constitutional-rights provisions and cannot therefore secure a minimum acceptable degree of stability of these meanings. Each of these aids, factors or considerations introduces an additional, potential source of controversy and discord as to what constitutional-rights provisions are supposed to mean.

---

34   *S v Zuma* 1995(2) SA 642; 1995(4) BCLR 401(CC) 411C-G (para, 17:412B-G) and *S v Makwanyane* 1995(3) SA 391; 1995(6) BCLR 665(CC) (paras, 9-10); See also the recent judgment in *Daniels v Scribante and Another* 2017(8) BCLR 949(CC) para, 24:958(B-D).

The first aid, namely the nature and larger objects of the Bill of Rights, creates an additional front of controversy about the meaning of the provision which is under consideration. This is so because interpreters might have different pre-understandings (including ideological outlooks) and expectations of the nature and larger objects of the Bill of Rights.

Some might view the Constitution and the Bill of Rights as a fundamentally stabilising force: a perfected whole of which the meanings now only have to be deduced and concretised to specific factual scenarios; a mechanism (as this concept is referred to above by Van der Hoeven and Sanford Levinson) that freezes time by controlling the future through the "hardness" of the language encoded in the Constitution. In this sense the Constitution (including the Bill of Rights) is essentially a means of ensuring limited government and stability through defending and protecting the rights in the Bill of Rights. The Bill of Rights and the Constitution in general must tie down government to protect the status quo (with regard to rights) against disruption. The metaphor of *entrenchment of rights* and the notion of *guaranteed rights* support this vision of the nature and larger objects of the Bill of Rights.

There might be a directly opposite view regarding the nature and larger objects of the Bill of Rights. Accordingly, the Constitution might be perceived as the foundation not for stability, but for large scale social and economic change with a view to dismantling the present society and replacing it with something entirely new. In terms of this view, the larger objects of the Constitution are not to tie down and accordingly ensure limited government but the exact opposite, namely to serve as an instrument for comprehensive governmental intervention with a view to giving effect to a programme of wide-ranging change.[35] This is what is envisaged by so-called transformative interpretation, which is discussed in the next section.

The second factor (aid), namely the language used to articulate the specific provision (right), is not an aid but rather an essential prerequisite for the entire interpretive exercise. The language used to articulate a provision provides access to meaning. However, precisely that is the central reason for different meanings about the provision to be interpreted. It is the only way to establish meaning and at the same time the reason why different meanings can be attached to the same subject matter. The citing of language used to articulate the specific provision or right as an aid, is in a sense based on a circular argument: the language used to articulate the specific provision gives rise to the problem of uncertainty of meaning, but this same problem is proposed as part of the solution.

The third aid is the historical origins of the provision or the concept to be interpreted as well as the history and background of the adoption of the Constitution. There is

---

35   See for example *Bato Star Fishing (Pty) Ltd v Minister of Environmental Affairs* 2004(7) BCLR 687(CC) 720D-722A (paras, 73-76); *South African Police Service v Solidarity (obo Barnard)* 2014(10) BCLR 1195(CC) paras, 29-30 1205 E-H, as well as the views expressed by Madala J in *Du Plessis v De Klerk* 1995(5) BCLR 658(CC) 729B-G (para, 157).

no certainty that the views on the historical origins of a provision will promote consensus on the correct meaning of constitutional provisions. On the contrary, interpretations of the history and background of the adoption of the Constitution are bound to further exacerbate the differences between the meanings of constitutional provisions. This is particularly true for South African history which is marked by deep differences of historical interpretations.

The Constitution might therefore be viewed, on the one hand as the basis for inter-communal reconciliation, but on the other hand as the basis for the large scale transformation of society, which might disrupt the prospects for reconciliation. By the same token it might also be viewed as the basis for compromise or, for redress that the collective "guilty" agent owes to "innocent" victims. Proceeding from a liberal-individualist ideological pre-understanding, the Constitution might be viewed as primarily an instrument for safeguarding individual dignity and individual rights; or, viewed from a (multi-)communitarian ideological pre-understanding, it might be perceived as an instrument for the accommodation of a variety of cultural, linguistic, religious and other communities; or viewed from yet another ideologically inspired pre-understanding, the Constitution might be regarded as the basis for the dissolution of such communities in order to be assimilated in a single homogenous South African *nation*. Once again inspired by a particular ideological pre-understanding, the Constitution might be viewed as the basis for establishing a distinctive South African rainbow nation, or conversely, as an instrument for Africanisation in order to establish an "authentic" autochthonous African state.

An essentially free-market ideological pre-understanding of the Constitution might be the basis for viewing it as an instrument slanting in favour of capitalist (or so-called neo-liberal) economic policies. Alternatively, viewed from another ideological perspective, it might be viewed as an instrument for meeting the needs of a mixed economic dispensation with a social democratic character. Viewed from a generally "progressive" or more specifically Marxist perspective, the Constitution might be viewed as an instrument for a revolutionary class struggle aimed at dismantling capitalism through a redeeming socialist revolution resulting in the establishment of a splendid classless society of equality. The Constitution can also be viewed from the perspective of a combination of reconciliation and transformation. From such perspective the Constitution would be perceived as an instrument for the promotion of reconciliation among previously conflicting communities through the transfer of economic assets from the "guilty" haves to the "innocent" have-nots; and in so doing promote economic equality. This, as the discussion of transformative interpretation in part 7.4 below will show, is the very founding stone of the South African brand of transformationism.[36]

---

36   This is what the argument of Langa, 2006:359 boils down to.

Most of these and many other outlooks stem from conflicting perspectives of the history of South Africa, which is a history prone to conflicting perspectives.[37] Exponents of all these perspectives could refer to specific provisions of the Constitution and in particular the Bill of Rights as support for claiming that the realisation of every particular claim finds expression in the constitutional text.[38] However, it is not the text itself that is so clear. The perceived clarity cannot be ascribed to the text as such but to the readers' understanding of the text, which is shaped by their particular ideologically-inspired pre-understanding of the text.[39]

The bottom line is that the historical origins and background of the provision or the concept to be interpreted, and in particular such origins and background pertaining to the adoption of the Constitution, are no (consensus-producing) aids at all. They cannot contribute to correct, accurate, basically objective and largely consensus opinions as to what constitutional provisions and the Constitution generally mean. The opposite obtains: it is not an aid but more correctly an additional source of discord about what the Constitution means. The Constitution in fact means many different and conflicting things to members of different interpretive communities; and there is considerable truth in the assertion that even though there is but a single text there are in fact a multitude of constitutions, each for every interpretive community.[40]

The forth of the above-mentioned aids is the meaning and the purpose of other rights associated with the right under consideration. No doubt other (associated) rights should also be considered, to avoid contradictions and to interpret the provision in question in proper context. Nevertheless, this does not necessarily suggest that consensus may be reached on the accurate and objective meaning of the provision in question. The direct opposite might obtain, namely that associated rights (might) add further problems of finding accurate and basically objective meanings. All provisions are marred by controversies surrounding their meaning, especially constitutional-rights provisions which are broadly and inevitably also ambiguously formulated. Each *associated* provision is therefore accompanied by specific meaning-controversies, thus increasing the uncertainty of the meaning under consideration. The point is that if the uncertainties surrounding the meaning of the first provision has to be determined with reference to associated provisions, which are marred by similar uncertainties and controversies, the extent of uncertainty simply expands

---

37   For an intriguing discussion of the deep division in South African historiography see generally Van Jaarsveld, 1984:6-7.

38   Different interpreters, approaching the text from different ideological pre-understandings, will be assisted in their claim that the texts clearly says what they claim it to say by reason of the fact that human rights have become almost completely free of any specific ideological content and remain beyond any exclusive ideological preferences or aversions. Human rights are like a sponge and would appear to absorb almost anything that rears its head, irrespective of the ideological discrepancies of those interests recognised as human rights. (See in this regard the observations by Szabo, 1982:19.)

39   See the observations made by Du Plessis, 2002:197.

40   Recalling the conclusion of Coombe, 1989:617.

as each associated right is added to the interpretive exercise. Associated rights and provisions can therefore make interpretive problems more intricate and their solution more difficult.

There is also another problem arising from the aid of associated rights and that is the question as to which rights and provisions are really associated ones. Whilst in the eyes of one interpretive community some rights would qualify as associated rights other interpretive communities might conclude otherwise.

The fifth aid suggests that constitutional provisions, specifically constitutional rights should be construed generously rather than legalistic, so as to afford every person entitled the full benefit of the Bill of Rights. This aid can hardly be of help because rights are often contradictory – more correctly, they are susceptible to different irreconcilable interpretations – because Bills of Rights usually include formulations originating from a variety of conflicting ideological perspectives,[41] which could become the source of interpretive battles. The battles can lead to compromises. However, more often than not, depending on the inclinations and relative strengths of the interpretive communities, one right is preferred and reigns victorious. The bottom line is that it is simply out of the question to construe all rights generously. A generous interpretation of one right often necessitates a restrictive interpretation, or disregard of another right. No wonder therefore that the Constitutional Court, notwithstanding its statement that rights should be construed generously rather than legalistically, subsequently conceded that such interpretation would often be (logically) impossible.[42]

On close analysis, it is clear that purposive interpretation is an ineffective means of establishing correct, basically objective and stable meanings. The opposite obtains if these aids are applied: the uncertainties about the meanings of constitutional provisions are deepened and give rise to multiple conflicting arguments among competing interpretive communities about the meanings of constitutional provisions; rather than producing clarity and basic consensus on meanings, interpretive battles are aggravated.

74

Transformative (transformationist) interpretation (as an ingredient of transformationism)

The so-called transformative approach (doctrine) to interpretation of the Constitution has gained ascendancy in the South African constitutional and

---

41   See the observations made by Szabo, 1982:19 referred to above. The various generations of rights – some liberal/free market and others socialist, underscore the point.

42   See for example *Soobramoney v Minister of Health KwaZulu-Natal* 1997(12) BCLR 1997(CC) 1702E-F (para, 17); *South African National Defence Union v Minister of Defence* 1999(6) BCLR 615(CC) 629G-630B (para, 2).

political discourse. It is an important ingredient of the encompassing ideology of transformationism or transformative constitutionalism, indicative of a so-called transformative vision of the Constitution. Such vision demands that everyone who is engaged in constitutional interpretation and legal interpretation in general to interpret the law and the Constitution with a view to accomplishing a transformed society. The term transformationism is preferred here since it reveals the profound ideological nature of the matter under discussion more candidly than the seemingly ideologically neutral and legal-like term of transformative constitutionalism.

The leftist United States of America scholar, Karl Klare,[43] in one of the most praised and romanticised writings[44] on transformationism in South Africa, described transformative constitutionalism as "a long term project of constitutional enactment, interpretation, and enforcement committed ... to transforming a country's political and social institutions and power relationships in a democratic, participatory, and egalitarian direction."[45] Thus viewed, a Constitution is not regarded as an instrument to restrain governmental power. On the contrary, it is an instrument for the achievement of fundamental change[46] – politically, socially, economically, culturally and intellectually. To that end all organs of state, the courts and the civil society must be conscripted and mobilised. The South African Constitution, in terms of this transformative understanding "(c)reates the legal framework for the fundamental transformation of unjust political, social, economic, and cultural relations in South African society."[47] The Constitution is not the supreme instrument for safeguarding continuity and stability of existing interests and rights. It is the direct opposite: the supreme weapon for guaranteeing the radical change of the existing political, economic, social, cultural and intellectual transformation; an instrument for an encompassing legally organised revolution. Accordingly, the Constitution must also be interpreted with a view to bring about such encompassing and far-reaching change.

Ironically, even though transformationism, as the discussion will show, has distinctively (leftist) revolutionary ideals, it bears striking commonalities with orthodox interpretation. Sanford Levinson and Van der Hoeven[48] we may recall, noted that the orthodox interpretation believes in the hardness – the undisturbed

---

43   Klare is an exponent of the Critical Legal Studies (CLS) movement that gained prominence in the United States during the 1980s.

44   Klare, 1998:146-188 at 153 et seq. in fact overtly romanticised about South Africa's caring, positive, participatory and multicultural, post-liberal constitution. Roux, 2009b:258-285 at 260 et seq., specifically at 263, 265 and 266 highlighted the vagueness and lack of exactness in Klare's argumentation.

45   Klare, 1998:146-188 at 150. Klare's article marked the beginning of a now mounting literature surrounding transformative constitutionalism and its ramifications – transformative adjudication and transformative interpretation. See for example: Langa, 2006:351-360; Moseneke, 2002:309-319; Pieterse, 2005:155-166; Liebenberg, 2006:3-36; Van der Walt, 2006:1-47. Albertyn & Goldblatt, 1998:248-276; Liebenberg, 2010:23-78.

46   Liebenberg, 2006:1-47.

47   Liebenberg, 2010:76.

48   Levinson, 1982:376; As to the insights of Van der Hoeven see the first part of this chapter.

certainty, objectivity and durability – of the meanings of constitutional provisions and perceived them as effective mechanisms which can be used to freeze time by controlling the future through the perceived hardness of language encoded in a monumental document. Ironically, transformative interpretation subscribes to the same belief. It also believes in the hardness of language of the written Constitution. In the case of transformative interpretation, the hardness of language is enlisted to guarantee transformationism's drive for constant revolution in the same direction.

Yet there are vast practical differences between the two approaches. The orthodox doctrine strongly slants towards interpretation of formulations that would favour the preservation of the status quo. In other words, orthodox interpretation would use the ostensible hardness of language and the certainty, clarity and stability of meanings to justify stability and continuity. Transformative interpretation on the other hand follows the opposite direction by favouring meanings that dismantle the status quo. In other words, transformative interpretation would enlist the ostensible hardness of language and the certainty, clarity and stability of meanings not to justify stability, but to justify fundamental change.

Under orthodox interpretation rights formulations are interpreted to justify the protection of existing interests. Under transformative interpretation the converse obtains; the Constitution is understood to mandate encompassing change: the restriction or nullification of (existing) rights and the recognition and advancement of rights and interests, perceived previously not to have been recognised.[49]

7.4.1 Homogenous egalitarian society

What does transformationism's ideal dispensation look like and how must the Constitution be interpreted to achieve and sustain the kind of society that transformationism hankered for? An authorative answer to these questions is provided by former Chief Justice Langa[50] and former Deputy Chief Justice Moseneke.[51]

The quintessential feature of the vision of the transformed constitution, that is, of the destiny of transformationism, is a full-fledged egalitarian society: a truly

---

49 Purposive interpretation cannot solve this clash between orthodox and transformative interpretation. It merely reformulates the clash of different terms: for orthodox interpretation, the overriding purpose of the Constitution, is the safeguarding of existing rights; for transformative interpretation it is the opposite namely the dismantling of the existing order and its replacement by a new dispensation – a new dispensation that more often than not, would require existing rights and interests to be sacrificed. See in this regard the statement by Ncgobo J as he then was. in *Bato Star Fishing (Pty) Ltd v Minister of Environmental Affairs and Tourism* 2004(7) BCLR 687(CC) para, 76:721F-G about the effect of the commitment of transformationism to equality. "The measures that bring about transformation will inevitably affect some members of the society adversely, particularly those coming from the previously advantaged communities. It may well be that other considerations may have to yield in favour of achieving the goal we fashioned for ourselves in the Constitution." The difficulties associated with the attainment of equality, Ncgobo J said, should not be underestimated. See also *South African Police Service v Solidarity (obo Barnard)* para, 78:1217H-1218B.

50 Langa, 2006:351-360.

51 Moseneke, 2002:309-319.

equal society based on (a particularly strong version of) substantive equality,[52] if not sameness – a classless socialist society which is essentially homogeneous in the public sphere.

Both Moseneke and Langa endorsed the views of Albertyn and Goldblatt in whose view the Constitution is the foundation for revolving South Africa into an egalitarian society. Transformation, Albertyn and Goldblatt stated, requires "(a) complete reconstruction of the state and society, including a redistribution of power and resources along egalitarian lines."[53] Equality as a value (in section 1 of the Constitution) and as a right (in section 9) are to them "(c)entral to the task of transformation."[54] Equality is the "foundational value" and "organising principle" of the new – the present and evolving – dispensation.[55] Particular emphasis is placed on the activist formulation in section 1 of the Constitution in which not equality, but the "achievement of equality" is posited as part of the value foundation of the Constitution.[56] Both Moseneke and Albertyn, as well as Goldblatt referred approvingly[57] as authority for their stance (that the transformative programme is essentially premised on and directed towards the achievement of substantive equality) to the statement by former Constitutional Court Justice Kriegler, who declared as follows in *President of the RSA v Hugo*:

> The South African Constitution is primarily and emphatically an egalitarian Constitution. The supreme laws of comparable constitutional states may underscore other principles and rights, but in the light of our particular history and vision for the future, a Constitution was written with equality at its centre. Equality is our Constitution's focus and organising principle.[58]

Transformationism's intimate association with substantive equality causes it to reject formal or notional equality in the words of Moseneke.[59] Hence, from a transformationist angle what is decisive is not equal opportunities but equal outcomes. Accordingly Moseneke declared:

> Unlike classical liberal jurisprudence, animated by individual autonomy and protection of property, the attainment of collective good, through redistributive fairness in an open and democratic society, informs transformative jurisprudence.[60]

Transformationism and the attainment and maintenance of actual substantive equality is a comprehensive project in which all branches of governmental power

---

52 Moseneke, 2002:315-316; Langa, 2006:252-254.

53 Albertyn &Goldblatt, 1998:249.

54 Ibid.

55 Ibid.

56 Ibid.

57 Moseneke, 2002:316 and Albertyn & Goldblatt, 1998:250.

58 *President of the RSA v Hugo* 1997(4) SA 1(CC) para, 74:740I-741B.

59 Moseneke, 2002:317.

60 Ibid.

and organs of the state, as well as the courts, have to pull their weight. The courts have their own specialised transformative role, namely that of interpreting the Constitution and adjudicating in a way which would most effectively achieve and maintain substantive equality.[61] Thus Moseneke declared:

> (t)ransformative adjudication must be put to the task of achieving (in conjunction with other organs of the state and diverse organs of civil society) social redistributive justice. The primary purpose of the Constitution is to intervene in unjust, uneven and impermissible power and resource distributions, in order to restore substantive equality ...[62]

The judiciary, Moseneke concluded, "(i)s commanded to observe with unfailing fidelity the transformative mission of the Constitution."[63]

The premise of the passion for an egalitarian society, as the gravamen of transformationism is the transformationists' imagined natural human condition. That natural condition is an egalitarian society, that is, a society marked by substantive equality, homogeneity and the absence of any significant difference.[64] In contrast, *in*equality is unnatural. Inequality is the dreadful consequence of an historical aberration in which the natural and only acceptable condition, namely that of equality is disrupted and replaced by one of inequality, hierarchy, heterogeneity, domination and abuse of the lower by the higher strata of society. The august mission of transformationism is to restore this egalitarian condition premised on fundamental equality and public homogeneity. It is to this laudable duty that judges are also called. They must read the Constitution in the revealing light of transformationism, namely as a solemn decree to restore the natural equality that was disrupted by the evils of history. It is against this background that Moseneke declared that the primary mission of the Constitution is that of intervening into the uneven state of power and resource distributions with a view to *restore* substantive equality.[65]

In the South African context the natural and classless condition of equality is viewed to have been disrupted by the vices of colonialism, of racial separation and a raft of concomitant evils, including sexism, patriarchy and generally any other causes of inequality. The main duty of the Constitution in this context is to dismantle the consequences of colonialism and racial separation and all the concomitant evils, so as to restore the natural egalitarian human condition.

---

61 Ibid, p.318.

62 Ibid.

63 Ibid, p.319 and Langa, 2006:358 also highlighted the joint responsibility of the courts in this regard.

64 See the remarks by Albertyn & Goldblatt, 1998:253 viewing difference not as a (natural) given but as something that is artificially created.

65 Moseneke, 2002:318.

As noted in Chapter 5, Chief Justice Mogoeng added his voice to this historical vision. According to Mogoeng, basing his view on a quote that turned out to be an Internet forgery, South Africa, and Africa in general, was in a paradisiacal state of peace, abundance and equality that was only uprooted by the terrifying arrival of white colonialists, who caused this splendid natural state to be uprooted and who are still wreaking havoc, yet now using devious tactics.

Transformationism proves to be based on a distinctively simplistic grand narrative - a crude historical imagery. It has a backward and forward looking perspective at the same time. It is backward looking in the sense that it looks back at a history, which in the interpretation of the South African brand of transformationism is one of inequality, abuse and domination, preceded by the primeval condition of natural equality; and it looks forward towards the restoration of the perceived splendid natural condition of equality. Transformationism is therefore presented as a programme of restitutionary, remedial and redistributive constitutionalism.

The seminal beginning of this (official) historical interpretation in the South African context is the postscript to the interim Constitution and the preamble to the 1996 Constitution discussed in Chapter 3. The postscript states that the Constitution provides a historic bridge between the past of a deeply divided society characterised by strife, conflict, untold suffering and injustice, and a bright future founded on the recognition of human rights, democracy and peaceful co-existence and development of opportunities for all South Africans, irrespective of colour, race, belief or sex.

The Constitutional Court is guarding over this interpretation of South African history with great care and has vehemently dismissed any historical interpretation that could cast doubt on the credence of the splendid society that the interim Constitution is claimed to have brought about.[66]

On close analysis, there is no substantive difference between an orthodox political ideology of socialism and transformationism. They subscribe to the naturalness of equality; are equally averse to (public) heterogeneity and both are equally committed to the establishment – in their thinking, the restoration – of substantive equality and homogeneity. The difference between the two is not conceptual but terminological.[67] Socialism is openly political. Transformative constitutionalism by contrast is covertly political and masquerades in juridical terms. It disguises its passions for a classless socialist society for which it struggles in less blatant and often neutral-like language of the law. This masquerading is in itself a political stratagem because the language of law and constitutionalism is seemingly more erudite and professional, more neutral and therefore more convincing and difficult

---

66   In *Helen Suzman Foundation v President of the RSA; Glenister v President of the RSA* 2015(1) BCLR 1(CC) for example provides a telling example of this, discussed in 5.2 elaborates on this point.

67   Klare, 1998:150; 151; 153 and 155 subscribed to distinctively purely socialist ideology.

to challenge than strait forward political ideology openly articulated in political and ideological terms.[68]

The courts cannot be passive and neutral bystanders in this. More specifically, the courts were called upon to part with what was termed their conservative, formalist, literalist and liberal legal culture, which was patently unsuitable in terms of transformationism's vision of the Constitution.[69] Moseneke specifically makes this point. What he terms "liberal legalism" in his view: "(b)alks at the idea of transformative adjudication."[70] Transformationism expressly calls on judges to accomplish political objectives. Accordingly, Moseneke declares that a transformative understanding of the Constitution has reconfigured the way in which judges should be doing their work. The Constitution thus viewed, invites judges into a new sphere of jurisprudential creativity and self-reflection about legal method, analysis and reasoning consistent with their transformative roles.[71] It is against this background that the classical principles of separation of powers and judicial independence and impartiality need to be reconceptualised. In this regard Liebenberg makes a call for what she referred to as a dialogic conception of adjudication,[72] in which there is no room for strict separation of powers and in which the *partiality* (instead of impartiality) of the judiciary, which closely co-operates with the legislature and the executive, is recognised and actively propagated.

This plea is in fact nothing new. It merely corroborates in overt terms the argument advanced in Chapter 6, namely that the three powers are usually unified in a single power elite.

It also affirms, as demonstrated in Chapter 6, that judicial impartiality is *regime-relative*. Judicial impartiality plays out only within ideologically set limits. In the present case, the call is for the judiciary *not* to be *im*partial, but to actively join the other branches of the ruling elite in the battle to achieve the goals of their shared ideology of transformationism, and thus to participate in achieving and then defending its socialist goals of a classless, substantively egalitarian and (publicly) homogenous society. In South Africa, inspired by the ideology of transformationism, the unity of powers and the call for an (ideologically) partial and active judiciary is overtly extreme.

---

68 (The advocates of) transformative constitutionalism are, however, not the sole delinquents in this. All political ideologies can and in fact do make themselves guilty of intellectual dishonesty of this kind. All can use the language of law and constitutionalism as a stratagem to pursue ideological goals under the useful cloak of this neutral-like and convincing language.

69 This lies at the core of Klare's argumentation in Klare, 1998:166 et seq.

70 Moseneke, 2002:315.

71 Ibid, p.318.

72 Liebenberg, 2010:66-71.

Klare's call for a change in legal culture[73] must be understood against this background. His call seeks to enlist judges and lawyers in general to join the enterprise towards the achievement (and eventual defence) of the classless, egalitarian, homogenous society and to seize on the opportunities that the Constitution, through transformative interpretation offers to achieve this goal.

Cadre deployment, the principle of representivity and official monoligualism, which as shown in Chapter 5, are crucial operative strategies for achieving the egalitarian goal of transformationism. Once the representivity principle is fully complied with, the vision of the transformed society will be realised. Then substantive equality will be in place because the economy, in terms of property, labour, business enterprise and management will be spread equally through society and unequal relations of power will be replaced by equality; and once the representivity is fully complied with, all organised spheres in society will be exact replicas of one another and will be reflective of the national population profile. This clearly leaves no room for the recognition of minority communities because they stand in the way of transformationism's notion and ideal of the egalitarian homogenous society. Minority communities should therefore actively be opposed and their claims countered. The judiciary should also play its part by interpreting the Constitution toward achieving the desired result. There is some room for a multitude of identities (especially cultural identities) in the private sphere and there is rhetorical yet specious recognition for heterogeneity, multiculturalism, differences and a multitude of identities,[74] but claims for actual recognition for minority cultural communities are often met with dismissive response. Then the transformative goal of a single homogenous substantively equal society takes precedence.

7.5

Transformative interpretation – the transformationist role of the Constitutional Court

The South African courts, more specifically the Constitutional Court, have on many occasions delivered judgments against government and organs of state, which in some instances have caused embarrassment to government and the ruling party. Amongst them is included a raft of judgments relating to the malfunctioning of the state administration and government. Also included are the numerous judgments against state departments, yet often not complied with, which eventually induced the Constitutional Court to rebuke the state for its chronic laxity. As a result the Constitutional Court was applauded in some quarters for what was regarded as proof of the Court's real and genuine independence and impartiality.

---

73   Klare, 1998:166 et seq.

74   See for example the statements by Sachs J in *Minister of Home Affairs v Fourie* 2006(1) SA 524; 2006(3) BCLR 355(CC) discussed below.

Then there is another set of judgments discussed in part 7.5.1 below, which also caused embarrassment to the government and the ANC. The judgments concerned resulted from disputes within the ranks and within the ideological assumptions of the dominant elite. Once again, these judgments were hailed for their perceived proof of the courts' impartiality and willingness to act independently. Once again, however, commitments to transformationism was not at stake in these cases. On the contrary, these Constitutional Court cases and occasionally other court cases as well, assisted the dominant elite (specifically the ANC) in its efforts to regain ideological coherence and to pursue transformationism more effectively than before, and to enable them to more effectively overcome challenges from opposition parties. These judgments are discussed in part 7.5.1.

The point is that it would be patently wrong to look upon any of these judgments as evidence of the Constitutional Court's *ideological* independence and impartiality. On the contrary, the jurisprudence of the Constitutional Court overwhelmingly proves that the Court is closely unified with the legislature, the executive, the ruling party, and other supporting formations within a single dominant political elite. The judgments discussed in part 7.5.2 prove the point. The courts, more specifically the Constitutional Court, have through their majority and unanimous judgments faithfully played their part in close conformity with (the rest of) the elite in promoting and defending transformationism. Occasionally majority judgments in favour of transformationism would go too far, thus leading to minority judgments in which the majority's transformationist extremes are criticised and rejected. These minority judgments are particularly insightful for their lucid exposure of the (majority of the) Court's unfailing co-operation towards the advancement of the ruling elite's transformationist drive.

7.5.1 Intra dominant elite hiccups and quarrels

The first judgment to be considered is that of the Constitutional Court in the so-called Nkandla-case.[75] In this judgment the court sternly rebuked the president (former president Zuma), as well as the caucus of the ruling ANC in the National Assembly for their constitutionally unbecoming conduct. The case emanated from findings and directives of the Public Protector regarding illegitimate public expenditure on the private homestead of president Zuma in Nkandla in KwaZulu-Natal. Parliament, more specifically the parliamentary caucus of the ANC, failed to heed to these findings and directives, and usurped the powers of review and eventually rejected the Public Protector's report, thus protecting Zuma and the ANC itself. In this judgment the Court, among other things, ruled this conduct unconstitutional and sharply reprimanded the parliamentary ANC.

---

75 *Economic Freedom Fighters v Speaker of the National Assembly and Others; Democratic Alliance v Speaker of the National Assembly and Others* 2016(5) BCLR 618(CC). See also the background discussion by Hoffman, 2016:202-231.

The impression that the court in this case acted from outside the dominant elite and gave a verdict against the dominant elite is glaringly mistaken.[76] None of the ideological commitments of transformationism was at stake. Moreover, the two opposition parties who were the applicants in the case shared with the ANC many of its basic ideological elements of transformationism. In fact, the EFF (the first applicant) and the ANC are of one mind regarding the confiscation of white-owned (farm) land and its redistribution among the black population. They had also joined forces to let the National Assembly pass a resolution to that effect on 27 February 2018. None of the ideological commitments of the dominant elite has been challenged by an outside challenger, such as in the cases discussed in part 7.5.2. On the contrary, the Nkandla-case involved a dispute *within* the dominant elite, namely about Zuma's conduct and about the protection that he received from the ANC's parliamentary caucus. Within this dominant elite – and this is really the gist of the matter – there were strong forces insisting on Zuma's resignation. These forces included a host of groups and individuals within the ranks of the ANC who were firmly committed to transformationism, yet deeply embarrassed at the deep-seated corruption associated with Zuma and his faction. Clearly the reason they wanted Zuma removed was not because, with Zuma out of the way, it would be easier for the ANC to change its ideological programme. On the contrary, they wanted Zuma to leave so that the ANC could regain its balance which would enable it to peruse transformationism with new vigour, free from the dissent and confusion caused by Zuma, which was precisely what came to pass after Zuma's removal from the presidency in February 2018. The Constitutional Court's judgment was to my mind legally beyond controversy. The point, however, is also that the Court's judgment implicitly, yet emphatically rendered assistance to the ANC, allowing the anti Zuma faction to gain the upper hand and in so doing for the ANC to regain its balance free from the encumbrances that Zuma caused. To think that the Court in this case suddenly became a new kind of institution, divorced from the dominant elite would be glaringly wrong. In this case the Court had to deal with a dispute arising *within* the dominant elite. As part thereof the court had to discharge its responsibility as a specialised element within that elite.

The second case to consider is that of *Black Sash Trust and Others v The Minister of Social Development and Others*,[77] often referred to as the SASSA judgment. SASSA is the abbreviation for South African Social Security Agency, an organ of state which was responsible for paying out state grants to approximately 17 million social security grant holders. The first respondent, the minister of social security, bears political responsibility for SASSA. In terms of an agreement between SASSA and Cash Paymaster Services (CPS) (the sixth respondent) the latter was responsible for payment of the state grants mentioned above. In 2013 in the case of *AllPay Consolidated*

76   Malan, 1 May 2016. Available: http://bit.ly/2Me63Sm

77   *Black Sash Trust v Minister of Social Development and Others (Freedom Under Law NPC Intervening)* (CCT48/17) [2017] ZACC 8 (17 March 2017).

Investment Holdings (AllPay 1) the Court found that the agreement between SASSA and CPS was constitutionally invalid because it had been concluded on the basis of invalid tender procedures.[78] The Court suspended its ruling of invalidity until 31 March 2017 so that SASSA could enter into a new five year contract or could make arrangements to shoulder the obligations itself *(AllPay 2)*.[79]

In November 2015 SASSA informed the Court that it would not enter an agreement with a service provider, but would make the arrangements to shoulder responsibilities itself. In April 2016, it transpired that SASSA could not honour its undertaking. Neither SASSA, nor the minister, took any steps to inform the Court accordingly in order to obtain new instructions from the Court. The minister, who had been made aware of this incapacity in October 2016, showed no interest in SASSA's progress with regard to the execution of the court order. In consequence, a catastrophe was looming large in view of the risk that no grants would be paid out after 31 March 2017, something which would amount to a massive infringement of the right to social security and appropriate social assistance under section 27 of the Constitution[80] and an accompanying social disaster. In an atmosphere of a looming national crisis and growing public outrage at the laxity of SASSA and the minister, the Court was at the eleventh hour approached to intervene in the matter. On 17 March the Court held that SASSA and CPS were under the constitutional obligation to ensure payment of social grants from 1 April 2017 until an entity other than CPS is able to do so. The suspension of the order made in *AllPay 2* was extended for another period of 12 months. SASSA and CPS were ordered to pay out the social grants. They had to comply with this responsibility under strict supervision of the Court in terms the structural interdict.

The situation that lead to the Court's interdict and the terms of the judgment and the interdict, were hugely embarrassing to SASSA, the minister and the governing party. The court's intervention, however, did not in any way go against the governing party's own policy or the ideological commitments of transformationism. On the contrary, the very notion of socio-economic rights such as those embodied in, for example sections 26 and 27 of the Constitution,[81] emanated from the ANC's own ideological convictions. It was precisely the ANC who, during the constitutional negotiations in the beginning of the 1990s pressed for these rights to be included in

---

78   *AllPay Consolidated Investment Holdings (Pty) Ltd v Chief Executive Officer, South African Social Security Agency* 2014(1) SA 604(CC); 2014(1) BCLR 1(CC) (AllPay 1).

79   *AllPay Consolidated Investment Holdings (Pty) Ltd v Chief Executive Officer, South African Social Security Agency* 2014(4) SA 179(CC); 2014(6) BCLR 641(CC) (AllPay 2).

80   The sub-section reads: Everyone has the right to have access to – (c) social security, including, if they are unable to support themselves and their dependents, appropriate social assistance. The Court in paragraph 8 of the judgment also referred to this right as the right to transformative empowerment.

81   The right to housing and the right to health care, food, water and social security.

the Bill of Rights.[82] Moreover, the ANC in its capacity as government gave effect to the benefits of these rights by establishing the vast system of social grants, which on close analysis is an integral element of transformationism. In the very first sentence of the judgment, the Court emphatically associated itself with this policy stating that one of the signature achievements of the present constitutional order was to establish a comprehensive programme of social assistance. What the Court therefore effectively did was to utilise its remedial powers to give effect to the enforcement of the very rights that the ANC wanted to be included in the Constitution as part of the programme of transformationism and which it eventually embodied in its social security system. The Court therefore did not go against the ANC (and the dominant elite in general) or any of its ideological convictions. On the contrary, it restored the necessary balance for the ideological programme to continue without the catastrophe that a discontinuation of payments would have caused. It did not double cross the ANC; it assisted it.

I briefly refer to three other judgments of the High Court and the SCA which fall in the same category as the two cases dealt with above. These cases also emanated from wrangles within the dominant elite. In *Democratic Alliance v Minister of International Relations and Cooperation and Others*[83] the High Court ruled that the decision of the national executive to withdraw from the International Criminal Court (ICC) without prior parliamentary approval was unconstitutional. Notwithstanding the fact that the application in this case was lodged by the main opposition party in parliament, the Democratic Alliance, it would be wrong to perceive of the judgment as a rebuke of the dominant elite.

The ANC government staunchly supported the establishment of the ICC and played a prominent part in the negotiations that led to the Court's formation. After the conclusion of the founding treaty that established the Court, it also quickly took steps to have the treaty ratified by Parliament and to pass legislation for the incorporation of the treaty into South African domestic law.[84] Only later it developed misgivings about the Court and that gave rise to the attempted withdrawal. However, there is no consensus within the dominant elite on this issue. On the contrary, there are forceful trends within the dominant elite which wanted South African to remain in the ICC.

The next case related to the refusal of the executive and the relevant criminal justice authorities to effect the arrest of the Sudanese president, Omar Al Bashir in execution of an arrest warrant of the ICC while he was on visit in South Africa

---

82   ANC, 1993. A Bill of Rights for a New South Africa. Available: http://bit.ly/2TvCcp5
     [Accessed, 20 August 2013].

83   *Democratic Alliance v Minister of International Relations and Cooperation and Others (Council for the Advancement of the South African Constitution Intervening)* (83145/2016) [2017] ZAGPPHC 53; 2017(3) SA 212(GP); [2017] 2 All SA 123(GP) (22 February 2017).

84   *Implementation of the Rome Statute of the International Criminal Court Act* 27 of 2002.

during 2015 to attend a meeting of the African Union. In this case the SCA in *Minister of Justice and Constitutional Development v Southern African Litigation Centre*[85] held that this failure was unconstitutional and at variance with South Africa's treaty obligations under the Rome Statute of the International Criminal Court. Once again, there is no consensus in the dominant elite on this question. On the contrary, there are many within the elite who vehemently reproached the executive decision not to arrest Al Bashir. When the SCA therefore ruled that it was unlawful (contrary to South Africa's treaty obligations) not to arrest Al Bashir they did not rule in favour of challengers from outside the dominant elite against the dominant elite.

From a political point of view both the cases on the attempted withdrawal from the ICC and the refusal to arrest Al Bashir concerned wrangles within the dominant elite that were ruled in favour of one faction and against an opposing faction in the dominant elite (granted that the successful faction was supported by forces outside the elite). Moreover, the case on the withdrawal from the ICC did not relate to the substance, that is, to the merits or the contents of the decision but to the procedure, namely failure to obtain prior parliamentary approval for the decision to withdraw. (The) government (of the time) sought to withdraw solely on the basis of an executive decision, which was inadequate. After the judgment government is still free to withdraw on the basis of suitable parliamentary procedure.[86] In the last case, *Earthlife Africa Johannesburg and Another v Minister of Energy and Others*[87] the High Court ruled the South African government's multi-billion nuclear transaction with Russia invalid. However, the judgment pertained only to procedural shortcomings, namely government's failure to have proper consultation before entering into an agreement. It did not touch on the matters of substance, that is, the merits of the agreement. Government is therefore still at liberty to proceed with an agreement on condition that the relevant consultation process takes place. The judgment therefore leaves untouched the government's ideological preferences, which in this case relates to foreign relations.[88] Moreover, this transaction was also a bone of contention within the governing elite and within the ANC. After the ouster of previous president Zuma, government resolved not to proceed with negotiations on the procurement of nuclear power from Russia.

---

85 2016(4) BCLR 487(SCA).

86 At the time of finalising the manuscript the matter still appears to be in political limbo.

87 *University of the Free State v Afriforum and Another* 2017(5) SA 227(WCC).

88 There are numerous judgments that fall into this category, namely cases in which the courts ruled against organs of state in relation to their failure to give effect to socio-economic rights. It began with the well-known judgment of the Constitutional Court in *Government of die Republic of South Africa v Grootboom* 2000(11) BCLR 1169(CC) and shortly after that the judgment in *Minister of Health v Treatment Action Campaign* 2002(10) BCLR 1033(CC). These judgments on the enforcement of the rights to housing, food, water, health and social security are integral to the ANC's transformationist ideology. They are an important part of the juridical embodiment of the ideological convictions of the ANC.

7.5.2 Transformationist interpretation in the Constitutional Court

In contrast to the above, judgments concerning challenges to certain features of the ideology of transformationism are a different matter altogether. In cases viewed to be challenges to transformationism, the Constitutional Court dutifully discharges its role and duty as an integral part of the dominant political elite. It delivers judgments that defend and promote – sometimes forcefully – the ideology of transformationism. I will deal with a set of six judgments during the period 2013-2017 in which the Constitutional Court invoked transformationist interpretation in favour of transformationism. More attention is paid to the last two judgments.[89]

I want to emphatically clarify the basis of my criticism of these judgments. In keeping with views on the nature of interpretation subscribed to in part 7.2 of this chapter these judgments are not critiqued on the basis of the Courts' erring in their interpretation of the objective meanings of certain constitutional provisions. As explained in some detail there is in fact no such objective meanings in the (constitutional) text. The discussion concerned is aimed at demonstrating that the Court was consistently partial in that it constructed meanings in keeping with the dominant elite's commitments to the ideology of transformationism. In doing so, the Court was emphatically (ideologically) partial in promoting the commitments of transformationism and fending off challenges from circles (viewed to be) opposed to transformationism. I do not seek to show how wrong the Court was (erring on some perceived objective meaning of the formulations of the Constitution). What I am trying to do is to show how consistently partial it was.

In the first case, that of *Agri South Africa v Minister for Minerals and Energy (Afriforum and Others as amici curiae)*,[90] the Court held that the commencement of the Mineral and Petroleum Resources Development Act (MPRDA),[91] which terminated the rights of mineral rights holders, did not amount to expropriation.[92] The Court, amongst other things, held that the termination of the rights was a *deprivation* as envisaged in section 25(1) of the Constitution. The state did not, as a result of this deprivation, acquire these rights for itself, the Court said, but merely for the benefit of third parties. Hence, it did not constitute *expropriation* as envisaged in section 25(2) which, unlike *deprivation*, is subject to compensation. The Court held that the state merely acted as a trustee which served as a conduit for channelling these rights to others

---

89 The cases discussed here were all decided by the Mogoeng Court. However, the tendency of the Constitutional Court going a long way to rule in favour of the dominant elite when challenged from outside the elite on matters of importance to the elite dates back to the era long before Chief Justice Mogoeng became the Chief Justice. Compare for example the legally highly questionable and heavily critiqued judgments in *New National Party of South Africa v Government of the Republic of South Africa* 1999(3) SA 191; 1999(5) BCLR 489(CC), *United Democratic Movement v President of the Republic of South Africa* 2003(1) SA 495; 2002(11) BCLR 1179(CC) and arguably also *Kaunda v President of the Republic of South Africa* 2005(4) SA 235; 2004(10) BCLR 1009(CC).

90 2013(7) BCLR 727(CC).

91 *Mineral and Petroleum Resources Development Act* 28 of 2002.

92 For a concise discussion of the history of this litigation see Van der Walt, 2013:201.

in terms of general principle of (economic) transformationism, which is part of the general ideology of transformationism. Since according to the Court's reasoning, this was a deprivation for which no compensation was due, it did not constitute an infringement of the right to property.[93]

The reasoning of the Court was unconvincing. The effect of the Act was clearly that the state acquired rights which previously vested in the holders of the mineral rights. There was an acquisition of rights in favour of the state which previously vested in the private mineral rights holders, namely the right to dispose of these mineral rights. The Court's view that the state had not acquired any right previously vested in private holders of these mineral rights, were idiosyncratic and illogical. In this regard Badenhorst stated as-follows:

> The denial by the CC of any acquisition whatsoever defies legal reality and logic insofar as an entitlement without an encompassing right, whether public or private in nature, or a right not being held by anybody is not possible. The fact that the State is, since enactment of the MPRDA, capable of granting rights to minerals to applicants can only mean that the state acquired former rights or entitlements or (as a conduit) is holding them on behalf of future successful applicants.[94]

The Court in fact failed to strike a fair balance between the right of private property owners and the notion of transformation. Why, one might ask, can transformationist goals not be reconciled with the compensation which is paid to owners whose rights are taken away, specifically within the context of a Constitution which does recognise the right to property? Badenhorst stated as follows:

> Despite the presence of a property clause and a statute authorising payment of compensation, the SCA and CC in the AgriSA line of decisions did not recognise that expropriation took place. These decisions do not enhance security of mineral tenure nor the sanctity of constitutional property in South Africa.[95]

In the final analysis, valuable assets were taken without compensation and the fine balance between protection of property and transformation was not maintained.[96]

Badenhorst's critique demonstrates that that there was ample room for the Court to interpret the relevant provisions – the property clause in the Constitution (section 25) and the relevant provisions of the MPRDA – in a different and more plausible way, namely in a way that would have been more protective of the deprived mineral rights holders. However, the Court opted for a strict transformationist mode of interpretation, emphasising the pursuit of transformation. This mode of interpretation squared with the goals of economic transformationism in keeping with that of the ideological convictions and objectives of the dominant elite.[97]

---

93 For critique of the arguments underpinning the judgment of the Constitutional Court and the SCA see Badenhorst, 2014:472-490; and Van der Vyver, 2012:125-142.

94 Badenhorst, 2014:279.

95 Badenhorst, 2014:280.

96 Ibid, p.82.

97 See paras, 63, and 69 and generally paras, 60-62; 65-66 and 68-70.

In the second judgment to be considered, namely the one in *South African Police Service v Solidarity abo Barnard*,[98] the Constitutional Court sided itself with the principle of representivity, which is a core element of transformationism. The fact that the promotion of the respondent (a top-performing white female police officer, who repeatedly qualified as the best candidate for promotion) would not have fostered the achievement of racial representation in accordance with the national population profile, was an important factor for the court deciding the matter in favour of the appellant. This is particularly apparent in the concurring minority judgment of Van der Westhuizen J who stated:

> The goal of equality is being promoted in this case through representivity. The National Commissioner has a duty to achieve equitable representation in SAPS but, as stated above, this implies a corollary duty not to aggravate existing over-representation. Ms Barnard's appointment would have aggravated unacceptably the already significant over-representation of white women at level 9. In summary, the impact on her dignity is not excessively restrictive and indeed reasonably and justifiably outweighed by the goal of the affirmative measure.[99]

Once again the Court had choices to decide the case in favour of the respondents as was convincingly argued, amongst others, by André Louw.[100] However, the Court justified and promoted the transformative ideological commitments and objectives of the dominant elite. Further judgments in the mould of *Barnard* followed, which reinforced the judicial endorsement of and support for the representivity aspect of the transformationist ideology.[101]

The third judgment which requires attention was delivered in *Helen Suzman Foundation v President of the RSA*; *Glenister v President of the RSA*.[102] In this case the dominant elite's historical grand narrative was defended by the Constitutional Court: a narrative of an evil past of untold suffering, inequality and discrimination from which salvation eventually came with the dawn of the present constitutional order

---

98   *AllPay Consolidated Investment Holdings (Pty) Ltd v Chief Executive Officer, South African Social Security Agency* 2014(1) BCLR 1195(CC).

99   *AllPay Consolidated Investment Holdings (Pty) Ltd v Chief Executive Officer, South African Social Security Agency* 2014(1) BCLR 1195(CC) para, 183. See also para, 66 of the (main) judgment.

100 See Louw, 2015:593-667 (Part I) and 668-733 (Part II); Rautenbach, 2015:431-443. Also see the indignant commentary by Du Plessis, 2014:6; Wiechers, 2014:12.

101 See for example *Solidarity and Others v Department of Correctional Services and Others* 2016(5) SA 594(CC). The court per Zondo J stated as follows: "In my view the application of the *Barnard* principle is not limited to White candidates. Black candidates, whether they are African people, Coloured people or Indian people are also subject to the *Barnard* principle. Indeed, both men and women are also subject to that principle. This has to be so because the transformation of the workplace entails, in my view, that the workforce of an employer should be broadly representative of the people of South Africa. A workplace or workforce that is broadly representative of the people of South Africa cannot be achieved with an exclusively segmented workforce. ... If, therefore, it is accepted that the workforce that is required to be achieved is one that is inclusive of all these racial groups and both genders, the next question is whether there is a level of representation that each group must achieve or whether it is sufficient if each group has a presence in all levels no matter how insignificant their presence may be. In my view, the level of representation of each group must broadly accord with its level of representation among the people of South Africa."

102 *Helen Suzman Foundation v President of the RSA; Glenister v President of the RSA* 2015(1) BCLR 1(CC).

in 1994, which is paving the way for a splendid new order now being ushered (and in part already established) in terms of the ideology of transformationism under the governing elite lead by the ANC. (Previously – before the dreadful evil order – there was according to Chief Justice Mogoeng, basing his view on a quote that turned out to be an Internet forgery, a marvellous almost paradisiacal natural dispensation of peace, tranquillity and equality in Africa and Southern Africa in particular, only to be upset by the evil forces of Western colonialism, which are in fact still ominously looming large in present-day South Africa.)[103] In this litigation, specifically the last part of this narrative – the splendid new order transformationist dispensation ushered in by the Constitution – was challenged, but forcefully protected by the majority of the Constitutional Court bench.

One of the appellants (Glenister) sought to present wide-ranging expert evidence in support of the proposition that there is a justified public perception that the South African Police Service (SAPS) is an exceptionally corrupt institution, managed and controlled by sections of a corrupt executive, deployed from the ranks of a corrupt ruling party in terms of its cadre deployment policies (which, as we have noted in Chapter 5, is part of the ideology of transformationism) that pays no regard for integrity and professionalism. Chief Justice Mogoeng supported by the majority, including deputy Chief Justice Moseneke and Zondo J (as he then was) in a strikingly indignant majority judgment struck out the allegation made by Glenister. They ruled the evidence Glenister sought to present to be *scandalous, vexatious or irrelevant* in terms of the rules of the law of evidence. Froneman J, supported by Cameron J in a minority judgment found the evidence relevant and admissible. The very idea that this situation – this wide-ranging condition of corruption – might exist, Froneman J correctly pointed out, will be scandalous for South Africa. That, however, does not entitle the courts (in the way the majority did) from barring concerned persons from seeking to present evidence to sketch the general condition of corruption in South Africa. Although the applicant's made grave assertions against what is held dearly under the Constitution that does not mean that the Court is entitled to simply turn a blind eye to it.

What on close analysis was at stake in this case was the very credibility of the redeeming transformationist grand narrative/history about South Africa that has been told first by the postscript to the interim Constitution, referred to in Chapter 3. The basis for the majority's view appears to have been founded not in the law of evidence but in something entirely different, namely its debunking of the transformationist grand narrative. The evidence that Glenister sought to present was certainly annoying, embarrassing and scandalising. It also relayed a story of

---

103 In various public addresses such as "From imitation to innovation: comparative perspectives on legal education" paper delivered at the 2018 *African law school leadership forum conference on legal education* in Cape Town on 6 March 2018. Available: http://bit.ly/2TdD6q9 [Accessed, 27 June 2018].
The importance of courageous free media in exposing and holding power to account paper delivered to the South African National Editors Forum (SANEF) on 23 June 2018. Available: http://bit.ly/2OL0Zqk [Accessed, 25 June 2018]. See further footnote 87 of Chapter 5.

a dreadfully malfunctioning South African state. It was an embarrassment to the veracity and the credibility of the transformationist grand narrative upon which the constitutional order – more specifically the very notion of transformationist constitutionalism – is based which has also repeatedly been told by the Constitutional Court itself.[104] The evidence was therefore annoying in that it showed that the grand narrative might be false, thus casting doubt not only on the veracity of the narrative itself but also on the narrators, which include the Constitutional Court. The evidence showed that the evangelical prediction of the forward-looking element of transformationism was based on very tenuous grounds; that the prediction was superseded by new events, that is, by a new narrative supported by strong evidence, that shows that the official transformationist grand narrative was in material respects untrue and that the new constitutional order was in part failing to fulfil the splendid (forward-looking) promise that transformationist constitutionalism makes. Clearly it was just too much for the majority to countenance such *heresy* against the official grand narrative. Hence, they silenced this insolent dissenting narrative suggested in the evidence of Glenister and pilloried it by imposing a cost order against the applicant, thus also showing all prospective doubters what might befall them when the official transformationist grand narrative is challenged. The majority used the vocabulary provided by the law of evidence (ruling the evidence inadmissible for its alleged irrelevance and its scandalous and vexatious nature) to protect the official narrative and to silence and punish the challenge to the official transformationist grand narrative.

At the time of finalising of the manuscript for this book evidence of unprecedented corruption was heard by the "State Capture" Commission.[105] This casts a new embarrassing light on the majority's rejection of the evidence that Glenister sought to lead in this case a few years before. This is evidence of the same kind that Glenister sought to lead – only exponentially more. In an ironic and embarrassing turn of events deputy Chief Justice Zondo now has to listen to evidence on the scandalous state of corruption which he and his colleagues on the Constitutional Court bench found too scandalous to listen to.[106]

The forth judgment, *FEDSAS v MEC for Education, Gauteng and Another (Equal Education as amicus curiae)*[107] is the culmination of a series of judgments[108] in which the Constitutional Court justified the increasing deterioration of the autonomy of school governing bodies of public schools in favour of the centralisation of power in

---

104 See for example *S v Makwanyane* 1995(6) BCLR 665(CC) para, 262:758C-G.

105 Judicial Commission of Inquiry into allegations of state capture, corruption and fraud in the public sector appointed by the President in terms of section 84(2)(f) of *the Constitution* by Proclamation 3 of 2018.

106 See Malan & Hoffman, 2019. Available: http://bit.ly/2YVCV40

107 2016(8) BCLR 1050(CC).

108 Most prominently *Head of Department: Mpumalanga Department of Education and Another v Hoërskool Ermelo and Another* 2010(2) SA 415(CC); 2010(3) BCLR 177(CC) and *MEC for Education in Gauteng Province and Other v Governing Body of Rivonia Primary School and Others* 2013(6) SA 582(CC); 2013(12) BCLR 1365(CC).

the hands of national and provincial authorities. In various provinces, specifically in the Gauteng province, these centralised powers are used to stamp out Afrikaans education in favour of homogeneity (in the form of Anglicisation), which as shown in Chapter 5, is one of the cornerstones of transformationism.

The present judgment is often referred to as the *Lesufi*-judgment named after the member of the Gauteng provincial executive council (MEC) for education and since the middle of 2018 the deputy leader of the ANC in the Gauteng province, Phanyaza Lesufi. The case, amongst other things, involved the dispute on whether or not the MEC had the power of allocating pupils (learners in the official state jargon) in schools in the Gauteng province.

This judgment justifies the increasing centralisation of powers of provincial education authorities, including the MEC, to have the final say in the placing of pupils in these schools. The Constitutional Court held the regulations passed in the Gauteng province to be consistent with the provisions of section 5(5) of the South African Schools Act[109] notwithstanding the fact that this provision vests these powers in the school governing bodies.

This decision comes against the backdrop of history of provincial authorities – occasionally quite blatantly – interfering in the powers of individual school governing bodies, specifically Afrikaans medium schools. The case was also decided against the backdrop of concerns that Lesufi would abuse his power to allocate English-preferring pupils to single medium Afrikaans schools, thus forcing these schools to become parallel or double medium schools. This concern was based, amongst others, on Lesufi blustering animosity against Afrikaans medium public schools in the public media.[110] The Constitution and the relevant legislation – section 5 of the South African Schools Act – afforded the Court ample space to decide the case in favour of the appellant, namely that this power in terms of the Act primarily falls within the authority of the school governing bodies. The Court, however, decided in favour of the MEC and in this way supported the centralising and homogenising ideology of transformationism.

The fifth case to which more attention is dedicated is that of *City of Tshwane Metropolitan Municipality v Afriforum and Another*,[111] the so-called street name case. In this case the majority of the Constitutional Court sided itself with the strong proclivities towards homogenisation and vehemently dismissed the case for the recognition of (Afrikaner) cultural diversity.

---

109 Act 84 of 1996.

110 Lesufi threatened in a television debate that he was "coming for" Afrikaans schools and that he was going to "crush" these schools.

111 2016(9) BCLR 1133(CC).

In the majority judgment delivered by Chief Justice Mogoeng supported by eight justices, Mogoeng emphatically sided with (the rest of) the ruling elite in subscribing to an anti-Afrikaner interpretation of South African history and a homogenous majoritarian-inspired vision of South African culture. In the same breath it roundly rejected the claim for the recognition of cultural diversity. The majority did so in spite of constitutional provisions that suggest recognition for the protection of cultural diversity.[112] In embracing this homogenising stance, the majority also went back on its own previous assertions, namely in *Minister of Home Affairs v Fourie*[113] referred to below in which the Court in support of the recognition of same sex marriages, subscribed to respect for diversity.

This street name case concerned an appeal against an interim order made by the High Court in favour of Afriforum, an Afrikaner civil rights movement against a local authority, the Tshwane Metropolitan Council prohibiting it from renaming a number of streets within its jurisdiction before a proper public consultation had run its course. The city of Pretoria falls within the territorial jurisdiction of the Tshwane Metropolitan Council and is home to the largest concentration of Afrikaners. Before the renaming, the streets concerned bore the names that reflected aspects of Afrikaner history held dear by many belonging to the Afrikaner cultural minority.

In its judgment the majority emphatically subscribed to transformationism. It also disregarded the established principles on the non-appealability of interim orders, which it branded as technicalities and an illegitimate stratagem to frustrate the realisation of the transformative project.[114] This disregard for established rules of procedure was strongly criticised in a minority judgment by the justices Froneman and Cameron.[115]

More importantly, and central to the present discussion, the majority also dismissed any claim for retaining Afrikaans names for public places as an illegitimate stratagem contrary to the constitutional project of transformationism. Retaining such names was also unjustifiable in terms of cultural rights of sections 30 and 31 of the Constitution.[116] Such names were tainted by an unjust history and not worthy of protection under the transformative Constitution. The majority drew on the Preamble to the Constitution and the value of Ubuntu, to which it

---

112 Sections 30 and 31 of the Constitution. See also the dicta of the *Constitutional Court in Minister of Home Affairs v Fourie* 2006(1) SA 524; 2006(3) BCLR 355(CC) referred to below.

113 2006(1) SA 524; 2006(3) BCLR 355(CC) at 1175B-F (para, 60-61).

114 The majority stated: Our peculiarity as a nation impels us to remember always, that our Constitution and law could never have been meant to facilitate the frustration of real justice and equity through technicalities ... Our Constitution was never meant to be a selectively recognised weapon, conveniently produced and used by some of us only when it could help advance sectarian interests through legal stratagems (Para, 18:1141G).

115 Paras, 83-99. See also Hoffman, 2016:11.

116 As argued in paras, 174-175 by justice Jafta who gave his own minority judgment which was endorsed by the majority judgment.

repeatedly referred.[117] However, not only the Preamble and Ubuntu, but the whole Constitution forms the corner stone for an encompassing transformative project. Thus the majority sharply rebuffing Afriforum, declared: "Our constitutional vision militates against a never-ending determination to oppose change to city, town or street names." The majority then proceeded: "Through the Preamble and the entire Constitution we impose on ourselves the duty to transform."[118] Moreover, according to the majority it was the duty of all to participate in pursuing the transformation of South African society,[119] instead of being *retentionist, one-sided, selective* and *sectarian*,[120] all epithets the majority used to dismiss Afriforum's argument for the retention of some of the names associated with Afrikaner history. South Africa had a dark past marked by injustice, racial discrimination and exclusion of the black majority. The transformative vision of the Constitution requires that this be completely replaced by a new society. Afriforum's case for the retention of some of the Afrikaner names was fundamentally anti-transformative and unequivocally vituperative to the Constitution's transformative vision. Hence, it was slated as an attempt to pamper the injustices of the past.[121]

The transformation project is closely connected also to culturally related matters such as the (re)naming of public places, (which according to the majority is still by far too Eurocentric and celebrating the past of only one segment of the population while disregarding the black majority.)[122] Thus the Chief Justice professed:

> We also need to take steps to breathe life into the underlying philosophy and constitutional vision we have crafted for our collective good and for posterity. That would be achieved partly by removing from our cities, towns, 'dorpies', streets, parks, game reserves and institutions names that exalts elements of our past that caused grief to other racial groups or reopen their supposedly healing wounds. Also, by removing even some innocuous names that give recognition only to the history, language, culture of people of one race ...[123]

It is conspicuously significant that not all Afrikaner names were unacceptable to the majority. On the contrary, the naming of places after Afrikaners, such as Beyers Naudé and Bram Fischer was desirable.[124] The reason for this is that these people joined the struggle against white minority rule with the ANC and related organisations – the

---

117 Reference was made to the Preamble in paras, 5, 9, 17 and 65 and to ubuntu in para, 11. Even though the postscript to the Interim Constitution (discussed in Chapter 3) was not referred to, its vision is emphatically reflected in what the Chief Justice proclaimed in this case.

118 Para, 14:1140F.

119 Para, 8:1139D.

120 Attitudes that the majority ascribed to the Afriforum's desire to retain some Afrikaans street names. (See para, 13:1140D-E and para, 18:1141H).

121 Para, 6 :1138F.

122 Para, 12, 13:1140C-F.

123 Para, 8:1139B-C.

124 Para, 14:1140G-H.

core of the dominant elite after 1994. In contrast the naming of other Afrikaners who did not have this congenial record towards the ANC is generally offensive to the present dominant elite. This emphatically attests to the Court's embrace of a single homogenous (majoritarian-based) historical interpretation and homogenous South African culture – an attitude, as discussed below, that was rejected in the dissenting judgment.

The minority judgment cast light on the intolerant implications of the majority. The minority criticised the majority judgment as intolerant to the diversity and difference, and to the culture of Afrikaners and white people in general. The minority disagree with Afriforum's view of history.[125] That, however, is no justification for saying that Afriforum's members' sense of belonging to particular places and experience of loss when such names are taken away, is not real and that it should not also be recognised by the Constitution.[126] Unfortunately, this was precisely what the majority implied, namely that Afrikaners do not enjoy (constitutionally-based) cultural protection and that they are required to conform to a single homogenous interpretation of history and a homogenous culture.

This creates an unacceptable state of affairs because according to the minority, the Constitution generally creates scope for recognising interests or rights based on a sense of belonging to the place where one lives, rooted in a particular history.[127] Once it is accepted that a right or interest of that kind may exist, "(i)t cannot be negated by either saying that the basis of the sense of belonging does not advance society as a whole, or that the basis of the enjoyment is so ephemeral that its loss can never be irreparable."[128] This, however, the minority charged is precisely what the majority judgment did.[129] The dissenting judgment went on to state that when Afriforum asserted a right of a sense of belonging and place based on a historically affinity to Pretoria, Afriforum's members have not done any wrong. They have not committed a crime.[130] The Preamble of the Constitution in the view of the dissenting judgment precisely allows Afriforum to make this claim:

> The Preamble to the Constitution states that South Africa belongs to all who live in it, united indeed, but 'in our diversity'... Indeed recognising and preserving cultural rights is important in our constitutional society. This helps to ensure that minorities, including cultural, linguistic or cultural minorities feel included and protected. This is not only to safeguard their interests. It is to preserve cultural diversity that is of value to the country's identity. Cultural rights, whether of the Islamic community, the Vha Venda or seTswana speakers, are integral to a sense of identity, self-worth and dignity.[131]

---

125 Para, 123:1167A.

126 Para, 123:1167B.

127 Para, 124:1167B-C.

128 Para, 125:1167D.

129 Para, 125:1167D.

130 Para, 126:1167E.

131 Para, 126:1167E-1168A.

Consider this, Froneman and Cameron stated: "What is the effect of a failure to embrace ubuntu ...? Does the person lose his or her constitutional protection?"[132] This, however, the two justices stated is precisely what the majority judgment suggests.[133] The charge that the majority judgment is premised on the pursuit of a single homogenous majority-based culture runs through the whole of the dissenting judgment. The majority judgment implies that "(a)ny reliance by white South Africans, particularly white Afrikaner people, on a cultural tradition founded in history, finds no recognition in the Constitution because that history is inevitable rooted in oppression."[134] Although that is most certainly the case, they said: "(t)he constitutional discountenancing of a cultural history many continue to treasure has momentous implications for a substantive portion of our population."[135]

What the dissenting judgment found concerning of the majority judgment is that no reliance by white South Africans, particularly white Afrikaner people, on any historically-rooted cultural tradition finds any recognition in the Constitution, because that history is inevitably rooted in oppression.[136]

What does this dismissal of constitutional protection mean in practical terms, Froneman and Cameron asked:

> Does it entail that, as a general proposition, white Afrikaner people and white South Africans have no cultural rights that pre-date 1994, unless they can be shown not to be rooted in oppression? How must that be done? Must all organisations with white South Africans or Afrikaners as members now have to demonstrate that they have no historical roots in our oppressive past? Who decides that, and on what standard?[137]

This question does not only pertain to whites or Afrikaners. Other groups were also oppressed: "It may also be of concern to those who take pride in the achievements of King Shaka Zulu, despite the controversy about his reign, and those who nurture the memory of Mahatma Gandhi's struggles in South Africa, despite some repugnant statements about black people."[138] The point, as emphasised in the minority judgment is that there are many cultural, religious or associational organisations in South Africa that have roots in our divided and oppressive past. Surely they cannot be treated as constitutional outcasts, merely because of a history tainted by bloodshed or racism.[139]

---

132 Para, 139:1170G.

133 Para, 139:1170G.

134 Para, 81:1159A-B.

135 Para, 89:1159B.

136 Para, 130:1168G-G.

137 Para, 131:1168G-H.

138 Para, 132:1168H-1169A (Footnotes removed).

139 Para, 134:1169D.

In contrast to the majority judgment, the dissenting judgment embraces the view that the Constitution should be interpreted as an instrument that allows for tolerance and respect for difference and diversity. It should not be dealt with as an instrument that insists on and imposes conformity to a single culture and a homogenous identity. Thus Froneman and Cameron declared that the Constitution does not impose an obligation on citizens, either by enjoining the adoption of the ubuntu world-view, or otherwise to be denied recognition.[140]

That is unfortunately exactly what the majority judgment suggests namely that what is referred to as the national project of attaining inclusivity, unity in diversity and reconciliation makes suspicious or doubtful the kind of sense of space and belonging that Afriforum claims for its Afrikaner membership.[141] This, according to Froneman and Cameron, distancing themselves from the majority, is not the way in which the Constitution should be interpreted. In their view the Constitution, they declared does not mandate the courts to impose a particular conception of this national project.[142] On the contrary, the Constitution in their view "(i)s broad and inclusive enough for our unity in diversity to survive even by recognising and including those who differ radically and wrongly from the one espoused in the first judgment, and for recognition that the historical past of white people also includes much not to be ashamed of."[143] Hence: "(r)ecognition and tolerance of difference, even radical difference, is what, in our view, the Constitution demands of us. It is not consonant with the values of the Constitution to deny constitutional protections to people because of the content of their beliefs, views and aspirations."[144] (The first judgment refers to the majority judgment.)

The minority judgment is in step with the views that the Constitutional Court took in the same-sex marriages case of *Minister of Home Affairs v Fourie*.[145] In this judgment the Court per Sachs J underscores (in glaring contrast to the majority judgment in the present case) the need for respect across difference. It stated that the right to equality does not presuppose the elimination or suppression of difference, but the "the affirmation of self, not the denial of self." Equality it stated did not imply homogenisation, but an acknowledgment and acceptance of difference, diversity and pluralism.

In view of Froneman and Cameron Afriforum should be given the same kind of space when cultural matters are at issue. Alas, in the present judgment relating to Afrikaans cultural claims the lofty acknowledgement and acceptance of difference, diversity and pluralism, and the laudable cause against homogenisation that was so prominent in the same sex marriages case were all forgotten.

---

140 Para, 137:1170D.

141 Para, 138:1170E.

142 Para, 138:1170F.

143 Para, 158:1174E-F. The "first judgment" refers to the majority judgment.

144 Para, 159:1174F-1175A.

145 Para, 160:1175B-F; Paras, 60-61 of the *Fourie* judgment.

Hence, there is a glaring inconsistency: in the case of gays and lesbians the values of respect and recognition for difference and diversity were found (quite correctly) to obtain. It was not at loggerheads with the transformationism. In the case of the claims of Afrikaners these same values were forgotten. The insistence on homogeneity was held to be imperative. That is what transformationism demanded.

The sixth – and last – judgment of the Constitutional Court at the date of completion of the present analysis is *Afriforum and Another v University of the Free State*.[146] The case arose from a decision of the Council of the University of the Free State (the University) to abolish the parallel-medium dispensation of tuition that was officially in place at the University since 2003, and to replace it with a unilingual English system. Before the University's decision Afrikaans was used alongside English. According to the parallel-medium system of tuition, separate classes were offered in English and Afrikaans. Initially Afriforum successfully challenged the University's decision in the High Court. However, the High Court's decision was overturned by the Supreme Court of Appeal (SCA).[147] Hence Afriforum appealed to the Constitutional Court. However, Chief Justice Mogoeng on behalf of the majority of the bench of the Constitutional Court refused to listen to the merits of Afriforum's argument. The majority dismissed Afriforum's application for leave to appeal in emphatic terms[148] and praised the University for its decision.[149]

The view of the majority was that the continued use of Afrikaans alongside English was incongruent with the transformative goals of the Constitution, in the same way as Afrikaans street names according to the majority in *City of Tshwane Metropolitan Municipality v Afriforum,* discussed above, were at variance with the objectives of transformationism. Froneman J supported by two other justices delivered a minority judgment in which he stringently criticised the majority judgment.

Afriforum's case was based on section 29(2) of the Constitution, which reads as follows:

> Everyone has the right to receive education in the official language or languages of their choice in public educational institutions where that education is reasonably practicable. In order to ensure the effective access to, and implementation of, this right, the state must consider all reasonable educational alternatives, including single medium institutions,

---

146 *Afriforum and Another v University of the Free State* 2018(4) BCLR 387(CC). In the course of 2017 there was a series of judgments in which the courts found the abolition of Afrikaans constitutionally justifiable. *Gelyke Kanse and Others v Chairman of the Senate of the Stellenbosch University and Others* 2018(1) BCLR 25(WCC) in relation to the University of Stellenbosch and *Afriforum and Another v Chairperson of the Council of the University of Pretoria and Others* (54451/2016) [2016] ZAGPPHC 1030; [2017] 1 All SA 832(GP) in relation to the University of Pretoria.

147 *University of the Free State v Afriforum and Another* 2017(4) SA 283(SCA). The High Court judgment is reported in *Afriforum and Another v Chairman of the Council of the University of the Free State and Others* (A70/2016) [2016] ZAFSHC 130.

148 Para, 39:400C-E.

149 Paras, 77-78:410A-E.

taking into account:
(a) equity;
(b) practicability; and
(c) the need to redress the results of past racially discriminatory laws and practices.

According to Afriforum, it was patently, reasonably practicable as envisaged in section 29(2) to provide tuition in Afrikaans. That it was "reasonably practicable to do so" was evident from the fact that Afrikaans tuition was delivered up to the time of the decision to replace it with single medium English tuition. There was a fairly large demand for Afrikaans tuition and the necessary Afrikaans language proficiency – academic staff proficient in Afrikaans – to meet the demand was available.

In step with the SCA the majority held that the proviso of reasonable practicality in section 29(2) has not been complied with in order to allow for tuition in Afrikaans. The notion of "reasonable practicality" had to be interpreted in a transformative way.[150] Hence, according to Mogoeng and his supporters, "reasonable practicality" was not a matter of reasonable achievability, but of achievability within and in conformity with the ideological parameters of a specific ideological model, namely that of transformationism. That would mean that even if it is reasonably possible to provide tuition in Afrikaans, it would still be unreasonable – and therefore unconstitutional – if it does not fall within the ideological constraints of transformationism.

Accordingly, the majority states as follows:

Reasonable practicability therefore requires not only that the practicability test be met, but also that considerations of reasonableness that extend to equity and the need to cure the ills of our shameful apartheid past, be appropriately accommodated. And that is achievable only if the exercise of the right to be taught in a language of choice does not pose a threat to racial harmony or inadvertently nurture racial supremacy. That goes to practicability.[151]

Against this backdrop the question was not merely whether it was reasonably achievable to use Afrikaans alongside English as a language of instruction. Instead, the question, according to Mogoeng and his supporters was whether "(t)he use of Afrikaans as a medium of instruction at the University had a comfortable co-existence with our collective aspiration to heal the divisions of the past or has it impeded the prospects of our unity in our diversity?" Has race relations, particularly among students, improved or degenerated as a consequence of the University's 2003 language policy? If not, would it be "reasonably practicable" for the University to relegate Afrikaans to low-key utilisation in a constitutionally-permissible way?[152]

---

150 Para, 48:402F-403B.

151 Para, 53:404C-D.

152 Para, 53:404D-E. (Footnotes removed).

In the absence of any evidence that has ever been provided to that effect, Mogoeng and his supporters without further ado, accepted the allegation of the University that the continued Afrikaans tuition would lead to racial segregation (Afrikaans classes were mostly white and English classes black or multiracial); caused inequality of access to knowledge with Afrikaans in a preferential position; entrenched racial exclusivity; and continued racial supremacy.[153] For the majority this contention put forward by the University, but for which no evidence had been adduced, was enough to justify the abolition of the existing rights of Afrikaans students to receive tuition in their own language as envisaged by section 29(2) of the Constitution.

Mogoeng, on behalf of the majority, was clearly anxious to avoid the perception that they were partial against Afrikaans. This explains why he was at pains to declare that they were in fact not partial.[154] This is indeed strikingly weird for Mogoeng to have said so since the impartiality of judges are usually assumed. It need not be avowed. Mogoeng's assertion that he was impartial clearly shows his apprehension of the risk that he might have been perceived as partial against Afrikaans as so real that he found it necessary to assert his own impartiality. Notwithstanding this claim to impartiality the way in which Mogoeng and his supporters went about consistently shows precisely how partial they in fact were, because in this case, in keeping with the judgments discussed above, the majority emphatically associated themselves with the (rest of the) dominant elite's commitment to transformationism and with a transformative interpretation of the Constitution – in the present case of section 29.[155] The majority subscribed to an interpretation that has to achieve "radical transformation of society" and viewed the language of instruction as a "transformational issue".[156] Specifically at the universities (such as the University of the Free State) which in a previous age was an Afrikaans university, there is a dire need for radical transformation. These universities:

> (w)ere exceedingly well-resourced for the exclusive or primary benefit of white Afrikaner students. And their inseparable and almost destiny-defining mandate; was to develop the Afrikaans language very well... African universities and languages were deliberately starved of resources and capacities critical for a similar developmental agenda.[157]

On close analysis, Mogoeng decided in favour of the University very early in his judgment when he described its decision to abolish Afrikaans as a measure to promote the "constitutionally-inspired transformational agenda".[158] In the context

---

153 See paras, 17, 18, 49, 50 and 53.

154 Para, 8:392G-I.

155 Amongst others paras 1, 2, 4, 7, 14, 48-50.

156 Para, 4:391G.

157 Para, 2:390F. Mogoeng also referred to African universities, that he said were starved. He did not identify these universities. It looks though as if this reference is in step with his drawing as authority on the Macaulay forgery where reference was also made to splendid African educational systems that were in existence in Africa before the arrival of the Europeans. For the reference see Chapter 5, footnote 86.

158 Para, 7:392F.

of the present case, the promotion of the transformative agenda once again entailed the pursuit of (a general South African) homogeneity.[159]

Mogoeng and his colleagues clearly failed to understand that their commitment to transformationism in this judgment betrayed their ideological bias, consequently making a travesty of their claim to impartiality.

In his minority judgment Froneman cast a long shadow over the credibility of Mogoeng and his followers' (claim to) impartiality. Even though Froneman did not reject the transformative approach to the interpretation of the Constitution, he subtly yet emphatically shows exactly how partial Mogoeng in fact was.

He pointed out that Mogoeng was biased in his historical contextualisation concerning language of instruction at South African universities because, in contrast to what Mogoeng claimed,[160] Afrikaans was patently not exclusively associated with colonialism, racism and apartheid.[161]

A second element of Mogoeng and his followers' one-sidedness in relation to their sketch of the historical context of the case is that they failed to acknowledge Afrikaans' own difficult uphill battle against the erstwhile imperialist domination of English – something that Froneman emphasised.[162]

Thirdly, the partiality of Mogoeng and his followers' is also patent from their strikingly selective favourable quotation from the report of the Gerwel-committee. (In 2003 the Gerwel-committee, mandated by the then minister of higher education gave advice on the use of Afrikaans at universities.) As Froneman pointed out,[163] Mogoeng and his supporters chose not to mention that Gerwel also advised that two universities – Stellenbosch University and North West University (Potchefstroom as it was then) – had to accept responsibility for the protection and promotion of Afrikaans. The majority's silence on this is particularly striking since it belies the view that the use of Afrikaans as a language of instruction could be identified with the anti-transformationism evils of racial segregation, unequal access to education, racial exclusivity and the continuation or causation of racial supremacy, and that it (the use of Afrikaans as medium of instruction) would lead to racial disharmony.

Fourthly, as Froneman also showed,[164] Mogoeng and his supporters failed to give a reliable account of the law pertaining to the present issue. They failed to take into account that the Constitution (in section 6(2)) requires the state to enhance the

---

159 Para, 14:393H-394B.

160 Paras, 1-7:389H-392B.

161 Paras, 90-95:312G-414C.

162 Para, 93:413E-414A.

163 Para, 90:412G-413B.

164 Para, 91:413C.

status and promote the use of the official languages.[165] The irresistible inference is that this provision was disregarded because it did not accord with Mogoeng's personal view of Afrikaans and Afrikaans tuition.

In the fifth place – yet another instance of an incomplete and opportunistically unreliable account of the relevant legal position – Mogoeng and his supporters chose to be unmindful of the international and foreign law relating to the present matter. These bodies of law afford compelling authority for the special measures in support of minority languages (such as Afrikaans). These bodies of law would afford support to Afriforum while weakening that of the University.[166] However, it clearly suited the transformationist prejudices of Mogoeng and his supporters to steer clear of international and foreign law authorities.

In the sixth place, there is the idiosyncratic mode of argumentation of Mogoeng and his supporters in relation to the view that Afrikaans tuition leads to racial segregation, unequal access to education, racial exclusivity, racial supremacy and racial disharmony. This is arguably the strongest indication of their ideological bias and prejudices against Afrikaans. For instance, Mogoeng accepted the allegations of the University without the slightest attempt to scrutinise the merits thereof, which would indeed have happened had the relevent evidence been adduced. Precisely this haphazardly random embrace of the University's allegations went against Froneman's grain.

This leads to the seventh indication of Mogoeng's partiality: If there were any truth in the allegation that evils, such as racial segregation, unequal access to education, racial exclusivity, racial supremacy and racial disharmony were caused by the use of Afrikaans as a language of instruction, the question arises as to who should be blamed. The University did not contend that the Afrikaans students were at fault. If Afrikaans (and parallel-medium tuition) did indeed contribute to the said evils, then clearly the University management was at fault by reason of, amongst other things, its negligence and failure to introduce appropriate remedial measures. If Afrikaans students, are not to be blamed, they obviously dare not be prejudiced by the acts and omissions of the University. It is untenable that the University should be allowed to prejudice other people (the Afrikaans students) for its (the University's) own impertinent conduct.

Froneman and his supporters found it unacceptable that blameless Afrikaans students should be prejudiced by the acts and omissions (of the University). He found it equally deplorable that the majority accepted the University's allegations without solid evidence. Hence, Froneman declared:

> On the papers, there is no suggestion that all, most or even a substantial portion of white Afrikaans-speaking students being taught in that language have been guilty of racial

---

165 The courts are in the present case included in the concept of "state" See Malan, 2016:20-59. Available: http://bit.ly/33u2g8Kf

166 On this see the observations of Froneman at para, 124:421E.

discrimination. Any unfair discrimination was instead that of the University in its provision of instruction to different language groups and control of other activities on campus. It is thus for the University to provide a factual and normative justification for depriving innocent users of an official language of the right to receive education in that language.

There are factual issues that are neither clear to me nor addressed in the main judgment. For example, if there were individual students or members of staff who were themselves guilty of racial discrimination, whether in the delivery and receipt of Afrikaans instruction or otherwise, why was it impracticable to discipline them? What exactly made it impossible to eradicate the racial discrimination? Did it have anything to do with the reaction to the continued use of Afrikaans in lectures by those who preferred another language? If so, was the reasonableness of that reaction assessed? Was an attempt made to address it by other measures?

In the absence of evidence that the students receiving instruction in the language of their choice were themselves guilty of racial discrimination in the receipt of that instruction, what is the normative justification for visiting a sanction upon them? It is not at all obvious to me – and the main judgment does not address this question directly.

All these questions should have formed part of this Court's own assessment of the legal question of racial discrimination. It may well be that, had the issues raised been fully ventilated, the conclusion of factual and normative impracticability would have been found justified. The applicants' failure to present practical alternatives may well have played an important part in that assessment.[167]

Hence, Froneman held that factual clarity first had to be obtained as a prerequisite for dealing with the juridical merits of the case. He declared:

> It would have served the interests of justice better to have granted leave to appeal after an oral hearing. A public hearing in this Court, where important and emotive issues are debated rationally and objectively, would have allayed any unjustified fears that people may harbour. The merits of the appeal should have been considered in a manner that took into account the wider context and the interests of those others to whom I have referred. This has not been done, to my deep regret.[168]

If Froneman had it his way, the case would have followed the following proposed course:

> I would have granted leave to appeal; allowed the appeal; reserved costs; and referred the matter back to the High Court in order to allow –
>
> (a) the University to present evidence on: (i) the nature and extent of any racial discrimination by students receiving instruction in Afrikaans; (ii) the nature and extent of any racial discrimination by staff lecturing in Afrikaans; (iii) the steps taken to address these acts of racial discrimination, in the form of disciplinary proceedings or other measures; and (iv) if none of these measures were taken, the reason for not doing so.
>
> (b) the applicants to present evidence on the practicable alternatives available to continue

---

167 Para, 113-116:418C-419A.

168 Para, 125:422A-B.

parallel medium instruction that would not result in indirect racial discrimination.[169]

In the final analysis, Mogoeng and his supporters essentially failed (refused) to adjudicate the case that was placed before them. This refusal emanated from their partial ideological preference in favour of transformationism – a transformative ideological approach to the interpretation of the Constitution. Hence, as in the case of the other five judgments dealt with above, transformationism resolved the dispute in favour of the ideological commitments of the dominant elite. In step with the previous five judgments the Constitutional Court once again proved itself to be the juridical arm of the dominant elite, defending and promoting the commitments of this elite. As in the five previous judgments, it was once again possible to interpret the Constitution (in the present case section 29(2)) in a way that would have justified public multilingualism, including the use of Afrikaans as a language of instruction, something which is quite apparent from the wording of the provision. However, the ideological commitment to transformationism (including the pursuit of homogeneity as subscribed to by the majority of justices of the Constitutional Court) foreclosed this alternative interpretation.

All these judgments graphically prove how the Court through transformative interpretation supported the ideological commitments of the dominant elite of which it is an integral part. These judgments were decided in accordance with the ideology of transformationism as described in part 7.4. There was no actual impartiality. On the contrary, there was ideological partiality in favour of the ideology of transformationism. What the Constitutional Court did in each of these cases was what Moseneke, as noted in part 7.4, declared what it had to do, namely "(t)o observe with unfailing fidelity the transformative mission of the Constitution," that is, in compliance with the ideology of transformationism and in close conformity with the other constitutive segments of the dominant elite. The Court acted in terms of the transformationist take on adjudication, which Sandra Liebenberg, as noted in part 7.4, called the dialogic conception of adjudication. That, on close analysis, can be called the (ideological) *partiality* (instead of impartiality) of the judiciary, which closely co-operates with the legislature, the executive, the ruling party and other supportive elements of the dominant political elite to proceed towards the achievement and defence of transformationism.

---

169 Para, 126:422C-E.

7.6

Conclusion

The preceding discussion leads to three conclusions.

7.6.1 Judicial interpretation of the Constitution

The discussion underscores that here is no inherent, objective and universal meaning in the formulations of the Constitution, including in constitutional-rights formulations. Moreover, there is also no interpretive method capable of discovering and securing objective, authentic and accurate meanings. Constitutional formulations do not speak for themselves. The meanings of the constitutional formulations are not directly known and there is no way to predict their impact with any measure of certainty. They are only vicariously known, namely through the interpretation by interpreters who are members of interpretative communities and who interpret formulations in accordance with the interpretive communities' ideologically inspired understanding of the Constitution: of why the Constitution was adopted, what it is supposed to say and destined to achieve. Moreover, the meanings of constitutional formulations only come to light at the moment they are interpreted. Different and changing meanings with concomitant and changing implications are also attributed to constitutional formulations in consecutive interpretive exercises.

As the discussion has shown, there are usually more than one interpretive community, each with its own ideologically inspired pre-understanding of the Constitution. In the case of South Africa's so-called transformative interpretation, which is grounded in the dominant elite's ideology of transformationism (a socialist ideology of egalitarianism and public homogenisation), has gained a dominant position.

The ideology of transformationism has amalgamated with purposive interpretation, in that transformationism regards the achievement of a socialist and basically homogenous society as the main purpose of the Constitution.

Whenever the courts are engaged in interpretation, they must interpret in a way that most effectively pursue the achievement of this kind of society and at the same time remove all stumbling blocks which are obstructing the achievement of this society.

In the final analysis, the meaning and implication of the Constitution including formulations that pertain to rights (constitutional-rights provisions) are an embodiment of what the dominant interpretive community say they mean and what their effects are.

Courts, more specifically the highest courts, are generally part of and a leading element in the dominant interpretive community. Their interpretations are ordinarily conditioned by the ideological commitments of the dominant elite. They are judicial interpretations that subscribe to and further the ideological commitments of the dominant elite of which they are part.

The courts' interpretations usually represent the most authorative, and erudite affirmations of the ideological commitments and objectives of the dominant elite. Unanimous or majority judgments of these highest courts, specifically in ideologically charged matters, are therefore a species of exercising political power that defends and promotes the preferred ideological and political goals of the dominant elite and correspondingly, condemns the challengers of the elite, namely political forces and interpretive communities of lesser strength.

Consequently, their interpretations – that what they say the Constitution means – are an important part of the weaponry of the dominant elite. The courts safeguard and entrench the position of the dominant elite by clothing their views and actions in the guise of constitutional legitimacy. The converse is that they, at the same time, supply the means for the constitutional de-legitimisation of the convictions and interests of sectors of society (and non-dominant interpretive communities) that stand outside this elite, by providing the constitutionally interpreted basis for the denial of interests and the violation of their rights (at least viewed from the perspective of the non-dominant sectors).

(Members of) non-dominant interpretive communities might differ from the interpretation of the dominant elite as reflected in the unanimous or majority judgments of the dominant majority interpretive community on the bench. They might be appalled by the conclusions that are arrived at by the dominant interpretive community and by the motivations for their judgments. They might be stunned by the meaning which the majority on the bench have managed to wring free from the text of the Constitution. Their counter-arguments against the interpretations and judgments might be intellectually and morally appealing; they might agree that the judgments of the dominant interpretive community on the bench were ill-conceived, unjust, unfair, partial, biased or illogical; they might view some judgments to be harsh or unfair towards a litigating party or against the interests of certain communities; they might view certain judgments to be harshly prejudicial to one party while unduly favouring another. In the final analysis, they might consider the judgments of the dominant interpretive community – the majority on the bench – to be patently wrong. Such rejections of judgments as *wrong* are totally irrelevant. They are simply beside the point. The crucial point is not that the interpretation and the finding of the majority on the bench were *right* or *wrong*. (After all, there is no universally objective standard to judge whether a decision was *right* or *wrong*). The pertinent point is that court decisions, in particular those of the Constitutional Court from where there is no further avenue of appeal, are authoritative, binding and final. They represent a decisive exercise of coercive political power, for which the constitutional order provides no remedy or relief. Such judgments constitute the exercise of judicial power which depending on its effects may cause coercion, domination, exclusion and finally an (obscured) act of violence against the losing party.[170] These are simply done deals – *res iudicata*. Nothing can be done about them, at least not within the parameters of the judicial system and the order as outlined in the written Constitution. These interpretations and judgments are simply a matter of *res perit domino*.[171] They are the effect of a constitutionally authorised judicial delict, legitimised in terms of the dominant ideological and political commitments – the convictions of the dominant interpretive community – of the constitutional order concerned.

Clearly then, interpretation is not a passive enterprise that merely brings the supposed inherent meanings in the Constitution to light. On the contrary, it is an active meaning-creating (constructing) project in which interpreters continuously attribute meaning to the formulations of the Constitution, which meanings they might change in consecutive judgments. In consequence, the interpretation, more specifically judicial interpretation of a Constitution and of constitutional-rights, is a distinctively ideologically and politically biased enterprise – in South Africa that of transformative interpretation in keeping with the ideology of transformationism.

7.6.2 Guaranteed judicial protection of individual rights?

Under the doctrine of statist-individualist constitutionalism, as indicated in Chapter 2, the Constitution is premised on the exclusive twosome consortium of the territorial state with undivided sovereignty and the abstract individual with universal individual human rights – the latter purporting to be the embodiment of justice. In consequence statist-individualist constitutionalism also rejects the constitutional recognition of (cultural) communities. It is anti-communitarian as we explained in Chapter 2. In consequence of statist-individualist constitutionalism's association of justice with individual rights, a bill of individual rights as interpreted and enforced by a so-called independent and impartial judiciary, is one of the key mechanisms of statist-individualist constitutionalism. This is why the judiciary is said to be the protector – the supreme guardian – of individual rights. This is also the most posed and recurrent claim in South Africa's constitutional discourse.

In Chapter 6 it is shown, amongst other things that the courts are in fact not as independent, impartial and effective as the doctrine of statist constitutionalism would have it. It is also pointed out that the courts, specifically the apex court together with the two other branches of governmental power (and a raft of other bodies, institutions and individuals) are usually unified in a single power

---

170 Recalling the rather harsh description by De Ville, 2000:18.

171 The loss of the thing is to the prejudice of the owner.

elite, informed by the same ideological assumptions, committed to achieving the same goals, yet organised on the basis of a division of labour performed in the separate branches.

In the present chapter, this truth has been affirmed from another angle, namely from an interpretive point of view. The courts, specifically the apex court (the Constitutional Court in the case of South Africa), being part of the dominant elite, also interpret individual rights in keeping with the dominant elite's shared ideological commitments and political goals.

Hence, when the court deals with rights formulations which in the context of the litigation in question would produce results that conform to and advance the ideological commitments of the dominant ruling elite (such as transformationism), they are highly likely to interpret in a way that favours the claimant of the right/s in question. Conversely, when the court deals with formulations that would produce results that clash with the ideological commitments of the dominant elite, the court will in all likelihood interpret and rule against the claimant of the right/s. The court will rule that the claim of the right in question is *bad in law.* The bottom line – and something which is often not grasped – is that the establishment of meaning and the application of rights formulations, sanctified as *entrenched, guaranteed and enshrined individual constitutional rights* (like all law) are functions of interpretation. Only once the rights are interpreted and applied – also by the courts – will it be clear whether, and if so to what extent they in fact guarantee the protection which statist-individualist constitutionalism claims. Thus viewed, it should be clear that the claim of guaranteed protection, though soothing and reassuring, is baseless – and false.

Within the South African context, following the transformative approach of interpretation which is anchored in the socialist ideology of egalitarianism and homogenisation, the legal position of property owners and of cultural and language minorities who are at the wrong side of this ideology is particularly precarious. Their interests hang in the balance. They cannot look up to the courts to protect their interests. Their rights are not guaranteed. In fact, the court acts as the body that finally attaches constitutional legitimacy to the restriction, deprivation and negation of their interests.

The question whether the *guaranteed individual human rights* adjudicated by the courts provide the necessary protection, has to be answered in the negative.

Constitutional provisions, more specifically constitutional-rights formulations, are soothing. They masquerade as entrenched, enshrined and guaranteed, and are generally hidden under a cloak of the faith-strengthening language of the doctrine of statist-individualist constitutionalism. However, they are always required to be interpreted and such interpretation might prove to be cause for utter dismay on the part of a person firmly believing that his/her rights were guaranteed and then being confronted with an interpretation by the dominant interpretive community revealing that his/her firm belief in guaranteed entitlement was totally unfounded.

In the final analysis, legal (more specifically constitutional) interpretation is clearly a matter of politics in a far more complex and pervasive fashion, than might generally be acknowledged. It is not a field of study divorced from the social and economic conditions that sustain it.[172] Through constitutional interpretation authoritative and binding meanings that are attributed to the Constitution are harnessed to further the ideological programme of the dominant elite, to legitimise its cause and to delegitimise challenging claims by ruling them unconstitutional and bad in law. It is therefore not incongruous to say that judgments can be and in fact often are acts of institutional violations of rights against groupings outside the dominant elite.

The interests of communities, especially of minority communities that fall outside the scope of the dominant elite, cannot adequately be protected by the judicial chamber of such elite. The interests of communities cannot be catered for by way of individual rights in accordance with the belief system and structures of statist-individualist constitutionalism. They have to be protected in a different way, namely through macro constitutional arrangements by vesting powers of self-government for such communities over their own autonomous corporate and territorial-based institutions. This question, however, falls largely beyond this book's central theme, namely the critique of statist-individualist constitutionalism. It is referred to only in passing in Chapter 9.

7.6.3   The supremacy of the Constitution

At the beginning of the discussion in this chapter, it was explained that the doctrine of supremacy of the Constitution has its own logically implied (complementary) doctrine of interpretation. It was referred to as the doctrine of orthodox or deductive interpretation. Applied to the Constitution, it implies that constitutional formulations – the language of the Constitution – provide direct access to the basically objective and certain, as well as stable, durable and predictable meaning of the text of the Constitution. It follows that all reasonable persons applying their minds when reading the Constitution would come to the same conclusion as to the meaning of what they read. One simply has to listen to the Constitution, as it were, and then act accordingly.

The Constitution is therefore an autonomous subject. Moreover, according to the doctrine of statist-individualist constitutionalism, it is a supreme subject. It speaks for itself – it speaks on its own behalf. If it does not do so, and if others – interpreters – can ascribe meanings to it, it is clearly not supreme anymore. The Constitution further does not *provide* for anything. If interpreters should convey

---

172   As Coombe, 1989:651-652 also observes.

what the Constitution says (and if that is binding), the interpreters may possibly claim supremacy, but the Constitution itself clearly cannot. On that score, the so-called supremacy of the Constitution is a fallacy.

The statist-individualist belief in the supremacy of the Constitution feeds on a complete lack of insight as to what interpretation entails. There are no objective, certain and stable durable and predictable meanings. The formulations of the Constitution only acquire and change meaning when they are interpreted by interpreters belonging to interpretive communities and informed by their (ideological) pre-understanding of what the formulations of the Constitution are supposed to mean. The meaning of the Constitution is therefore an expression of interpretive activity – a continuous activity of meaning creation and recreation by interpreters who pretend that they have found in the Constitution what the Constitution itself claims to be saying.

The Constitution does not bear inherent meaning. It is no living organism regardless of sometimes delightful popular but misleading metaphors about the so-called *growth of the constitution* or the *living constitution* suggest. The Constitution is not alive. Hence, it can also not be powerful, let alone supreme. It is a passive document, to which active interpreters ascribe meaning. The meanings that the dominant interpretative community ascribes to the Constitution are (for the moment) authoritative and binding. To the extent that power might come into the picture, it is the power of the prevailing interpretive community; not the power of the Constitution, let alone the supreme power of the so-called supreme Constitution.

UNIVERSAL INDIVIDUAL RIGHTS

8.1

Introduction

Individual rights are so important to statist-individualist constitutionalism that the constitutional discourse is almost entirely consumed by the focus on individual rights. Hence, when a supreme Constitution includes a comprehensive bill of individual rights, it is readily believed that the Constitution safeguards basically all human interests and in so doing guarantees a full-fledged system of justice and constitutionalism.

This belief is part of the general belief system of statist-individualist constitutionalism as outlined in Chapter 2. According to this belief (encapsulated amongst others in the eighth belief of the doctrine of statist-individualist constitutionalism), the Constitution is premised on the exclusive twosome consortium of the sovereign territorial state and the abstract individual with universal human rights.[1] (In consequence, the Constitution is anti-communitarian and has an anti-pluralist

---

[1] A series of French scholars in the decades immediately following the French Revolution and the Napoleonic era were the first to comment on this phenomenon. See for example Guizot, 1977:162; 155; 165. This process had its early origins with the emergence of kingship in twelfth century Europe reaching full sway during the era of Louis XIV and cardinal Richelieu. Both of these kings and the common subjects wanted to rid the political order of intermediary as embodied in the aristocracy (Guizot, 1977:80), thus forming something akin to a partnership in favour of state centralism and individualism. (See further on this Malan, 2012a:33-63.)

proclivity.)[2] The third mechanism of statist-individualist constitutionalism, namely bills of individual rights, is the supreme embodiment of this belief.

This chapter extends the critique of statist-individualist constitutionalism into the field of so-called individual rights. The critique challenges statist-individualist doctrine on its own terms. It will be shown in part 8.3, which contains the main thrust of this chapter, that rights ordinarily portrayed by statist-individualist constitutionalism as genuinely individual are by far not all that individual; they have a distinctive communitarian character. Communities are often a prerequisite for individual rights and are generally essential for safeguarding justice. In consequence, for statist-individualism to be true to its claim to secure justice through individual rights it should account in its system for the communal element inherent in such rights.

Part 8.2 of this chapter places the importance of individual rights in proper historical context, explaining the rise of the abstract individual and the accompanying doctrine of universal human rights. This is an intricate history.[3] The present discussion on the rise of the abstract individual cannot therefore pretend to be comprehensive. It merely provides a broad outline for part 8.3, which contains a critique of abstract universal individual human rights.

8.2

The way to the abstract individual and universal human rights

Individual persons have always existed. However, the abstract universal individual, distanced and abstracted from his/her community (to the extent that communities are recognised at all), essentially the same and equal to all other individuals having the same rights, is a recent phenomenon. The notion of universal human rights – unalienable universal rights – vesting equally in all individuals solely on account of their being individual people, is of recent origin. It is to a large measure an incidence of the statist-individualist constitutionalism.

The abstract universal individual was unknown to Classicism, the Middle Ages and to a considerable extent also to modernity. For the most part, the individual was either completely unknown or only of marginal importance to modern political philosophy and legal thinking. Classical notions of law, including natural law, were

---

2 This is encapsulated in the ninth belief on statist-individualist constitutionalism described in Chapter 2. It is because of this emphasis on the individual rights that the discourse of statist-individualist constitutionalism is so preoccupied (the seventh belief) with micro-theory. It is further based upon a deductive (orthodox) view of interpretation, which usually deals with individual rights, discussed in Chapter 7. The assumption is that rights exist at two levels, the level of the individual and the level of the nation state. Groups other than the nation (or the population of the state) could be ignored. See Van Dyke, 1974:725-741 at 726. Van Dyke is but one of many commentators who made this observation. Compare for example Vincent, 1987:186.

3 This history is the subject of an enormous and mounting body of scholarship. Among the many works dealing with this issue count Gillespie, 1992; Dupré, 1993; Gregory, 2012; Milbank, 1992.

not associated with universal individual rights.[4] Law was associated with the idea of justice as encapsulated in the Greek notion of dikaion and dike.[5] These notions were identified with a dispensation of justice and just outcomes (for the whole). Rights were concrete and specific rather than abstract and universal and were associated with specific persons and circumstances. Roman (private) law, for example was not a system of general abstract subjective rights; it consisted of a variety of divergent and specific remedies – actiones, interdicta, exceptiones and other remedies – for specific situations and often only for specific persons, whose legal statuses were different and unequal.[6] Only once the abstract universal individual was construed, did it become possible to conceive of a doctrine of abstract universal individual human rights.[7] In keeping with this, the notion of natural law also underwent a rationalistic metamorphoses, by morphing into a deductive "science," that is, a system of fixed and unchangeable universal principles from which solutions for specific problems were logically deduced.[8]

Everyone who somehow contributed towards the eventual establishment of the doctrine of abstract universal human rights – theoreticians such as Thomas Hobbes, John Locke, Jean-Jacques Rousseau, Emmanuel Kant, Thomas Paine and other articulators of the doctrine – subscribed to the fundamental equality, if not sameness of all people. Recent constructions of models of justice based on the notion of the abstract individual, such as those of John Rawls, attest to this.[9] Such constructions do not account for specific persons in concrete cultural and other community contexts. Being abstract universalist constructions, they purport to account for all concrete individuals. They do so in that they claim that all concrete situations and persons have been factored into the abstract universalist model. As individualistic systems they are inherently exclusive of communities. It is precisely on that account that Jeremy Bentham in 1789, the same year as the beginning of the French Revolution, could declare:

> [T]he community is a fictitious body, composed of the individual persons who are considered as constituting as it were its members. The interest of the community then is, what? The sum of the several interests of the members who composed it.[10]

If this assertion has not altogether excluded communities from a model of justice, it at least diminished communities to such a marginally insignificant position that

---

4   Arnold, 1979:78-79.

5   Vincent, 2010:40.

6   See in general for example Van Zyl, 1977.

7   Vincent, 2010:43.

8   Thus d' Entreves, 2017 declares as follows with respect to Hugo Grotius: "If natural law consists in a set of rules which are absolutely valid, its treatment must be based upon an internal coherence and necessity. In order to be a science, law must not depend upon experience, but on definitions, not on facts, but on logical deductions. Hence, only the principles of the law of nature can properly constitute a science. Such a science must be constructed by leaving aside all that undergoes change and varies from place to place."

9   As explained in Rawls, 2009. For a discussion on this see Malan, 2012a:156-165.

10   Bentham, 1967:iv.

they did not qualify for conceptualisation about justice. If the concession would have been made that there are such things as communities, they are nevertheless not important enough to be factored into models of morality or justice, because individual rights are comprehensive enough to account for all interests – also those of (so-called) communities.[11]

It may be claimed that the rudiments of the abstract individual go back to the eleventh century, that is, to the beginnings of Western Christian civilisation,[12] and that its emergence had four phases. At first, there were the early beginnings during the High Middle Ages up to approximately 1200; then came the second phase, which became particularly pronounced in the fourteenth century with the rise of nominalism. Since the sources of the beginning phase are particularly subtle, a little more attention is dedicated to that. Thirdly, after nominalism, the spotlight shifts to the sixteenth and seventeenth centuries, more specifically the individualist impact of the scientific and philosophical revolutions, the Reformation and the individualistic upshots of the territorial state. Fourthly, concise attention is dedicated to the revolutionary period of the eighteenth century with its final upshots in the period after World War II.

In Western culture, Colin Morris stated the "discovery" of the individual is one of the most important events of the period 1050-1200. He explains:

> It was not confined to any one group of thinkers. Its central features may be found in many different circles: a concern with self-discovery; an interest in the relations between people, and in the role of the individual within society; an assessment of people by their inner intentions rather than by their external acts. These concerns were, moreover, conscious and deliberate. "Know yourself" was one of the most frequently quoted injunctions.[13]

However, the individual whom Morris speaks of, was worlds away from the modern day abstract universal individual. The individual of the period 1050-1200 was in the domain of religion and culture. This abstract universal individual was, at most, glimmering in the distant future. "Individuals" to the extent that this is an apt description at all, were people with specific roles, places, capacities, responsibilities and acting in specific and serving in specific offices within larger wholes such as the family or the tribe, the town, or the larger communities of the polis, the church or within any other particular community.[14] The individual who was emerging in

---

11   Juristic persons can also be entitled to some rights. To that end any juristic person is regarded as an individual of sorts. Communities, in contrast to juristic persons, however, do not have any entitlements under the doctrine of statist-individualist constitutionalism.

12   There may be many views as to when Western-Christian civilisation really originated. It may be argued that the origins go back to Classicism. I subscribe to the view though that the present Western Christian civilisation, although it had its roots in Classicism, finally established itself in the eleventh century. Contemporary Western Christian civilisation might be viewed a successor civilization of Classic Mediterranean root civilisations which is constituted by Judaea-Christianity, Greek philosophy and science, and Roman law and statecraft.

13   Morris, 1972:158.

14   See for example the first two chapters Siedentop, 2014.

the era 1050-1200 was to a considerable extent the spinoff of currents in Christian theology. Francois Guizot explains that it was the church which paved the way for an individual intellectual space and for the independence of individual thinking.[15] The emerging canon law also played an important part in this regard. This "individual" was one who stood before God as a sinful person; an "individual" characterised by his/her congruent subordination to the Almighty God and in equal participation in the body of God; on proper analysis not really equal individuals but rather equal dependent souls.[16] Moreover, although these individuals might possibly have been abstracted from their families, they were still inextricably bound to the close knit community of the church. There was a liturgical community of ceremonies in which each faithful Christian believer played his/her designated part.[17]

Moreover, only converted Christians were regarded really to have souls in the true sense of the word and only they were members of the community of God – the populus Dei.[18] The papal revolution of the last years of the eleventh century and the monarchical governmental structure of the Roman Catholic Church (in contrast to the worldly power), was as it were the concrete – and visible – embodiment of religious individualisation. It was a community consisting of the association of individual souls under the authority of the governmental structures of the church – in the final analysis of the pope.[19] At the same time, this monarchical structure of the church set the precedent for a similar dispensation which later, from the twelfth century onwards, emerged in the guise of rudimentary state structures (initially around the person of the prince) in conjunction with individuals in the worldly (political) sphere.

The period around the papal revolution witnessed the emergence of some other forms of individuality – individuality on intimate and inner levels of the person. The focus was on the inwardness of the individual self, the spiritual identity, a desire to self-knowledge as the path towards God. The realisation of personal guilt, sinfulness, consistent guilt confession and self-reproach were prominent in these elements of inward individuality.[20] Peter Abelard's work on ethics, provides, according to Morris, a typical insight into these elements.[21]

Also other dimensions of this kind of inward individualisation dawned during the High Middle Ages: The discovery of intimacy and romantic love – a kind of love that placed a very high score on service to the loved one.[22] In this period the genre of

---

15 Guizot, 1977:96.

16 Siedentop, 2014:61; 102; 110; 122; 131; 141; 173; 190. See further Morris, 1972:10.

17 Morris, 1972:26-29.

18 Siedentop, 2014:155, 158. See further Morris, 1972:10.

19 Siedentop, 2014:238; 255; 263.

20 Morris, 1972:64-78.

21 Ibid, p.66-67. See on St Abelard, Copleston, 1972.

22 Morris, 1972:76; 108 et seq. Siedentop, 2014:193.

the autobiography (that was almost unknown to Classicism) and the self-portrait appeared on the scene.[23] The High Middle Ages also witnessed the emergence of the ode to personal friendship. Cicero's reflections about friendship did exert an influence on this. However, the thinking on personal friendship of this era emerged from a common mind that derives from a shared participation in Christ's love,[24] something that was particularly prominent in monastery life. In literary works peoples' personal feelings were articulated. There was also a focus on heroes and heroic deeds. This too placed individuality on the foreground,[25] yet not an abstract individuality, but an exceptional and unique individuality, which distinguished the hero from the common people. This promoted the idea of the individual, but not of equality.

New learnedness, thanks to a renewed interest in the classical Greek and Roman intellectual heritage, also subtly contributed towards the emergence of the individual. Scholastic scholars were not only believers; they were also enquiring minds set on elucidating their ability to understand.[26] Utilisation of the rational faculties, though anchored in the Classical intellectual tradition, necessarily also implied individual effort and achievement. The keener interest in the Classical languages, especially Latin, played an important part in contributing towards nuanced and sharper formulation.[27]

The emergence of the individual was not entirely limited to the inward dimension. The basis had also been laid for public expression of the individual person, which had an impact on the political and legal spheres. From the twelfth century onwards the genre of satire started to find its place in the repertoire of the literary world. It was used as a means of criticism against the organised church.[28]

New studies of the Justinian *Corpus Iuris Civilis* that began in the twelfth century in Northern Italy placed the individual person – more specifically the individual mind – under new focus. In canon law, which had its roots in the *Corpus Iuris Civilis*, the voluntary individual will emerged in law of contract and criminal law. Consensual individual wills regardless of formalities became the autonomous basis for the formation of contractual obligations.[29] This contrasted with Roman law of contract that, in addition to the requirement of consensus, also required compliance with strict formalities before contractual liability would arise, as for instance the

---

23   Morris, 1972:79-99.

24   Ibid, p.106.

25   Ibid, p.135-136.

26   Guizot, 1977:117.

27   Morris, 1972:7-9.

28   Morris, 1972:122 et seq; 132.

29   Siedentop, 2014:230; 232. Also further in general Guizot, 1977:106-107.

uttering of formal words and the actual handing over of the thing sold in the case of certain contracts of sale and other formal acts which were required in the case of many contracts – real contracts (*contractus re*), *contractus verbis*, etc.[30]

In the field of criminal law there was a similar development. Instead of regarding merely the punishable act (*actus reus*) as the basis for criminal liability, the reproachable individual mind in the form of *dolus* or *culpa* to constitute mens rea now became the basis for criminal liability.[31] The expression of the individual will also become the basis for the law of succession in private law, strikingly encapsulated in the word "will", for the testament of the testator.[32] Consensual individual wills also became the basis for marriage.

Lastly in the legal field, the development of the law of associations (*Genossenschaftsrecht*) took place. The expression of the individual will was the basis for the formation of corporations – structured permanent and autonomous (juristic) persons that were formed separate from the individual members. This was significant both economically and political-constitutionally.[33] These associations stimulated the professions and trading activities. The significance of this in the constitutional sphere was that the association did not stem from some kind of royal charter; the source of the association was the convergence of personal wills that created the association. Association was part of the answer to – a check and balance against – royal and other forms of princely political power.

It was mentioned above that Christian theology with its emphasis on personal salvation had an individualistic flavour. Sin, for example, was something that was increasingly a matter for the individual conscience. It was not punishable per se by some worldly authority (unless of course it was also a crime). Mythical theologies that placed the emphasis on intimate personal experiences and feelings and personal intimate bonds with God, emerged during the thirteenth and fourteenth centuries,[34] thus giving further impetus to individualisation.

Social conditions since the second half of the eleventh century subtly supported the emergence of individuality. The overarching factor in this was the rise of Western European population numbers. This era also saw the emergence of cities after the long period of ruralisation that followed on the demise of the Western Roman Empire. Urban centres created the cradle for new professions, new economic activities and an expanding spectrum of personal choice.[35]

---

30 See for example Van Zyl, 1977:275-285.

31 Siedentop, 2014:230; Morris, 197:278.

32 Siedentop, 2014:239.

33 Ibid, p.234.

34 Morris, 1972:152 et seq.

35 Siedentop, 2014:265-277; Morris, 1972:121 et seq.

The earliest signals for viewing the law in the subjective sense, that is, as rights vesting in individual persons originated only with the work of the Glossators in the twelfth century.[36] This assisted in the formation of the basis of the nominalist philosophy of the fourteenth century emanating from the work of, amongst others, William of Ockham and Jean Gerson. According to some commentators, William of Ockham caused a legal revolution using a semantic strategy. Whilst law had always been viewed as an objective system of justice, William gave law a new interpretation, namely of law as a subjective system of rights, that vested in people in their individual capacity.[37] Thus Andrew Vincent stated:

> The nominalist attack on universals and metaphysics is seen as working parallel with similar changes in moral and political life, thus forming a key background to the more modern obsessions with individualism and subjective right.[38]

William of Ockham opposed the encompassing metaphysical system of Thomas of Aquinas. His (William's) nominalism (in keeping amongst others with the Franciscan views of the time) impacted on conceptions about God, political authority and the individual. The common factor on all three terrains was that of free-willing sovereignty.[39] In the place of Thomas' rational God within the totality of a comprehensive metaphysical system, God now under the sway of nominalism morphed into a complete sovereign free God.[40] In keeping with the free and sovereign God, people too, now became free-willing (and equal) individuals. Siedentop explains:

> Human freedom and God's freedom were becoming mutually reinforcing characteristics. That is why contingency and choice, rather than eternal ideas and a priori knowledge, loom so large in his thinking.[41]

Nominalism also announced the removal – the abstraction – of the individual from the encompassing metaphysical system. According to the metaphysical order there are not really (free) individuals but rather people occupying places in the metaphysical cosmos. Nominalism, in contrast, now allowed for the free individual person. The free individual provided the backbone for a new moral philosophy. According to that, the integrity of the free individual conscience must be recognised and protected.[42] People cannot be forced to perform good deeds. If one does what is good only when forced to do so, that is not really good. Moral rectitude (and wickedness) is possible only if it emanates from free individual decision-making.

---

36   See for example the insights of Tierney, 1997:30-42.

37   Vincent, 2010:12; 17; 39-43. Tierney, 1997:30-42 disputes this view and shows that the work of the Glossators, more specifically of the canonists, already subscribed to the view of subjective rights two centuries before. See further in general on the work of William of Ockham Antonites, n.d:185-208 and Copleston, 1972:230-256.

38   Vincent, 2011:43.

39   Vincent, 2011:306-320.

40   Siedentop, 2014:306-308.

41   Ibid, p.309.

42   Ibid, p.316.

On that score, individual freedom of choice is regarded as the moral prerequisite for genuine moral (and immoral) conduct. People are after all only capable of praiseworthy in contrast to evil deeds if such deeds arise from individually willed decisions rather than from a predetermined role played within a universal whole.

Nominalism also stimulated convictions about natural human equality. Instead of the natural inequality of different people within a larger whole, free individuals now more than before become equals before God.[43] The Christian idea of equality actually stood in opposition to the classical idea of inequality for more than a millennium, but with William it acquired new energy.

The nominalist moral philosophy forged new conceptions about law. More specifically it gave further impetus to individual rights. From the new focus in the *Corpus Iuris Civilis* in the twelfth century, Canonist jurists interested themselves for a period of 200 years in what with hindsight appeared to be transformation of natural law from a system of objective justice to a system that placed the emphasis on subjective rights. In William of Ockham and nominalism this transformation clearly acquired the meaning of individual rights – inborn individual rights,[44] which in later centuries, (more specifically at the end of the eighteenth century) acquired the stamp of unalienable individual rights.

Nominalism therefore caused a turn-about in the way law was conceived of. Instead of viewing natural law, as almost always before, as an objective universal legal order, bound to the upholding of justice, it now became a system of subjective rights accruing to free-willing individuals. Hence, it is aptly declared:

> The nominalist attack on universals and metaphysics is seen as working parallel with similar changes in moral and political life, thus forming a key background to the more modern obsessions with individualism and subjective right.[45]

Moreover, the rights also started to include civil rights enlisted as a defence against arbitrary force exercised by absolutist princes – rights that could not be waived because they were regarded as inborn and inalienable rights.[46]

Nevertheless nominalism also helped in establishing the basis for princely absolutism, vested in the free will of the sovereign prince. Thus French king Louis le Hutin declared in 1315 that French subjects were unequal as the case concerned fell to be dealt with under feudalism, but they were equal subjects of the French ruler.[47] This mode of thinking, in terms of which only the state and the individual enjoyed recognition in constitutional law has gradually achieved dominance in statist-individualist constitutionalism.

---

43   Ibid, p.210-311.

44   Ibid, p.313.

45   Vincent, 2011:43.

46   Siedentop, 2014:316-17.

47   Ibid, p.312.

Nominalism also impacted on the views relating to the practice of science. On account of the verification principle it was now assumed that existing knowledge could be disproved on account of new reliable experience (evidence), and that knowledge could on that score be expanded.[48] In consequence, the role of the rational and observing individual who could find new truths, was gaining increasing importance. This paved the way for the forthcoming scientific and philosophical revolution.

Three potent forces during the sixteenth and seventeenth centuries contributed towards a profound conversion towards individual centralisation: the scientific and philosophical revolution, the Reformation, and the centralisation of political power in the emerging sovereign territorial states.[49]

The scientific and accompanying philosophical revolutions that were already germinating in the preceding era followed as a product of a general cultural climate. If specific figures have to be singled out as protagonists of this changing climate, the names of Copernicus, Kepler, Galileo and Newton present themselves. The scientific revolution which occasioned the enormous knowledge leaps brought about a dramatic change in the traditional understanding of reality. The basis for this new understanding and the mode of knowledge expansion were twofold. First, there was sharp observation and analysis. This empiricist impulse is associated primarily with Francis Bacon, however, it also derives from figures, such as William of Ockham. Secondly, there is the sense-making and organising intellectual activity that proceeds purely from the sovereign human intellect, that is, from rationalism, which is primarily associated with figures such as Rene Descartes. Descartes' famous statement "I think, therefore I am" is, as Richard Tarnas, the great historian of Western intellectual history declares, the "[e]pochal defining statement of the modern self."[50] This person – this "self" – that Tarnas speaks of is an individual person not bound into and, as it were, constituted by his/her community, but a person who is the exact opposite: removed and abstracted from communities. In fact, it was believed that the new science was made possible owing to individualisation – an abstraction of the "I" from the "we".

The Church reformation brought an end to the erstwhile empire/church world whole (the *Republica Christiana/Rykskerklike wêreldgeheel*) in Western Europe. The religious wars that followed on the schism in the church terminated the many centuries long erstwhile visible general church community. This gave rise to the institutional dispersion and individualisation in the Christian world, as religion morphed into a direct personal relationship of the faithful individual with God, without the intermediate authority of the church and its office bearers.[51] Tarnas said the Reformation was:

---

48   Ibid, p.313.

49   See the discussion by Tarnas, 2010:223-324.

50   Ibid, p.75.

51   The effect of this in conjunction with the rise of the territorial state is discussed in Malan, 2012a.

(a) new and decisive assertion of rebellious individualism – of personal conscience, of "Christian liberty," of critical private judgment against the monolithic authority of the institutional Church [...] on another level the Reformation's revolutionary declaration of personal autonomy served as a continuation of the Renaissance impulse – and was thus an intrinsic [...] element of the overall Renaissance phenomenon.[52]

In time the Reformation led to the secularisation of religion which enabled every person (and not the church authorities) to adopt a belief system which was most acceptable to him or her. To quote Tarnas again:

The self increasingly became the measure of things. Truth increasingly became truth-as-experienced-by-the-self. Thus the road opened by Luther would move through to Pietism and Kantian critical philosophy and Romantic philosophical idealism to, finally, the philosophical pragmatism and existentialism of the late modern era.[53]

The chasm in the church was directly linked to the third major force towards individualism in this period, namely the emergence and final establishment of the sovereign territorial state. The rise of the state came over a long period, as smaller, semi-autonomous polities – feudal units, principalities, republics and cities – lost authority in favour of the emerging sovereign territorial state under powerful dynasties.[54] England and France were the first sovereign territorial states.

Owing to the religious wars, it was hardly possible for political units to have a homogenous character. The denominational differences were simply too deep and divisive. Hence, political units were no longer regarded as suitable entities to accommodate (religious) communities. Political units could only accommodate individual subjects regardless of their religious persuasions or loyalties. In time, the emerging territorial states were only accommodating individuals and no communities.

The emphasis on the individual was in this era prominent among for example, the Levellers in England, more specifically in accordance with the notion of the individual's "self-ownership" – a notion that can be traced back to the thirteenth century and which has reached its zenith in modern libertarian convictions. It was accordingly quite natural for individuals to have full-scale ownership of themselves, more correctly unqualified personal self-determination with the implication, amongst other things, that all forms of government not premised on personal consent had to be rejected.[55]

Moreover, the belief was established (stimulated amongst other things by the continuous violent struggles of the time in Western Europe and England), especially in the work of Thomas Hobbes, that humankind was nothing more

---

52 Tarnas, 2010:241.

53 Ibid, p.243.

54 See the discussion in Malan, 2012a:33-63.

55 See the discussion in Casey, 2017:448-449; 840-844 and Sabine, 1971:477-481.

than an aggregate of people who were locked in a never-ending state of mutual suspicion and continuous damaging strife. This sorry state could only be overcome by the sovereign power structure of governmental power of the territorial state in order to at least establish formal peace – a truce as it were – among the mutually belligerent individuals.

The outcome of this is the contemporary anti-communitarian statist-individualist doctrine which is based on the acknowledgement of only the (sovereign) state and the abstracted individual (essentially the same as all other individuals) accompanied by the emphatic rejection of the claims of communities, and even more so, their very existence. This conception of the state was in this era articulated in political theorising by Michel de l'Hôpital and Jean Bodin in France, and by William Berkeley and ultimately by Thomas Hobbes in England.[56] At the same time, the case for the constitutional accommodation of communities (alongside individuals) avidly advocated by Johannes Althusius was emphatically dismissed.[57]

The individualising upsurge of the time can be encapsulated in the involvement of three prominent figures: René Descartes, Martin Luther en Thomas Hobbes.

Descartes, who posited the rationalistic, actively reasoning individual opposed to everything outside this individual agent – the "extension" – and independently in command of the extension.

Luther removed the authority of the church between God and man and placed the faithful individual in a direct undisturbed relationship with the Almighty sovereign God.

Hobbes who no longer recognised any actual existing human communities, but only mutually hostile individuals in a state of incessant war with each other (*bellum omnia contra omnes*), and panting for the intervening state – the Leviathan or mortal god – who had to bring and maintain some calm among the battling individuals.

Clearly there were still communities, but in view of the events of this era their recognition became anomalous. The foundations for the sovereign atomist world were laid and their implications played out during the revolutionary period of the last quarter of the eighteenth century (the great upheavals of the American and French Revolutions). During the American and French Revolutions, the notion of abstract equal individuals, already prominent in the brute individualism of figures such as Hobbes, came to full fruition in inalienable inborn individual human rights. These rights were solemnly sermonised by the leading ideologues and in the founding

---

56   See the discussion in van Malan, 2012b:65-93.

57   Johannes Althusius' work is contained in *Politica: Politics methodically set forth and illustrated with sacred and profane examples* (an abridged and translated version) edited and translated from Latin by Frederick S Carney (Liberty Fund Indianapolis 1994). See also the discussion of Althusius' work in Malan, 2017b:1-27 and Malan, 2017a:1-35.

documents of these revolutions. Among the official revolutionary documents count the French Declaration of the Rights of Man and the Citizen of 1789 as the most prominent. Article 1, amongst other things, proclaims that men are born free and remain equal in rights. Article 2 proclaims the conservation and imprescriptible (individual) rights of man the singular goal of political association.

The social conditions in the British colonies in the North America and in time the United States of America, represented an important step on the path of the doctrine of the universal individual, essentially equal to all other individuals. Alexis de Tocqueville,[58] who toured the United States of America, made important observations about this. Equality of free individuals, unconstrained by differences and hierarchies of rank and class which the former colonists had left behind in old world in England and Europe, was established as the unchallenged socio-political doctrine and mode of living in the United States of America. Equality of individuals was not only a doctrine, but became the essential character of the social order. Due to the rise of the United States of America this became a potent force for the establishment of the idea of universal equal individual human rights based on the notion of the abstract universal individual.

Individual human rights are associated with the essence of the statist-individualist Constitution. A constitution without a comprehensive collection of inalienable inborn individual human rights is not a constitution at all.[59] One and a half century after the tumultuous revolutionary era, the doctrine of abstract universal individual human rights (based on the notion of the abstract universal individual) made a universal claim in positive law. That was when the General Assembly of the United Nations on 10 December 1948 passed the Universal Declaration of Human Rights, which in its turn influenced numerous state Constitutions and international rights instruments.[60]

These inalienable inborn human rights were affirmed in emphatic written formulations.[61] In keeping with the doctrine of statist-individualist constitutionalism these rights are also dealt with pre-politically (and extra-politically). Their absolute integrity must be beyond reproach. In consequence, no political decision is allowed

---

58   See De Tocqueville, 1988.

59   Accordingly, article 16 of the French Declaration of the Rights of Man and the Citizen provides "Any society in which the guarantee of rights is not assured, nor the separation of powers determined, has no Constitution."

60   See the *Universal Declaration of Human Rights of the United Nations* of 10 December 1948 in provisions as outlined in articles 1 and 2. The preamble commences with the words: "Whereas recognition of the inherent dignity and of the equal and inalienable rights of all members of the human family is the foundation of freedom, justice and peace in the world ..." Article I provides that all human beings are born equal in dignity and rights. Article 2 provides that "(e)veryone is entitled to all the rights and freedoms set forth in this Declaration, without distinction of any kind, such as race, colour, sex, language, religion, political or other opinion, national or social origin, property, birth or other status."

61   Friedrich, 1974:87 observes that these rights are not natural at all. If so, there would have been no need to protect them in a constitutional document.

to impact on them.[62] The inviolability of the sovereign, abstract and unbounded individual and the unrestrained free will to which the individual is entitled to, is the default position of the notion of abstract universal individual human rights.[63] Within the framework of the abstract universal individual and the doctrine of equal, universal, individual human rights no one has any distinctive place to occupy, role to play, capacity to fulfil, responsibilities to discharge or to act in accordance with the duties associated with a particular (public) office. All have exactly the same universal rights solely because they are individual people. Precisely for that reason these rights are deliberately called human rights.

The importance of the protection of the interests of people also conceived as individuals is beyond doubt. It is one of the gains of modernity.[64] However, the fixation of statist-individualist constitutionalism on the abstract individual and universal individual human rights (alongside the state) and the accompanying rejection of communities are for at least four reasons patently misplaced.

First, constitutionalism without the recognition of communities is inconceivable. Justice – the core objective of constitutionalism – without the recognition and active accommodation of communities is unsustainable.

Secondly, a system of power balance based on the effective checks and balances that safeguards a balanced constitution and limited government cannot be achieved without the recognition and active accommodation of communities.

Thirdly, the notion of universal individual human rights based on the notion of the abstract individual do not account for core aspects of societal reality, namely the reality that people are not simply abstract individuals with equal (human) rights which they may enforce against other individuals. As members of communities (communal wholes) they occupy specific places, play roles, fulfil capacities, discharge specific responsibilities and act in accordance with the duties associated with particular (public) office according to their distinctive talents, professions, standings and statuses.

Fourthly, the very idea of individual rights is also questionable. The enjoyment of what is called individual rights is only sustainable within a communal framework. Hence, in the absence of communities, these so-called individual rights are simply dead letter. Quite frankly there are no (exclusive) individual rights.

In the next part of this chapter, the notion of individual human rights is critiqued. This will be done mainly with reference to the South African discourse on this question, but also with reference to pointed references emanating from elsewhere

---

62   In theoretical expositions the best example of this is most probably the John Rawls' *original position.*

63   See the observations by Vincent, 2010:17 with reference to Kant, Bentham en Hart.

64   This I specifically and repeatedly stated in Chapter 10 of *Politocracy – An assessment of the coercive logic of the territorial state and ideas around a response to it.*

in the world. The first aspect mentioned above is by implication also covered in this discussion. Together with the second aspect it is dealt with in more detail in the last chapter. The third aspect fall beyond the scope of this book. I hope to deal with that at a later stage.

8.3

Individual rights without communities

On account of the doctrine of abstract individualism (and the exclusive recognition of abstract individual rights), statist-individualist constitutionalism, also in the South African discourse, bases its assault on communities on two grounds. The first is the redundancy (or individualist reductionist) ground and the second the definition (or legal subjectivity) argument. The first argument claims that the legal protection of communities is redundant and unnecessary. The second claims that a community is not susceptible to clear legal definition as a legal subject and for that reason cannot be the bearer of rights. These two arguments will now be discussed and rebutted.

8.3.1 The redundancy argument

According to the redundancy argument, individual rights (and rights exercised by juristic persons) fully cover the terrain of rights protection. The belief was based on the argument that since cultural communities (assuming that their existence is not altogether rejected) consist of individual members, and that as long as the individual rights of the members are protected, protection of the community would be redundant. Stated differently, that when individual rights are protected, the communities to which individuals might belong automatically attract the benefit of such protection, thus affording protection to communities unnecessary.[65] In the same vein, the South African Law Commission, though conceding that there might be collective interests, proclaimed that in the final analysis all rights vest in and are enforced by individuals. It claimed quite emphatically that "(n)either in legal theory nor in legal practice is it correct or necessary to recognise these values as anything other than individual rights in a Bill of Rights. After all, every individual member of the group subscribing to these values can enforce them ..."

In some academic circles similar views are harboured. Some jurists contend that legal science precludes the possibility of community rights protection, claiming that something like language rights can juridically speaking be protected only as the rights of individuals.[66] The objection to the legal protection of cultural

---

65 Hartney, 1991:294; See also unpublished address by Mr Justice Olivier, former head of the South African Law Commission at Justice College, Pretoria on 15 May 1992:9-10.

66 Du Plessis, 1987:133. This is a particularly superficial and in the final analysis a profoundly wrong view. See Malan, 2014:66-84.

communities is purported to be based on what was sanctified as legally scientific and philosophical grounds. A collectivity, such as an ethnic, language or cultural community cannot be defined as a legal subject, and they can therefore neither be the bearers nor enforcers of any rights. Hence, both substantive law and procedural law lack the conceptual framework for dealing with community claims in the form of rights.

Lourens du Plessis, on the basis of what he erroneously put forward as a philosophical perspective, insisted that since an ethnic or cultural community is not juridically definable, there is no such thing as community rights or interests worthy of protection.[67] The South African Law Commission cherished similar scruples.[68] It acknowledged the importance of certain interests of (minority) communities but nevertheless found the difficulty or impossibility to define a community as a legal subject, to be, what it called a fundamental legal problem and stated that "(f)rom a legal point of view before there can be any question of an enforceable right in respect of any person, there must also be a legal subject, a persona juris, to whom the right belongs. After all, this is obvious."[69]

Distinguishing between interests, which the Commission conceded communities might have, and rights, which they could never have, the Commission stated:

> In that sense it is possible to speak of a group interest, but juridically it is not a group right. It remains an individual right which an individual can protect in a court of law although he upholds the value together with other individuals.[70]

I now proceed to show that the redundancy argument is ill-conceived and without substance.

The claim that individual rights exhaust all rights protection and therefore provide an encompassing system of justice is profoundly erroneous. A bill of individual rights, no matter how comprehensive, falls way far short of securing justice. Justice and

---

67   Du Plessis, 1988:17. Du Plessis stated: "*Omdat 'n etniese groep of volk 'n maatskap en daarom juridies ondefinieerbaar is, bestaan daar ook nie so iets soos regtens beskermenswaardige etniese groepe of regsbelange nie.*" (Own translation) See also Coetzee, 1983:6-7.

68   SA Law Commission Project 58 *Group and human rights. Summary of interim report* (Aug 1991) para, 13.5.

69   SA Law Commission Project 58 *Group and human rights. Summary of interim report* (Aug 1991) Para, 13.4. Sieghart, 1992:367-368, specifically dealing with the question of the rights of peoples, added two further objections to the recognition of collective rights: First: that it is difficult to identify the entities that are obliged to respect the rights of peoples, and secondly, he fears that the rights of peoples might pose a danger to individual human rights, which might become subservient to the rights of peoples.

70   To this Mr Justice Olivier under whose supervision the Law Commission conducted its inquiry added procedural objections arguing that groups were incapable of enforcing rights. How would a group (for example Afrikaners), pursue their legal action, he asked: "Must all Afrikaners sign the power of attorney to institute an action, who is going to pay the legal costs and against whom must execution be taken in the event the action is unsuccessful?" (own translation). Olivier, 1992 unpublished address by Mr Justice Olivier, former head of the South African Law Commission at Justice College, Pretoria on 15 May 1992:9-10. (Original Afrikaans text: "*Moet alle Afrikaners die volmag teken om 'n aksie in te stel, wie gaan die koste betaal en teen wie moet eksekusie gehef word as die aksie verloor word?*") Olivier, who later served as a judge of the Supreme Court of Appeal, headed the team conducting the inquiry into human and group rights.

constitutionalism also require the constitutional recognition and accommodation of communities. Moreover, it will be shown that the constitutional recognition of communities is indispensable for the protection of individual persons. The rejection of the protection of communities therefore also reneges on what is usually referred to as individual rights.

The claim that all rights are exclusively individual and that the protection of the (rights of) communities is redundant overlooks the fact that a vast field of interests are in fact not reducible to any specific individual/s. On close analysis, many rights nominally conceived as individual are in fact rather collective or communal since they are dependent on a community of similarly positioned people who belong to the same community and who share common interests. Moreover, there are certain seemingly individual rights that cannot be enjoyed individually, but only collectively, that is, in community with other similarly placed people belonging to the same community.[71] Individual rights contained in a Bill of Rights therefore do not exhaust the entire field of rights protection, which means that even when all so-called individual rights that one can conceive of have been recognised, there remains a vast field of legally protectable interests still to be accounted for.[72] These rights pertain to interests that are supra-individual; they do not vest in a single individual to the exclusion of other individuals and never fall within the exclusive control of any single individual person.[73] These rights relate to interests that are non-severable in that they cannot be divided into separate individual interests:[74] they are never only mine, but always ours. When one person benefits from these interests, others simultaneously also benefit, and when one person suffers as a result of the violation of these interests, others also suffer similar prejudice.

These interests have an inherently communal dimension. They can never be exercised exclusively by one person alone. They require a community of similarly interested people and are always exercised within a collective setting. Several seemingly authentic individual rights can be cited to demonstrate these points.

The right to freedom of association immediately comes to mind in this context. The widely held belief seems to be that this entails a freedom to exercise an abstract, universal, individual right. To exercise such right is considered to be a function of individual choice. Upon such assumption, association (the formation, continuation and termination of association) is viewed to result purely from the exercise of individual choices. If that is so, association is a mere derivative of individual choice. However, this conception of the right to freedom of association is inaccurate and incomplete, since it disregards the essential communitarian basis of the right. The

71   Burgers, 1990:72-73.
72   Green, 1991:326.
73   Hartney, 1991:298.
74   McDonald, 1991:218.

protection of the right to freely associate does not only entail freely exercising individual choices. On a more fundamental level, it involves the protection of the integrity of the communities which people belong to and the right to freely associate is therefore non-existent in the absence of a community. Association takes place within communal settings. In consequence, the right to freedom of association, in the first place, revolves around the maintenance of the integrity of communities. It is impossible to conceive of the exercise of the right to freedom of association in an exclusively individual way. To associate is clearly not merely an involvement of a single person. It is inherently a reciprocal activity. The exercising of the right to freedom of association must therefore obviously always presuppose and imply the mutually cooperative involvement of similarly positioned people who comprise the community concerned. When the right is exercised, a number of similarly placed people (and never only one person) benefit, and when the right is infringed, the ensuing harm does not befall a single person but ordinarily a collection of such similarly positioned people.

Moreover, families and cultural, linguistic or religious communities do not arise as a result of the exercise of individual choices to associate. On the contrary, people are born within family units which are part of these communities, and even though they might later on decide to rescind their ties (and to dissociate), they ordinarily remain in their communities. To state that they are members of these communities is inapt. It lacks appreciation of what is really at stake. To say that people belong to their communities, suggests a far more appropriate understanding of the matter. Members of a community (or communities) experience their community as a space and place available to them where they are truly at home; where they enjoy the benefit of understanding and positive engagement with others; where they feel safe and secure; and from where they can draw upon available sources to develop a sense of direction in pursuit of happiness. Hence, association is clearly not only a matter of sovereign individual choice. On close analysis, it is rather a matter of continued belonging to existing communities. Existing communities are therefore the prerequisite for (the right to) freedom of association. If communities are disrupted as a result of programmes of social manipulation such as those aimed at so-called nation building, the prerequisite of freedom of association is undermined, thus making it impossible to exercise the right to enjoy that freedom.

The same argument obtains to the right to freedom of expression. Freedom of expression is an inseparable element of a broader interactive process with other similarly positioned people. When there are no other people to whom the expression can be addressed the expression is rendered impossible and so is the exercise of the right. Exercising the right requires an understanding audience of similarly positioned and interacting addressees. The right to freedom of expression is therefore community-dependent, which means that a collective dimension is an indispensable prerequisite and ingredient for the existence and enjoyment of the right. Both the rights to association and expression depend upon a community of people. Such community is a crucial part of the goods/assets to which these rights pertain and without which they cannot be exercised.[75]

The right to profess and practice religion is hardly conceivable in purely individualistic terms. Religious goods/assets, that is, the belief system and a religious community within which someone is born, or to which a person subscribes and may join, are key requirements for practicing religion (that is, to exercise religious rights). These goods provide the myths and the intellectual, social, and psychological space without which religious practice would be barely possible. Essential aspects of the professing and more so, of the practising religion, take place mainly within the context of a (religious) community of people and in the absence of a community such involvement is seriously curtailed. When the religious right of a single person is violated, the religious rights of fellow believers, whose religious practices depend upon the existence of a religious community, also suffer. Denise Réaume aptly articulates this truth when she states:

> Although in some aspects their relationship with God may be capable of individual enjoyment, there are also many aspects of their religious practice, including communal worship and celebration of sacred events, which require the joint participation of others to make them valuable. No one person can have the good unless at least some others also enjoy it.[76]

Language and cultural rights are also not susceptible to individual reductionism.[77] Language and cultural rights can be exercised only in communicative interaction with other people of the same culture and speakers of the same language. The enjoyment of these rights is possible only within the cultural and linguistic contexts within which people of the same language can interact. It requires other people of the same language between whom interaction can take place. By far the greatest value of a cultured community, says Réaume quite correctly, is that it inherently involves the presence of other people who have similar interests and with whom one can interact and share that culture.[78] The exercise of the right therefore presupposes a community of people, in this case of people sharing the same culture, that is, a cultural community. It is never an exclusively individual matter. Emphasising the communal element of cultural (and other rights), Rodoolfo Stavenhagen aptly observes:

> However, when we refer to cultural rights, as well as to many social and economic rights, a collective approach is often required, since some of them can only be enjoyed in community with others and that community must have the possibility to preserve, protect

---

75   Taylor, 1993:176 states in this respect that the French language can be seen as a collective resource that individuals may make use of.

76   Réaume, 1998:16.

77   See the illuminating observations on language and religious rights by the eminent South African philosopher Degenaar, 1987:247.

78   Réaume, 1998:10.

and develop what it has in common. Beneficiaries of these rights may be individuals but their content evaporates without the preservation and the collective rights of groups. The rights pertain to persons belonging to specific cultures and shaped by these cultures, who engage in collective action, who share common values, and who can only be the bearers of these common values by joining with other members of their group.[79]

Culture is an interactive and participatory[80] good/asset par excellence, involving a multitude of active and passive participants who simultaneously produce and consume, create and utilise the products and qualities of culture. The practising of culture (that is, the exercising of cultural rights) is not directed towards the achievement of some final result. Its value lies in the fact that it is a continued process in community with others belonging to the same community. In the absence of such community the essential element of the right simply falls by the wayside. The sharing with others of the cultural experience is a vital aspect of cultural practice and thus an important element of the exercise of cultural rights.

Culture, the object of cultural rights, Réaume reminds us:

(c)onsists in participating in the production of those artefacts which constitute a cultural society. But there is no end product because in a sense, those artefacts are never completed but are continuously reinterpreted and recreated by each generation. This process is the essence of the cultured society and can only take place through, not simply because of, the involvement of many.[81]

In the case of political rights, a communal dimension is once again essential. Political rights, like all the rights already mentioned, are also dependent on (interactive) communication and therefore come to nothing in the absence of a (political) community. Moreover, the existence and maintenance of political rights presuppose structures and procedures shared by everyone within the political community. Political rights which are sustained by these procedures and structures are often not reducible to the interests of a particular individual, to the exclusion of others and if those structures and procedures are ineffectual, everyone forming part of the political community simultaneously suffers. The conclusion is once again that when the right is exercised, a multitude of people are instantaneously and similarly benefiting and when it is violated the resulting prejudice in the same way strikes at a multitude of interdependent people and is not limited to a single person. The above seemingly individual rights – and the list can be extended considerably – never protect the individual interests of a single person to the exclusion of others. These rights always protect shared goods and assets from which never only one, but always a multitude of persons belonging to the same community simultaneously benefit.[82]

---

79 Stavenhagen, 1995:68.

80 Réaume, 1998:10.

81 Réaume, 1998:10-11.

82 See e.g. Green, 1991:328 at 321; Hartney, 1991:293-314 at 298 and Réaume, 1998:18-19.

All these rights are of value only when there are communities within which they can be exercised. They have a meaningful content only when shared with others of the same community and when that community is involved in the enjoyment thereof. Their value lies in shared enjoyment without which they are meaningless or at least severely impoverished and infringed.[83]

Since these goods and assets are shared by a community of interdependent people and the rights pertaining to them are therefore of a communal nature, it is impossible to force them into the straitjacket of individual reductionism and thus into the doctrine of abstract universal individual rights, and in so doing, to reduce them to separated atomised abstract individuals. These goods and assets can only vest in a multitude or a collection of people who have shared interests in these goods, who together and in a relationship of mutual dependence exercise the rights pertaining to these goods. These goods and the rights pertaining to such goods vest in the totality of the community in question and never separately in one individual.

A crucial factor that further underscores the communal nature of the above rights and which makes it even more impossible to reduce them to the interests of separate individuals is that no individual can fully dispose of or do away with the goods protected by these rights. The goods and assets to which these rights pertain are in themselves aspects of the (cultural-political) tradition which is more durable than an individual's own life span. Precisely this is one of the important reasons why these goods cannot be disposed of or dispensed with by any single individual. At birth these goods and assets – language, religion, culture and often even political structures, etc. – already exist and on death they remain behind. A person is, as it were, born into these legal goods and when he or she passes away he or she leaves them – albeit possibly in changed form – behind.[84]

Having rebutted the redundancy claim which is premised on the doctrine of the abstract individual, the focus now turns to the legal definition (legal subjectivity) argument.

8.3.2   The definition (legal subjectivity) argument

According to the definitional (legal subjectivity) objection to the legal recognition of communities, there is a strict rule that the recognition and legal accommodation of (legal) interests must always begin with a clear definition of the legal subject. Exact definition of the legal subject is an absolute precondition for the recognition of rights. Accordingly, only once clear subject definition has been achieved, can the question of the possible recognition of rights of the subject in question be considered.

---

83   Stavenhagen, 1995:63-78.

84   See for example the discussion in Malan, 2014a:72-80.

This objection to the legal recognition of communities coincides logically with the doctrine of abstract individual human rights. The notion of the (atomistic) individual is the sole archetype – the only model – for legal subjectivity and, finally for the recognition and enforcement of legal interests[85] which can only take the form of individual-like rights. Stated differently, when the question of legal recognition is considered, the very first, and strict threshold-question that is raised, is whether the entity that seeks legal protection can be defined in a similar way as the individual. The individual legal subject and the procedural rules which are applied to enforce individual rights therefore provide the only framework in terms of which the broad question of legal recognition and accommodation can be dealt with.

The individual legal subject is precisely defined: their lifespan begins at a specifically defined moment and terminates at an equally precise moment. Moreover, it is clearly distinguished from other individual legal subjects and consequently the difficulty of vague and uncertain boundaries between them never arises. Thanks to clear definition, the individual legal subject is easily accommodated by both substantive and procedural law (private law and law of civil procedure to be exact).

Proceeding from this premise, the legal protection of any community is summarily dismissed. A community unlike the individual, cannot be delineated with precision. Hence, it is unclear precisely who is claiming legal protection and how the rules of enforcement, such as the rules of civil procedure would be dealing with it.[86]

There is as little substance in this second objection to the legal recognition of communities as there is in the first – the redundancy objection – because the notion of the (atomistic) individual does not provide the only juridical model for the recognition and enforcement of people's interests. On the contrary, this is but one of various ways of accounting for the interests and the promotion of justice. The rejection of the legal accommodation is simply oblivious of various other, specifically non-individualist approaches to securing justice.

Aptly conceptualised law is a set of institutions and facilities that respond to the legitimate needs of people. These institutions and facilities enable people to realise their needs and interests.[87] What we refer to as individual rights is one such institution. When viewing law in this way – as an evolving set of institutions and facilities – the focus of the legal inquiry turns to the objects of law instead of, and

---

85   Elsewhere I argued that this approach proceeds from a typically and rather limited private law conception of the law that feeds on the notion of abstract individual rights. To a large extent the individual person and private law are two sides of the same coin. Private law is there in the first place for individuals and for regulating individual relations. (Malan, 2008a:437.)

86   See the objection raised by unpublished address by Olivier, 1992:9-10.

87   Hart, 1994:27.

over and above subjects of law,[88] that is, instead of legal subjectivity on which the legal subjectivity objection is so singularly fixated.

It has also been indicated that the enjoyment of language, cultural, association, expression, religious and many other rights cannot be enjoyed by a single person to the exclusion of others; they are enjoyed instead in community with others, sharing, for instance, the same language, culture or religion, and belonging to the same cultural, linguistic, or religious community. The exercise of these rights is therefore dependent upon the existence of communities – language, cultural and religious or whatever other community. It is crucial to understand that these cultural and language communities are themselves the very goods and assets – the resources with respect to which rights pertaining to, for instance, language, culture, free association and free expression are exercised, on the basis of the same logic that real rights are exercised with respect to things (res) and intellectual property rights are exercised with respect to intellectual property assets. The existence and the well-being of these objects – res (corporal things) and intellectual property assets – are the prerequisite for the exercise of the relevant rights. By the same token, the very existence and well-being of communities are the prerequisite for individual people exercising rights pertaining to culture, language and religion. Consequently, these communities have to be secured since they are the indispensable legal goods and assets, that is, the legal objects, without which the enjoyment of the rights relating to culture, language and religion and other rights would be impossible.[89]

However, communities are not necessarily in good shape. They might be languishing and therefore cannot serve as the resources – the objects – for the enjoyment of rights. The livelihood and vibrancy of communities are dependent on institutions that sustain them: they depend on institutional maintenance. Communities need, as Stavenhagen emphasised, institutions and facilities that provide and demarcate the social boundaries and define the spaces of social relationships by which membership is attributed[90] within which individual identity takes a particular form,[91] and within which their rights can be enjoyed meaningfully. In other words, communities need various forms of structured organisation. The following examples may be cited:

σ   People belonging to cultural communities need educational institutions and facilities, within which language and educational rights (also the association, cultural and expression rights) can be practically enjoyed. They also need the necessary

88   This outlook on communities as subjects of law is inspired in part and is comparable to the well-developed system of subjective rights in Western European private law, in terms of which rights are distinguished in terms of the objects that they pertain to, namely res as the object of real rights, obligations as the objects of personal rights; personality as the object of personality rights and intellectual goods property as the objects of the intellectual property (immaterial property) rights.

89   See in this regard the illuminating observations by Stavenhagen, 1995:66-67.

90   Ibid.

91   See in general on the communitarian view of individual identity and how individual identity is defined within the spaces occupied by communities Gardbaum, 1992:701-705; Van Blerk, 1998:196-198.

self-determination, that is, the competence to decide autonomously on culturally sensitive matters which are of importance to the well-being of such community.

σ   People belonging to religious communities need religious institutions for the enjoyment of, for instance, religious, associational, expression rights.

σ   People belonging to language and cultural communities need means of organised communication, such as mass media enabling the enjoyment of cultural language and expression rights.

σ   People belonging to any of the various sexual minority communities[92] need legal facilities recognising and legally stabilising (long-term) relationships in the same way as heterosexual people need legal facilities for heterosexual relationships.

σ   A cultural/linguistic community, specifically a minority community might be in need of autonomous rule over a particular territory, more specifically a metropolis,[93] which enables it to protect all interests associated with such community, including its cultural and economic well-being, and its physical safety, specifically in the face of homogenising programmes that threatens the cultural survival of such community or laxity of state governments towards the physical safety of such community.

The examples are numerous. The truism common to all these instances is that institutions and facilities are indispensable for the protection of communities – institutions that on close analysis serve as the concrete embodiment of these communities. These institutions stabilise and provide the organisational bulwark for the safety of these communities. Thus viewed, communities provide the raw resources/goods/assets for the enjoyment of rights, whilst institutions and facilities for these communities, such as schools, universities, radio stations, television channels, territories over which communities exercise self-management to protect, stabilise, organise and invigorate these communities. For as long as adequate and well-functioning institutions are in place, meaningful enjoyment of rights becomes and remains a reality.

84

Conclusion

The discussion brings to light that communities need not necessarily be viewed as aspiring subjects of rights. Viewed from the perspective of the rights discussed above – association, expression, rights relating to language, culture, religion (and possibly also other rights) – communities assume the guise of the objects and not the subject of such rights. They constitute the goods, assets and resources in respect

---

92   This would be the so-called sections of the LGBTI groupings.

93   For the importance of a metropolitan basis for maintaining a minority language see Malan in *Taalverval met besondere verwysing na die ideologieë en praktyke van verstaatliking* (Language deterioration with specific reference to the ideologies and practises of statism) Malan, 2014b:462-480.

of which rights are exercised and without which individual identity is restricted and what is called individual rights, cannot be enjoyed. If a community is left without any institutions or if its institutions are destroyed by homogenising governmental programmes. Once that happens, the very legal objects (resources and goods) on which the rights to culture, language, expression, religion, individual identity and many other rights depend, are allowed to vanish resulting in the large-scale violation of individual rights.

Once it is understood that communities assume the character of the objects of rights, it becomes quite obvious that the insistence on exact subject definition as a precondition for the recognition of rights and for legal protection is a glaring misconception based on an erroneous premise as to the juridical nature of cultural (and other) communities. Precise subject definition is required only if law is approached from the viewpoint of the doctrine of abstract universal individual rights which illegitimately reduces legal protection and justice to the individual and to individual rights. The insistence on precise subject definition as a precondition for rights protection has nothing to do with legal science (let alone legal philosophy) as Du Plessis so speciously stated. It is nothing more than an outgrowth of an ideologically-driven error based on the restricted doctrine of abstract individual rights.

It has been established that communities assume the character of the objects of rights and that the well-being of those objects depends on an infrastructure consisting of institutions and facilities that keep those objects alive and stabilise, protect, and strengthen them. In consequence, individual persons, together with other persons who belong to the same community, are enabled to enjoy the rights concerned. When it is an institution or facility for a non-hegemonic (minority) community, it will obviously set certain boundaries and define the spaces identified for the enjoyment of rights by members of the community concerned. Members of a minority community – those regarding themselves as belonging to that community or those who associate with it – will be making use of those spaces: they will utilise the benefits and enjoy the rights ensuing from the relevant institutions and facilities created for that community. Those belonging to such communities are making use of the institutions and facilities thereby formally define themselves as part of that community. The rest will obviously be self-excluded in this way. In this way the community is defined on a continuous basis. A cultural community will have certain basic and long-term characteristics of a cultural nature. The same holds true for any other kind of community. The exact boundaries of such communities can, however, never be exactly defined. It will never be possible to determine precisely which and how many individuals are belonging to it. Its boundaries will always be vague and changing. Exact demarcation – definition – will never be possible. However, since we are not dealing here with communities as subjects of rights the absence of exact definition is legally entirely irrelevant and of no consequence at all.

This perspective of the juridical reality proceeding from the objective side of law underscores the vital importance of institutions and facilities for individual rights. Hence, it also brings to light something that would otherwise have remained unnoticed if one would operate within the constraints of the doctrine of abstract individual rights, namely that individual rights could come under attack not only in consequence of a direct assault on the interests of a specific individual bearer of rights. Other persons could also come under indirect attack. This would occur when governments were pursuing homogenising nation building strategies and then either neglecting communities by failing to allow, provide or maintain institutions and facilities for them, or by actively attacking such communities by destroying their institutions and facilities or by preventing their establishment and functioning. In all these cases of indirect assault communities would be debilitated and eventually destroyed. At the same time, the very goods and resources without which individual rights are not possible would also be destroyed and individual rights violated. Indirect assaults, for example those in pursuit of nation building programmes, are ordinarily much more damaging because they violate the interest not only of one, but of a multitude of people belonging to the communities concerned.

In the final analysis, the statist-individualist fixation on individual rights to the exclusion of communities constitutes a failure to comprehend the importance of communities as a prerequisite for justice and constitutionalism. Justice – and constitutionalism – is achievable only when due recognition is also given to communities – something that the doctrine fails and in fact refuses to do. There are no so-called legally scientific, let alone legal philosophical grounds for rejecting the legal accommodation of communities. Such dismissive behaviour arises from nothing more than a constrained reductionist doctrine, namely that of the abstract atomist individual accompanied by universal individual rights, which is part of the broader doctrine of statist-individualist constitutionalism.

Apart from assuming the character of the objects of individual rights as outlined above, communities clearly can also assume the quality of subjects. This, however, takes one beyond the sphere of individual rights. Communities as subjects place one in the sphere of the macro arrangements of a constitution as described in Chapter 2. In this scenario a community constitutes the body-politic. The body-politic is the collective subject of self-determination providing for legislative, executive, administrative and other forms of power exercised by virtue of macro constitutional arrangements relating to power allocation and checks and balances. This falls largely beyond the focus of this book, namely a critique of statist-individualist constitutionalism.

*   *   *

This concludes the last of five chapters in which the belief system of the doctrine of statist-individualist constitutionalism has been critiqued. It has been shown that the beliefs upon which the doctrine of statist-individualist constitutionalism as set out in Chapter 2.4 is premised are without substance. It was also demonstrated that the three constitutional mechanisms representing the embodiment of the belief system of modern-day statist-individualist constitutions are flawed. From the five preceding chapters it should be clear that:

σ So-called supreme Constitutions are in fact not supreme. In consequence, entrenchment and conformity mechanisms accompanied by strict amendment requirements, are not capable of securing the actual supremacy of the constitution and safeguarding it from profound changes, even though such changes are not reflected in the constitutional text. The constitution changes on an on-going basis and these mechanisms are not capable of arresting these changes.

σ Judicial independence and impartiality premised on the notion of separation of powers are metaphorical rather than real. More fundamental and decisive than the separation of powers is the actual *unity of the three (separate) powers*, who, though separated in terms of institutions, personnel and functions, are ordinarily firmly unified in one single power elite: integral segments of one and the same dominant political leadership, informed by the same ideological assumptions, committed to achieving the same goals.

σ Individual rights, interpreted by the judiciary fall way short of achieving justice. As a result of judicial interpretation, which is a deeply ideological and political exercise, individual rights often prove to be very disappointing and not guaranteeing the interest they are believed to guarantee. Individual rights, moreover, fall way short of safeguarding justice. Over and above individual rights the achievement of justice also requires that communal interests – of language, culture, religion – be recognised and protected.

The belief system of statist-individualist constitutionalism and its accompanying mechanisms fall way short of securing justice and constitutionalism. This was also demonstrated with reference to South Africa's vaunted statist-individualist supreme Constitution. Following upon debunking the belief system of statist-individualist constitutionalism, the last chapter of the book – Chapter 9 – provides a brief outlook beyond statist-individualist constitutionalism.

Beyond Statist-Constitutionalism

Pointers to Politocratic Constitutionalism

9.1

Introduction

In the preceding five chapters it was shown that the belief of statist-individualist constitutionalism in the supremacy of the written Constitution was unfounded and that the mechanisms of statist-individualist constitutionalism could not sustain the claim of supremacy and durability of the Constitution. The constitution is changing continually in step with the dominant socio-political forces in society. Statist-individualist constitutionalism does not live up to the commitments of constitutionalism. It suffers from essentially two basic flaws, which are both direct consequences of its erroneous doctrinal foundations: It cannot sustain a system of justice; and cannot provide a system of distribution of power, accompanied by effective checks and balances capable of securing limited government and a balanced constitution. Both flaws emanate from the same cause, namely the failure to (sufficiently) accommodate communities.

As a result, in the first place, of its flawed belief in the abstract individual with so-called individual universal human rights, adjudicated by the courts (combined with its dismissal of communities) statist-individualist constitutionalism lacks the essentials for securing justice. These essentials have been described from two different angles set out in Chapters 7 and 8.

As a result, in the second place, of its flawed belief that the threefold separation of governmental power is capable of securing adequate power distribution and a system of mutual checks and balances, statist-individualism in fact fails, as shown in Chapters 6 and 7, to secure a plausible system of power-limitation, power distribution and checks and balances. That is the very reason why it falls short of securing a balanced constitution and effective public office-bearing for the benefit of all (the whole). Its shortcomings pave the way for a partisan constitution contrary to the commitment to justice for the whole, which lies at the very core of the idea of constitutionalism.

Power distribution and controls and the operation of checks and balances in pursuance of the doctrine of statist-individualist constitutionalism are all state-departmentalised. The courts and other seemingly independent and impartial bodies are in the final analysis essentially departments of state under the control of the dominant political elite. This obtains in particular to South Africa under its statist-individualist Constitution where all the centres of power and the apparatus for checks and balances – including the judiciary – are in the final analysis rooted in state structures dominated by the power apparatus of one and the same dominant political elite embodied in the ruling party. The various centres of power are not the shining embodiment of an effective system of balance of power and of checks and balances as statist-individualist constitutionalism would claim. To some extent it is exactly the opposite. As shown in Chapters 6 and 7 the judiciary is at best a superficial check on the rest of the dominant elite, namely a check and balance *within* the constraints of the partial ideological consensus of the elite. On fundamental issues, it cannot function as a check and balance, simply because it cannot exercise a check and balance to itself, that is, the dominant political elite of which the judiciary is an integral ingredient and within which it serves as a specialised role player.

This concluding chapter ventilates in brief the basic ingredients for an improved version of constitutionalism, more true to the essentials of constitutionalism. To that end, one has to step outside the paradigm of territorial statism and outside the statist-individual straitjacket of statist-individualist constitutionalism (and obviously also outside statist-collectivism which is part of the broader paradigm of statism outlined in Chapter 2.2.) One must and into the sphere of a different mode of thinking which is positioned in opposition to the statist paradigm. The outline is not comprehensive. It provides only some pointers in the right direction to be followed.

9.2

Autonomous, self-sustained communities; a multitude of governmental centres

In order to achieve the essentials of constitutionalism as described in Chapter 1 it is necessary to conceptualise communities alongside rights-bearing individuals and alongside, or even instead of the state. This will in particular open up an avenue to accomplish justice and a plausible system of power checks and balances. An improved constitutionalism is fundamentally (multi-)communitarian, or politocratic as it is named elsewhere.[1] The communities envisaged here are in the first place autonomously governed and self-sustaining cultural, linguistic and local communities. Secondly, and equally important, they include a broad spectrum of professional, business, educational, religious, socio-economic, cultural associations and interest groups of civil society in general, organised in their own self-supporting and autonomously governing institutions, and who rely on their own property as the patrimonial guarantee for their autonomy.

Autonomously governed self-sustained communities, who are all part of a larger pluralist (or federal) whole, are the essential addition of politocratic constitutionalism. Multi-communitarian – politoctaric – constitutionalism is not a new concept. As indicated in Chapter 2, even when statist-individualism was at its strongest there had always been critical counter trends. In fact, there is a rich tradition of non-statist, pluralist and communitarian thought in which the notion of free association/s (*Gesellschaft*) and corporation/s (Korporation) have a pivotal position. In this tradition, communities are subscribed to as the indispensable prerequisite for genuine constitutionalism. Many theorists such as Johannes Althusius, Otto von Gierke, Neville Figgis, to mention but three classical communitarian thinkers are prominent in this context.[2] Also pertinent are the views of for example Edmund Burke and Alexis de Tocqueville and many others who may be categorised broadly within the frame of "pluralist political thinking". The discussion below draws on this thinking.

9.2.1 A classical constitutional moment: Regnum and Sacerdotium

At this stage it is necessary to make some observations on a singularly important moment in the conceptualisation of constitutionalism. This was the constitutional arrangement[3] in Western Christianity often called the *papal revolution* dating back to the last decades of the eleventh century. This constitutional arrangement which is reverberating to this day ushered in the all-important jurisdictional and power distribution between the ecclesiastic and temporal spheres of power; taking place between the Western church and the empire – Regnum and Sacerdotium. So important was this constitutional arrangement that it prompted Harold Berman to state:

> The very separation of ecclesiastical and secular authority was a constitutional principle of the first magnitude, which permeated the entire system of canon law.[4]

---

1   For an explanation of the term politocracy (and politocratic constitutionalism). See Malan, 2012a:272 and Vincent, 1987:186.

2   For a concise discussion of this topic, see Vincent, 1987:181-217.

3   I fully agree with Harold Berman that a constitutional arrangement is at hand here. Not only the exercise of power within the church (in terms of canon law), but in particular also the division of power between the church and the empire, was arranged as a result of the papal revolution. The authority of both was delineated and restricted. It reflects all the characteristics of a true constitutional arrangement. As Berman, 1983:213-214 asserts: "The very separation between ecclesiastical and secular authority was a constitutional principle of the first magnitude, which permeated the entire system of the canon law."

4   See Berman, 1983:214.

The papal revolution[5] originated in the early papacy of Pope Gregory VII (Hildebrand, Pope: 1073-1085) and came to fruition with the Concordat of Worms in 1122. Prior to the revolution, emperors often appointed and dismissed popes and other high-ranking clerical officials, convened synods of the church under their (the emperor's) chairmanship and in some instances even issued canons of both a theological and a legal nature.[6] In the mid-eleventh century, successive emperors had again exerted considerable power in church affairs[7] causing the church to be dealt with as an integral part of the empire in a way that reminds of the inferior position that the Eastern Orthodox Church of Constantinople found itself in vis-à-vis the (Eastern) empire. In the years preceding the papacy of Gregory VII opposition against this mounted within the ranks of the church.[8] When Gregory eventually became pope, he forthwith issued a papal decree in pursuance of which the church *liberated* itself from the imperial authority. In terms of the decree, the pope would be elected by the senior clergy without any imperial mandate. At the same time, the selection of senior clerical officials would fall within the jurisdiction of the pope and be pertinently excluded from the emperor's jurisdiction. By appealing to what the position of the church was claimed to be at an earlier stage,[9] in contrast to the authority that it later renounced in favour of the empire, the pope endeavoured to establish the integrity of the church as a corporate structure, free from the power of temporal authorities. This led to an acrimonious struggle between the emperor (Henry IV) and Gregory, in which Gregory eventually turned out victorious. The conflict between the pope and the emperor – successors to the two initial antagonists – ended in a compromise in 1122, with the Concordat of Worms. This compromise established the *freedom of the church* and finally settled the constitutional arrangement for the *Republica Christiana*. Following this, there would be a clearly defined division of power between empire and church, although the two entities would cooperate as components of one unit, comprising empire and church.

The doctrine of the two swords had, in reality, already been in existence long before the papal revolution. However, it was now formulated anew. In this relationship, the church merely comprised the parish of (temporary) pilgrims progressing towards final, everlasting salvation. Henceforth the doctrine attained a political and, more specifically, a constitutional nature in the sense that it effected an arrangement between church and empire – pope and emperor. The church, in its capacity as

---

5   Ibid, p.99 et seq explains in detail why it was indeed a full-scale revolution.

6   Ibid, p.484.

7   In fact, in the century preceding 1059, when the church opposed lay investiture for the first time, the emperor appointed 21 of the 25 popes of that period himself and he also dismissed several. See Berman, 1983:91.

8   A church council that was called by Pope Nicolas II, decreed for the first time in 1059 that the pope had to be elected by the cardinals. See Berman, 1983:94.

9   In typical fashion, the legitimacy of this papal revolution, similar to that of subsequent revolutions like the Lutheran Revolution, was sought in the practices of the ancient past. The revolution was therefore regarded as a restoration (and correction) of a bygone order. See Berman, 1983:112-113.

a temporal corporate political and legal entity, carried the spiritual sword, which was not only concerned with the great beyond. In addition, it exerted authority over a plethora of earthly matters, such as church property, the activities of the clergy, family relationships, business morality and the like.[10] In this way the church consolidated its position. On account of the efforts of Gratian, the Camaldolese monk of the twelfth century, founder of the canon law[11] and author of the *Concordantia discordantium canonum*, which was the foundation for the church inter alia acquiring its own legal system – the *Corpus iuris canonici* (canon law). The establishment of the church's own legal system clearly signifies the autonomy of the church, divorced from the empire[12] functioning under the supervision of the pope.[13]

There are at least five matters in this settlement which are of crucial importance for constitutionalism:

1. the separation of powers and jurisdictions;
2. the checks that the two centres exerted over each other;
3. each jurisdiction had its own legal system and judicial system;
4. the custodians of each legal system had its own legal profession, namely the civil jurists in relation to the temporal law, and the canon jurists in relation to canon law; and
5. the property arrangement, more specifically regarding the fact that the church was a property owner – in time it would become one of the largest property owners in Western Europe (and the British Isles), thus providing the material guarantee for the church's independence.

It is very important to note that the basis for these five crucially important ingredients is the fact that it had a communal, more particularly a multi-communal, basis, namely the temporal and the ecclesiastical community.

For many reasons, going back to various phases in history, the church has lost perhaps most of its erstwhile constitutional role. The chasm brought about by the

---

10 Ibid, p.521.

11 Ibid, p.187.

12 Ibid, p.202-203.

13 Copleston, 1972:303. On the other side stood the empire. Although the empire, as an integral part of the totality of empire and church, was by its nature Christian, it could, in view of the church's autonomy over religious matters, concentrate on temporal matters - politics. As part of the church's claims against the emperor, Gregory VII also declared that the pope had the capacity to express judgments in respect of both ecclesiastical and temporal matters. Innocent III (Pope: 1198-1216), probably the most powerful of all popes, maintained that in their capacity as the successors to Saint Peter, popes had jurisdiction over all religious and temporal matters concerning the adjudication of allegations of sin. He regarded the temporal authority of the emperor as completely inferior to the pope's authority, since it was the pope who had transferred the imperial crown of Byzantium to the West and was responsible for the fact that the emperors could exercise their authority by the grace of the pope. Although the temporal powers exercised by Innocent III were never to be surpassed by any other pope, papal political claims reached a theoretical pinnacle during the papacy of Boniface III (Pope: 1294-1303), when the *Bull Unam Sanctum* was promulgated in 1302. In terms of this decree, all temporal (political) authority had to be exercised under the supervision of the pope.

Reformation in the sixteenth century was the first major event in this reduced role. The emergence of a large variety of organised formations of civil society is another reason. This caused the church to become only one of a variety of non-state role players The wide-ranging process of secularisation provides the most comprehensive general explanation for the diminished role of the church (more correctly of churches). Moreover, in terms of some theological doctrines, there is in fact no notable constitutional role to be played by the church holding that the church should remain completely outside of all politics.[14] Nevertheless, organised religion – churches more specifically – are not a spent force within the framework of constitutionalism. For that reason they are referred to in part 3.4 below, together with other institutions of civil society as a constitutional role player.

Medieval constitutionalism was not limited to the grand jurisdictional separation between temporal and ecclesiastical spheres of power. It was also distinctively pluralist in that it comprised a large variety of jurisdictions and power centres each exercising power over its own domain as well as keeping one another in check. This includes manorial, feudal, royal, urban jurisdictions,[15] as well as the age old commercial law – the *lex mercatoria* – that existed in the field of trade and manufacturing.[16]

In the work of Johannes Althusius, this encompassing medieval federalism-like thinking still loomed large. At the same time, Althusius laid the foundations for a comprehensive (multi-)communitarian constitutionalism. This was an anticipatory response in part to the territorial statism and to statist-individualist constitutionalism that was establishing itself at the time when Althusius was delivering his work at the beginning of the seventeenth century. Althusius' ideas place the kind of a multi-communitarian thinking which is touched on in this chapter in proper perspective. It shows that there has for very long been an alternative tradition of constitutional thinking, which presently, in an era where there are signs of increased post-statism, is regaining relevance. The discussion now turns briefly to Althusius' thinking. This is linked with observations on the politicratic thinking as set out in Chapter 10 of *Politicracy*.[17]

Thereafter, the discussion turns to power checks and balances. This is in response to the inadequate (and often failing) state-departmentalised checks and balances as described in Chapters 6, 7 and in part implicitly touched on in Chapter 8. Finally, observations are made about the importance of (private) property for sustaining constitutionalism. The discussion in this chapter is limited to a selected set of observations forming the basis for a politocratic constitutionalism.

---

14   See Malan, 2012a:54.

15   Berman, 1983 thoroughly discussed the plurality of the various jurisdictions.

16   See for example Hosten, Edwards, Nathan & Bosman, 1979:365.

17   Althusius, 1994. Althusius' views has been receiving considerable attention since the beginning of the 1980. I recently discussed his constitutionalism in two articles, namely, Malan, 2017a:1-27; and Malan, 2017b:1-35.

9.2.2 Althusius' Politica

Politocratic constitutionalism resonates with the constitutionalism articulated in *Politica*,[18] the work of Johannes Althusius in 1603. The *Politica* represents a mode of thinking – the beginning of a counter-tradition – which was sharply at variance with that which underpins the modern (territorial) statist paradigm and statist-individualist (and statist-collectivist) constitutionalism. Althusius' ideas was in opposition to those of Jean Bodin and was also in the nature of a comprehensive anticipatory response to Thomas Hobbes. Althusius' work was soon superseded by the victorious territorial state and finally by statist-individualist constitutionalism. It almost fell into complete oblivion. Yet, it remained an important source for pluralist constitutional and political thinking. In recent decades, against the backdrop of an increasing trend of post-statist thinking and practice in which communities – cultural, local, religious and linguistic – are forcefully (re)-claiming constitutional recognition and in which alternatives for statist-individualist constitutionalism are sought, Althusius' thinking has regained considerable renewed attention. It is also an important background to the politocratic response to statist-individualist constitutionalism.

For Althusius, resonating Aristotle, commonwealths are a natural and fundamental given. Man is by nature gregarious, born for cultivating society with fellow human beings. People are not inherently separated from one another and therefore incapable of acting to the mutual benefit of one another.[19] On the contrary, people by their very nature eagerly strive for association. Echoing Aristotle, Althusius states that those who do not wish to live in society or are not in need of anything because all their needs are satisfied in abundance, are not part of the commonwealth. Any person meeting this description is either a beast or a god.[20]

Althusius is viewed as the founder of the federal idea in modern political thinking.[21] His federalism consists of a set of associations, beginning with the smallest association, starting with the family, then collegia (guilds), cities and provinces, with the ecclesiastical associations also forming a distinctive part of the larger encompassing constitutional order, and ending with the encompassing empire. This order (echoed in *Politocracy*) is built up from below, that is, from the smallest to the most encompassing entity, not the other way around. The smaller can still exist without the larger ones, but the more encompassing structures are not viable without the smaller ones.

---

18 Althusius, 1994 with an introduction by Carney; Elazar, 1994.

19 Althusius, 1994:2-23. Goosen, 2015 developed a wide ranging apology for communitarian politics in which he rejects the absence of community as essentially an anomaly. See specifically section A of the book under the heading *"Monsters en mense"*.

20 Althusius, 1994:25. Also see Goosen, 2015:section A, who expands on this question in considerable detail.

21 Elazar, 1994:xxxvii.

His system therefore entailed a holistic bottom-up federal constitutionalism that provides for the pluralisation of government among the members of a commonwealth in which all higher levels of authority are as a matter of principle constituted on the basis of consent from below. He proposes a multitiered constitutional system – a community (the commonwealth) of multiple communities. The particular communities are to be sustained by consent among their constituent members, and the universal community – the commonwealth – is built and sustained from below, namely by the smaller communities. All communities are to be interconnected by universal principles of association, representation, and sovereignty. His system provides for shared or co-sovereignty which is to be divided up from the smallest fellowship to the universal Christian commonwealth (in sharp contrast to the notion of unilateral and undivided state sovereignty of the unitary territorial state). Accordingly, there should be balanced power-sharing among different constituent communities. The particular interests are clearly autonomous but not sovereign on their own and somehow completely separated from other particular interests. They are bound together in the universality of the common enterprise, encapsulated in the encompassing commonwealth. Following the subsidiarity principle (echoed in *Politocracy*), all particular powers should be allocated at the lowest possible level of responsibility. At the same time, these powers are still limited according to universal standards of solidarity.

The notion of communities forms the very core of Althusius' constitutional thinking. It is the cure in anticipation for the two flaws of statist-individualist constitutionalism, namely for its failure to secure justice and its failure to provide a system of distribution of power, accompanied by effective checks and balances, capable of guaranteeing limited government and a balanced constitution.

Clearly, Althusius' constitutionalism cannot simply be transplanted into our modern-day thinking on constitutionalism. One obvious reason would be that we cannot envision the idea of empire in our day and age as Althusius could in the last phases of the encompassing Christian republic – the *Republica Christiana*. The most important reason, however, is that Althusius' delivered his work before the advent of the individual and of individual rights which only came to full fruition in the twentieth century. The requirement of individual rights would now be essential. Modern constitutionalism cannot be sustained without it. However, for its multi-communal basis and for its opposition to territorial statism, it remains an important point of departure for politocratic constitutionalism.

9.2.3 Politocracy

Politocracy defines a comprehensive politico-constitutional order: multispherical government by the citizens of every political community over the specific *res publica* – the commonwealth – of the relevant community.[22]

In politocractic constitutionalism there is no single centralised sovereign *locus* of government, established in terms of the demands of the territorial state and for the sake of its intact maintenance and veneration. The territorial state does not form the dominating structure of government power. Government authority is spread out and there is a variety of public identities all enjoying legal recognition. There is a dispensation of maximal joint government. Provision is made for government authority, ranging from small, restricted communities to the most comprehensive one, that is, government power for and by the most *habitative* (see below) and local communities, stretching to larger and more comprehensive government for a more encompassing community. In a politocratic constitution, public political identity is of a plural nature. Public political allegiance, which under statist-individualist constitutionalism at present is only owed to the state, is divided and relativised. It is primarily due to the more habitative of communities, and only thereafter to the more comprehensive political communities. Democracy is radicalised. Governing in respect of habitative issues takes place on a habitative government level. It is not dictated from elsewhere. Matters of a more comprehensive nature are governed at a more comprehensive level.

On close analysis, three species of habitative communities may be distinguished. In the first place, a community may simultaneously be local and cultural, that is, a homogeneous cultural community, which is concentrated in the same location. That would be a *local cultural community*. This is the community with the most encompassing commonwealth with the most comprehensive mutual ties among its citizens (the richest *res publicae*).

Secondly, a habitative community may be a *local community* in which a culturally heterogeneous community, sharing the same territory, is closely connected by means of other (local) ties, despite their cultural heterogeneity.

Thirdly, a habitative community may be a culturally homogeneous community, differing from the first type in that it is not concentrated in one place, but where its members share close cultural ties in spite of the fact that they are not congregated in one location. That would be a *translocal cultural community*.

Irrespective of the nature of the habitative community, politocracy aims to award maximal self-government to all of these communities. Each of these habitative communities controls its own type of *res publicae* – public affairs common to the citizenry of the community concerned – which is jointly shared by all the citizens of such community.

---

22 Discussed in detail Malan, 2012a:Chapter 10.

We do not, however, only belong to habitative communities, but are also members of many other, and more comprehensive, communities – geographical, demographical and cultural. These kinds of communities are bound by ties of communal public interests and issues, differing from the ties that connect habitative communities. In conformity with their specific nature, the more encompassing communities have their own *res publicae*.

Our public identity should be determined by the fact that we are simultaneously members of all of these communities and, depending on the kind of issue involved, government authority – the power to take binding decisions and execute them – should be vested at all of these levels. There are matters that may be denoted as typically habitative, regional, subcontinental and even more comprehensive issues. In other words, there are various typically habitative, regional, subcontinental, or more comprehensive *res publicae*. However, there are also many matters of simultaneous importance in more than one of these domains. It will often have to be determined at which level of government the relevant issue has to be addressed. Joint government at various levels will in many cases be indispensable. The crux of the matter is that there is no single sovereign government. There is plainly no single sovereign statist government that the statist paradigm (in its most unaccommodating form) could claim for itself.

Politocracy rejects the atomised hypothesis, namely that there are only atomised individuals (without any real communal ties) and the state. From a politocratic vantage point this is a fundamentally erroneous view of the human condition and way of life. All individual existence, identity, values and achievements and most rights are firmly anchored in communities. In the absence of communities, no individual existence would be possible. Therefore, politocracy is constructed on a (multi-)communitarian basis.

At the very core of politocracy lies the authentic constitutional tenet of power distribution and mutual checks and balances, fending off the risk of power centralisation and safeguarding justice. This is so because politocracy as was noted, is a system of multispherical government by the citizens of every political community over the specific *res publicae* of the relevant community.

9.3

Checks and balances

The (multi-)communitarian federalism (as for example outlined in *Politica* and in *Politocracy*), goes a long way towards promoting the aim of justice. Since politocracy is based on government authority distributed to a variety of communal governments, limited government and mutual checks and balances necessarily occupy a crucial place in politocratic constitutionalism. The remainder of the discussion of this chapter expands on the question of power limitation and (mutual) checks and balances.

Statist-individualist constitutionalism also subscribes to power checks and balances. The big flaw of the checks and balances of statist-individualist constitutionalism as shown in Chapters 6 and 7 is that they are compromised by their state-departmentalisation, thus lacking the autonomy to perform their checking and balancing function. As the South African experience over recent decades shows, the power centres for checks and balances, including the judiciary, are rooted in state structures dominated by the power apparatus of one and the same dominant political elite embodied in the ruling party. It is important that vigorous centres of power, which provide the infrastructure for checks and balances, vest not only within, but also outside the organogram of state structure.

Important among these structures are the family, the autonomous professions and trade and industry sectors, educational institutions, religious institutions, organised civil society, and the media.

9.3.1 The family

The family has always played a crucial part in all traditional social orders. It often occupied an important part in socio-political and constitutional philosophising about the most suitable (and natural) political order. This was the case in classical philosophy, for example in the thinking of Aristotle, and scores of political thinkers since that time. The family occupied this important position until the rise of the abstract individual and the concomitant emergence of statist-individualist constitutionalism.

The thinking of Althusius is of specific importance in this context. Unlike Thomas Hobbes (the harbinger of the abstract individual – and of modern statist-individualist constitutionalism), Althusius posited the importance of the family. Hobbes's system made no provision for any entity other than the abstract atomist individual (and the state). The family which played an important part in Althusiun constitutionalism is very important in the (multi-)communitarian, politocratic alternative to statist-individualist constitutionalism. The family was the first entity – the first community – in Althusius' grand federalism.

To Althusius, the family is a natural association based on necessity and affection.[23] This family should not be confused, with the modern nuclear family (*Afrikaans: gesin*). It is a broader association of kinship that includes more distant relatives and could also include allies and friends, sharing close bonds. But why, one may tend to ask, are families politically significant; why are they an essential ingredient of the constitutional order; and why are they so crucial for constitutionalism? How can it be explained that they form part of the constitutional order, yet do not have a public nature?

---

23   Althusius, 1994:28.

Althusius noticed the first signs of the statist totalitarian peril in terms of which private life, commerce and civil society would be dealt with as mere subordinate segments of and therefore susceptible to subjugation to state-centralised political control. That peril would fully materialise if the families and civil society would dissolve into an aggregate of atomised and vulnerable individuals, all dependent on the centralised and homogenising state, devoid of the protection that affectionate families once provided and are arguably more capable of providing than the state itself. To Althusius families and guilds (*collegia*), that is, commercial and professional associations, even though emphatically private (non-statist), were the seedbeds of the public association and were therefore politically and constitutionally of significance.[24]

In Althusius' system families, and not individuals, are the natural seedbed (certainly not an arbitrary social construct) for the larger public associations.[25] Each family provides psychological, social and economic safeguards to its members. They provided the semi-autonomous (mutual) symbiosis for their members within the family structure. Families are wholes in which basic roles, places and responsibilities are assumed by each of its members – fathers, mothers, children, etc. Each member of the family benefits from the physiological and economic protection generated by the collective contribution of all, each according to her/his assigned role. In this way, individuals are spared the vulnerable existence of being in a condition of dependence on a distant and impersonal Leviathan, who has come to materialise in the modern territorial state in which individuals have rights only vis-à-vis the state, which, depending on its strength and willingness, might or might not be successfully enforced against the state.

The family providing this protection enables its members to participate as self-reliant active citizens in the public affairs of the body-politic instead of vulnerable, dependent, individual clients in need of the state's care in terms of rights, more particularly socio-economic rights which the centralised state is trusted to provide.[26]

State-sponsored *human rights* have increasingly engendered individual dependence on the state. The rights are primarily enforceable against the state. The addition of every new right adds another new pair of undesired consequences: A stronger state

---

24 Althusius, 1994:32 stated: Furthermore, some persons wrongly assert that every symbiotic association is public, and none private. Now this axiom stands firm and fixed: all symbiotic association and life is essentially, authentically, and generically political. But not every symbiotic association is public. There are certain associations that are private, such is conjugal and kinship families, and collegia. And these are the seedbeds of the public association. Whence it follows that the private association is rightly attributed to politics.

25 Althusius, 1994:31.

26 It is one of the main themes of De Tocqueville, 2008:13-14, 24-27, etc., who elaborates at length on the real risk that a society consisting only of individuals without strong intermediary communities and institutions may be particularly prone to absolutism.

that has to comply with the needs of dependent individual consumers; and more severely dependent individuals looking up to the state to safeguard a livelihood. Hence, every new right, especially every new socio-economic right adds yet another dimension to individual dependency on the state government.[27] In consequence individuals increasingly forfeit their capacity as true citizens[28] and instead assume the dual negative identity of subjects and consumers caught up in a relationship of dependency and subordination to government. As needy subjects and consumers they find themselves in a dependent commercial relationships in which the identity of buyer, tenant, borrower, or whatever other commercial identity, but never the identity of (active) citizenship assumes increased prominence.

It is not possible to resurrect the family to its pre-modern form, as conceived by someone like Althusius. Moreover, it is not feasible in our time to conceive of the family (or any other social structure) in a way that suppresses individual expression. However, the thinking of Althusius clearly reveals the importance of the family:

σ   as a bulwark – to perform a check and balance – against the power structures of the centralised state;

σ   as the primary natural structure entailing a variety of complementary roles fulfilled by the various family members towards social and psychological security for members and the foundation of education for children;

σ   as the basis for economic autonomy; and

σ   a benefit of real, active citizenship instead of subordinate dependency in the form of rights-clientilism.

Even though the family is not entirely revivable in its erstwhile form, the cultivation of autonomous family bonds providing for interdependent roles of family members, are clearly, not only significant from a private (law) point of view, but also as a constitutional rampart. Strong families are a constitutional matter of the first order.

9.3.2 Commerce, industry and the professions

In the next sub-sections follows a brief discussion of the checks and balance function of an important selection of institutions. They all have the following common denominators.

1.   All are corporate bodies, enjoying a life of their own, distinct from those of their members and therefore (potentially) transcending the duration of the life of their members. Their corporate nature enables them to accumulate patrimonial and human capital which would outlast the life span of their members.

---

27   Malan, 2012a:233-236.

28   Citizenship signifies the ability to participate independently with all other citizens in the joint endeavour of governing the polity. This view of citizenship is derived from Aristotle's view on citizenship and citizenly virtue. In Aristotle, 1962:Book III, Chapter 13:131 he explains that a citizen "... has a share both in ruling and in being ruled." In Book III, Chapter 12:103 he clearly states that a citizen is someone who is entitled to participate in the exercise of both consultative and judicial authority. See further Aristotle, 1962:Book III, Chapter 5 and p.112.

2. It allows the corporate bodies to provide members the protection of the corporate veil, that is, it affords these bodies, through their representatives, the power to act on behalf of the corporate bodies concerned without compromising the interests of individual members.

3. The corporate bodies are autonomous. They are self-governing and self-regulating. They control access to the trade, industry or profession concerned; they determine and prescribe/require training, impose standards, prescribe/require licensing, provide for disciplinary measures and take all other necessary steps relating to the trade, industry or the profession concerned.

4. Lastly, corporate bodies are entitled to acquire and hold any right including the right, of ownership of any property. They often are, as they are entitled to be, large property owners. Their own property is in the final analysis the strategic guarantee for their autonomy.

Professional, vocational, trade and industrial corporate-organised bodies also ought to be exclusive. Access to these formations is controlled and qualified. Membership depends on compliance with the distinctive professional, vocational, academic, manufacturing, commercial and other criteria of each formation. Access to and participation in these elitist formations are not based on equality; on the contrary, they are based on compliance with certain minimum thresholds - requirements pertaining to qualifications, experience and performance. They are based on inequality, not equality. These are the requirements to be met in order for these elitist institutions to be formed, to function and in the final analysis, also to perform their constitutional checks and balance responsibilities.

Self-governing and internally self-regulating vocations, including the widest range of professional, arts and business formations are crucially important constitutional mechanisms and prerequisites for constitutionalism.[29]

The arguments advanced in this section apply to both commerce and industry as well as the professions. Among the professions are also other vocations such as artisans. The focus of the first part of this section is commerce and industry. Thereafter the spotlight shifts to the professions. Specific reference will be made to the legal profession.

Trade and industry

The idea of a national (state) currency, and macro-economic figures such as the gross domestic and national product, growth rates, national interest rates, sovereign debt, rate of un/employment and other figures create the impression that the economy is somehow a statist affair. That, however, is a misconception.

29　This was also an important element in *Althusian constitutionalism*. See Althusius' discussion on the guilds (collegia) in Althusius, 1994:33-38. Althusius' discussion was by far not purely theoretical. Guilds were an important part of the late Medieval constitutionalism.

This misconception came about as a result of the operation of the statist paradigm which requires economic activities to be viewed through the prism of the state.

The statist paradigm in which economic activities are conditioned, like the statist paradigm within which constitutionalism has been reduced to statist-individualist constitutionalism, only came about with the establishment of the territorial state. The economy – economic enterprise, including industry, trade and services – is not statist. It is a general human activity, playing out over a spectrum ranging from local and community-based, on one extreme, to semi-global or global-based, on the other. It is certainly not statist in the first place.

On a fundamental level, economic activities have nothing to do with the state. Trade and industry for example may be and were for long periods of time conducted in accordance with the internally agreed norms of the economic sector in question. Trade and industry regulated their relations and resolved disputes among business enterprises and among clients and customers on the basis of their own mutually agreed practices and customs.

This was the basis for the *lex mercatoria* (law merchant), which was an autonomous commercial legal system, specifically in Western and central Europe and the British Isles. Its origins in all probability went back millennia whence it had developed until the rise of the territorial state in the seventeenth century[30] and met its final demise only with the advent of the first comprehensive legal codifications in Europe's territorial states at the beginning of the nineteenth century.[31]

Even though the *lex mercatoria* might not have been as independent from the political authorities as is often believed,[32] it was at least partially autonomous, thus falling outside the ambit of any specific political jurisdiction. It was not formulated and promulgated by any specific political ruler and its operation was not linked to any political jurisdiction – king, lord or parliament. Hence, it could and did largely exist independent of the fate and vagaries – the rise, change or demise – of political jurisdictions.[33] Disputes were mediated and adjudicated and sanctions, including excommunications were internally imposed and executed in terms of internally agreed voluntarily norms. The procedural rules of the *lex mercatoria* were simple and disputes adjudicated quickly. The *lex mercatoria* remained a distinctive legal system with a supranational character distinguishable from the various territorial legal systems. It existed throughout the whole of Europe with only limited local variations.[34]

---

30   Hosten, Edwards, Nathan & Bosman, 1979:545.

31   For a comprehensive discussion on the ancient and modern *lex mercatoria* see Booysen, 1995.

32   Michaels, 2007:453-454.

33   Hosten, Edwards, Nathan & Bosman, 1979:542.

34   Ibid, p.544.

In the era of intensified cross-border contractual relations thanks to improved technology, private power generation, the Internet and the vast drop in the costs of long-distance transport, it has now become much easier for trade and industry to be conducted in the absence of and without the help of state authorities.

This provides the basis for business sectors to organise themselves as potent autonomous forces and to conduct checks and balances on organs of state, thereby playing an important constitutional role. The bottom line is that the role of private business is not limited to commerce and manufacturing. On the contrary, when organised business seriously engages in acting as an autonomous force by counterbalancing state governments, it in fact fulfils an important constitutional responsibility.

Professions

Like trade and industry, there are also no inherent affiliation between the professions and other vocations on the one hand, and the state, on the other. The professions in fact constitute autonomous fields of activity, clearly distinguishable from the state. Moreover, they are also trans-state, operating across state boundaries. They function in terms of standards of training, apprenticeship and professional practices and are regulated by the norms of best professional practice relevant to the particular profession in question and fundamentally regardless of the statist boundaries that might be existing between the members of the particular profession. The commonalities that bind professionals together might be in existence notwithstanding the statist identity assigned to them in terms of their passports and identity documents.

Members of each profession have better knowledge and insight than anybody else, including organs of state, on what the best standards and practices of the profession in question are; what the training and educational requirements for the particular professional sector would be; and what the best standards for suitable professional conduct within that profession should be. They are also best positioned to enforce such norms and practices. Precisely for that reason members of a profession should be acting in accordance with standards set by them and governed by freely-formed autonomous bodies comprising voluntary members of the profession concerned.

The legal profession which should be playing an important role in carrying out the checks and balances responsibility was in Western Europe for centuries bound together by the common Roman law tradition and a common mode of learnedness and practices regardless of where the lawyer in question was practicing. The basis for this was a common Western-European legal learnedness premised on the Roman civil code (the *Corpus Iuris Civilis*) which was the basis of the legal curriculum in basically all Western and central European universities. The various lawyers might have had political loyalties towards the communities where they hailed from or where they lived. Professionally, however, they were members of a common profession, characterised by overarching norms of professional excellence regardless of where they might have been based.

In England the legal profession played an even stronger independent role. The legal profession was the product, guardian and servant of the common law. The common law was not the product of acts of the political sovereign – prince or parliament – but the common law of the citizenry. It did not derive from the political sovereign. On the contrary, at its zenith it was the most potent constitutional check on the aspiring sovereign.[35]

Among the various professions the autonomy of the legal profession stands out as particularly important from the point of view of constitutionalism. The legal profession stands at the very centre of politics because important parts of the law, more specifically public law, provide the means in and through which governments package and enforce their political will. It is precisely for that reason that the checks and balances function of the legal profession is particularly important. The legal profession should not be a mere state departmentalised adjunct to government – an obsequious servant of the state or dominant political elite. On the contrary, the organised legal profession should assume the nature of an autonomous *estate* – a social force,[36] that is, an autonomous self-regulating profession with authority over its own training, licensing and discipline. Its independence should also imply an orientation of independence towards the state government and towards business. Moreover, it implies at least a minimum measure of independence towards clients.[37] The client's interests should not be pursued at all costs, especially if such pursuit would constitute a failure of justice. That is so because the primary responsibility of jurists and the very point of constitutionalism should remain loyalty towards and the pursuit of justice.[38] That is where the constitutional responsibility of jurists and of the organised legal profession lies.

The independence of the legal profession has been avowed in various international instruments, for example the *Basic principle on the role of lawyers* adopted by the *Eighth United Nations Congress on the prevention of crime and the treatment of offenders* held from 27 August-7 September 1990 in Havana, Cuba. Article 24 provides:

> Lawyers shall be entitled to form and join self-governing professional associations to represent their interests, promote their continuing education and training and protect their professional integrity. The executive body of the professional associations shall be elected by its members and shall exercise its functions without external interference.[39]

---

35 This was graphically demonstrated in 1608 in the Bonham's case when Edward Coke on the basis of the common law and having applied "artificial" reasoning, ruled the executive action King James I "unconstitutional and invalid". See for example Malan, 2012a:229-231.

36 Terminology borrowed from Gordon, 1988:9.

37 The discussion of Gordon, 1988:1-83 is in large part dedicated to this issue.

38 See the reference made to Roman lawyer, Celsius made in Chapter 1.

39 United Nations Human Rights: Office of the High Commissioner *Basic Principles on the Role of Lawyers* http://bit.ly/2yT39K1 [Accesses 30 November 2017].

Also in 1990 the International Bar Association (IBA) resolved that: "The independence of the legal profession constitutes an essential guarantee for the promotion and protection of human rights and is necessary for effective and adequate access to legal services: An equitable system of administration."[40]

Various judgments of the courts, both in South Africa and abroad, subscribe to the principle and several academics and practitioners also strongly endorse it.[41]

Authoritarian-leaning governments are aware of the potential potency of an autonomous and independent-minded legal profession as a check and balance on government. For that reason they might have a strong urge and tendency to annex – state-departmentalise – the legal profession as a bulwark for legitimising and enforcing political and ideological programmes. This is in fact a very old phenomenon,[42] which in present juristocratic societies have gained even more traction.

At the same time, it is as important for the legal profession to understand and fulfil its crucially important responsibility to act as a check and balance against a centralising government and ideologies of homogenisation, and in doing so, to defend and promote constitutionalism.

The legal profession in South Africa have always successfully been regulated by autonomous bodies for attorneys and advocates. Lately this has changed, fundamentally when the Legal Practice Act[43] was adopted. The Act is part of the mechanics to promote the ideology of transformationism, referred to in Chapters 5, 6 and 7. It provides the legislative framework for the transformation of the legal profession in South Africa. It pays lip service to enhance the independency of the legal profession. However, through the regulating Legal Practice Council and Provincial Councils, it goes a long way to basically state-departmentalise the profession by placing it under the control of government and the ruling party. Certain provisions of the Act, Patrick Ellis and Albert Lamey stated, appear to encroach upon the principle of the independence of the legal profession.[44] What has been said here about the legal profession also applies in principle to all other professions.

Autonomy, however, does not mean sovereignty. Hence, autonomous bodies do not mean sovereign independent bodies, sovereign professions or sovereign business sectors. Hence, these bodies, and in consequence the professions and business sectors,

---

40   file:///C:/Users/u04186516/Downloads/IBA_Resolutions_Standards_for_the_Independence_of_Legal_
      Prof_1990.pdf [Accessed, 30 November 2018].

41   See Ellis & Lamey, 2017:1.3-1.9.

42   Rulers of emerging absolutist monarchies were for example strongly inclined to appoint jurists with
      university-based legal training and influenced by the absolutist conceptions constructed from the codification
      of Justinian, who furthered the absolutist claims of such rulers. (Ritter, 1964:21-22).

43   Legal Practice Act 28 of 2014.

44   Ellis & Lamey, 2017:1-5.

must be subject to external correction when things go wrong in the professions or business sectors concerned. Autonomous governance and self-regulation therefore do not exclude a carefully defined role for suitable political organs to exercise checks on behalf of the broader public. Such checks should come into play, only in pursuance of the subsidiarity principle, which will apply, when the autonomous governing institutions prove to be malfunctioning.[45] Moreover, checks over the professions and business formations, aside from the autonomous self-governing function of the bodies for the profession or business sector concerned, need not in the first place necessarily be exercised by organs of state. They can most probably better be exercised by suitable formations of civil society, including consumer organisations, the governing bodies of other professions and business sectors, trade unions, the media and other formations of civil society.

The bottom-line is that self-governing and internally self-regulating professions are essential ramparts in support of constitutionalism. The state-departmentalisation, including strict state-regulation of business and the professions is a serious infraction of constitutionalism. State-departmentalisation and strict state regulation caused overt state-centralisation and control. It flies in the face of the idea of limited government, which is inherent in constitutionalism. It strips the professions and business of their self-government and self-regulating competency, as a result of which they forfeit their constitutional function to act as a check and balance on the state government to the detriment of the very idea and practice of constitutionalism.

9.3.3 Educational institutions, universities in particular

Universities are institutions of higher, specifically theoretical learning, research and reflection. Together with other educational institutions they provide the basis for professional life. Their theoretical and reflective orientation dictates that they should maintain a balanced distance from other bodies, institutions, interest groups and society in general. This, however, does not mean that universities should become self-serving institutions isolated from society and from other bodies, institutions and interest groups mentioned above. On the contrary, their distance is precisely what should allow universities to guard and promote their integrity as universities. Hence, they should not be an extension of the state, political authorities, professions, communities, doctrines and ideologies. They should also not be a mere microcosm of society or of any particular community. More specifically, universities should not be mere adjuncts or obedient servants of any institution, political party, trade union, pressure group, etc. They should in particular not be state-departmentalised. The role of the head of a university should never be equated with that of the head of a state department and academic staff should not be perceived and they should not be acting as robed public servants or as champions for government or political party policies or ideologies. Neither should universities be rootless globalised

---

45   The notion of correction and subsidiarity. See Malan, 2012a:282-286.

institutions, totally divorced from and with no role to play in their communities and with nomadic academic staff with a similar non-committal globalised orientation. In the final analysis, universities should remain faithful and dedicated to their task of not only generating and disseminating knowledge at the highest possible level but also of fostering a culture commensurate with the highest principles within the vital sphere of civilisation where they are destined to function. To this end, universities should simultaneously be involved in as well as remain distanced from society and from government. An important element of what is referred to as a critical orientation or critical thinking has much to do with this distanced orientation. They should therefore maintain a distant involvement or orientation.

This distanced orientation allows universities to be true to their telos as institutions of higher learning, yet at the same time positioned to fulfil their constitutional responsibility as a check and balance on forces and formations such as homogeneous totalitarian ideologies, authoritarian-leaning, centralising governments and ruling parties. Devoid of that and being in a too cosy relationship with government, the state and the ruling party, or any authoritarian-leaning formation, may cause universities to lose their independence and in consequence to also forfeit their constitutional position and their check and balance function.

Universities are a very distinctive product of Western Christian civilisation.[46] It is important to bear in mind that contemporary universities have their roots in their medieval predecessors. The roots and subject matter of the learnedness endeavour are founded on Biblical scriptures, Greek science and philosophy and Roman law and administration and eventually also in modern science and scholarship.[47] The mere fact that the learning of the universities had this threefold-base: Christian theology, Greek-based science and philosophy, and Roman-based law and statecraft, instead of only a single basis, cultivated a constitutional mode of thinking and practice in Western universities. The fact that it was not solely religious-based – that philosophic and juristic learning was conducted alongside Christian theology – meant that counterbalances were built into university curricula and also that politics could not be reduced to an exclusive theocracy. On the other hand, philosophical and legal learnedness were conditioned by Christian theology. That resulted in the culture of university learnedness being broadly Christian, yet distinctively *not* theocratic (theogarchic). This obtains to Western civilization and Western politics in general.[48] Although founded on broad Christian convictions, yet not theocratic, it was not entirely secular either. The various foundational forms and branches of learnedness: religion, philosophy, science and law, create a system of coherent multi-knowledge constitutionalism, essentially Christian-based, yet not theocratic.

---

46   The rudiments of a university culture were present in the Arabic world but never really got off the ground.

47   Their curriculum was not limited to theology, law and philosophy. They also engaged in a variety of other subjects such as medicine, astronomy, physics, etc. Some of these universities emphasized only one faculty and not others. Paris was for example known for its theological studies in contrast to Bologna, known for its focus on law.

48   See for example the discussion on the *Republica Christiana* in Chapter 2 of Malan, 2012a.

Religious institutions played an important part in the formation of universities having stemmed from monastic and more importantly cathedral schools. That applies specifically to those universities where theology was the main thrust of academic activity. However, even at these universities theological studies were not mere extensions of the formal church organisation. The distanced orientation - the autonomous studiousness – of the university became a salient feature of the universities. Although both the church and political authorities as well as society in general benefitted from university learning and from graduandi delivered by the universities; and although the universities were an integral part of the whole of society, they at the same time also functioned at a distance and to some degree in a relationship of tension with both the church and the temporal authorities. The universities were almost an autonomous centre of political authority. Consequently Previté-Orton stated:

> It is hard to overrate the influence of the Universities on the life of the central Middle Ages, which gave rise to the dictum that there were three powers to guide the world, the Sacerdotium, the Regnum and the Studium.[49]

Modern constitutional practice does not specifically focus on the macro-constitutional function of universities as centres of authority and accordingly also not on the check and balance responsibility of universities. Instead the focus is rather on the individual rights of the scholar, researcher or scientist. This is all very well but inadequate. The academic institutions themselves should also enjoy (macro)-constitutional recognition by allowing them to discharge their constitutional responsibility. They should be autonomous and self-regulating. They should enjoy autonomy in determining their curricula, appointments, research themes and standards. They should also have the freedom to differ from each other. Universities should not be standardised and uniform. Their differences are crucial in allowing them to express alternative and conflicting opinions and thereby fulfilling their constitutional responsibility more comprehensively. This does not mean that each university should be entirely independent. They should be universities in interaction with other universities and other educational institutions, and with the professions, political authorities and organised civil society.

Finally, universities will be able to act autonomously only when they have a varied material basis. They should not be financially dependent on the state. They should preferably by financed by a variety of sources, thus allowing them to be autonomous and different from each other, which are prerequisites for fulfilment of their constitutional responsibility.

The need for educational integrity and autonomy dictates that universities should not be the product of state enterprise. If state-departmentalisation occurs universities are unable to discharge their constitutional responsibility. Universities should be

---

49   Previté-Orton, 1952:626.

the product of educational, professional, commercial and societal enterprise, with the state possibly also a role player among many others.

The autonomous university capable of executing its constitutional responsibility in the way as concisely explained above, should serve as example for all other educational institutions.

At the time of finalising this manuscript the constitutional position of South African universities is precarious. In accordance with the transformationist ideology referred to in Chapters 5 and 7, universities like other levers of power and authority are in the process of increasingly being subjected to state and party rule. Universities are required to subscribe and give effect to this ideology and to adjust their curricula accordingly. This totalitarian approach displays blatant disregard for the constitutional role of universities. What is even more appalling is that university leadership – councils, senates, vice chancellors and other university leaders seem to be oblivious of the constitutional role of universities. University leadership should protect the integrity and essential roles of universities, instead of acquiescing universities' descend into mere extensions of the government and the ruling party in their imposition of the ideology of transformationism.

9.3.4 Formations of civil society

Modern-day socio-political reality has seen the rise of organised civil society – a vast array of multifarious formations and institutions – some essentially permanent, some ad hoc, some multi-issue and other single-issue, some more private, others rather social, others civil, political religious, cultural or economic and many more. From a constitutional point of view, this is a significant development. Formations of civil society together with all the other institutions thus far referred to, are positioned to fulfil important constitutional responsibilities, each – either big, small, strong, or weak – constituting a centre of power, authority and influence for the benefit of their membership and whoever might be benefitting from their activities. At the same time, they act as a check and balance on all other centres of power, specifically on government.

Associations – corporations in the terminology of Otto von Gierke – of civil society can do what individuals are incapable of doing. They provide the protective shelter for their members and their following. Many individuals do not have the ability to articulate and advocate the causes that they identify with. They are perhaps not knowledgeable enough or they lack the communicative skills to get actively involved. Even more important is the fact that most individuals on their own are socially and economically simply too vulnerable to speak out. They are cowed into silence by the precarious position of being single individuals. Self-sufficient organisations of civil society drawing on monetary contributions from their members overcome all these stumbling blocks. They give individuals the power and the voice which they would otherwise not have had. Whilst individuals on their own are ordinarily not capable of playing any constitutional role – of acting as a check and balance on other formations and on government – organisations of civil society make that possible.[50]

To a considerable extent the church, referred to in part 9.2.1 above, serves as the paradigmatic example for the constitutional role of organisations of civil society. For that reason religious institutions such as churches are also included among civil society formations which are now under discussion here. Given the paramount constitutional role of the church in a previous era, it might be argued, not without merit, that (the) church(es) should also in present-day conditions qualify for discussion under a separate heading.

It is important to emphasise that civil society as such is an essentially meaningless abstraction. Civil society defined as merely all people outside the state structure is of no constitutional significance. An arbitrary conglomerate of just any number of people has at most very fleeting and feeble commonalities, if any at all.

For that reason the reference here is to *formations* or *organised spheres* of civil society (associations or *Genossenschaften* in Von Gierke's German formulation) not simply to *civil society* in general. These organised spheres or formations are constitutionally significant. People with common identities and/or interests may organise themselves in a formation in order to articulate, defend or advocate whatever issues they may have in common. These common issues by which they are bound are the very cause for their formation. However, as from the moment of creation of the formation the members of the formation are apart from all other people. Every specific formation of civil society and all formations of civil society together, are marked by their distinctive features, namely the issues which have caused them to join together in their respective formations. These issues distinguish them from all other people. They are not distinguished because they are representatives of society in general; they are distinguished because of their personal distinctive (peculiar, unique) features.

The very idea of civil society is therefore entirely dependent on formations of the widest variety of specific interest groups and communities. Any insistence that a formation of civil society would be representative and representing the entire (all of) society, would mean that the creation of any formation within a society would prohibit the creation of any further formations in that society. Such prohibition would also be an assault on civil society as such and therefore also on the very notion of constitutionalism. This is the constitutionally detrimental effect of the transformationist ideology (including representivity) referred to in Chapters 5 and 7.

---

50   The formation of American constitutionalism clearly owes much to this kind of vibrant organisation-based civil society. See the description by De Tocqueville, 1988:215 et seq on the vibrancy of civil society in the various states of the United States of America in the 1830s, as well as the phenomenon of strong local town democracy which particularly impressed him and on which he repeatedly commented of the exceptional.

94

Property

Where does private property fit into all of this? The answer is that private property serves as the guarantee for the autonomy of individuals, as well as for all organised spheres of civil society. A(n) (individual) man of straw without property, who is dependent on someone else to keep him alive does not have the freedom of his own views, or, at least the freedom to openly express those views.[51] The Afrikaans/Dutch expression says it all: "*Wiens brood men eet, diens woord men spreek.*" You cannot bite the hand of those who feed you. In the final analysis your views can hardly differ from those of the person who feeds you.

Without their own material means organised spheres of civil society, such as those that have been referred to in this chapter cannot act autonomously. They are incapable of autonomous government and self-regulation, and unable to discharge their constitutional responsibility to act as a check and balance against a rights-infringing and power hungry government. Without their own property, state-dependent individuals also lack the necessary freedom-mindedness to join and strengthen organised spheres of civil society.

This is something movements, parties and governments steeped in an unflinching belief in centralisation and homogeneity are keenly aware of. That is why they are opposed to private ownership and inclined to socialist proclivity. They know that autonomous institutions such as the ones discussed above are the only genuine checks and balances on government and the paramount guarantee for constitutionalism. These parties and governments are generally not content only with their governmental authority; they want more. They want to be the main or sole property owner.

Socialist governments, therefore, have a very special preference for an aggregate of atomised state-dependent individuals. They are equally averse to materially well-sourced autonomous institutions of civil society. Socialist movements seize property, levy inordinately high taxes, oppose testator freedom and encumber or completely prevent succession, thus confiscating the citizenry's material means. In that way they seek to ensure that people are stripped of the material prerequisite for a sense of independence and that there are no organisations of civil society to act as a rampart against overt governmental power. In short, socialist governments confiscate property so as to secure, for themselves, unrestrained power without the annoyance of countervailing checks and balances.

On close analysis, governments that accumulate property for themselves and which to that end confiscate private property are inherently anti-constitutionalist. Thus viewed, socialism is no mere economic matter. Neither are its anti-private property

---

51   See for example the observations by Van Hayek, 1960:123-124.

programmes a matter which impact only on private law and private property. On the contrary, it goes to the very core of constitutional law. The socialist assault on private property is inherently incongruent with the very notion of constitutionalism. A socialist government cannot be a constitutional government. They are mutually exclusive.

The combination of autonomous institutions of civil society and private property are, therefore, the main rampart against rights-threatening centralised governments and movements, especially socialist governments and movements.

For constitutionalism to be sustained private property is crucial for individuals, families, business and for institutions of civil society. These institutions have to be in a position to accumulate material assets in the form of protected property which serve as the prerequisite for these institutions to perform the check and balance function.

The protection of property therefore lies at the very core of the constitutional idea. It provides the oxygen for free, active and politically participating citizens, and forms the basis for the autonomous institutions of civil society which secures freedom by acting as check and balance against bad government.

John Adams, we noted in Chapter 1 stated: "Power must be opposed to power, force to force, strength to strength, interest to interest, as well as reason to reason." These oppositions of various forms of power encapsulate the essence of checks and balances. The centres for exercising such checks and balances should not be limited to state institutions, including the judiciary. They have to include the widest variety of autonomous non-statist institutions whose viability can be sustained only on the basis of their own property and the property of their members.

*   *   *

Statist-individualist constitutionalism is premised on a fallacious belief system. The mechanisms it offers for securing justice and a balanced constitution are flawed and inadequate. It is ironic that the South African constitutional order, once so lavishly praised for all its splendid statist-individualist hallmarks, has descended into an order which turned out to be a striking specimen of a system displaying the flaws of statist-individualist constitutionalism. These flaws are innate, in all statist-individualist Constitutions, but they are usually not that visible. However, in the South African constitutional order their presence are too glaring to go unnoticed. That, paradoxically enough, is of great value because it affords the opportunity to identify and assess the deficiencies of statist-individualist constitutionalism and to broaden our horizons towards the pursuit of better ideas and systems of constitutionalism - beyond the straitjacket of statist-individualist constitutionalism, not only in South Africa, but elsewhere as well.

BIBLIOGRAPHY

Books and Journal Articles

Aarnio, A. 2011. *Essays on the Doctrinal Study of Law*. Dordrecht: Springer. https://doi.org/10.1007/978-94-007-1655-1

Abraham, H.J. 1999. *Justices, Presidents and Senators: A History of the US Supreme Court Appointments from Washington to Clinton*. Lanham: Rowman & Littlefield.

Ackerman, B. 1997. The rise of world constitutionalism. *Virginia Law Review*, 83:771-797. https://doi.org/10.2307/1073748

Ackermann, B. 2007. Oliver Wendell Holmes Lectures: The Living Constitution. Harvard Law Review, pp.1737-1812.

Albertyn, C. & Goldblatt, B. 1998. Facing the challenges of transformation: difficulties in the development of an indigenous jurisprudence of equality. *South African Journal for Human Rights*, 14(2):248-176. https://doi.org/10.1080/02587203.1998.11834979

Alexy, R. 2004. The Nature of Legal Philosophy. *Ratio Iuris*, pp.155-156. https://doi.org/10.1111/j.1467-9337.2004.00261.x

Alexy, R. 2008. On the Concept and the Nature of Law. *Ratio Iuris* ,21(3):281-299. https://doi.org/10.1111/j.1467-9337.2008.00391.x

Althusius, J. 1994. *Politica: Politics methodically set forth and illustrated with sacred and profane examples*. Edited and Translated from Latin. Introduction by F.S. Carney. Forward by D.J. Elazar. Indianapolis: Liberty Fund.

Andrew, W.G. 1968. *Constitutions and Constitutionalism*. Toronto: Van Nostrand.

Antonites, A.J. (n.d.) *Middeleeuse wysbegeerte*. Navorsings- en publikasiekomitee. Pretoria: Universiteit van Pretoria.

Aristotle. 1962. *The politics*. Book VII. Translated into English by T.A. Sinclair. Middlesex: Penguin.

Arnold, C. 1979. Analysis of rights. In: E. Kamenka & A.E. Tay (eds.). *Human Rights*. London: Edward Arnold.

Badenhorst, P. 2013. Expropriation of 'unused old order rights' by the MPRDA: you had nothing! *Tydskrif vir die Hedendaagse Romeins-Hollandse Reg*, 2013(76):472-490.

Badenhorst, P. 2014. A tale of two expropriations: Newcrestia and Agrizania. *De Jure*, 2014(47):258-282.

Barak, A. 2002-2003. A Judge on Judging: The Role of the Supreme Court in a Democracy. *Harvard Law Review*, pp.19-162.

Bennett, T.W. 2011. Ubuntu: an African equity. *Potchefstroomse Elektroniese Regsblad/ Potchefstroom Electronic Law Journal*, pp.29-60. https://doi.org/10.4314/pelj. v14i4.2

Bennett. T.W.; Munro, A.R. & Jacobs, P.J. 2018. *Ubuntu – an African jurisprudence.* Cape Town: Juta.

Bentham, J.1967. Principles of morals and legislation. In: E.A. Burtt. *The English philosophers from Bentham to Mill.* New York: The Modern Library.

Berlin, I. 1969. *Four Essays on Liberty (Two Concepts of Liberty).* London: Oxford University Press.

Berman, H. 1983. *Law and Revolution: The Formation of the Western Legal Tradition.* Cambridge MA: Harvard University Press.

Bickel, A.M. 1962. *The Least Dangerous Branch: The Supreme Court at the Bar of Politics.* Indianapolis: Bobbs-Merrill.

Bilchitz, D. 2010. Citizenship and community: explaining the right to receive basic municipal services in Joseph. *Constitutional Court Review*, pp.45-78.

Bingham, J.W. 1912. What is the Law? *Michigan Law Review*, 1. (Reprinted in B.S. Summers, 1991. *American Legal Theory.* Dartmouth: Aldershot.) https://doi.org/10.2307/1275560

Bodenheimer, E. 1974. *Jurisprudence: The Philosophy and Method of Law.* Cambridge MA: Harvard University Press. https://doi. org/10.4159/harvard.9780674733107

Booysen, H. 1995. *International transactions and the international law merchant.* Pretoria: Interlegal.

Bork, R.H. 1971. Neutral Principles and Some First Amendment Problems. *Indiana Law Journal*, pp.1-35.

Boukema, P.J. & Meuwissen, D.H.M. (eds.). 1976. *Grondwet en Grondwetsherziening.* Zwolle: Tjeenk Willink.

Boulle, L. Harris, B & Hoexter, C. 1989. *Constitutional and Administrative Law.* Cape Town: Juta.

Bozeman, A. 1976. *Conflict in Africa.* Princeton: Princeton University Press.

Brassey, M. 1998. The Employment Equity Act: Bad for employment and bad for equity. *Indiana Law Journal*, pp.1359-1366.

Bray, E. & Joubert, R. 2007. Reconciliation and peace in education in South Africa: The constitutional framework and practical manifestation in school education. In: *Addressing ethnic conflict through peace education.* New York: Palgrave Macmillan. https://doi.org/10.1057/9780230603585_5

Budlender, G. 2005. Transformation of the Judiciary: The Politics of the Judiciary in a Democratic South Africa. *South African Journal for Human Rights*, pp.715-724.

Burgers, J.H. 1990. The function of human rights as individual and collective rights. In: J. Berting, P.R. Baehr & J.H. Burgers (eds.). *Human rights in a pluralist world: individuals and collectivities.* Middelburg: Netherlands commission for UUNESCO and Roosevelt Study Center.

Burns, J.H. (ed.). 1988. *The Cambridge History of Medieval Political Thought.* Cambridge: Cambridge University Press. https://doi. org/10.1017/CHOL9780521243247

Burtt, E.A. 1967. *The English philosophers from Bentham to Mill.* New York: The Modern Library.

Buttleritchie, D.T. 2004. Critiquing modern constitutionalism. *Appalachian Journal of Law*, 3:37.

Calland, R. 2013. *The Zuma Years: South Africa's Changing Face of Power.* Cape Town: Zebra Press.

Cameron, E. 1982. Legal Chauvinism, Executive Mindedness and Justice: L.C. Steyn's Impact on South African Law. *South African Law Journal*, pp.38-75.

Carlyle, R.W. 1928. *A History of Medieval Political Theory in the West - Vol 3: Political Theory from the Tenth Century to the Thirteenth Century.* Edinburgh: Blackwood.

Carlyle, R.W. 1936. *A History of Medieval Political Theory in the West - Vol 6: Political Theory from 1300 to 1600.* Edinburgh: Blackwood.

Casey, G. 2017. *Freedom's progress? A history of political thought.* Exeter: Imprint Academic.

Choudhry, S. 2010. "He Had a Mandate": The South African Constitutional Court and the African National Congress in a Dominant Party Democracy. *Constitutional Court Review*, pp.1-86.

Coetzee, C.J. 1983. Groepe en kategorieë in Suid-Afrika. *Woord en Daad*, 23(252):6-7.

Connor, W. 1971-1972. Nation-building or nations-destroying. *World Politics*, pp.319-355. https://doi.org/10.2307/2009753

Coombe, R.J. 1989. Same as it ever was: rethinking the politics of legal interpretation. *McGill Law Journal*, 1989(34):604-662.

Copleston, F.C. 1972. *A history of Medieval philosophy.* London: Methuen.

Cornell, D. 2004. A call for a nuanced constitutional jurisprudence: Ubuntu, dignity and reconciliation. *SA Publiekreg/ Public Law*, 19(1):666-675.

Cornell, D. 2009. Ubuntu, pluralism and the responsibility of legal academics to the new South Africa. *Law and Critique*, 20(1):43-58. https://doi.org/10.1007/s10978-008-9041-y

Crawford, J. 1988. *The rights of peoples.* Oxford: Claredon Press.

D'Entreves, A.P. 2017. *Natural law.* London: Hutchinson & Co.

Dahl, R. 1957. Decision-making in a Democracy: The Supreme Court as a National Policymaker. *Journal of Politics and Law*, pp.279-295.

Dallmayr, F. 1992. Hermeneutics and the rule of law. In: G. Leyh. (ed.). *Legal hermeneutics: history, theory and practice.* Berkeley: University of California Press.

De Benoist, A. 2000. The first federalist: Johannes Althusius. *Telos*, 18:25-58.

De Montesquieu, C.L. De Secondat. 2002. *The Spirit of Laws, Book II, Book XXX.* Translator from French into English not indicated. New York: Prometheus Books.

De Tocqueville, A. 1988. *Democracy in America.* Hertfordshire: Wordsworth Classics of Word Literature.

De Tocqueville, A. 2008. *The Ancient Regime and the Revolution.* London: Penguin.

De Ville, J.R. 2000. *Constitutional and statutory interpretation.* Johannesburg: Interoc Consultants Pty Ltd.

De Villiers, B. 2004. Comparative studies of federalism: Opportunities and limitations as applied to the protection of cultural groups. *Tydskrif vir die Suid-Afrikaanse Reg/ Journal of South African Law*, pp.209-234.

De Vos, P. & Freedman, W. (eds.). 2014. *South African constitutional law in context.* Oxford: Oxford University Press.

Degenaar, J. 1987. Nationalism, liberalism and pluralism. In: J. Butler, R. Elphick & D. Welsh (eds.). *Democratic liberalism in South Africa: Its history and prospect.* Middletown: Wesleyan University Press.

Devenish, G.E. 2003. The Doctrine of Separation of Powers with Specific Reference to Events in South Africa and Zimbabwe. *Tydskrif vir die Hedendaagse Romeins-Hollandse Reg*, pp.84-99.

Diamond, S. 1971. The rule of law versus the order of custom. In: R.P. Wolff (ed.). *The rule of law.* New York: Simon and Schuster, pp.115-144.

Dobner, P. & Loughlin, M. 2007. *The Twilight of Constitutionalism.* Oxford: Oxford University Press.

Donnelly, J. 1982. Human rights and human dignity: An analytical critique of the Non-Western conception of human rights. 76. *American Political Science Journal*, pp.303-316. https://doi.org/10.1017/S0003055400187015

Dreyer, P.S. Plato (427-347). 1981. In: A.M. Faure (ed.) *Die Westerse Politieke Tradisie.* Pretoria: Academica.

Du Plessis, L.M. 1987. 'n Regsteoreties-regsfilosofiese peiling van die menseregtehandvesdebat in Suid-Afrika. *Journal for Juridical Science*, 12(2):124-144.

Du Plessis, L.M. 1988. Filosofiese perspektief op 'n menseregtehandves in Suid-Afrika. In: J.V. van der Westhuizen & H.A. Viljoen. *A bill of rights for South Africa*. Durban: Butterworth.

Du Plessis, L.M. 2002. *Re-interpretation of statutes*. Durban: Butterworths.

Du Plessis, L.M. 2015. Theoretical (dis-) position and strategic leitmotivs in constitutional interpretation in South Africa. *Potchefstroomse Elektroniese Regsblad/Potchefstroom Electronic Law Journal*, 18(5):1332-1365. https://doi.org/10.4314/pelj.v18i5.03

Du Plessis, T. 2014. 'Gelykheid hoër geag as vryheid'. Rapport Weekliks. 7 September 2014. p.6.

Dupré, L. 1993 *Passage to Modernity - An Essay on the Hermeneutics of Nature and Culture*. New Haven: Yale University Press.

Du Toit, P.; Swart, C. & Teuteberg, S. 2016. *South Africa and the case for the renegotiation of the peace*. Stellenbosch: AFRICAN SUN MeDIA. https://doi.org/10.18820/9781928357148

Du Toit, Z.B. 1999. *Die Nuwe Toekoms: 'n Perspektief op die Afrikaner by die Eeuwisseling*. Pretoria: J.P. Van der Walt.

Dunn, J. (ed.). 1993. *Democracy: The Unfinished Journey – 508 BC-AD*. Oxford: Oxford University Press.

Dworkin, R. 1977. *Taking Rights Seriously*. London: Duckworth.

Dworkin, R. 1986. *Law's Empire*. London: Fontana Press.

Dworkin, R. 1992. Law as interpretation. In: W.J.T. Mitchell. *The politics of interpretation*. Chicago: University of Chicago Press.

Dyzenhaus, D. 1982. L.C. Steyn in Perspective. *South African Law Journal*, pp.380-393.

Ehrlich, E. 1936. *Fundamental Principles of the Sociology of Law*. Translated from the original German by W.L. Moll. Cambridge MA: Harvard University Press.

Elazar, D.L. 1994. Althusius' Grand Design for a Federal Commonwealth. In: J. Althusius, *Politica: Politics methodically set forth and illustrated with sacred and profane examples*. An abridged and translated version edited and translated from Latin by F.S. Carney. Indianapolis: Liberty Fund.

Elkins, Z.; Ginsburg, T. & Melton, J. 2004. *The endurance of national constitutions*. New York: Cambridge Law Press.

Ellis, P. & Lamey, A.T. 2017. *The South African legal practitioner - A Commentary on the Legal Practice Act*. Durban: Lexis Nexis.

English, R. 1996. Ubuntu: the quest for an indigenous jurisprudence. *South African Journal for Human Rights*, pp.641-648.

Falk, R. 1988. The rights of peoples (in particular indigenous peoples). In: J. Crawford. *The rights of peoples*. Oxford: Claredon Press.

Feldman, S.M. 1991. The new metaphysics: the interpretive turn in jurisprudence. *Iowa Law Review*, 76:661-699.

Feldman, S.M. 1996. The politics of postmodern jurisprudence. *Michigan Law Review*, 95(1):166-202. https://doi.org/10.2307/1290133

Figgis, J.N. 1960. *Political thought from Gerson to Grotius 1414-1625*. Cambridge: Cambridge University Press.

Fish, S.E. 1980. *Is there a text in this class? The authority of interpretive communities*. Cambridge: Harvard University Press.

Fiss, O.M. 1993. The Limits of Judicial Independence. *University of Miami Inter-American Law Review*, pp.57-76.

Fombad, C.M. 2011. Constitutional Reforms and Constitutionalism in Africa: Reflections on Some Current Challenges and Future Prospects. *Buffalo Law Review*, pp.1007-1109.

Fombad, C.M. & Murray, C. 2010. *Fostering constitutionalism in Africa*. Pretoria: Pretoria University Law Press.

Fourie, E. 2016. Constitutional values, therapeutic jurisprudence and legal education in South Africa: Shaping our legal order. *Potchefstroomse Elektroniese Regsblad/Potchefstroom Electronic Law Journal*, 19(1):1-26. https://doi.org/10.17159/1727-3781/2016/v19i0a732

Friedrich, C.J. 1963. *Man and His Government.* New York: McGraw-Hill.

Friedrich, C.J. 1974. *Limited Government – a Comparison.* New Jersey: Englewood Cliffs.

Fukuyama, F. 2011. *The Origins of Political Order from Prehuman Times to the French Revolution.* London: Profile Books.

Fuller, L. 1998. Summarised by A.E. van Blerk. *Jurisprudence: An Introduction.* Durban: Butterworths.

Gadamer, S.E. 1980. *Is there a text in this class? The authority of interpretive communities.* Cambridge: Harvard University Press.

Gadamer, H.G. 1989. *Truth and method.* (Translated by Joel Weinsheimer and Donald G Marshall). London: Sheet & Ward.

Gardbaum, S.A. 1992. Law, politics and the claims of community. *Michigan Law Review.* 1992(90):686-760.

Gillespie, M.A. 1992. *The theological origins of modernity.* Chicago: University of Chicago Press.

Goosen, D. 2015. *Oor gemeenskap en plek – anderkant die onbehae.* Pretoria: FAK.

Gordon, R.W. 1988. The independence of lawyers. *Boston University Law Review,* 1988(68):1-83.

Gordon, A. & Bruce, D. 2007. *Transformation and the Independence of the Judiciary in South Africa.* Braamfontein: Centre for the Study of Violence in South Africa.

Green, L. 1991. Two views on collective rights. *Canadian Journal of Law and Jurisprudence,* 4(2):315-327. https://doi.org/10.1017/S0841820900002952

Greenberg, D; Katz, S.N.; Oliviero, M.B. & Wheatley, S.C. (eds.). 1993. *Constitutionalism and democracy: transitions in the contemporary world.* Oxford: Oxford University Press.

Gregory, B.S. 2012. *The Unintended Reformation - How a Religious Revolution Secularized Society.* Cambridge, MA: Harvard University Press. https://doi.org/10.4159/harvard.9780674062580

Griffin, S.M. 1990. Constitutionalism in the United States: From Theory to Practice. *Oxford Journal of Legal Studies,* 10(2):37-61. https://doi.org/10.1093/ojls/10.2.200

Griffin, S.M. 1995. Constitutionalism in the United States: From Theory to Practice. In: S. Levison. *Responding to Imperfection: The Theory and Practice of Constitutional Amendment.* Princeton: Princeton University Press, pp.200-220. https://doi.org/10.1515/9781400821631.37

Griffith, J.A.G. 1979. The Political Constitution. *Michigan Law Review,* pp.1-21. https://doi.org/10.1111/j.1468-2230.1979.tb01506.x

Grimm, D. 2007. The achievement of constitutionalism and its prospects in a changed world. In: P. Dobner & M. Loughlin. 2007. *The twilight of constitutionalism.* Oxford: Oxford University Press.

Grimm, D. 2009. Constitutions, Constitutional Courts and Constitutional Interpretation at the Interface of Law and Politics. In: B. Iancu (ed.). *The Law/Politics Distinction in Contemporary Public Law Adjudication.* Utrecht: Eleven International.

Guizot, F. 1977. *The history of civilization in Europe.* London: Penguin.

Gumede, W.M. 2005. *Thabo Mbeki and the Battle for the Soul of the ANC.* Cape Town: Zebra Press.

Habermas, J. 1988. Law and Morality. In: S.M. Mc Currin (ed.). *The Tanner Lectures on human values, VIII.* Cambridge: Cambridge University Press. p.260.

Haffajee, K. 2013. South Africa: the transition to violent democracy. *Review of African Political Economy,* pp.589-604. https://doi.org/10.1080/03056244.2013.854040

Haffajee, F. 2015. *What if there were no whites in South Africa?* Johannesburg: Picador Africa.

Hahlo, H.R. & Kahn, E. 1968. *The South African legal system and its background.* Cape Town: Juta.

Hamilton, A.; Madison, J. & Jay, J. 1961. *The Federalist Papers.* New York: Mentor Books. https://doi.org/10.4159/harvard.9780674332133

Hart, H.L.A. (ed.). 1983. *Essays in Jurisprudence and Philosophy.* Oxford: Oxford University Press. https://doi.org/10.1093/acprof:oso/9780198253884.001.0001

Hart, H.L.A. 1994. *The Concept of Law*. Oxford: Oxford University Press.

Hartney, M. 1991. Some confusion concerning collective rights. *Canadian Journal of Law and Jurisprudence*, 4(2):293-314. https://doi.org/10.1017/S0841820900002940

Hobbes, T. 1985. *Leviathan*. London: Penguin Books.

Hoexter, C. 2007. *Administrative Law in South Africa*. Cape Town: Juta.

Hoffman, P. 2016. *Confronting the Corrupt*. Cape Town: Tafelberg.

Hoffman, P. 7 Augustus 2016. 'Naam-hofsake jag die wind'. *Rapport Weekliks*. p.11.

Holdsworth, W.S. 1937. *A history of English law*, Vol. VIII. London: Methuen.

Hosten, W.J.; Edwards, A.B.; Nathan, C. & Bosman, F. 1979. *Inleiding tot die Suid-Afrikaanse reg en regsleer*. Durban: Butterworth Legal Publishers.

Hueglin, T.O. 1999. *Early modern concepts for a late modern world – Althusius on community and federalism*. Waterloo: WLU Press.

Hueglin, T.O. & Fenna, A. 2015. *Comparative federalism: A systematic inquiry*. Toronto: University of Toronto Press.

Huntington, S.P. 1991. *The third wave: Democratisation in the late twentieth century*. Oklahoma: University of Oklahoma Press.

Jacob, H.; Blankenburg, E.; Kritzer, H.M.; Provine, D.M. & Sanders, J. 1996. *Courts, Law and Politics in Comparative Perspective*. New Haven: Yale University Press.

Jellinek, G. 1919. *Algemeine Staatslehre*. Berlin: Julius Springer.

Johnson, R.W. 2009. *South Africa's brave new world: The beloved country since the end of apartheid*. Johannesburg: Penguin.

Johnson, R.W. 2015. *How long will South Africa survive? – The looming crisis*. Johannesburg: Jonathan Ball.

Jolowicz, H.F. 1954. *Historical Introduction to the Study of Roman Law*. London: Cambridge University Press.

Jung, C.F. 1974. *Limited government – A comparison*. New Jersey: Englewood Cliffs.

Kamenka, E. & Tay, A.E. (eds.). 1979. *Human Rights*. London: Edward Arnold.

Keevy, I. 2009. 'Ubuntu' versus the core values of the South African Constitution. *Journal for Juridical Science*, 34(2):19-58. https://doi.org/10.4314/jjs.v34i2.63129

Kelsen, H. 1961. *General Theory of Law and State*. Translated from the original German by A. Wedberg. New York: Russel & Russel.

Kelsen, H. 1967. *Pure Theory of Law*. Translated from the original German by M. Knight. Berckley: University of California Press.

Kennedy, D. 1997. *A Critique of Adjudication (fin de siécle)*. Cambridge MA: Harvard University Press.

Klare, K. 1998. Legal culture and transformative constitutionalism. *South African Journal of Human Rights*, 14(1)1998:146-188. https://doi.org/10.1080/02587203.1998.11834974

Koller, P. 2014. On the Nature of Norm. *Ratio Iuris*, pp.155-75. https://doi.org/10.1111/raju.12040

Kriegler, J. 21 April 2013. 'A Lonely Life on the Bench'. *Sunday Times*. p.5.

Kriek, D. 1983. In: Van Vuuren and Kriek (eds.). *Political Alternatives for South Africa: principles and perspectives*. Johannesburg: Macmillan.

Kymlicka, W. 1991. Liberalism and the politicisation of ethnicity. *Canadian Journal of Law and Jurisprudence*, pp.239-256. https://doi.org/10.1017/S0841820900002927

Labuschagne, J.M.T. 1988. Minagting van die hof: 'n Strafregtelike en menseregtelike evaluasie. *Tydskrif vir die Suid-Afrikaanse Reg/Journal for South African Law*, pp.329-342.

Lancaster, L. 2016. At the heart of discontent – measuring public violence in South Africa. *ISS (Institute of Security Studies)*, Paper. p.292.

Lane, M. 2014. *Greek and Roman Political ideas*. London: Pelican.

Langa, P. 2006. Transformative constitutionalism. *Stellenbosch Law Review*, 2006(17):351-360.

Larkins, C.M. 1996. Judicial Independence and Democratization: A Theoretical and Conceptual Analysis. *American Journal of Comparative Law*, pp.605-626. https://doi.org/10.2307/840623

Levinson, S. 1982. Law as literature. *Texas Law Review*, 1982(60):373-403.

Levinson, S. 1995. *Responding to Imperfection: The Theory and Practice of Constitutional Amendment*. Princeton: Princeton University Press. https://doi.org/10.1515/9781400821631

Liebenberg, S. 2006. Needs, rights and transformation: Adjudicating social rights. *Stellenbosch Law Review*, 2006(17):5-36.

Liebenberg, S. 2010. *Socio-economic rights – adjudication under a transformative constitution*. Johannesburg: Juta.

Llewellyn, K.N. 2008. *Jurisprudence: Realism in Theory and Practice*. London: Routledge.

Locke, J. 1992. *Of civil government (second treatise)*. South Bend Indiana: Regnery/Gateway Inc.

Loughlin, M. 2007. What is constitutionalism. In: P. Dobner. & M. Loughlin. *The twilight of constitutionalism*. Oxford: Oxford University Press.

Louw, A. 2015. "I am not a number! I am a free man!" The Employment Equity Act, 1998 (and other myths about the pursuit of "equality", "equity" and "dignity" in post-apartheid South Africa). *Potchefstroomse Elektroniese Regsblad/ Potchefstroom Electronic Law Journal*, (18):593-667; 669-773. https://doi.org/10.4314/pelj.v18i3.05

MacCormick, N. 1974. Law as Institutional Fact. *Law Quarterly Review*, pp.102-129.

MacCormick, N. (et al). 1985. *World Congress on Philosophy of Law and Sociology: Conditions of Validity and Cognition in Modern Legal Thought*. Stuttgart: Steiner.

Macintyre, A. 1981. *After virtue*. New York: Bloomsbury Academic.

Mahommed, I. 1999. Address by Mr Justice Mahommed, Chief Justice of the Supreme Court of Appeal on Accepting the Honorary Degree of Doctor of Laws at the University of Cape Town on 25 June 1999. *South African Law Journal*, pp.853-857.

Malan, K. 2004. Die reg se afhanklikheid van mag: Magswanbalans as voorwaarde vir die positiewe reg en die regstaat. *Tydskrif vir die Hedendaagse Romeins-Hollandse Reg*, 67:474-479.

Malan, K. 2005. The Unity of Powers and the Dependence of the Judiciary. *De Jure*, pp.99-115.

Malan, K. 2006. Faction Rule, Democracy and Justice. *SA Public Law/Publiekreg*, 21:142-160.

Malan, K. 2007. The inalienable right to take the law into our own hands and the faltering state. *Tydskrif vir die Suid-Afrikaanse Reg/Journal for South African Law*, pp.642-654.

Malan, K. 2008a. The Deficiency of Individual Rights and the Need for Community Protection. *Tydskrif vir Hedendaagse Romeins-Hollandse Reg*, pp.415-437.

Malan, K. 2008b. Observations and suggestions on the use of the official languages in national legislation. *SA Publiekreg/Public Law*, pp.59-76.

Malan, K. 2009. Observations on the use of the official languages for the recording of court proceedings. *Tydskrif vir die Suid-Afrikaanse Reg*, pp.141-155.

Malan, K. 2010. Observations on representivity, democracy and homogenization. *Tydskrif vir die Suid-Afrikaanse Reg/Journal for South African Law*, (3):427-449.

Malan, K. 2011. The discretionary nature of the official language clause of the Constitution. *SA Publiekreg/Public Law*, pp.381-407.

Malan, K. 2012a. *Politocracy – An assessment of the coercive logic of the territorial state and ideas around a response to it*. Pretoria: Pretoria University Law Press.

Malan, K. 2012b. The rule of law versus decisionism in the South African constitutional discourse. *De Jure*, 45(2):272-305.

Malan, K. 2012c. 'n Oorweging van die kragte wat inwerk op die betekenis en toepassing van die diskresionêre taalklousule van die Suid-Afrikaanse grondwet. *Litnet Akademies*, pp.55-78.

Malan, K. 2014a. An analysis of the legally protectable interests pertaining to language. *Tydskrif vir die Suid-Afrikaanse Reg/Journal for South African Law*, (1):66-84.

Malan, K. 2014b. Taalverval met besondere verwysing na die ideologieë en praktyke van verstaatliking. *Tydskrif vir Geesteswetenskappe*, 54(3):462-480.

Malan, K. 2014c. The suitability and unsuitability of Ubuntu in constitutional law – inter-communal relations versus public office-bearing. *De Jure*, pp.231-257.

Malan, K. 2015a. Die begrip 'amptelikheid' van 'n taal in die lig van onlangse buitelandse reg. *Tydskrif vir die Hedendaagse Romeins-Hollandse Reg*, pp.116-120.

Malan, K. 2015b. Die dinamika van die hedendaagse oppermagtige grondwet beskou in die lig van voor- en vroegmoderne opvattings van regsoppergesag en populêre soewereiniteit. *Tydskrif vir die Hedendaagse Romeins-Hollandse Reg*, (78):248-266.

Malan, K. 1 Mei 2016. 'Dié Hof se visie is dieselfde as die ANC'. *Rapport Weekliks*.

Malan, K. 2016a. Considering an appropriate language policy for judicial proceedings in South Africa. *Revue de Droit Linguistique/ Journal for Language Law*, 2016(3):20-59.

Malan, K. 2017a. 'Johannes Althusius' Grand Federalism, the Role of the Ephors and Post-Statist Constitutionalism. *Potchefstroomse Elektroniese Regsblad/ Potchefstroom Electronic Law Journal*, (20):1-31. https://doi.org/10.17159/1727-3781/2017/v20i0a1344

Malan, K. 2017b. The Foundational Tenets of Johannes Althusius' Constitutionalism. *Potchefstroomse Elektroniese Regsblad/ Potchefstroom Electronic Law Journal*, (20):1-35. https://doi.org/10.17159/1727-3781/2017/v20i0a1344

Marshall, G. 1971. *Constitutional Theory*. Oxford: Claredon Press.

Matthee, H. 2013. Assessing and promoting human rights in South Africa. South African Monitor Report, 1.

Matthee, H. 2014. Democratic decline and state capture in South Africa. South African Monitor Report, 2.

Matthee, H. 2015. Zuma's hybrid regime and the rise of a new political order. South African Monitor Report, 4.

McDonald, M. 1991. Should communities have rights? Reflections on liberal individualism. Canadian Journal of Law and Jurisprudence, 4(2):217-237. https://doi.org/10.1017/S0841820900002915

McIlwain, C.H. 1910. The High Court of Parliament and its supremacy. New Haven: Yale University Press.

McIlwain. C.H. 2007. Constitutionalism: ancient and modern. Indianapolis: Liberty Fund.

Mclouglin, M. & Walker, N. (eds.). 2007. The Paradox of Constitutionalism: Constituent Power and the Constitutional Form. Oxford: Oxford University Press.

McRae, K. 1979. The plural society and the Western tradition. Canadian Journal of Political Science, 675-688. https://doi.org/10.1017/S0008423900053579

Michaels, R. 2007. The true lex mercatoria: law beyond the state. Indiana Journal of global legal studies, 2007(14):447-469. https://doi.org/10.2979/gls.2007.14.2.447

Milbank, J. 1992. Theology and Social Theory: Beyond Secular Reason, 2nd edition. Malden Massachusetts: Blackwell Publishing.

Mill, J.S. 1962. Considerations on representative government (ed. E.B. Acton). London: T.M. Dent & Sons.

Moerane, M.T.K. 2003. The Meaning of Transformation of the Judiciary in the New South African Context. South African Law Journal, pp.708-718.

Mokgoro, Y. 1998a. Ubuntu and the law in South Africa. Buffalo Human Rights Law Review, (4):15-23.

Mokgoro, Y. 1998b. Ubuntu and the law in South Africa. Potchefstroomse Elektroniese Regsblad/Potchefstroom Electronic

Law Journal, 1(1):16-27. https://doi.
org/10.17159/1727-3781/1998/v1i1a2897

Mommsen, T. & Krueger, P. 1985. *The Digest
of Justinian.* Latin-English translation
and edited by A. Watson. Philadelphia:
University of Pennsylvania Press.

Mootz, F.J. 1994. The new legal hermeneutics
review essay: legal hermeneutics: history,
theory and practice. *Vanderbilt Law Review,*
1994(47):115-143.

Morris, C. 1972. *The discovery of the individual
1050-1200.* London: SPCK.

Moseneke, D. 2002. The fourth Bram Fischer
memorial lecture – transformative
adjudication. *South African Journal on Human
Rights,* 2002(18):309-319. https://doi.org/10
.1080/02587203.2002.11827648

Motala, Z. 11 December 2011. 'SCA: Beware
Politics Masquerading as Law'. *Sunday
Times.* p.5.

Müller, F. 1991. Basic questions of
constitutional concretization. *Stellenbosch
Law Review,* 10(3):373-403.

Mullet, C.F. 1932. Coke and the American
revolution. *Economica,* 12:457-471.
https://doi.org/10.2307/2549144

Mureinik, E.A. 1994. A bridge to where –
introducing the interim Bill of Rights.
SA Journal on Human Rights, 10(1):31-48.
https://doi.org/10.1080/02587203.1994.1
1827527

Murphy, W.F. 1993. Constitutions,
constitutionalism and democracy. In:
D. Greenberg, S.N. Katz, M.B. Oliviero &
S.C. Wheatley (eds.), *Constitutionalism and
democracy: transitions in the contemporary
world.* Oxford: Oxford University Press.

Neumann, F.L. 1986. *The Rule of Law: Political
Theory and the Legal System in Modern Society.*
Warwickshire: Berg.

Niiniluotu, I. 1985. Truth and Legal Norms. In:
N. MacCormick, (et al). *World Congress on
Philosophy of Law and Sociology: Conditions
of Validity and Cognition in Modern Legal
Thought.* Stuttgart: Steiner, pp.168-190.

Nisbet, R. 1990. *The quest for community:
A study in the ethics of order and
freedom.* San Francisco: Institute for
Contemporary Studies.

Norman, N.J.E. 2013. *Edmund Burke -
The visionary who invented modern politics.*
London: William Collins.

Ntsebeza, D.B. 25 July 2004. 'Why Majority
Black Bench is Inevitable'. *Sunday Times.*
p.19.

O'Brien, D.M. 1988. *Judicial Roulette: Report of the
Twentieth Century Fund Task Force on Judicial
Selection.* New York: Priority Press.

O'Regan, K. 2005. Checks and balances
reflections on the development of the
doctrine of separation of powers under the
South African Constitution. *Potchefstroomse
Elektroniese Regsblad/Potchefstroom Electronic
Law Journal,* 8(1):1-30. https://doi.
org/10.4314/pelj.v8i1.43460

Oakeshott, M. 2006. *Lectures in the history of
political thought.* Exeter: Imprint Academic.

Olivecrona, K.N. 1971. *Law as Fact.* London:
Steven & Sons.

Olivier, M. 1992. Unpublished address.
Pretoria: Justice College. On file
with author.

Paine, T. 1996. *Rights of man.* Hertfordshire:
Wordsworth.

Parekh, B. 2000. *Rethinking multiculturalism:
cultural diversity and political theory.*
Cambridge Massachusetts: Harvard
University Press.

Pennington, K. 1988. Law, Legislative
Authority and Theories of Government
1150-1300. In: J.H. Burns (ed.).
*The Cambridge History of Medieval
Political Thought.* Cambridge: Cambridge
University Press.

Peretti, T.J. 2002. Does Judicial Independence
Exist? The Lessons of Social Science
Research. In: S.B. Burbank & B. Friedman
(eds.). *Judicial Independence at the Crossroads:
An Interdisciplinary Approach.* Sage:
Thousand Oaks.

Pestieau, J. 1991. Minority rights: Caught
between individual rights and peoples'
rights. *Canadian Journal of Law and
Jurisprudence,* pp.361-373. https://doi.
org/10.1017/S0841820900002988

Pfaff, R. & Schneider, H. 2001. The Promotion of Administrative Justice Act from a German Perspective. *South African Journal for Human Rights*, pp.56-90. https://doi.org/10.1080/02587203.2001.11827617

Pieterse, M. 2005. What do we mean when we talk about transformative constitutionalism? *SA Publiekreg/Public Law*, 2005(10):155-166.

Pitkin, H.F. 1987. The Idea of a Constitution. *Journal of Legal Education*, 39:167-169.

Plaut, M. & Holden, P. 2012. *Who Rules South Africa? Pulling the Strings in the Battle for Power.* Johannesburg: Jonathan Ball.

Plucknett, F.T. 1927. Bonham's Case and Judicial Review. *Harvard Law Review*, 40:30-70. https://doi.org/10.2307/1330126

Preuss, U.K. 2007. Disconnecting constitutions from statehood: Is global constitutionalism a viable concept?' In: P. Dobner. & M. Loughlin. 2007. *The twilight of constitutionalism.* Oxford: Oxford University Press.

Previté-Orton, C.W. 1952. *The shorter Cambridge Medieval history*, Volume I. Cambridge: Cambridge University Press.

Radbruch, G. 2006. Statutory Lawlessness and Supra-Statutory Law (1946). Translated from the original German by B. Litschewski & L. Paulson. *Oxford Journal for Legal Studies*, 26(1):1-11. https://doi.org/10.1093/ojls/gqi041

Rautenbach, I. 2015. Requirements for affirmative action and requirements for the limitation of rights. *Journal of South African Law*, 2015(2):431-443.

Rawls, J. 1971. *A Theory of Justice*. Oxford: Oxford University Press.

Réaume, D. 1998. Individuals, groups and rights to public goods. *University of Toronto Law Review*, 38:1-24. https://doi.org/10.2307/825760

Rickard, C. 18 July 2004. 'The Bench is Closed to Pale Males, Struggle Credentials or Not'. *Sunday Times*. p.16.

Rickard, C. 21 April 2002. 'Is the Price for Transformation Too High?' *Sunday Times*. p.16.

Ritter, G. 1964. Origins of the modern state. In: H. Lubasz (ed.). *The development of the modern state.* New York: Macmillan Co.

Roets, E. 2018. *Kill the Boer – government's complicity in South Africa's brutal farm murders.* Pretoria: Kraal.

Röling, B.V.A. 1962. *International Law in an Expanded World.* Amsterdam: Djambateen.

Roodt, M. 2018. *Broken Blue Line 3: The involvement of the South African police service in serious and violent crime in South Africa.* Johannesburg: South African Institute of Race relations.

Rosenberg, G.N. 2008. *The Hollow Hope: Can Courts Bring About Social Change?* Chicago: Chicago University Press. https://doi.org/10.7208/chicago/9780226726687.001.0001

Rousseau, J. 1968. *The Social Contract.* English translation and introduction by Cranston. London: Penguin Books.

Roux, T. 2009a. Principle and Pragmatism on the Constitutional Court of South Africa. *International Journal of Constitutional Law*, pp.106-138. https://doi.org/10.1093/icon/mon029

Roux, T. 2009b. Transformative constitutionalism and the best interpretation of the South African constitution: distinction without a difference. *Stellenbosch Law Review*, 20(2):258-85.

Roux, T. 2013. *The Politics of Principle: The First South African Constitutional Court, 1995-2005.* Cambridge: Cambridge University Press. https://doi.org/10.1017/CBO9781139005081

Sabine, G.H. 1971. *A History of Political Theory.* London: George G. Harrap & Co Ltd.

Sartori, G. 1962. Constitutionalism: A Preliminary Discussion. *American Politics and Science Journal*, pp.853-864. https://doi.org/10.2307/1952788

Sartori, G. 1962. *Democratic Theory.* Detroit: Wayne State University Press.

Seton-Watson, H. 1977. *Nations and states.* London: Methuen.

Shapiro, M. 1963-1964. Political Jurisprudence. *Kentucky Law Journal*, pp.294-345.

Siedentop, L. 2014. *Inventing the individual: The origin of Western liberalism.* London: Penguin.

Sieghart, P. 1992. *The international law of human rights.* Oxford: Oxford University Press.

Simeon, R. 1998. Considerations on the design of federations: the South African Constitution in comparative context. *SA Publiekreg/Public Law*, pp.46-72.

Simeon, R. & Murray. C. 2001. Multilevel government in South Africa: An interim assessment. *Publius Journal of Federalism*, pp.65-92. https://doi.org/10.1093/oxfordjournals.pubjof.a004921

Snyman, K. 2002. *Criminal Law.* Durban: Butterworths.

South African Law Commission. 1991. Projec 58. Group and human rights. Summary of interim report.

South African Institute of race Relations. 2015. *Broken Blue Line: The involvement of the South African Police Service in serious and violent crime in South Africa.* Johannesburg: Institute of Race Relations, pp.6-8.

South African Institute of Race Relations. 2016. *How to win the war on crime in South Africa: A new approach to community policing.* Johannesburg: Institute of Race Relations. pp.21-24.

South African Institute of Race Relations. 2017. *South Africa Survey 2017.* Johannesburg: Institute of Race Relations.

Stavenhagen, R. 1995. Cultural rights and universal human rights. In: A. Eide, C. Krause & A. Rosas (eds.). *Economic, social and cultural rights: A textbook.* Dordrecht: Martinus Nijhof.

Steytler, N. 2001. Concurrency and co-operative government: The law and practice in South Africa. *SA Publiekreg Public Law*, pp.240-254.

Strange, S. 1995. The defective state. *Daedalus*, 124(2)55-74.

Strauss, L. 1953. *Natural Right and History.* Chicago: University of Chicago Press.

Szabo, I. 1982. Historical foundations of human rights. In: Karel and Alston & K. Vasak. *The international dimension of human rights.* Westport Connecticut: Greenwood Press, pp.11-40.

Tarnas, R. 2010. *The passion of the Western world - understanding the ideas that have shaped our world view.* London: Pimlico.

Taylor, C. 1993. *Reconciling the solitudes: Essays on Canadian federalism and nationalism.* Montreal: McGill-Queen's University Press.

Tempelhoff, E. 1 Augustus 2012. 'Water-hofbevel: Rade wil wéér Appèl Aanteken'. *Beeld.* p.4.

Tierney, B. 1982. *Religion, law and the growth of constitutional thought 1150-1650.* Cambridge: Cambridge University Press. https://doi.org/10.1017/CBO9780511558627

Tierney, B. 1997. *The idea of natural rights: Studies in natural rights, natural law and church law.* Cambridge: William B. Eerdman.

Tushnet, M. 2009. *The Constitution of the United States of America: A Contextual Analysis.* Oxford: Hart.

Van Blerk, A.E. 1998. *Jurisprudence: An introduction.* Johannesburg: LexisNexis.

Van den Bergh, G.C.J.J. 1982. *Wet en Gewoonte: Historische Grondslagen van een Dogmatisch Geding.* Deventer: Kluwer.

Van der Hoeven, J. 1958. *De Plaats van de Grondwet in het Constitutionele Recht.* Zwolle: Tjeenk Willink.

Van der Hoeven, J. 1976. De Waarde van de Grondwet. In: P.J. Boukema & D.H.M. Meuwissen (eds.). *Grondwet en Grondwetsherziening.* Zwolle: Tjeenk Willink.

Van der Vyver, J.D. 2012. Nationalisation of mineral rights in South Africa. *De Jure*, 45(1):125-142.

Van der Walt, A.J. 2006. Legal history, legal culture and transformation in a constitutional democracy. *Fundamina*, 12(1):1-47.

Van der Walt, A.J. 2013. *Juta's Quarerly Review of Constitutional Property Law.* Johannesburg: Juta.

Van der Westhuizen, J.V. & Viljoen, H.A. 1988. *A bill of rights for South Africa*. Durban: Buttworth.

Van Drunen, D. 2003. *Law and Custom: The Thought of Thomas Aquinas and the Future of the Common Law*. New York: Peter Lang.

Van Dyke, V. 1974. Human rights and the rights of groups. *American Journal of Political Science*, 74(18):725-741. https://doi.org/10.2307/2110557

Van Dyke, V. 1976-1977. The individual the state and ethnic communities in political theory. *World Politics*, pp.343-369. https://doi.org/10.2307/2010001

Van Hayek, F. 1960. *The constitution of liberty*. London: Routledge.

Van Jaarsveld, F.A. 1984. *Omstrede Suid-Afrikaanse verlede: Geskiedenisideologie en die historiese skuldvraagstuk*. Johannesburg: Perskor.

Van Zyl, D.H. 1977. *Geskiedenis en beginsels van die Romeinse privaatreg*. Durban: Butterworth.

Van Zyl, D.H. 1977. *Geskiedenis en beginsels van die Romeinse reg*. Durban: Butterworth.

Vasak, K. & Karel and Alston. 1982. *The international dimension of human rights*. Westport Connecticut: Greenwood Press

Venter, F. 2010. *Global features of constitutional law*. Nijmegen: Wolf Legal Publishers.

Vilhena, O.; Baxi, U. & Viljoen, F. (eds.). 2013. *Transformative constitutionalism: Comparing the apex courts of Brazil, India and South Africa*. Pretoria: Pretoria University Law Press.

Vincent, A. 1987. *Theories of the state*. Oxford: Blackwell.

Vincent, A. 2010. *The politics of human rights*. Oxford: Oxford University Press.

Voet, J. 1955. *Commentary on the Pandects*. Paris Edition 1829. Translated from the original Dutch by P. Gane. Durban: Butterworth.

Von Holdt, K. 2013. South Africa: the transition to violent democracy. *Review of African Political Economy*, pp.589-604.

Walzer, M. 1995. Pluralism: A political perspective In: W. Kymlicka (ed.) *The rights of minorities*. Oxford: Oxford University Press, p.140.

Weber, M. Staatsformen. 1962. In: H.D. Betz, D.S. Browning, B. Janowski & E. Jüngel. *Die Religion in Geschichte und Gegenwart*. Tübingen: J.C.B. Mohr.

Wechsler, H. 1959. Towards Neutral Principles of Constitutional Law. *Harvard Law Review*, pp.1-35. https://doi.org/10.2307/1337945

Welsh, D. 2004. Democratic challenges and the opportunities for South Africa. *Politeia*, pp.5-21.

Wesson, M. 2011. Reasonableness in Retreat? The Judgment of the South African Constitutional Court in Mazibuko v City of Johnnesburg. *Human Rights Law Review*, 11(2):390-405. https://doi.org/10.1093/hrlr/ngr002

Wesson, M. & Du Plessis, M. 2008. Fifteen Years On: Central Issues Relating to the Transformation of the South African Judiciary. *South African Journal on Human Rights*, pp.187-213. https://doi.org/10.1080/19962126.2008.11864952

White, J. 1998. Open democracy: has the window of opportunity closed? *South African Journal on Human Rights*, 14(1):65-76. https://doi.org/10.1080/02587203.1998.11834969

Wiechers, M. 7 September 2014. 'Nog van koers af ondanks goeie wet'. *Rapport Weekliks*. p.12.

Wolff, R.P. (ed.). 1971. *The rule of law*. New York: Simon and Schuster.

Wood, G. 1993. Democracy and the American Revolution. In: J. Dunn (ed.) *Democracy: The unfinished journey*. Oxford: Oxford University Press.

Case Law

(Unless otherwise indicated case law is cited with reference to the South African and the Butterworths Constitutional Law Reports.)

AfriForum and Another v University of the Free State 2018(2) SA 185; 2018(4) BCLR 387(CC).

Afriforum and Another v Chairperson of the Council of the University of Pretoria and Others 2017(1) All SA 832(GP).

Afriforum and Another v Malema and Others 2011(6) SA 240; 2011(12) BCLR 1289(EqC).

Afriforum and Another v University of the Free State 2018(2) SA 185; 2018(4) BCLR 387(CC).

AllPay Consolidated Investment Holdings (Pty) Ltd v Chief Executive Officer, South African Social Security Agency 2014(1) SA 604; 2014(1) BCLR 1(CC).

AllPay Consolidated Investment Holdings (Pty) Ltd v Chief Executive Officer, South African Social Security Agency 2014(4) SA 179; 2014(6) BCLR 641(CC).

Association of Personal Injury Lawyers v Heath 2001(1) SA 883(CC).

Bangindawo & others v Head of the Nyanda Regional Authority 1998(2) SACR 16(TK).

Barkhuizen v Napier 2007(5) SA 323; 2007(7); BCLR 691(CC).

Bato Star Fishing (Pty) Ltd v Minister of Environmental Affairs 2004(4) SA 490; 2004(7) BCLR 687(CC).

Bhe and Others v Magistrate, Khayelitsha, and Others 2005(1) SA 580; 2005(1) BCLR 1(CC).

Black Sash Trust v Minister of Social Development and Others (Freedom Under Law NPC Intervening) 2017(3) SA 335; 2017(5) BCLR 543(CC).

BTR Industries South Africa (Pty) Ltd v Metal and Allied Workers Union 1992(3) SA 673(A).

City of Tshwane Metropolitan Municipality v Afriforum and Another 2016(6) SA 279; 2016(9) BCLR 1133(CC).

Daniels v Scribante and Another 2017(4) SA 341; 2017(8) BCLR 949(CC).

Dawood and Another v Minister of Home Affairs and Others; Shalabi and Another v Minister of Home Affairs and Others; Thomas and Another v Minister of Home Affairs and Others 2000(3) SA 936; 2000(8) BCLR 837(CC).

De Lange v Smuts 1998(3) SA 785; 1998(7) BCLR 779(CC).

Democratic Alliance v Acting National Director of Public Prosecutions 2012 (3) SA 486; 2012(6) BCLR 613 (SCA).

Democratic Alliance v Minister of International Relations and Cooperation and Others (Council for the Advancement of the South African Constitution Intervening) 2017(3) SA 212; 2017(2) All SA 123(GP).

Democratic Alliance v President of the RSA 2012(1) SA 417; 2012(3) BCLR 291(SCA).

Democratic Alliance v President of the RSA 2013(1) SA 248; 2012(12) BCLR 1297(CC).

Dikoko v Mokhatla 2006(6) SA 235; 2007(1) BCLR 1(CC).

Du Plessis v De Klerk 1996(3) SA 850; 1996(5) BCLR 658(CC).

Economic Freedom Fighters v Speaker of the National Assembly and Others; Democratic Alliance v Speaker of the National Assembly and Others 2016(3) SA 580; 2016(5) BCLR 618(CC).

Freedom under Law v Acting Chairperson of the Judicial Service Commission 2011(3) SA 549; 2011(3) All SA 513 (SCA).

Gelyke Kanse and Others v Chairman of the Senate of the Stellenbosch University and Others 2018(1) BCLR 25; 2018(1) All SA 46(WCC).

Glenister v President of the Republic of South Africa and Others 2011(3) SA 347; 2011(7) BCLR 651(CC).

Government of die Republic of South Africa v Grootboom 2001(1) SA 46; 2000(11) BCLR 1169(CC).

Head of Department: Mpumalanga Department of Education and Another v Hoërskool Ermelo and Another 2010(2) SA 415; 2010(3) BCLR 177(CC).

Helen Suzman Foundation v President of the RSA; Glenister v President of the RSA 2015(2) SA 1; 2015(1) BCLR 1(CC).

Hlantalala v Head of Western Tembuland regional Authority & Others 1998(2) All SA 85(Tk).

Hoffmann v South African Airways 2001(1) SA 1; 2000(11) BCLR 1211(CC).

Joseph and Others v City of Johannesburg and Others 2010(4) SA 55; 2010(3) BCLR 212(CC).

Judicial Service Commission v Cape Bar Council 2013(1) SA 170; 2012(11) BCLR 1239(SCA).

Koyabe and Others v Minister for Home Affairs and Others 2010(4) SA 327; 2009(12) BCLR 1192(CC).

Masethla v President of the RSA 2008(1) SA 566; 2008(1) BCLR 1(CC).

MEC for Education in Gauteng Province and Other v Governing Body of Rivonia Primary School and Others 2013(6) SA 582; 2013(12) BCLR 1365(CC)

Minister of Constitutional Development and Another v South African Restructuring and Insolvency Practitioners Association and Others 2018(5) SA 349; 2018(9) BCLR 1099(CC).

Minister of Finance v Van Heerden 2004(6) SA 121; 2004(11) BCLR 1125(CC).

Minister of Health v Treatment Action Campaign 2002(5) SA 721; 2002(10) BCLR 1033(CC).

Minister of Home Affairs v Fourie 2006(1) SA 524; 2006(3) BCLR 355(CC).

Minister of Justice and Constitutional Development v Southern African litigation Centre 2016(3) SA 317; 2016(4) BCLR 487(SCA).

National Coalition for Gay and Lesbian Equality v Minister of Home Affairs 2000(2) SA 1; 2000(1) BCLR 39(CC).

National Coalition for Gay and Lesbian Equality v Minister of Justice 1999 (1) SA 6; 1998 (12) BCLR 1517 (CC).

New National Party v Government of the Republic of South Africa and Others 1999(3) SA 191; 1999(5) BCLR 489(CC).

Nyathi v Member of the Executive Council for the Department of Health Gauteng 2008(5) SA 94(CC); 2008 (9) BCLR 865(CC).

Port Elizabeth Municipality v Various Occupiers 2005(1) SA 217; 2004(12) BCLR 1268(CC).

President of the Republic of South Africa v SA Rugby Football Union 2000(1) SA 1; 1999(10) BCLR 1059(CC).

President of the RSA v Hugo 1997(4) SA 1; 1997(6) BCLR 708(CC). https://doi.org/10.1016/ S1353-4858(97)90015-5

Qozeleni v Minister of Law and Order and Another 1994(3) SA 625; 1994(1) BCLR 75(E).

S v Makwanyane and Another 1995(3) SA 391; 1995(6) BCLR 665(CC).

S v Zuma 1995(2) SA 642; 1995(4) BCLR 401.

Satchwell v President of the RSA 2002(6) SA 1; 2002(9) BCLR 986(CC).

Section 27 v Minister of Basic Education 2013(2) SA 40; 2013 (2) BCLR 237 (GNP).

Shabalala and Others v Attorney-General, Transvaal, and Another 1996(1) SA 725; 1995(12) BCLR 1593(CC).

Solidarity and Others v Department of Correctional Services and Others 2016(5) SA 594; 2016(10) BCLR 1349(CC).

Solidarity obo Barnard v South African Police Service 2014 (2) SA 1; 2014(1) All SA 319(SCA).

Soobramoney v Minister of Health Kwazulu Natal 1998(1) SA 765; 1997(12) BCLR 1696(CC).

South African Association of Personal Injury Lawyers v Heath and Others 2001(1) SA 883; 2001(1) BCLR 77(CC).

South African National Defence Union v Minister of Defence 1999(4) SA 469; 1999(6) BCLR 615(CC).

South African Police Service v Solidarity obo Barnard 2014(6) SA 123; 2014(10) BCLR 1195(CC).

The Citizen 1978 (Pty) Ltd and Others v McBride (Johnstone and Others, Amici Curiae) 2011(4) SA 191; 2011(8) BCLR 816(CC).

Thint (Pty) Ltd v National Director of Public Prosecutions, Zuma v National Director of Public Prosecutions 2009(1) SA 1; 2008(12) BCLR 1197(CC).

Union of Refugee Women v Private Security Industry Regulatory Authority 2007(4) SA 395; 2007(4) BCLR 339(CC).

United Democratic Movement v President of the Republic of South Africa 2003(1) SA 495; 2002(11) BCLR 1179(CC).

University of the Free State v Afriforum and Another 2017(4) SA 283; 2017(2) All SA 808(SCA).

Van Rooyen v The State 2002(5) SA 246; 2002(8) BCLR 810(CC).

Zuma v Democratic Alliance and Others 2014(4) All SA 35(SCA).

Zuma v National Director of Public Prosecutions 2009(1) BCLR 62; 2009(1) All SA 54(N).

Foreign case law

African Court on Human and Peoples' Rights

Kevin Mgwanga Gumme et al v Cameroon African Commission on Human and Peoples' Rights, Communication 266/2003. Available: http://bit.ly/1otpofD

European Court of Human Rights

Mentzen alias Mencena v Latvia 2004 application no 71074/01, admissibility decision of 7 December 2004. Available: http://bit.ly/1pxGhTR

High Court of India

Kesavananda Bharti v Union of India 1973(4) SCC 225.

Constitutions

Basic Law of the Federal Republic of Germany, 1949.

Constitution of the Republic of India, 1949.

Constitution of the Republic of Kenya, 2010.

Constitution of the Republic of South Africa Act, 200 of 1993.

Constitution of the Republic of South Africa, 1996.

Constitution of the United States of America, 1787.

Constitution Seventeenth Amendment Act, 2012.

International Instruments

International Covenant on Civil and Political Rights (ICCPR) of 1966.

Universal Declaration of Human Rights of the United Nations of 1948.

Legislation

Broad Based Black Empowerment Act, 53 of 2003.

Commission for the Promotion and Protection of the Rights of Cultural, religious and linguistic Communities Act, 19 of 2002.

Employment Equity Act, 55 of 1998.

Implementation of the Rome Statute of the International Criminal Court Act, 27 of 2002.

Judicial Service Commission Act, 9 of 1994.

Legal Practice Act, 28 of 2014.

Mineral and Petroleum Resources Development Act, 28 of 2002.

National Unity and Reconciliation Act, 34 of 1995.

National Health Act, 61 of 2003.

Promotion of Access to Information Act, 4 of 2000.

Promotion of Administrative Justice Act, 3 of 2000.

Promotion of Equality and Prohibition of Unfair Discrimination Act, 2 of 2000.

Repeal of the Black Administration Act and Amendment of Certain Laws Act, 28 of 2005.

South African Police Service Act, 68 of 1995.

Internet sources

Advocate, (Columnist). 2013. *Which White Judges?* Available: http://bit.ly/3075FYQ [Accessed, 20 August 2013].

ANC. 1992. *Ready to Govern: ANC Policy Guidelines for a Democratic South Africa.* Available: http://bit.ly/2Z3a9yh [Accessed, 23 August 2013].

ANC. 1993. *A Bill of Rights for a New South Africa.* Available: http://bit.ly/2TvCcp5 [Accessed, 20 August 2013].

ANC. 1993. *A Bill of Rights for a New South Africa.* Available: http://bit.ly/2TvCcp5 [Accessed, 20 August 2013].

ANC. 1998. *The State, Property Relations and Social Transformation.* Available: http://bit.ly/2MRFqlH [Accessed, 3 September 2013].

Black Lawyers Association. 2013. *Home Page.* Available: http://bit.ly/2YP9ekX [Accessed, 3 September 2013].

Burger, J. 2013. *Kan die Polisie die Toename in Geweldadige Openbare Verset Hanteer?*

Available: http://bit.ly/2Tx1LGc
[Accessed, 20 September 2013].

Calland, R. 2013. *JSC's Attitude Opens Door for Conservatism.* Available: http://bit.ly/2YYKrPR [Accessed, 3 September 2013].

Du Plessis, C. 2013. *Appointing Judges Not About Merit Alone - Mogoeng.* Available: http://bit.ly/2N6kA26 [Accessed, 19 November 2014].

Gerber, J. 2013. *Bestes nie Altyd Regters - Gaan nie net oor Verdienste.* Available: http://bit.ly/2TxNhpG [Accessed, 20 September 2013].

Ginwala, F.N. 2008. *Report of the Inquiry into the Fitness of Advocate VP Pikoli to Hold the Office of National Director of Public Prosecutions Commission of Inquiry.* Available: http://bit.ly/2KvXPCZ [Accessed, 19 November 2014].

Hefer, O. 2013. *'n Politieke Kleur vir die Regbank.* Available: http://bit.ly/2Z9cVGu [Accessed, 20 August 2013].

Hoffman, P. 2013. *RDK Moet Gou Leer Lees.* Available: http://bit.ly/2TyJ6tL [Accessed, 20 August 2013].

Judicial Service Commission. 2010. *Summary of the Criteria Used by the Judicial Services Commission when Considering Candidates for Judicial Appointments.* Available: http://bit.ly/2OLzNrI [Accessed, 19 November 2014].

Kriegler, J. 2009. *Can Judicial Independence Survive Transformation? A Public Lecture Delivered by Judge Johann Kriegler at the Wits Law School.* Available: http://bit.ly/2YZsUXG [Accessed, 29 April 2010].

Malan, K. & Hoffman, P. 2019. *How the ConCourt dropped the ball on systemic corruption.* Available: http://bit.ly/2YVCV40 [Accessed, 19 March 2019].

Malan, K. 2016. *Dié Hof se visie is dieselfde as die ANC.* Available: http://bit.ly/2Me63Sm [Accessed, 24 April 2019].

Mogoeng, M. 2015. *Appointing judges not about merit alone - Mogoeng.* Available:

http://bit.ly/2YKzOk6 [Accessed, 4 January 2017].

Mogoeng, M. 2018. *The importance of courageous free media in exposing and holding power to account.* Available: http://bit.ly/2OL0Zqk [Accessed, 25 June 2018].

Motala, Z. 2011. *Divination Through a Strange Lens.* Available: http://bit.ly/2YJYAkv [Accessed, 4 April 2011].

Mpshe, M. 2009. *Why I Decided to Drop the ZumaCharges.* Available: http://bit.ly/2Z2yGUh [Accessed, 23 September 2013].

Rabkin, F. 2013. *Smuts Resigns from JSC in Wake of Furore Over Document.* Available: http://bit.ly/2KxUlzM [Accessed, 23 September 2013].

Rickard, C. 2012. *How Biased Commission Picks Judges.* Available: http://bit.ly/31CHwK8 [Accessed, 19 August 2013].

Smuts, I. 2013a. *The JSC Needs to Establish Why so Many Excellent Practitioners Do Not Apply.* Available: http://bit.ly/2KKBErq [Accessed, 19 November 2014].

Smuts, I. 2013b. *Transformation and the Judicial Service Commission - Discussion Paper for the JSC, April 2013.* Available: http://bit.ly/2N7dcDs [Accessed, 19 November 2014].

Staff Reporter. 2011. *Mantashe Defends ANC Cadre Deployment.* Available: http://bit.ly/2OZVww0 [Accessed, 23 September 2013].

Tolsi, N. 2013. *JSC Conflict Laid Bare by Inconsistency.* Available: http://bit.ly/2YP5KTP [Accessed, 23 September 2013].

United Nations Human Rights: Office of the High Commisioner. *Basic Principles on the Role of Lawyers.* Available: http://bit.ly/2YNDNfO [Accesses, 30 November 2017].

INDEX

www.ingramcontent.com/pod-product-compliance
Lightning Source LLC
Chambersburg PA
CBHW080643270326
41928CB00017B/3172